cultivation and catastrophe

THE *CALLALOO* AFRICAN DIASPORA SERIES

Charles Henry Rowell, *Texas A&M University*
Series Editor

The *Callaloo* African Diaspora Series focuses on literary and cultural productions in the contexts of the history and cultural politics of peoples of African descent in the Americas, the Caribbean, and Europe. Like the quarterly journal *Callaloo*, the *Callaloo* African Diaspora Series is a forum for artists and intellectuals producing challenging and seminal books that help illuminate the African Diaspora as a multidimensional site of evolving complexity, a location speaking, in part, through its literary and cultural productions that are informed by a number of indigenous traditions, which in turn inform and shape cultural productions across the globe.

cultivation
and catastrophe

The Lyric Ecology of
Modern Black Literature

SONYA POSMENTIER

Johns Hopkins University Press
Baltimore

This book has been brought to publication with the generous assistance
of the Abraham and Rebecca Stein Faculty Publication Fund.

Johns Hopkins Paperback edition, 2020
2   4   6   8   9   7   5   3   1

Johns Hopkins University Press
2715 North Charles Street
Baltimore, Maryland 21218-4363
www.press.jhu.edu

The Library of Congress has cataloged the hardcover edition of this book as follows:

Names: Posmentier, Sonya, 1975– author.
Title: Cultivation and catastrophe : the lyric ecology of modern Black literature / Sonya Posmentier.
Description: Baltimore : Johns Hopkins University Press, 2017. | Series: The Callaloo African
   diaspora series | Includes bibliographical references and index.
Identifiers: LCCN 2016041516| ISBN 9781421422657 (hardcover) | ISBN 9781421422664 (electronic)
   | ISBN 1421422654 (hardcover)
Subjects: LCSH: American literature—African American authors—History and criticism. |
   American literature—20th century—History and criticism. | Caribbean literature—Black
   authors—History and criticism. | Caribbean literature—20th century—History and criticism |
   Nature in literature. | Ecology in literature. | Blacks—Caribbean Area—Intellectual life—20th
   century. | African Americans—Intellectual life—20th century. | African diaspora. | BISAC:
   LITERARY CRITICISM / Semiotics & Theory. | LITERARY CRITICISM / American / African
   American. | NATURE / Ecology.
Classification: LCC PS153.N5 P675 2017 | DDC 810.9/896073—dc23
   LC record available at https://lccn.loc.gov/2016041516

A catalog record for this book is available from the British Library.

ISBN-13: 978-1-4214-3793-4
ISBN-10: 1-4214-3793-7

Special discounts are available for bulk purchases of this book.
For more information, please contact Special Sales at specialsales@press.jhu.edu.

For Jess, Mina, and Asa

In memory of Smokey and Milton Posmentier and Baldev and Kamala Bhatia

Contents

coda
Unnatural Catastrophe
The Ecology of Black Optimism in M. NourbeSe Philip's *Zong!*

Acknowledgments

A friend once told me that if I became a literary scholar, I should prepare myself for a solitary existence, but *Cultivation and Catastrophe* has always insisted on a social life.

The earliest readers for the materials that have become this book were my dissertation advisors, Daphne Brooks, Simon Gikandi, and Susan Stewart. I owe first and greatest thanks to them for inspiring the questions I undertake here and encouraging even my most idiosyncratic leanings. It was in Susan's graduate seminar on pastoral that I began to imagine a different landscape for black poetry, and it was with her encouragement that I sought answers to my questions in a wide array of materials while holding onto poetry. Daphne has reminded me at every turn about the broader purpose of this work: to tell the story and do right by the people in it. I'm grateful for this urging and for the model her work has provided for listening, looking, and reading "in the break." I thank Simon for piling books in front of me, for urging me to pursue the aesthetic afterlife of the provision ground as modern, and for his honesty at crucial moments. I hope the pages of this work will manifest my debt to the scholarly work of these mentors, whose example I strive daily to approximate.

At Princeton University I was lucky as well to benefit from the teaching, mentorship, and friendship of Jeremy Braddock, Edouardo Cadava, Anne Cheng, Diana Fuss, Josh Kotin, Meredith Martin, James Richardson, Alexandra Vazquez, Timothy Watson, Susan Wheeler, Amanda Wilkins, and Tamsen Wolf in whose seminars, offices, and homes this project had its origins. I am particularly grateful to Valerie Smith and Bill Gleason for bringing me into the profession by inviting me to teach with them and to Cornel West for the example of his teaching and his mind. Pat Gugliemi was an ally in everything. Shirley Tilghman, as university president, made a crucial intervention on my behalf that let me know it might be possible to be a mother and a scholar, for which I will be grateful all my life. This book also would not exist without the important earlier mentorship of Mary Kay Glazek, Garret Hongo, Molly Pollak, and Michael Thurston.

The Department of English at New York University, where I am fortunate to go to work every day, has been an ideal intellectual home. I could not have asked for more generous interlocutors than Maureen McLane and Elizabeth McHenry, who read the entire manuscript and helped to see it through an important pivot in its transformation from dissertation to book. Nicholas Boggs, Jini Kim Watson, and Greg Vargo read and offered feedback on individual chapters of the book. Many other colleagues have taken the time to discuss portions of the work with me through seminars, in conversation, or in print, especially Tom Augst, Jennifer Baker, Bill Blake, Una Chaudhuri, Pat Crain, Patrick Deer, Carolyn Dinshaw, Elaine Freedgood, Toral Gajarwala, Jay Garcia, Philip Brian Harper, Julia Jarcho, Wendy Lee, Peter Nicholls, Urayoán Noel, Crystal Parikh, Lytle Shaw, Pacharee Sudinharaset, Simón Trujillo, and Robert Young. I owe much that is worthy here to their willingness to think with me. Some of these ideas developed in conversation with students in graduate and undergraduate seminars at Princeton, The College of New Jersey, and NYU. Discussions with Kesi Augustine, Bernadette Davis, Ricardo Dunn, Allie Lehrer, Briana Meeks, Tara Menon, Sidney Paige Patterson, Gabrielle Royal, Olga Shkolnikov, and Andrew Schlager were especially significant. On two occasions I had the privilege of sharing work formally with my own colleagues, at the Department of Social and Cultural Analysis Faculty Colloquium and the Farm-To-Text Colloquium in the English Department. I thank Carolyn Dinshaw and John Linstrom and Kimberly Adams, respectively, for creating those opportunities and engaging my work. David Hobbs and Sidney Paige Patterson provided invaluable research support, and Mina Row stepped up to help at a crucial moment. How lucky I am to have had such a supportive department chair in Christopher Cannon, a remarkably attentive mentor in Jini Kim Watson, and guidance and support at every turn from Patricia Okoh-Osene, Taeesha Muhammed, Shanna Williams, Mary Mezzano, Alyssa Leál, and Lissette Florez.

An extraordinary group of fellow-traveling friends have read or talked with me about parts of this book and supported its development over the years: Veronica Alfano, Greg Londe, Anne Hirsch Moffit, Mary Noble, Britt Rusert, Alexendra Vazquez, the 2011–2012 graduate fellows of the Princeton Institute for International and Regional Study, and especially Alicia Christoff, Michelle Coghlan, Briallen Hopper, and Lindsay Reckson, who became family to me at Princeton. Late-night-lyric talks with Rachel Galvin became panels, roundtables, articles, poems, and now books. I owe a great deal of the thinking in this book to Adrienne Brown, who has read it from its earliest to its most recent days and without whose sharp, expansive, and creative interaction I cannot imagine writing anything. Nadia Ellis was the first to see the seed of something worthwhile in this project, and I am grateful for her continued intellectual companionship and impassioned writing. My decades of friendship and intellectual exchange with Rachel Price have sustained me emotionally and intellectually, and chapters of this book are the better for her poetic mind and high standards as a reader. It has been a delight to discover a shared interest in environmental history and humanities with my friend Debbie Coen. I have found in Vanessa Agard-Jones, Laurie Lambert, Imani Owens, Anjuli Raza Kolb, and Gillian White new readers and friends with whom I look forward to many years of exchange. Finally, I am lucky to share this writing life and so much more with Melanie Conroy-Goldman, Casey Kait, and Stephen Weiss.

Many of the chapters in this book developed from conference papers and presentations. I'm grateful to the colleagues with whom these conversations have taken place at the annual conferences of the American Studies Association, the Modern Language Association, the American Comparative Literature Association, the Association for the Study of Worldwide African Diaspora, the Caribbean Studies Association, the Caribbean Philosophical Association, and the Northwestern Radical Poetics Symposium. I thank the Department of English at Williams College, and the Race and Ideology Workshop at the University of Chicago for inviting me to present portions of the work that eventually became this book. Over the years, talking with and listening to poets (some of them also scholars) about their work has been an important part of my process. I am grateful every day for the poetry of Kamau Brathwaite, M. NourbeSe Philip, and Derek Walcott—and also for NourbeSe Philip's generosity in taking the time to speak to me in Toronto many years ago. In addition to the poets about whom I have written in this book and the many others about whom I might have written, I am grateful to Major Jackson, Fred Moten, Mendi Obadike, Evie Shockley, and Tracy K. Smith for their poetry and conversation over the years.

I was fortunate to receive fellowships and grants in support of my research. The costs of production were aided by a generous grant from the Abraham and Rebecca Stein Faculty Publication Fund of the Department of English at New York University. Sean Goudie and Priscilla Wald allowed me to be part of the first cohort of fellows in the First Book Institute at Penn State's Center for American Literary Study. In addition to spearheading this visionary program, Sean was an ideal reader for my work on Brathwaite and for the project as a whole, and Priscilla has doled out much professional wisdom. Shirley Moody-

Turner also offered generous feedback, as did the cohort of fellows: Adrienne Brown, Todd Carmody, Danielle Heard, Sarah Juliet Lauro, Semaine Lockwood, Ted Martin, and Christen Mucher. A Goddard Junior Faculty Fellowship at NYU allowed me necessary release from teaching and service so I could focus on my research, and a Career Enhancement Fellowship from the Woodrow Wilson Foundation extended that time. In that context, Brent Hayes Edwards gave generously of his time and was an invaluable source of guidance. I am grateful to librarians and archivists at the Beinecke Rare Book and Manuscript Library at Yale University, the Moorland-Spingarn Research Center at Howard University, the Thomas Fischer Rare Book Library at the University of Toronto, the Library of the Spoken Word at University of the West Indies-Mona, the National Library of Jamaica, the Schomburg Center for Research, and the American Folklife Center at the Library of Congress and in particular to Renu Barrett, Todd Harvey, Sean Mackoyan, and Frances-Anne Solomon.

I thank Charles Rowell, the series editor for the Callaloo African Diaspora Series, not only for shepherding this book into material existence but also for doing much for the study of black diasporic culture and of poetry and for his unflagging commitment to amplifying the conversation at the intersection of those fields. I also wish to thank Matthew McAdam, my editor at Johns Hopkins University Press, for believing in this project and seeing it through, as well as Catherine Goldstead and MJ Devaney. The two anonymous reviewers who read this manuscript with such care were ideal interlocutors who had a rich understanding of my aims, and I hope I have done justice to their insightful suggestions for revision.

My family, in the words of Zora Neale Hurston, "hauled the mud to make me." My father, Eric, has answered my questions about wind and water and has been a sympathetic ear regarding life in the academy. My mother, Loveleen Posmentier, taught me that it's possible to love my work. My brother Raoul knows the whole story. I wish also to thank Xiahong Feng, Marti Long, Seth Row, Connie Row, and the late Clark Row. I am also grateful for the love and attention with which Rosalia Ruiz, Laura Hill, Nanci Tischler, Lisa Taylor Hebert, and the teachers at U-Now Day Nursery, Little Missionary Preschool, and PS 3 have cared for my children during these years, which enabled me to write and teach. Finally, I must thank Asa and Mina for sharing me with this project, which came into being along with them, and my husband, Jess Row, whose discipline is my daily example and whose love has made this work possible in material and immaterial ways. This book is theirs.

Every effort has been made to identify, contact, and acknowledge copyright holders. I gratefully acknowledge permission to reprint works cited within:

"Will You Be There?," by Shelton Alexander, from *When the Levees Broke: A Requiem in Four Acts*. Reprinted by permission of the author.

Excerpts from "Annie Allen," "Beverly Hills, Chicago," and "In the Mecca," by Gwendolyn Brooks. Reprinted by consent of Brooks Permissions.

Excerpts from "The Catt," by Frank Collymore, and the foreword to *BIM*, Volume 3, No. 9 (1949). First appeared in the *BIM* magazine, Barbados, and have been reprinted with permission of *BIM: Arts for the Twenty-First Century*.

Excerpts from "The Schooner Flight," "The Sea Is History," and "The Star-Apple Kingdom," previously published in *Collected Poems, 1948–1984*, by Derek Walcott. Excerpt from "Forty Acres," previously published in *White Egrets*, by Derek Walcott, from *The Poetry of Derek Walcott, 1948–2013*, by Derek Walcott, selected by Glyn Maxwell. Copyright © 2014 by Derek Walcott. Reprinted by permission of Farrar, Straus and Giroux, LLC, and Faber and Faber, Ltd.

Excerpts from "The Antilles" and "The Muse of History" from *What The Twilight Says: Essays*, by Derek Walcott. Copyright © 1998 by Derek Walcott. Reprinted by permission of Farrar, Straus and Giroux, LLC.

For excerpts from "The Flood," "The Flood, the Red Cross, and the National Guard: I," and "The Flood, the Red Cross, and the National Guard: II," as well as figure 4.1, the publisher wishes to thank the Crisis Publishing Co., Inc., the publisher of the magazine of the National Association for the Advancement of Colored People, for the use of this material first published in the July 1927, January 1928, and February 1928 issues of *Crisis Magazine*.

"Backwater Blues," by Bessie Smith. Copyright ©1927 (Renewed), 1974 Frank Music Corp. All Rights Reserved. Reprinted by Permission of Hal Leonard, LLC.

"Muddy Water." Words and Music by Harry Richmond, Peter DeRose, and Jo Trent. Copyright © 1926 by Sony/ATV Music Publishing, LLC, De Rose Music (ASCAP) and Music Sales Corporation (ASCAP). Copyright Renewed 1954. All rights on behalf of Sony/ATV Music Publishing, LLC, administered by Sony/ATV Music Publishing, 424 Church Street, Suite 1200, Nashville, TN 37219. International copyright secured. All rights reserved. Reprinted by permission of Hal Leonard, LLC, Bienstock Publishing Company, on behalf of Redwood Music, Ltd., Songwriters Guild of America on behalf of De Rose Music and Music Sales Corporation.

"Ma Rainey" and "Cabaret" from *The Collected Poems of Sterling A. Brown*, selected by Michael S. Harper. Copyright © 1980 by Sterling A. Brown. Reprinted by permission of Elizabeth A. Dennis.

Excerpts from *Shar: Hurricane Poem*, by Kamau Brathwaite. Copyright © 1990 Edward Kamau Brathwaite. Reprinted by permission of the author.

Zong! Copyright © 2008 by M. NourbeSe Philip. Published by Wesleyan University Press. Used by permission.

Selections from this book have appeared in slightly different form in the publications and are reprinted here with permission of the publishers:

Chapter 1: Posmentier, Sonya. "The Provision Ground in New York: Claude McKay and the Form of Memory." *American Literature* 84, no. 2 (June 1, 2012): 273–300. doi:10.1215/00029831-1587350.

Chapter 3: Posmentier, Sonya. "The Slave in the Great House." In *Race and Real Estate*, ed. Adrienne Brown and Valerie Smith, 294–312. Oxford: Oxford University Press, 2015.

cultivation and catastrophe

Introduction

CATASTROPHE

In the final moments of its second act, Spike Lee's epic 2006 documentary of Hurricane Katrina, *When the Levees Broke*, features a particularly gruesome series of photographs of dead bodies bloated and stiff, on land and in water, clothed, unclothed, and covered with sheets. The camera settles at last on images of makeshift graves, crosses, and pennants marked with Sharpies in lieu of headstones, while the mournful score composed by Terence Blanchard echoes in strings.[1] Here, in the still center of the film the camera pans up, as if from the burial ground, to spoken word poet Shelton "Shakespear" Alexander reciting in front of St. Vincent de Pau cemetery:

> Blessed are the ones who sacrificed their lives to save us, you truly are dedicated, and
> Blessed are the ones who cried, your tears will not be wasted, and
> Blessed are the ones that were lost and displaced, and whose houses were knocked
>   off its foundation by winds and tidal waves, cemeteries turned into mazes,
>   caskets coming out of their graves like they were in Texas and sitting sideways,
> Days for days, from sin,
> Skeletal remains, remain scattered and unclaimed and that's a shame
> Bush said he accepted the blame so tell me, why they playing games with the money
>   trying to give us the change?

The story has been told, and the devastation has been made visible, but the film's narrative cannot yet propel itself forward, so Lee turns to lyric poetry.

This poetic interlude forwards the broader work of the four-hour film: to connect for viewers the event of the storm, whose physical and environmental end point is most spectacularly visualized in the images preceding the poem, and the long-reaching social and political causes and consequences of human suffering in Louisiana and beyond. The poem acts as a hinge between the first two acts, which tell the story of the storm, and the second two acts, which delve into the political aftermath, including the evacuation and the resulting diaspora. But rather than continue the narrative, the juxtaposition between the repetitive beatitudinal structure and the descriptive language that exceeds that structure suggests the representational challenges brought about by the flood. Alexander concludes:

> I told you that I'd be here.
> What's important is that I came.
> I'm leaving. But I'll be back again.
> Will you be there?

The image of Alexander and the cemetery gates fades into that of an open road lined with debris, alluding to the future progression of the film and the people of New Orleans. The poem evokes the migrations that Katrina, like previous storms, would yield. But the final moment of the poem suspends that progression, figuring the poet's presence in a circular collapse of past ("I came"), present ("I'm leaving"), and future ("I'll be back again.") The poem itself is the caesura, a rhythmic pause characteristic of lyric poetry, providing a break between the film's focus on the local conditions of New Orleans in the first half and its attention to diaspora—the loss of human bodies to the waters and the scattering of human lives—in the second. The film and the break in it remind us of the different forms diaspora takes: the movement of bodies, the movement of sound and text, and the movement of seeds and storms. These parallel and intersecting movements define the landscapes through which this book travels.

In this volume, I uncover how black writers in the twentieth century have responded to environmental alienation resulting from the vexed legacy of the plantation, urbanization, and various forced and free migrations. In the arc from beatitude to curse and back again through song and prayer, Alexander's poem enacts an oscillation between social death and social life that has shaped black cultural expression over the last century. If Orlando Patterson coined the term "social death" to describe the structure and aftermath of slavery, and more recent scholarship has insisted on the persistence of social death beyond the institution of legalized slavery itself, the concept takes on different meaning in black writing that wrestles with environmental experience in the twentieth century.[2]

At the intersection of social and environmental history there has emerged a rich body of black literary response to natural and agricultural experiences, whether the legacy of enforced agricultural labor or the destruction and displacement brought about by a hurricane, that have wrought and sustained social death. Through extended analysis of works by Claude McKay, Bessie Smith, Sterling Brown, Zora Neale Hurston, Frank Collymore, Gwendolyn Brooks, Derek Walcott, Kamau Brathwaite, Lloyd Lovindeer, and M. NourbeSe Philip, this book demonstrates how writers and lyricists have countered the alienation brought about by social and environmental catastrophe by voicing a poetics of survival, repair, and generation. Black literary accounts of historical rupture and cultural continuity have long constituted an important response to environmental experience and ecological change. In turn, the imperative to account for environmental experience, far from being a curious nostalgic throwback to the plantation, forms one basis for black modernity in the twentieth century.

The key terms of this study, "cultivation" and "catastrophe," do not oppose one another but intersect: in the United States and the Caribbean, cultivation in the form of enforced agricultural labor has been a social catastrophe in and of itself; environmental catastrophes in turn have yielded rich traditions of art, music, and poetry. Hence the simultaneity of cultivation and catastrophe animates Shelton "Shakespear" Alexander's insistence on his living presence in the space of death. These terms function in part as metaphors for human experiences of growth and displacement and in part as descriptions of agricultural and natural processes that have had material and ecological implications for black communities and their environments. Hurricanes, for example, play a central role in black diasporic literature, and in this book, because they retrace the motion of the transatlantic slave trade and the violence and loss of the middle passage, forming off the coast of West Africa and making landfall in the Caribbean archipelago and the southern United States, taking different forms as they touch different shores. But they are equally significant as material forces that cause economic destruction and exacerbate racial and other inequities. As such, these storms are an apt figure for an understanding of black diaspora as constituted by a shared history, on the one hand, and by distinctive, at times uneven, geographic, economic, and cultural forms on the other.[3]

The other environments and literary modes I encounter in this oeuvre of twentieth-century black writing—the landscapes of the plantation and provision ground, the topography of the archipelago, pastoral and georgic modes, the blues, the archive—similarly foreground the tension between particular and expansive expressions of blackness. I name such spaces of bounded aesthetic innovation "lyric ecologies," establishing a relationship between lyric and ecology on the level of both content and form. I am interested in the way poems recount, contain, and respond to ecological experience—by which I mean the relationships between human and nonhuman organisms and the management and use of natural and agricultural resources. Mindful of Samantha Pinto's useful instruction that "our own interpretive strategies" for analyzing diaspora "must shift not away from form and structure but toward it" (*Difficult Diasporas*, 9), I focus less on how black literature takes up "nature" as its subject and more on how black writing yields theories of environmental relation rooted in the particularities of black history, black experience, and black aesthetics.[4] To that end, I am also interested in lyrics as ecological: that is, in how poems sometimes mimic or approximate organic forms and processes often associated with enclosure, preservation, self-sustainability, and internal relation, forms that can exceed their own boundaries, and that may in turn yield new models for social and ecological relation.

Virginia Jackson has referred to the idealization, abstraction, and dehistoricizing tendencies of twentieth-century critics' approach to the qualities often associated with lyric poetry, many of which I draw on in my discussion of lyric ecologies (brevity, the fictional subjectivity of an individual lyric speaker, the suspension of temporal progression, the proximity to song), as the "lyricization" of poetry. Indeed, she insists that the process of "lyricization" has itself produced what we now call "lyric," an abstracted, transparent, ahistorical generic category that obscures the local, personal, and historical conditions that produce more specific genres, and the way such specific forms are used by poets.[5] After Jackson's intervention and the subsequent analyses guided by the methods of historical poetics that Jackson and Yopie Prins's *The Lyric Theory Reader* offer, it is hard to talk about lyric without the worry that I will reproduce the kind of dehistoricizing discourse that (rightly) concerns Jackson, Prins, and other scholars of historical poetics. (My concern is perhaps itself a version of what Gillian White has called "lyric shame.") But I refer to near-sonnets by Claude McKay and Gwendolyn Brooks, documentary poems by Sterling Brown, musical lyrics by Bessie Smith and Lloyd Lovindeer, long poems by Brooks and Derek Walcott, and fragmentary book-length poems by Brathwaite and M. NourbeSe Philip as lyric precisely to index the richly historical debates that have arisen around the characteristics typically associated with lyric. I do not invoke the qualities of lyric poetry as "givens" inherited from a much older European classical tradition but rather as vital modern concerns about the capacities of literary genre. Whereas Jackson and Prins define the history of modern lyric reading almost entirely as a product of "Anglo-American" (by which, it seems, they mean white American and European) criticism ("General Introduction," 1), I attend to a different history of the lyric generated on the margins of American and European modernity.

Cultivation and catastrophe also describe different models for thinking about time, and in particular black historical experience. This book posits a theory of lyric time that encompasses both historical continuity and the ruptured time of what Édouard Glissant calls "nonhistory," the time fractured by the slave trade and its legacy (*Caribbean Discourse*, 61–62). I focus on lyric ecologies—whether in the form of a poem or in the relationship of the poem to novels, dancehall, the blues, and other forms of expression—because of the way lyric time reorients the temporality of black history. As a form that mediates between the musical and the textual, lyric poetry also indexes the difficulties of transcribing and preserving on the page that which is extraliterary, including both sonic and environmental experience. *Cultivation and Catastrophe* uncovers the possibilities and limits of poetic forms as archives for black diasporic culture that is textual, sonic, performative, intangible, concrete, preserved, and partial. As I draw lines around these lyric ecologies, defining closed systems for study, I know that the lines are permeable and impermanent.

As intersecting frameworks for approaching black diasporic experiences, cultivation and catastrophe allow us to see people of African descent in the eastern United States (from the Mississippi to the Atlantic coast, but especially in the southern Black Belt) and in the Caribbean as common inhabitants of an heterogenous zone.[6] I don't call this zone the postcolony, although I draw on postcolonial studies. Nor am I describing only a black Atlantic, circumatlantic, or archipelagic region, although all of these models come to bear on my analysis: parts of the United States well inland from the coast fall within the scope of this study, such as Gwendolyn Brooks's Chicago and Bessie Smith's Mississippi delta. Further, whereas previous Atlantic frameworks have maintained a theoretical focus on the circulation of human lives and cultural materials, I contend that ecological characteristics and processes (the trade winds, the hurricane, the flood), agricultural products, and landscapes are equally definitive of black diaspora. I speak often of the plantation and the plantation zone, but I also attend to cities like New York, Chicago, and Kingston. The area under study here includes apartment complexes whose histories and architecture have been produced by local housing policies and transregional migrations and also watersheds (the mid-Atlantic, the south-Atlantic gulf, the Tennessee, the upper and lower Mississippi, the Hope River in Jamaica) that cross state and sometimes national borders. It is not my goal to establish a fixed geographic region of study but rather to bring into focus a dynamic, cross-cultural, extranational zone defined by the shared processes of growth and destruction to which its inhabitants are subject and in which they participate. One premise for this book is geographer Katherine McKittrick's important assertion that "black matters are spatial matters" (*Demonic Grounds*, xiv), but equally significant is the work that McKittrick and others have done to denaturalize the association between specific places and black diasporic identities.[7] Thus, *Cultivation and Catastrophe* does not concern itself with the comparison of national cultures but rather with the language, literature, and sound that stretches (to borrow a term from Jahan Ramazani) and travels within this dynamic zone.[8]

NATION LANGUAGE / NATURE LANGUAGE

Having defined the geographic parameters of this study as permeable and elastic, discrepant with the geopolitical boundaries of the nation state, I nonetheless want to note that Caribbean writers articulating a poetics in the waxing days of independence from European colonialism often sought homologies between environmental experiences and national or regional identities. In their essays from the 1970s and 1980s, Sylvia Wynter (from Jamaica), Kamau Brathwaite (from Barbados), and Édouard Glissant (from Martinique) turned to their local geographies and to shared regional experiences of weather, climate, and agriculture to define Caribbean writing for a new generation and for emerging nations.

For many of these writers, black subjectivity is inseparable from geography and, further, from questions of literary form. One necessary theory of the intimacy between geography and black life is to be found in Wynter's early essay, "Novel and History, Plot and Plantation" (1971), a work that has been, until recently, more often taken up as narrative or political theory than as ecological theory.[9] Her essay helps us see how agricultural language shapes nationalist formulations and how engagement with the geographical history of the plantation has defined literary forms and literary genres. For Wynter, the West Indian writer must engage in a caretaking rather than a property-based relation to the earth in order to make an "indigenous" claim to the land and has the capacity to do so because of his or her historical double relation as both laborer and commodity. Wynter identifies the agricultural basis for this relation in the "inevitable and inbuilt confrontation between the plantation" and what she calls "the plot," subsistence gardens farmed by enslaved laborers and later peasants for their "use value" in survival ("Novel and History, Plot and Plantation," 102). Perhaps most significantly for our purposes, this dual relation produces an aesthetics as well as a politics; that is, Wynter argues, the Caribbean novel necessarily partakes in the tension between the market economy and its critique. Wynter's framing of modern blackness in relationship to plantation geography

performs a *critical reterritorialization* that I take up in chapter 2.[10] I investigate
the precise terms of the connection between agricultural geography and literary
genre both later in this introduction and throughout part 1, but I invoke Wynter
here to introduce the broad sense in which the plantation has an epistemological afterlife in Caribbean literary theory.

Throughout and beyond the 1970s other Caribbean thinkers continued to
take up the problem of geography as a determining factor in black postcolonial
life and in the production of literature. As Elizabeth DeLoughrey has observed,
we can identify an important tension in this era of Caribbean environmental
thought between the ongoing intimacy with the earth Wynter celebrates and
the alienation from the landscape emphasized by Martincan poet and theorist
Édouard Glissant.[11] The plantation and plot do not so much define competing
models for establishing Caribbean nationhood as they give shape to a diasporic
poetics. Whereas Glissant renders cultivation as a figure for emergent Caribbean regional politics in the set of essays collected in the 1981 *Caribbean Discourse*, in the 1990 *Poetics of Relation*, the *racine* (root) gives way to the *rhizome*,
an environmental trope he borrows from Deleuze and Guattari to figure Caribbean errantry. Glissant's transformation of environmental metaphor from static
to relational (root to rhizome) indicates a critical shift I want to enact in the
readings that follow in this book, from thinking of natural and agricultural
tropes in black writing as figurations of nationalist discourse to imagining more
elastic formations of identity and belonging that emerge in relationship to specific surroundings.[12]

Glissant advocates an understanding of Caribbean history as a "nonhistory"
that is unintelligible within the framework of Western linear progressivism and
defined instead by processes of detour and rupture (*Caribbean Discourse*, 61–62).
In *Caribbean Discourse*, linking literary "nonhistory" with the chronotope of the
Caribbean, Glissant naturalizes literary form in relationship to the specificity
of the Caribbean season. Like other writers of his generation searching for a
language of authenticity, of "lived rhythms" (109), Glissant uses environmental
metaphor to describe the relationship between literature and experience.

Enacting what Timothy Morton might term a form of ecomimesis, Glissant
wants to collapse the space between the environment and the poem in order to
address the failure of Western realist modes to contain Caribbean experience.[13]
Part of the problem, according to Glissant, has to do with a persistent presen-
tism in books that represent the "miserable reality of our countries," which he
attributes to a failure to account for "*the function of the landscape*" (105, emphasis
in original). Glissant's starting point is alienation—that is, rupture between the

people and the land, between nature and culture. To attend to this rupture, this catastrophic break, is the work of literature, and it is a work that writers cannot fully achieve within the constraints of Western literary form—whether the realist novel (which, he contends, works well for Balzac or Zola but can only be the basis of a "wretched substitute" in the Caribbean) or the European sonnet (105–6). In order to understand the "deepest meanings" of the landscape, writers must align poetic form to the climatic experience of the Caribbean:

> These observations are linked to the problem of the rhythmic structure of the literary work. The pattern of the seasons has perhaps shaped, in the works of Western literature, a balanced rhythm between neutral zones of narrative that are periodically crossed by explosive flashes that arouse the emotions and bring "revelation." . . . To aim for spectacular moments, or twists in the narrative, for "brainwaves," is perhaps for our writers to perpetrate at the technical level an unconscious and unjustified submissiveness to literary traditions alien to our own. Technical vigilance is here not a question of splitting hairs. (106)

Glissant relegates Caribbean poetics to "monotony, a plainsong," on the grounds of its seasonal structure—that is, the pattern of weather over time that governs environmental experience. In a (curiously) nationalist, even an essentialist, moment, Glissant suggests that to repair the rupture between land and humans, Caribbean writers must overcome their "literary submissiveness to literary traditions alien to their own" and instead seek to express "the unvarying season (the absence of a seasonal rhythm)." "Technical vigilance" is environmental vigilance (the need to watch the "obsessive rhythm" of Caribbean nature).

Thus, to account for the historical experience and the geography of black diasporic subjects is for Glissant a matter of literary genre. It seems that to repair the break, to survive in literature, is necessarily to reject "alien" forms (the sonnet, for instance) and find a way of writing that is more fully mimetic of what Glissant calls the "monotony" of Caribbean time. Calling for "a new economy of expressive forms," Glissant notes that "neither poem nor novel are for that matter our genres" (106, 106n1). Here Glissant echoes an ethno-environmental mimeticism that was common among Caribbean intellectuals during the 1970s, a period of national and regional self-definition.[14]

If *Caribbean Discourse* seeks a kind of reflection between landscape and aesthetics, *Poetics of Relation* attends to misalignment itself (opacity, not reflection) as a form of Caribbean expression. In this later work Glissant elaborates his poetic response to environmental alienation as a way of describing not only Caribbean identity but also environmental relation. The originary rupture of

Poetics of Relation is "The Open Boat," a meditation on the middle passage, "the first uprooting" (8). Beginning thus, it is no wonder that when he calls for at last "an aesthetics of the earth," Glissant is careful to qualify "aesthetics":

> Yes. But an aesthetics of disruption and intrusion. Finding the fever of passion for the ideas of "environment" (which I call surroundings) and "ecology," both apparently such futile notions in these landscapes of desolation. Imagining the idea of love of the earth—so ridiculously inadequate or else frequently the basis for such sectarian intolerance—with all the strength of charcoal fires or sweet syrup.
>
> Aesthetics of rupture and connection. (151)

The environmental mimesis proposed in *Caribbean Discourse* becomes here a problem of slippery relation. Yet we cannot slip out of territory ("planted," "legitimated," limited) and into land (limitless) without understanding the plantation system. In "Closed Place, Open Word," Glissant sets out to understand the paradoxes of the plantation system's economic and geographic structure: the "Plantation's will to autarky" and "its dependence, in reality, in relation to the external world," its enclosure and its repetition. If this structure allowed the survival of the plantation system beyond its historical limit, it also produces the structure and geography of black diasporic expression, the "creative marronage" exerting itself at the margins of European "literature of illusion" (70–71). If in *Caribbean Discourse* Glissant expresses skepticism about the capacity for poetry to perform and produce this marronage, a skepticism rooted in the "limitations" of written literature (108), *Poetics of Relation* instead articulates "why we stay with poetry" (9) as an open and capacious form of expression. Ecological language rooted in the geography of Martinique allows Glissant to derive his central aesthetic structure from the particular geography and history of the Caribbean while also imagining relation, a potential for comparison and connection both within and beyond the archipelago.

Cultivation and Catastrophe follows in the wake of the model of environmental relation Glissant elaborates in *Poetics of Relation*, a model acknowledging the limits of ecomimesis or the idea that the relationship between nature and culture is a transparent one.[15] But I want to insist at the same time that there is a congruity between the essays in *Caribbean Discourse* and those in *Poetics of Relation*, and to highlight the intellectual history through which forms of diasporic belonging emerge in response to particular "surroundings." Attention to the context in which these ideas were circulating will be especially important in relationship to the claims I make in part 2 of this book, in which I argue that environmental catastrophe brings to the fore not only crises of representation but crises of preservation. In readings of poetry as an intermedial genre, I argue that poetry can be one response to this crisis, functioning as a lyric archive of social and environmental history. Attempts to theorize black environmental experience likewise constitute such an archive, produced in the ephemeral contexts of lecture halls, classrooms, and out-of-print periodicals, marking an "aesthetics of rupture and connection."

The publication and presentation history of the essays collected in *Caribbean Discourse* highlights the very problem of particularity, or the "local," within the diverse geographies and languages of the Caribbean.[16] They were originally adapted from works published in France (mainly) and the United States and from lectures given in Panama, Jamaica, Martinique, Canada, Guadalupe, Cuba, and the United States. Glissant's "The Quarrel with History," for example, in which he elaborates his idea of nonhistory, was delivered as a lecture at Carifesta 1976, a pan-Caribbean festival of the arts hosted that year in Kingston, Jamaica, in response to Edward Baugh's essay "The West Indian Writer and His Quarrel with History." The question of how to relate particular national and geographic histories to one another while striving for a collective cultural consciousness was at the heart of Carifesta as a whole in its founding years (the first Carifesta was held in Guyana in 1972), as it was at the heart of Glissant's oeuvre. In his contribution to the symposium on West Indian literature, Glissant insists on the need for a methodological approach to "collective consciousness" that would be other than "a totalitarian philosophy of history" (*Caribbean Discourse*, 62).[17] At stake in Glissant's impulse toward collectivity and repair are three different kinds of relation: the connections among different nations, locations, and cultures within the Caribbean; "the creative link between nature and culture" (63); and "the complex reuniting of writing and speech" (143). Glissant's poetics of relation, then, has always been conceived in connection with nations, mediation, and environmental relation. What might happen when this distinctly "Antillean" theory of culture and ecology is "stretched" beyond its regional framework?

THE HURRICANE DOES NOT ROAR IN PENTAMETER
The same five-day symposium on West Indian literature featured Bajan poet Kamau Brathwaite's lecture titled "National-Language in West Indian Poetry" in which he first opined that "the hurricane does not roar in pentameters" (*History of the Voice*, 10).[18] But in a Harvard lecture hall in 1979, Brathwaite delivered a different version of the lecture that had originated in conversation with Glissant and other Caribbean writers. In this new context, he defined the region of

his poetic making like this: "The Caribbean is a set of islands stretching out from Florida in a mighty curve. You must know of the Caribbean at least from television, at least now with hurricane David coming right into it" (6). The published book form of the lecture, titled *History of the Voice* (1984), offers a foundational theory of the relationship between language and culture as well as a significant modern theory of the relationship between nature and culture. Speaking and writing in the first decade of West Indian independence from British colonization, Brathwaite coins the term "nation language" as a way of defining a regional vernacular literary voice, an alternative to the violent experience of reading and writing in an inherited colonial language. But Brathwaite characterizes nation language as geographically and temporally dynamic, intercultural, and coming into being. In doing so he names a notion that helps us read the diasporic form not only of poetry we commonly understand as postcolonial, that which emerged in the later part of the twentieth century out of nations newly independent from European colonizers, but also of black modern poetry more broadly.

Unifying anxieties over translation of environmental experience, translation of national or regional experience, and translation from stage to page, a footnote simultaneously archives the history of the text and the history of environmental catastrophe: "This talk was presented at Harvard University, Cambridge, Massachusetts, late in August 1979. Hurricanes ravish the Caribbean and the southern coasts of the United States every summer. David (1979) was followed by Allen (1980), one of the most powerful on record" (*History*, 6n). Brathwaite's footnote is remarkable because it refers to the shared environmental experience of a region including both the southern United States and the Caribbean, suggesting an expanded definition of nation that encompasses the African diaspora. The footnote translates from Caribbean catastrophe to American classroom, signaling difference as a constituent element of diasporic experience.[19] The footnote also suggests that the search for a "national" (in the broad or elastic sense in which Brathwaite defines it) poetry is a search for a way to reconcile aural and textual experience.

Having evoked the hurricane as the signature environmental experience of the region, Brathwaite returns to it as a figure for the problem of literary mimesis that he and other Caribbean writers of his generation faced. "The hurricane does not roar in pentameters," he famously contends, "and that's the problem: how do you get a rhythm which approximates the *natural* experience, the *environmental* experience" (*History*, 10, emphasis in original)? Why is the hurricane the signal feature of "our experience"? To take Brathwaite too literally risks falling prey to mimetic fallacy, whereby we naturalize, romanticize, or nationalize the relationship between race and region. In the intimacy between "our experience" and the weather, we can hear the echo of a colonial tradition which fails to separate the bodies and minds of the enslaved people from their climates (given, of course, the irony that the very condition of Africans in the Americas is that of having been separated from their climates).

Colonial descriptions of the West Indies are replete with racialized formulations of the West Indian climate as claiming its inhabitants (both enslaved and free). Edward Ward's 1698 critique of Jamaica, for instance, equates the climate with the community of white colonists there, describing the "character of Jamaica" as follows: "Subject to Turnadoes, Hurricans, and Earthquakes, as if the Island, like the People, were troubled with the *Dry Belly-Ach*" (an affliction of the inhabitants which Ward attributes to the excessively sour fruits of the island) ("A Trip to Jamaica," 88–89). John Singleton's recounting of a hurricane and a black funeral in adjacent episodes in "A General Description of the West-Indian Islands" naturalizes both processes—tying them to the oceanic. Singleton initially emphasizes the "calm deportment" of the enslaved mourners and the "gentle waves" of their procession, but eventually the "frantic" energy of the funeral sequence echoes the description of the storm that immediately precedes it.

Unlike Ward and Singleton, physician-poet James Grainger demonstrates an acute awareness of the West Indies as a nonnative environment for Africans in *The Sugar-Cane*: "Woud'st thou secure thine Ethiop from those ails, / Which change of climate, change of waters breed / and food unusual?" (4:119–20). Grainger's concerns about "transplanting" African slaves from their native landscapes and Ward and Singleton's equation of the West Indian climate and character equally trouble modern readers, as both rely on naturalized conceptions of racial identity. Grainger cautions planters in St. Kitts that "in mind, and aptitude for useful toil, / The negroes differ" according to the particular African geography, climate, and culture from which they have been removed (4:38–39). He goes on to detail the particular pros and cons of enslaved laborers from particular places, slipping between climate and culture as explanations of the various taxonomies he outlines. Men from Cormantee are "bred too generous for the servile field" because at home they hunt and fight while "their wives plant rice, or yams, or lofty maize." The women, in turn, make good field-workers. Workers from Mundingo, he contests, are especially prone to worms owing to the unfamiliar food and climate of the West Indies. Grainger suggests an equiv-

alence between experience (i.e., how the slaves are "bred") and geography in accounting for labor fitness: "the sunny Libyan" apparently defines both the dis-
position and the climate of the enslaved Africans he deems most flexible in their
use value (4:40–121).

This kind of taxonomic thinking shares its logic with the strategies of cultural dominance that pervaded the colonial slave trade. Richard Ligon, in *A True
and Exact History of Barbados* [1657], cites three reasons why the Africans, although they outnumber "the Christians," did not rise up in rebellion:

> The one is, They are not suffered to touch or handle any weapons: The other, That
> they are held in such awe and slavery, as they are fearfull to appear in any daring at . . .
> Besides these, there is a third reason, which stops all designs of that kind, and that is,
> They are fetch'd from severall parts of *Africa*, who speake several languages, and by
> that means, one of them understands not another: For, some of them are fetch'd from
> *Guinny* and *Binny*, some from *Cutchew*, some from *Angola*, and some from the River of
> *Gambra*. (20)

The colonial equation between climate and culture parallels colonial assumptions about language and community. If building an enslaved labor force out of
disparate linguistic populations was a deliberate strategy to prevent the formation of community among the slaves, it also became the foundation for racist
theories of Africans' cultural inferiority: divorced from their mother tongue and
fatherland, this line of thinking goes, Africans and their descendants had *no* culture, *no* language, *no* weather. Twentieth-century writers and scholars have
been faced with the challenge of having to acknowledge the historical reality of
these displacements (albeit with significant qualifications to Ligon's oversim-
plified theory) while at the same time insisting on the viability of the black languages and cultures that nonetheless emerged from this history.[20]

It might seem surprising, then, that Brathwaite would develop his theory of
nation language in relationship to climate, echoing the powerful colonial language of cultural and racial supremacy he wishes to refute and redefine. Indeed,
if we read Brathwaite's definition of "nation" in a geographically limited sense,
we might understand his formulation as trapped within the colonial logic of mimesis. However, the very structure of the weather complex makes it difficult
for us to read Brathwaite's "hurricane" as an insistently local or national figure
for resistant poetic voice. I want to suggest instead that the hurricane is a particularly apt and powerful figure for poetic language because of its status as a
phenomenon that travels and yet takes different forms as it touches different

shores. Brathwaite's call for poetry worthy of hurricanes is a future-oriented call for a circulatory, collective poetics that acknowledges the geographic range and the violence of the hurricane's motion.

The tension between the experience of violence and disruption, on the one hand, and expressive possibilities for containing and reproducing that experience, on the other, is an example of what Gordon Rohlehr refers to as "the problem of the problem of form." It is also a tension in contemporary theories of black historiography between which I aim to find some common ground: what Jared Sexton and others have called Afro-pessimism, the theory that black diasporic subjects are conscripted within a modernity that enslaves, and what Moten describes as black optimism, the idea of blackness as a persistent, resistant overturning of Western civilization, whose aim is also the recognition and reconstruction of its own possibilities.[21] Brathwaite's own "Shar/Hurricane Poem," to which I return in chapter 6, gives voice to the hurricane's still center and to its motion:

> For the stone of this island to be bombed
>
> by this wind & all this. all this. water
>
> O longshore late light duppy Kingston nights
>
> wood
> has become so useless. stripped. wet .
> fragile . broken . totally uninhabitable
> with what we must still build

Composed in the immediate aftermath of Hurricane Gilbert, four years after the *History of the Voice* was published, these lines conflate the human action of bombing with the action of the hurricane, but the punctuation and abrupt enjambments also recall the hurricane's destruction as an interruption of "habitable" human temporality. The poem continues, grimly, to tell us "what we must still build": a poetic memory of "a half-a-million shaved off from the auction block/curled & cut off from their stock /without even that sweet scent of resin on a good day." The image the poem builds is of slaves "curled & cut off"; it is an image of detachment but also one that brings history into the conditional possibility of the future, through the still "eye" of the poem.

Natural disaster poses a spatial problem for Brathwaite: how to represent the regional experience of an environmental phenomenon (hurricanes, not snow). In this sense, writing about catastrophic experience brings challenges similar to those of representing a natural and agricultural environment steeped in history (the focus of my first three chapters). But the rhythm of the hurricane is also a way of marking time in opposition to the violence of colonial history. As a theory of poetic language and environmental mimesis, then, Brathwaite's contention that the hurricane does not roar in pentameter gives rise to the two animating questions of *Cultivation and Catastrophe*: how have black writers in the twentieth century formally represented ecologies haunted by the legacies of enforced agricultural labor, and how can poetic time account simultaneously for the growth (cultural and agricultural) and the catastrophic breaks that have shaped black historical experience?

LYRIC SPACE AND TIME

In this book I contend that poetry, and lyric poetry in particular, offers a way of thinking about catastrophic rupture as a temporal alternative to what Homi Bhabha calls the "continuous progressivist myth of Man" (*The Location of Culture*, 340). Bhabha challenges what he views as the predominance of ideas of "progress" in Western modernism by emphasizing an alternative "temporal dimension" (201). While Bhabha frames his call for "another time of writing" (202) as a rethinking of postcolonial *narrative,* it is worth noting that although he begins with analyses of Nadine Gordimer and Toni Morrison (and returns often to *Beloved*, a text in which narrative reveals its own limits), he resolves the questions he raises in his final chapter with a reading of a poem by Derek Walcott and concludes the book with a discussion of a poem by Sonia Sanchez, the lyrics of Ella Fitzgerald, and finally "the rhythm of the Sorrow Songs" in Du Bois (202–3, 255–56). Thus, when Bhabha concludes that "we must not merely change the *narratives* of our histories, but transform our sense of what it means to live" (256, emphasis mine), it is hard not to imagine that sense residing in song. He must borrow a term from prosody, "caesura," which describes the rhythmic pause in a poetic line, to describe "the time-lag of cultural difference" from which the human emerges (340). The "time-lag" in turn brings to mind Adorno's formulation of lyric as bearing "the quality of a break or rupture" ("Lyric Poetry and Society," 59). It is through this break, rather than in spite of it, that the lyric poem engages society, and it is this alienated engagement that for Adorno defines the lyric as a modern form. Lyric speaks from the caesura, the temporal break, and is opposed to "the continuous progressivist myth of man." Lyric poetry disrupts temporal progression even as it, in Bhabha's words, "keeps alive the making of the past" (364). In describing Bhabha's "*temporal* caesura" (340) as part of, according to Adorno, "what we mean by lyric" (59), that is, as a form characterized by a break or rupture—I do not mean to suggest that it is transhistorically or essentially so. Rather, I want to suggest that the social and environmental history of the black Atlantic—characterized by a break, a rupture—has in part produced an idea of lyric time.

For literary scholars in a wide range of subfields, one significant preoccupation of modern life is the need to understand catastrophic events—whether the violent dislocation of the slave trade or the dramatic devastation of a hurricane—within the scale of human time. For example, Lauren Berlant proposes in *Cruel Optimism* that "crisis ordinariness" better describes our current experiences of disappointment, suffering, and loss than does trauma theory, which emphasizes the singular catastrophic event (10), while Rob Nixon suggests in *Slow Violence and the Environmentalism of the Poor* that we need to slow down in order to perceive the pace of environmental disaster that is not catastrophic in the sense of a sudden turn or event but instead part of the everyday. These theories run parallel to and are interconnected with scientific attempts to account for an environmental change—for example, the emergence of the term "anthropocene" to account for the unprecedented intersection of recorded and geological history in our current age, or the theory of "punctuated equilibrium" that evolutionary biologists introduced half a century ago to account for changes in species and ecosystems.[22] Such theories remind us of the need to approach historiographic problems as spatiotemporal.

Scholars of black diaspora have long wrestled with a similar set of questions about how to engage the history of plantation slavery in the present. Elizabeth DeLoughrey's important comparative study of the oceanic, *Routes and Roots: Navigating Caribbean and Pacific Island Literatures*, elucidates "the ways in which diaspora space is conceptualized in relation to modern time" (52). Katherine McKittrick's *Demonic Grounds* argues that the geography of the transatlantic slave trade shaped black women's contemporary political and cultural formation. Building on this work, and entering into conversation with new projects by McKittrick and by Christina Sharpe on the chronotopes of enslavement, *Cultivation and Catastrophe* shifts the ground of this discussion by placing problems of literary genre at its center.[23] In his rereading of C. L. R. James's classic text *The Black Jacobins*, David Scott argues that the postcolonial present demands "another way of thinking about history and historical change." Scott describes this "other way of thinking" in literary terms. Specifically, he suggests that we give up constructing (critically) what Hayden White calls "romantic emplotments" that narrate the resistance of the oppressed and attend instead to "the story-form of tragedy," which, he contends, can account for the transformed conditions of modernity (*Conscripts of Modernity*, 131). For Scott the conscripting structure of the plantation shapes modernity and thus demands this new "story-form."[24] In calling for "story-form" Scott echoes countless theorists from Bhabha to Henry Louis Gates Jr. to Farah Griffin, who have laid the groundwork for identifying different strategies of narrating the black struggle for freedom. African American literary critics and postcolonial scholars have long expressed the need for new ways of thinking about space and time together. In this scholarship, narratives of cultural or national identity, along with narrative as a genre, constitute the foundation for black discourses of freedom.

In spite of poet Phillis Wheatley's status as a foremother of African American literature, early prose narratives form the backbone of a tradition deeply concerned with genealogy, identity formation, and progress. Major critics and theorists seek out and recuperate such narratives as constitutive of African American identity. Some obvious examples are Henry Louis Gates Jr.'s recuperative literary projects, such as the single-volume *Classic Slave Narratives*, which have made texts in the African American narrative tradition widely available, as well his recent efforts to bring together genealogical research and storytelling in *African American Lives* (2004) and the PBS documentaries based on that collection. Gates reminds us that "in the long history of human bondage, it was only the black slaves in the United States who . . . created a *genre* of literature that at once testified against their captors and bore witness to the urge of every black slave to be free and literate" (introduction, ix–x). Similarly, as Jahan Ramazani and Brent Edwards have pointed out, narrative fictions—novels—are at the center of postcolonial studies, often to the exclusion of a serious theoretical engagement with poetics.[25]

Given the predominance of narrative, how have writers gone beyond the "story-form" in imagining forms that can account for the conflicting experiences of constraint and generation that emerge within the plantation zone? In raising this question, I am not only suggesting that we need to consider genres other than the novel, story, or autobiography; while this is certainly the case, there are many important critical accounts of black poetry and black genre that do just this.[26] Rather, I am arguing specifically that lyric modes of representation allow us to comprehend the spatiotemporal displacements that have originated and perpetuated this time and place of modernity by going outside "emplotment" altogether.

Given the significance of the plantation and the "plot" for the rest of this book, it is worth returning to Sylvia Wynter's foundational account of the plantation's afterlife in "Novel and History, Plot and Plantation." Implicit in Wynter's analysis of the gardening "plot" as a space of potential critique is a pun on "plot" to describe both these gardens and the work a novel does against its superstructure through narrative. For Wynter, the Caribbean novel embodies the tension between the plantation and the plot insofar as it constitutes "the critique of the very historical processes" of colonization and works to "restore the written past to a people who had only an oral past" (97). However, while Wynter explicitly embraces the Caribbean novel as the formal embodiment of the provision ground, the essay makes a curious turn toward its end. Juxtaposing the history she associates with "indigenous plot values" against "the official history of the superstructure; the only history which has been written" (101), she does not cite a section of *A New Day*, the V.S. Reid novel that has been her primary focus, but instead insists that "the plot too has its own history, a secretive history expressed in folk songs" and chants. She includes excerpts from such songs, describing, for example, a Kumina ritual chant centered around Paul Bogle, the leader of the Morant Bay rebellion. These examples suggest that the provision ground produces something *else* we might call history, a plot that is not plotted but sung and chanted.

The implicit possibility that what Wynter calls the "indigenization" of Caribbean literary culture takes place not through the novel but through other genres and potentially other media becomes more explicit in another essay Wynter published a year earlier, "Jonkonnu in Jamaica," which traces the origins and transformations of an important Jamaican ritual dance associated with the planting, harvest, and fertility of yams. Here, indigenization, or "the rooting of the African in the New World" that connects people to the earth, is a process that unfolds through performance and the circulation of oral culture rather than in the form of written narrative. Wynter also makes a distinction between plot and plantation in this essay that becomes the basis for "Novel and History, Plot and Plantation": "the [plantation] would give rise to the superstructure of civilization in the Caribbean; the [plot] to the roots of culture" (37). Wynter uses "roots" metaphorically to indicate connection to West African tradition and more literally to demonstrate a material link between specific agricultural processes and the dance. She observes that the leap in dance follows the growth pattern of the yam: "the dancer identifies with the planted. The taller the leap, the taller the yams, the more flourishing" (42).

Wynter's thinking of the provision ground in relationship to performance provides one ground for an ecological poetry, where the poesis in question takes place in the lines between text, movement, and song. Each section of the essay on Jonkonnu begins with an epigraph, and while the early epigraphs consist mostly of descriptive passages (from a range of vantage points) about the dances and about agricultural practices, these give way eventually to quotations from songs and poetry, as in this excerpt from a song collected by ethnomusicologist Martha Beckwith:

> Last year me turn out
> I hope you well
> We went a war, edo edo
> You went a war,
> Me no gone 'way yet
> I hope you well,
> Till we meet a Canoe-lean-a-hill
> Kia-money dead, I hope you well

Offering no interpretation, Wynter instead follows the excerpt immediately with a question: "What of descriptions of the actual dancing of the Jonkonnu festival?" (41). The question points to the distance between epigraph and description and in turn to the distance between such description and the dance itself. Wynter notes that interpretations of the Jonkonnu can be "lost" as the contexts for the dances shift. Only the song lyrics, reproduced throughout Wynter's text, offer the rhythm and the sound of the dance. By way of recourse to the poetic line and the chant, Wynter walks the line between that textual approximation (to borrow a term from Brathwaite, which I will elaborate in part 2 of this book) and the sounds, sights, and sites of these performances. Wynter's attention to the significance of rhythm takes us beyond the superstructure/substructure architecture of narrative into a sonic landscape.[27] She traces the boundary between performance and written forms, a boundary I associate in particular with lyric.[28]

We might think of this boundary as a kind of aesthetic parallel to the economic, social and ecological boundary of the plantation that Glissant defines as its "structural weakness" as well as its generative potential. He offers us a view of the perimeter and a way into the lyric ecologies that are the focus of this book:

> The plantation is one of the bellies of the world, not the only one, one among so many others, but it has the advantage of being able to be studied with the utmost precision. Thus, the boundary, its structural weakness, becomes our advantage. And in the end its seclusion has been conquered. The place was closed, but the word derived from it remains open. (*Poetics of Relation*, 75)

In the first half of this book I ask what can be made from within the confines of the plantation geography and economy. Chapter 1, "Cultivating the New Negro: The Provision Ground in New York," contends that agricultural tropes, in particular what Wynter calls the "plot," were central to framing the black modernity of the New Negro Movement. The chapter positions Claude McKay's poems from the Jamaican and U.S. publication periods (before and after 1919, respectively) in the aesthetic tradition of the provision ground, a space on the edge of the plantation granted to the enslaved for subsistence crops, in which artistic beauty both depended on and exceeded the economic and social constraints of that space. Against readings of McKay's U.S.-published poetry as "romantic," on the one hand, or "universal," on the other, I argue that his sonnets emerge from both a historicized lyric tradition and the particular landscape and language of McKay's childhood, embedded within a transnational historical framework. This reading of McKay's poetry opens a space for a revised account of the New Negro period and of Alain Locke's anthology *The New Negro* (1925): the anthology reflects a diasporic consciousness that draws on the agricultural language of Booker T. Washington while also anticipating the radical aesthetic theories of Sylvia Wynter.

As a transnational figure, difficult to associate with one place or another, McKay is an ideal subject for exploring the way poets use the language of cultivation to construct diasporic subjectivities. But of course such mobility does not characterize all or even most black writing in the twentieth century.[29] If, as Wynter put, it the "provision ground ideology would remain based on a man's relation to the earth" ("Jonkonnu in Jamaica," 37), what was to become of this ideology once humans were displaced from the agricultural spaces that produced it? Would the provision ground continue to provide a viable model for the "roots of culture" or would other lyric ecologies emerge? The diffuse period spanning from World War II to the Black Arts and Caribbean Artists Movements would produce multiple answers to these questions, cultivating a profound sense of difference among the fractured geographies of diaspora. Chapter 2, "Cultivating the Nation," explores poetry, periodicals, and cultural criticism of this period that attempts to reground black lyric voices in a region, city, or country. In the early decades of the U.S. periodical *Phylon*, criticism of American poetry abstracted blackness from agricultural spaces in order to serve universalist claims to citizenship in the American literary sphere. At the same time, West Indian writers and editors were engaging in critical reterritorialization to ground their poetries in time and place in *BIM*, a Barbados-based journal, and *Savacou*, a Jamaica-based journal. Turning to the work of U.S. poet Gwendolyn Brooks, chapter 2 concludes by asking whether the urban enclave can function as an ecology for lyric experimentation.

But what if the property relations that have outlived slavery always determine our affective responses to the landscape? Through a reading of Derek Walcott's mid-career poems in *The Star-Apple Kingdom* (1979), chapter 3 asks how poetry represents and counters the alienation Glissant describes between black subjects and their environments. These are the poems in Walcott's oeuvre in which he most deeply engages the political and ecological ramifications of decolonization, tourism, and federation and its failures. The title poem in particular powerfully critiques colonial policies and legacies of the slave-era plantation for the postcolonial era. Unlike Walcott's later and better-known *Omeros*, often read as a national epic, these earlier poems use lyric strategies to engage the senses, juxtaposing the sensory experience of imperfectly assembled fragments against the desensitizing violence of history and situating the archipelago as the geographic form of black historical experience.

In the second half of this book, "Catastrophe," I explore environmental disasters as meteorological and anthropogenic events with vast social, political, and economic consequences; as figures for diasporic experience, beginning with the slave trade; and as spatiotemporal structures that have informed poetic practice and theory. The extreme violence of natural and unnatural disasters brings about not only a crisis of representation (how can we make art in such degraded times?) but also a crisis of preservation (how can we retain and maintain the materials of culture?) In the book's final three chapters I uncover a diasporic archive of musical response to environmental catastrophe as the basis for black lyric aesthetics. Figurative and literal hurricanes are a particular focus because of the ubiquity of these catastrophes in the global South, their persistence in the literature, and the shared path of the hurricane and the Atlantic slave trade. But I also consider how continuous local flooding, ongoing ecological degradation, and destructive earthquake vibrations figure the slow violence of black historical experience.

Brathwaite conjures the hurricane as a figure for an imagined or hoped-for postcolonial West Indian poetry, but his recourse to catastrophe helps us understand the cultural production of a broader archipelago. Natural disaster proves an equally transformative basis for the writers and lyricists associated with the New Negro renaissance in the United States, Sterling Brown, Bessie Smith, and Zora Neale Hurston, whose work is the focus of chapters 4 and 5. In chapter 4, "Continuing Catastrophe," I delve into musical and poetic responses to the 1927 Mississippi River flood, often known as "the Great Flood," whose massive destruction of farmlands, waterways, and communities throughout the Mississippi delta disproportionately affected black Americans. Given that natural disaster brings to the fore the paradoxical spatial crises of displacement and immobility, these modern lyric responses to catastrophe offer a new thinking of time that captures the "continuing catastrophe" figured by the floods. Focusing on sound in poetry (a focus that sustains the rest of the book) I establish both Bessie Smith's flood blues and Sterling Brown's flood blues poems as lyric ecologies whose formal properties account for the spatial and temporal displacements brought about by the floods. To account for the incommensurability between sonic and environmental experience, on the one hand, and textual representation, on the other, these lyricists turn not to transmission or transcription but to "approximation," a term I borrow from Brathwaite and elaborate on to describe the relationship of poetry to both sound and climatic experience.

Although Brathwaite seems to claim a natural or inherent relationship between cultural, regional, or national identity and certain forms of weather, the power of these tropes ultimately lies in their geographic scope and dynamic form, both of which are taken up in Zora Neale Hurston's 1937 novel *Their Eyes Were Watching God*, a narrative of the female protagonist's social and romantic development in rural Florida. Chapter 5, "Collecting Catastrophe," travels from the Mississippi watershed of Brown and Smith to the Florida "muck," where Hurston situates a devastating hurricane in the context of Jim Crow and the historical violences of the slave trade, plantation slavery, and colonialism. Uncovering the diasporic musical archive that informs Hurston's historical sense, I show how a transnational community of workers makes audible the geography and the beat of the hurricane, voicing a lyric interruption of the central narrative. For Smith, Brown and Hurston, all collectors and transcribers of musical folk culture, the uneasy exchange between musical and textual expressive forms defines the possibilities of black culture amid the devastations of disaster.

In chapter 6, "Collecting Culture," I propose that lyric poems can function as archives, preserving and transforming histories of rupture. I return to Jamaica, this time in the aftermath of Hurricane Gilbert in 1988, listening to Lloyd Lovindeer's smash dancehall hit "Wild Gilbert" alongside Brathwaite's 1990 poem *Shar*. Gilbert destroyed Brathwaite's home and archive of musical and literary culture in Irish Town, Jamaica. Brathwaite laments this loss in a context in which black culture has developed over and against suppositions that it already lacks history, rootedness, or an authentic relationship to its own cultivation. I contend that *Shar*, his work of mourning, both represents and ameliorates postmodern anxieties over the threatened print culture associated with what has often been described as simultaneously vanishing and incipient Caribbean history.

Finally, a coda entitled "Unnatural Catastrophe" takes us from the edge of the sea into the bottom of the ocean, the site of an eighteenth-century slave ship massacre and the source of M. NourbeSe Philip's book-length poetic response to that violence, *Zong!* (2008). Dwelling there, I posit that we not think of natural disaster as "social disaster" but rather reverse those terms to look at human violence as ecological in a formal sense. I test the limits of poetic "ambience" as a deracinated, dehistoricized category of experimental poetics and environmental writing and suggest instead that the ecological poem can be understood in relationship to a racial history of the Atlantic.

Although its meaning in common parlance is something like "disaster," or, in a geographical context, "cataclysm," the primary definition of "catastrophe" according to the *OED* is dénouement, "the change or revolution which produces the conclusion or final event of a dramatic piece." So there is no better place to begin than with the etymology of this "overturning," which suggests, among other things, the turning of soil before the planting of a new crop. Its root word "strophe," of course, is not only the Greek word for "turn" but also for the poetic unit of a stanza, "a series of lines forming a system." Catastrophe, then, is always involved with art making. It contains not only the finality of death and displacement but the making of form in the first place.

part 1 cultivation

one

Cultivating the New Negro
The Provision Ground in New York

TRANSPLANTING BOOKER T. WASHINGTON

In 1912 Claude McKay traveled on a United Fruit Company boat from Kingston, Jamaica, to Charleston, South Carolina. From there, he went to Tuskegee, Alabama, and then, six months later, as if following in the footsteps of American freedmen, to Kansas and later New York. The poet's brief education in agronomy in the halls of Booker T. Washington's Tuskegee Institute remains something of a mystery, even to McKay scholars and biographers. What can it mean that McKay, a self-described vagabond and radical darling of the Harlem Renaissance credited by some as breaking "the mold of the Dialect School and the Booker T. Washington compromise," came to the United States to learn from the Tuskegee wizard himself—that figurehead of conciliation, southern black pride, and rootedness?[1]

In his published autobiography, *A Long Way from Home*, McKay omits mention of the experience at Tuskegee entirely. His only known comment on the institute came some five years after his departure, noting his unhappiness with the "semi-military, machinelike existence there" (65). McKay's biographers have imagined that the reasons for his disappointment in Tuskegee include the strict regimen, the lack of intellectual stimulation and emphasis on vocational training, and the racism he encountered in the deep South.[2] Tyrone Tillery also speculates that "Tuskegee's practical curriculum did not appeal to McKay, whose real reason for attending the school had been to further his creative writing career" (*Claude McKay*, 23). If we are to accept Tillery's theory for the departure, we must assume a dichotomy between a "practical curriculum" focused on agriculture and McKay's poetic ambitions. Washington himself might have clung to such a dichotomy, touting practical over cultural growth. Where McKay's motivations are concerned, however, it is not quite so easy to separate the two. I begin at a point in McKay's itinerary through that place which, according to Booker T. Washington, "was distinguished by the colour of the soil. The part of the country possessing this thick, dark, and naturally rich soil where the slaves were most profitable, and . . . taken there in the largest numbers" (*Up from Slavery*, 63). How would McKay bring this soil into relation with that of his native Clarendon, Jamaica? And how would the shared history of plantation slavery to which Washington refers inform attempts of later writers to define the Black Belt as a region of poetic possibility and autonomy?

It is no small irony that McKay's "vagabondage" began at the institute founded by Booker T. Washington, the preeminent African American figure of stasis and rootedness. And yet to read McKay in relation to Washington is to uncover the former's role as a quintessential figure of diaspora, precisely because of his literary representations of the "soil" Washington so vociferously elevated. It is also to reframe Washington's shaky legacy for modern blackness in relationship to the global geography of diaspora.[3] Critics of Washington emphasize, among other things, his resistance to black migration from the South to urban centers at the very moment when black people were claiming their newfound freedom and mobility.[4] Indeed, early in *Up from Slavery*, Washington clarifies his wish that upwardly mobile black Americans in the Reconstruction era "get a foundation in education, industry, and property" rather than seek "political preferment," controversially locating progress in "Mother Nature" (54). While Washington heralds the toothbrush and modern laundry techniques alike as crucial tools for the development of his people, "the soil" has pride of place in his theory of education and political progress, and "the country districts" of the South are the capital of Washington's imagined community.

> How many times I wished then, and have often wished since, that by some power of magic I might remove the great bulk of these people into the country districts and plant them upon the soil, upon the solid and never deceptive foundations of Mother Nature, where all nations and races that have ever succeeded have gotten their start,—a start that at first may be slow and toilsome, but one that nevertheless is real. (53)

The agricultural terms of Washington's wish operate simultaneously as a literal plan for his school and as a metaphor for national and racial progress, moving "up from slavery," uniting the early senses of culture associated with the tending of plants and animals with the later abstracted sense of culture as social progress. Having established agricultural industry as a cornerstone of Tuskegee Institute, Washington uses the language of farming figuratively, casting himself as the farmer and "the great bulk of these people" as the seed he would "plant . . . upon the soil." If agricultural labor offered an opportunity for turn-of-the-century African Americans to uproot, as it were, the remnants of the plantation economy by replacing cotton crops with sustainable family and community farms, by owning land rather than sharecropping, the very vocabulary of this assertion suggests a parallel literary transformation for Washington and subsequent generations of African American writers. At stake here is not only Washington's ability as a farmer to plant new crops of utilitarian value or his ability as an educator-activist to draw hundreds of teachers and students (as well as thousands of dollars) from the urban centers of the North to the "country districts" of the South—a kind of transplanting in and of itself—but his ability *as a writer* to "plant" by "*by some power of magic*" the roots of his people. For all of Washington's pragmatic ambitions, he wished for something beyond the use value of the land. Washington was interested not only in the cultivation of the land but also in writing as an alternative labor, a process of cultivating himself "up from slavery." He called for the "power of magic," a language that would allow black Americans access to the land and its cultural as well as agricultural products.

Washington was well aware of objections to manual labor. Upon telling some of the first teachers at Tuskegee that they would be clearing some land to plant a crop, he "noticed that they did not seem to take to it very kindly. It was hard for them to see the connection between clearing land and an education. Besides, many of them had been school teachers, and they questioned whether or not clearing land would be in keeping with their dignity" (72). If it was hard for the teachers to see the connection "between clearing land and an education," it was hard for Washington, in spite of his personal history, to acknowledge "the connection between clearing land," slavery, and postslavery labor exploitation.

Washington's vision of the "country districts" that would magically reconnect black descendants of slaves to the land radically departs from the representation of such districts by Washington's staunchest critic, W. E. B. Du Bois. In *The Souls of Black Folk*, Du Bois documents the "bitter disappointment" that accompanied the unfulfilled "vision of 'forty acres and a mule,'" "the righteous and reasonable ambition to become a landholder," through the description of his journey into what Washington might have called the "country districts" of Georgia (32). For Du Bois, the Black Belt is a space of pure devastation, marked by histories of genocide, violence, environmental degradation and—especially since the Civil War—economic devastation. Paradoxically, he can only describe "country life" by reference to the city:

> Once upon a time we knew country life so well and city life so little, that we illustrated city life as that of a closely crowded country district. Now the world has well-

nigh forgotten what the country is, and we must imagine a little city of black people scattered far and wide over three hundred lonesome square miles of land, without train or trolley, in the midst of cotton and corn, and wide patches of sand and gloomy soil. (89)

In Du Bois's account, one outcome of postwar migration and industrialization is the largely bereft "country" landscapes, which can only be described in terms of their lack of modernity and technological advancement (no "train or trolley"). To be a black person in the country is to be isolated ("scattered" and "lonesome") and immobile. The products of this "gloomy soil" are those of the plantation monoculture that evolved during slavery, cotton, and corn. Du Bois's "gloomy soil" contrasts dramatically with Washington's description of the Black Belt as that region where the soil was "naturally rich."[5] For Du Bois, the fact that the soil's richness was directly related to the slaves being "most profitable" would render the landscape not only agriculturally and economically but symbolically destitute. His other descriptions of the Black Belt are similarly bleak, although varied. Du Bois searches for (and finds) culture, but his text evidences and historicizes the alienation Glissant would later describe between black subjects and the land, carefully narrating not only the roots of that alienation in the enslaved past but also its continuity in the emancipated present. We might understand Du Bois's and Washington's very different approaches to cultivation— as irreparably bound to the history of the plantation during slavery and then the labor of sharecropping, on the one hand, and as the basis for alternative forms of "rootedness," on the other—as marking the limits of the range of possibilities that become available to later writers attempting to inhabit, recover, or transform the geography of the plantation.

If Du Bois manifests the sense of alienation that pervades the postslavery plantation, Washington seeks a (conservative) politics of repair in the hope that an intimacy with nature might allow black Americans to transcend the evils of human history. In his celebration of the "never deceptive foundations of Mother Nature" Washington draws a stark contrast between the authenticity of the soil and the (implied) unreliability of human nature. His wish also suggests a model for global connectedness as one basis for black life in the United States. Even as he hopes to hold fast to the "country districts" of the U.S. South, Washington insists on the universality of "Mother Nature": "where all nations and races that have ever succeeded have gotten their start." Shifting his rhetoric quickly from the local ("districts") to the global ("all nations and races"), Washington gives voice to an idea of black life in the "country districts" that is surprisingly transnational even as it also elides the global history of transatlantic slavery by rendering a transnational geography via comparison rather than continuity.

Washington himself did not stay put in the "country districts," traveling, for instance, to the White House and to northern cities to raise funds for his southern school. Indeed, in McKay's words, Washington's "fame has spread all over the *world*" (*My Green Hills of Jamaica*, 83, emphasis mine). Houston Baker has rightly pointed out that Washington allowed himself a "public mobility" that he seemed to withhold as a possibility for the "black-South Mass."[6] But to suggest that this rendered both Washington and the mass culturally "inert" is to deny the palpable presence of Washington's "magic" of cultivation in the literature of writers who are part of Baker's canon of cosmopolitan Afro-modernity. In stirring the specter of Washington here, my point is not to insist on his literary influence in any conventional sense. Rather, I draw attention to McKay's interest in Washington to demonstrate how, in spite of Washington's resistance to "travel," the spirit of his agricultural discourse does migrate in the literary imaginations of later black writers.

Du Bois's political and economic radicalism would ultimately take hold among writers of the subsequent generation most closely associated with the New Negro Movement, including McKay. But where "some power of magic" was concerned, the soil of the Black Belt, and the processes through which it produced not only corn and cotton but culture remained "rich" ground for a poetics. Among some writers in subsequent generations the "connection between clearing land" and plantation slavery engendered a strong resistance both to what Du Bois calls Washington's "gospel of work and money" (*The Souls of Black Folk*) and to "Mother Nature" as the subject of literature. Yet in the aftermath of slavery, migration, and industrialization, features of the natural world have persisted in the poetry and poetics of the African diaspora during the modern period and beyond.

What forms would this literature take? After enslavement, how have writers understood the plantation geography as anything other than the space of containment and violence through which Du Bois traveled? By what "power of magic," what poetics, could these undeniably ruined landscapes of enslavement be transformed into sites of empowerment and possibility? It makes a certain sense that after the failures of Reconstruction in the United States, Du Bois and Washington would have to wrestle with the legacy of the postslavery plantation for economics, politics, and art. But what of the group of writers who were shaped by the very migrations Washington resisted and Du Bois urged, away from the plantation geography?

These questions preoccupy me in the first three chapters of *Cultivation and Catastrophe*, in which I explore the afterlife of the plantation in poems by McKay, Gwendolyn Brooks, and Derek Walcott, as well as Alain Locke's influential 1925 anthology *The New Negro* and pivotal issues of the periodicals *Phylon* (United States), *BIM* (Barbados), and *Savacou* (Jamaica). Taking Booker T. Washington's celebration of the soil as one unlikely basis for black creativity in the modern period, the remaining sections of this chapter demonstrate how even in the context of the decidedly urban New Negro Movement, writers continued to draw on the language and forms of cultivation to evoke the connections and ruptures of diasporic blackness.

Critics have long identified the rural as a major preoccupation of New Negro thought but in doing so have tended to juxtapose a regressive pastoralism against progressive modernity. Bernard Bell, for instance, coins the term "Afro-American pastoral" to describe the "implicit contrast between country and city life" that he and other critics in the late 1960s identified as a signal feature of African American literary race consciousness (*The Afro-American Novel and Its Tradition*, 113–14). The tension between urban and rural experience dates back to pastoral's classical origins. According to Leo Marx, the dialectic between idyll and industry that shapes the pastoral design resonates especially powerfully in the American or "New World" context because of America's status as an idealized landscape in the European imagination (*The Machine in the Garden*, 26–33). Extending Marx's theme, Robert Bone represents pastoral as the ideal mode for the expression of African American double consciousness, importantly prioritizing the rural context of the early twentieth-century African American literary tradition. Although he acknowledges the dualism at the heart of Renaissance pastoral, Bone ultimately consigns the mode to the realm of pure nationalism and defines its trajectory as "recoil" from white cosmopolitan values (*Down Home*, xii–xvii).[7] Paradoxically, by drawing attention to Afro-American pastoralism as a nationalist counterpoint to cosmopolitanism, this strain of criticism would set the stage for later accounts of black modernism that would (reactively) ignore or minimize the presence of the natural world in black literature altogether.[8]

At the same time, within postcolonial and Caribbean studies there has emerged a discourse that understands the plantation as constitutive of black modernity, insofar as its economic, social, and ecological structure gave rise to resistant cultural practices.[9] By placing McKay at the center of this discourse I foreground how an anticolonial ecological poetics emerging from the Caribbean also shaped the legacy of the plantation in black U.S. literary culture. Offering a counterexample to Alain Locke's description of the great migration and the accompanying New Negro Movement as "a deliberate flight not only from countryside to city but from medieval America to modern" ("The New Negro," 6), McKay's poetry uncouples the modern from the urban, distinguishes temporal progress from spatial migration, and wrests black modernity from the nation-state.

For McKay as well as subsequent generations of black diasporic poets, the need to occupy, dwell within, escape, and transform the geography of slavery involved a parallel need to revise essential (and essentialist) assumptions about organic form.[10] In McKay's hands, colonial form gives rise to a postcolonial poetics of errantry through its encounter with environmental form. The sonnet in particular (etymologically, "a little sound" made up of "rooms," according to the *OED*) is an apt form for exploring the geography of containment and freedom in the moving landscapes of the postslavery plantation. Insofar as the spatial histories of the plantation in the United States and the Caribbean have crucially informed black production of poetic space, we can understand the ecological to be a defining feature of modern lyric in the black world.

THE PROVISION GROUND

Drawing particular attention to McKay's upbringing in Jamaica and to the way his work circulated, I read McKay's poems, including those published after his emigration, in the tradition of the provision ground.[11] Provision grounds were plots of land on plantation outskirts that some Jamaican planters allotted to enslaved workers for subsistence farming. McKay's poetry offers a particularly striking example of the postslavery aesthetics of the provision ground because he writes as a colonial subject who has been profoundly shaped by colonial education and because his works in Harlem test the geographic limits of the provision ground as a specifically West Indian (and even more specifically Jamaican) phenomenon.[12] The provision ground, the space of semiautonomous cultivation, provides McKay with an ecological model for transforming the colonial lyric form.

The economic purpose of the provision system was to allow enslaved people to cultivate their own food staples, freeing the enslavers from the need to feed the laboring population. Enslaved laborers in Jamaica, however, produced not only ground provisions for their own consumption but also tree fruits and excess staples for trade within an informal, internal marketing system. Historians have debated the economic and social meaning of the provision system. Whereas some have argued that provision grounds sustained the populations that maintained them, B. W. Higman insists that, at least by 1807, there was no significant correlation between provision grounds and a decrease in slave mortality (*Slave Population and Economy in Jamaica*, 129). And to the extent that the provision grounds maintained a healthy and productive laboring population, scholars have emphasized the self-interest inherent in enslavers' support (or reluctant acceptance) of such spaces.[13] Finally, it has been argued that planters used representations of the provision grounds as "evidence" of the slaves' happy state, so as to defend slavery and perpetuate the plantation economy.

Simon Gikandi suggests that the value of these spaces for slaves transcended these economic or even mortal questions. Gikandi draws our attention to the beauty (as opposed to the utility) of these gardens, establishing the provision grounds as sites of resistance to the masters' economic purpose and as spaces where an autonomous black culture could grow (*Slavery and the Culture of Taste*, 241–43). Gikandi also reads the eighteenth-century provision ground as evidence of the ability of the enslaved to control time in ways that subverted the imperatives of the plantation. Against Orlando Patterson's and Michael Craton's assertions that their historical disconnection from the traditions and culture of their ancestors rendered the enslaved descendants of Africans socially dead, Gikandi argues that freedom from the thickness of history afforded them a creative "space for maneuver" (245).[14]

How would this environmental relation take literary form in the twentieth century? In this chapter I look beyond the novel for the literary provisioning described in Sylvia Wynter's important theory of the "plot" or "provision ground" as that which "give(s) rise" to "the roots of culture" ("Jonkonnu in Jamaica," 37).[15] In the dialect couplets of McKay's early poem "Quashie to Buccra," the inverted georgic logic of "Flame-Heart," and the boxy constraint of his Harlem sonnets, I discover a "language of the landscape," to borrow Glissant's term (*Caribbean Discourse*, 146), that operates outside of "plot" (in a narrative sense) altogether, a modern poetic space for aesthetic experimentation and anticolonial critique.

Uncovering the presence of the provision ground in McKay's poetry reveals the cultural continuity between his earlier agricultural practice and his poetic practice. I seek more than analogy here, for McKay's lyric agency is inseparable from his environment: in preparation for his trip, McKay tells us, "I did a lot of planting. With the help of the peasants I planted yams and conga peas, black-eyed peas and red peas as well as sweet potatoes, yams and like things" (*My Green Hills of Jamaica*, 83). As the financial foundation for McKay's journey to become a poet, cultivation is literally at the root of his poetic production and is a key poetic process through which he transformed his Jamaican identity into a diasporic one. Provision grounds were not universal to the British slave-holding colonies; as a particularly robust feature of Jamaican plantation economy, they formed the basis of an internal market system among laborers that has outlived enslavement and constitutes a source of local pride and identification. Although there were subsistence gardens in the North American colonies, no such developed system took hold. But by transplanting the poetics of the provision ground across the sea, McKay transformed the sign of the local tropics into a global poetics.

THE CARIBBEAN NEW NEGRO

McKay was one of the iconic figures of the Harlem Renaissance, an artistic and literary movement whose very name evokes an urban image of black modernity. To unearth cultivation as the motivation and method for McKay's modernity requires that we revisit the rural Jamaica of his youth and that we detour through the Black Belt, broadly construed as the transnational landscape of Atlantic slavery. Scholars have begun to attend to McKay's status as a transnational figure, turning to his cosmopolitan vagabondage, his Marxist internationalism, and his Jamaican upbringing to challenge his status as an "African American" writer and exploring the literary implications of his experience as what Michelle Stephens calls a "traveling black male subject" (*Black Empire*, 169).[16] But narratives of McKay's career as a transnational wanderer tend to emphasize his participation in an urban, cosmopolitan modernity (at least after his departure from Jamaica), while readings of the rural in his poetry consign McKay's natural imagery to a romantic and often provincial mode. Winston James both elucidates the agricultural economy of McKay's childhood home of Clarendon Hills and, in readings of McKay's early Jamaican poems, demonstrates McKay's fidelity to representing the sometimes-harsh economic realities of peasant life (*A Fierce Hatred of Injustice*, 3–11, 59–67). He also cautions against overly simplistic readings of the rural-urban dichotomy in McKay's first two books (133). Nonetheless, he describes some of McKay's early depictions of the Jamaican countryside as "idealized." Critical accounts of natural or agricultural themes in McKay's American poetry (written after McKay emigrated in 1912) read these works as sentimental, nostalgic, and romantic, contrasting them to what they see as the more radical or militant poems he published during the same period in *Harlem Shadows* and in American periodicals.[17]

In order to trace the surprising routes of poetic tropes rooted in the plantation geography, I wish first to emphasize the mobility of McKay's work and the
diversity of the circles through which it traveled—a diversity that extended not
only along the path of McKay's movement in the United States and Europe but
back to Jamaica. Inquiry into McKay's literary relationships with various white
American audiences (principally readers of radical leftist publications like the
Liberator and the *Masses*), black American writers, the founders of *négritude*,
and a diverse Jamaican audience reveals that from his earliest publications in
Jamaica in 1912, his poems nourished a certain type of white liberalism as well as
international black language and literature, and Jamaican vernacular culture.[18]
McKay was hostile to the members of Harlem's black intelligentsia, and felt oppressed by their bourgeois expectations. In a 1928 letter to Langston Hughes,
he complains that "their opinion will be conditioned by that of the whites. . . .
Whether you give them revolutionary thought or revolutionary depiction of life
there is no difference in their attitude. If they accepted 'If We Must Die' it was
because a radical white organ printed it *first*."[19] In fact, although he rejected a
certain type of white opinion (in the same letter he is openly derisive about a
New York Times review of *Home to Harlem*) McKay went so far as to say he cared
more about the response of the leftist *Masses* writers and editors than that of the
black elite literary establishment.[20]

 This is not to say that McKay felt he had no audience among black Americans. As readers of each other's work, McKay, Hughes, Jean Toomer, Wallace
Thurman, Zora Neale Hurston and others of their generation constituted a
kind of mobile, bohemian counterpublic.[21] They sent each other books, wrote
poems in the margins of their letters, and griped about their elders and patrons
and publishing venues. "Honestly," McKay wrote to Hughes, "I value your opinion above any of the Negro intellectuals." In turn, McKay sought to influence
Hughes, encouraging him to travel abroad and to "be more colloquial" in his poetry.[22] Additionally, many critics have shown that McKay's writing and his presence in France during the 1920s exerted a major influence on *négritude* (indeed,
in Aimé Césaire's estimation, McKay was the single most important progenitor
of the movement).[23]

 Although McKay himself never returned to Jamaica, his work also remained
a force on the literary scene there and in the life of his family. As Raphael Dalleo
has argued in his fine reading of *Banana Bottom*, McKay was invested in the notion of a literary public sphere in Jamaica (*Caribbean Literature and the Public
Sphere*, 96–121). The publication history of his poems in Jamaica, before and
after expatriation, bears out McKay's long-distance participation in such a

sphere. Six poems from *Harlem Shadows* appeared in J. E. Clare McFarlane's groundbreaking anthology of Jamaican poetry, *Voices from Summerland*, and the political journal *Public Opinion* (associated with the rise of the People's National Party) reprinted "If We Must Die" in 1939.[24] In the same year that Winston Churchill supposedly appropriated McKay's militant critique of American racist violence as a rallying cry against the Nazis, the editors of *Public Opinion* brought the poem back to Jamaica as part of their effort to define an emerging radical national literature. [25]

Long after his expatriation, McKay also continued to participate in Jamaican literary discourse through the newspapers. Kingston's *Gleaner* and *Jamaica Times* (whose literary editor, Tom Redcam, was McKay's friend) introduced McKay's early poems to Jamaican readers. After he left in 1912, McKay continued to publish his dialect poems in the *Gleaner*, and in 1913 he carried on a lively debate in the pages of that paper regarding the status of Jamaican (and American) dialect poetry.[26] The *Gleaner* also reprinted McKay's American poems, reviews of his work, and tales of his adventures abroad. Although the *Gleaner* was the mouthpiece of the Jamaican plantocracy, McKay made use of the paper to broadcast a nationalist message to a diverse audience. As McFarlane has pointed out, McKay's books were too expensive for circulation among the masses (*A Literature in the Making*, 84). Indeed, his brother Tommy complained in a 1929 letter to Claude that, "I have not read them for I am too poor to buy them. They are sold at profiteering rates in Jamaica. From you left Jamaica I have not seen anything of your writings except what I got from the newspapers."[27] The letter underscores Winston James's contention that the newspapers made McKay's poems available to "ordinary Jamaicans," many of whom first discovered McKay's poems in the papers (*A Fierce Hatred of Injustice*, 140). Phrases from McKay's poems also, in McFarlane's words, "passed from lip to lip and have become household words" (*A Literature in the Making*, 84). Thus, after his emigration, McKay's poems continued to "feed" not only a white American market hungry for a certain kind of postslavery stereotype, but also McKay's Jamaican family, insofar as he supported his daughter and niece on the earnings from his work and writing in America, an interracial Jamaican literary community, and a diasporic black reading public.[28] This broader publication context crucially indicates McKay's continued entanglement with the family, community, and environment of his youth.

As fruits or commodities in their own right, McKay's poems circulated within a Jamaican economy as well as a British and American one, deeply connected to the landscape and its cultivation in a real, not merely nostalgic, sense, long after

McKay's departure. In 1919, at least one copy of a number of Max Eastman's the *Liberator*, the leftist magazine for which McKay would eventually become an editor, "containing a page of sonnets and songs by Claude McKay" found its way to Jamaica and into the hands of the *Gleaner* editors, who in turn reprinted three of the poems, praised them as Wordsworthian, and insisted that one of them "proves that Claud [sic] McKay is really a poet" ("Jamaica Poet Praised"). The *Gleaner* published McKay's poems, including "De Gub'nor's Salary," and reviews of his books alongside features such as "Coolie Labour in the West Indies" (reporting on a visit from the Indian government to inquire into the status of immigrant laborers), a piece by a "Philosopher" titled "Growing Citrus Fruit in This Island for The Markets Abroad," and a religious sermon by Reverend Ernest Price titled "Effects of Disaster," among other things.[29] This history of his poems' continued circulation after his expatriation underscores the ongoing proximity between McKay's poetry and the documentation of Jamaican agricultural life and also implicitly suggests that his well-known poem, "The Tropics in New York," may have had a similarly international audience, an audience beyond the white American left that was the readership for the *Liberator*.

Tracing the circulation of "The Tropics in New York" in the 1920s in a different sense yields a vibrant map of the plantation geography's transnational afterlife in the black literary imagination. Having originally been published in the *Liberator* and then reprinted in both the English and U.S. versions of McKay's volumes (*Spring in New Hampshire* and *Harlem Shadows*, respectively), "The Tropics in New York" was reprinted in 1925 in Alain Locke's *New Negro* anthology as well as the March 1925 special issue of *Survey Graphic* magazine, "Harlem: Mecca of the New Negro," out of which *The New Negro* originated. The poem's placement in the journal brings to the fore McKay's status as a West Indian poet. In *Survey Graphic*, "The Tropics in New York," appears on the same page as W. A. Domingo's prose essay of the same title, as if to serve as an illustration of that essay, which explores tensions in New York City's black community between West Indian immigrants and southern African American migrants. The poem also appears symmetrically opposite another McKay poem, "Subway Wind," locating this exploration of West Indian identity firmly in New York City. "Tropics" and "Subway Wind" are modified English sonnets (abbreviated and elongated, respectively) and so can be seen as products of McKay's cultivation as a British subject.[30] They demonstrate both his acculturation to and transformation of the form. In turn, these poems invite us to reframe the constitution of black geography in Locke's *New Negro* anthology, to which I turn in the final section of this chapter.

"ALDOUGH DE VINE IS LITTLE, IT CAN BEAR":
"QUASHIE TO BUCCRA" AND THE LANGUAGE OF LANDSCAPE

Before we turn to read "The Tropics in New York" in detail, it is useful to trace the relationship between the provision ground and McKay's earlier poetry, written while McKay was still in Jamaica. Published with an introduction and heavy annotation (explanatory notes and a glossary) by Walter Jekyll in McKay's 1912 collection of Jamaican dialect poems, *Songs of Jamaica*, McKay's "Quashie to Buccra" offers an early critique of postslavery Jamaican agricultural economy. In the poem, a black laborer complains that his white boss does not properly value the fruits of his labor, engaging an antipastoral tradition to critique the production of subsistence crops and the "pretty" landscape that accompanies them. Demonstrating how postplantation labor practices sustain the agricultural economy, McKay produces an aesthetic countereconomy by establishing a mimetic relationship between poetic composition and agricultural labor. Like many of the poems in *Songs of Jamaica*, "Quashie to Buccra" is written in Jamaican patois, and critics have argued that it exemplifies the challenges of representing black authorial subjectivity in dialect.[31] While it is not my purpose here to defend McKay's use of dialect, I wish to draw attention to the relationship between cultivation of the landscape and cultivation of poetic language in the poem.

"Quashie to Buccra" raises the possibility of beauty within the agricultural landscape of early twentieth-century Jamaica only to acknowledge the way that beauty is compromised by harsh economic reality. The crop that is the focus of the poem, however, is not cane produced on plantations for export but rather "sweet petater"—a ground provision for local consumption and market trade, which, in part by virtue of its easy confusion with the African-derived yam, has long been a quintessential symbol of black sustenance and survival.[32] Evoking the spectral presence of slavery, the poem places itself not so much within the plantation fields as within the provision grounds.

McKay's early poem suggests the inextricability of ground provisions from the economic confines of the colonial plantation and at the same time uncovers the cultural power of black labor. The poem, spoken in the voice of Quashie, a laborer, to Buccra, his boss, opposes the hard work of field labor against the "tas'" of the crops their labor produces:

You tas'e petater an' you say it sweet,
But you no know how hard we wuk fe it;
You want a basketful fe quattiewut
'Cause you no know how 'tiff de bush fe cut. (19)

The speaker accuses his imagined auditor of undervaluing the product, offering only a "quattiewut" for something worth more. The opposition between the first and second lines ("you say it sweet,/But you no know") renders "tas'e" contingent on labor and on full knowledge and valuation of that labor. The pun "no know" doubly negates the "sweet" flavor of the potato, and the poem sets out to correct the knowledge gap (a gap underscored by the off-rhyme between the two lines of the couplet: "sweet" and "it"). But the poem never settles the question: will knowledge of the hard labor of cultivation make the potato sweeter? Or drain it of its sweetness?

At stake in this ambivalence is not only the cultivation of the sweet "petater" that Buccra "tas'e" and enjoys ("an' you say it sweet") but also the cultivation of poetic taste. The poem attests to the role of agricultural labor in the formation of colonial poetic taste, even as it questions the nature of that taste. After establishing the intensity of Quashie's physical labor, McKay connects the potential futility of that labor to the potential futility of language:

De bush cut done, de bank dem we deh dig,
But dem caan' 'tan' sake o' we naybor pig;
For we so moul' it up he root it do'n,
An we caan' 'peak sake o' we naybor tongue. (19)

The "naybor pig" and the "naybor tongue" equally frustrate the endeavors of the laborers: to build banks for burying the tubers and to speak. We can take "naybor" here to refer to competing laborers, who, like the poem's speaker, seek to make a living from the land and whose gossip or chattiness prevents Quashie from speaking. But we might also read "we naybor tongue" as a figure for colonial language in relation to the speech of the poem. This interpretation is particularly evocative when we think of McKay's complicated choice to write and publish "dialect poems" early in his career, a decision McKay's English mentor Walter Jekyll encouraged and subsequent generations of West Indian writers alternately derided and celebrated.[33] Buccra's "tas'e," it would seem, erases not only black labor but black language ("An' we caan 'peak"). In this vein, Michael North and others conclude that McKay is trapped within the double bind of modernism—between the rock of an oppressive standard written English and the hard place of dialect that white writers have appropriated for minstrelsy.[34]

I argue instead that through the doubleness of language, "Quashie to Buccra" engages the double bind of history that the provision ground evokes. The poem dramatizes the question that laborers face of whether or not to participate in an alternative economy with ties to the plantation economy, given that despite this tie, it offers the possibility of temporal and spatial control. In this context of the provision ground as semiautonomous space of cultural production, the double bind becomes a form of double consciousness, imbued with both a sense of historical burden and a sense of creative possibility. While the poem thematizes the loss of linguistic power in the face of colonial language, it also demonstrates the power of literary expression and literary form.

In his writings on the topic, McKay asserts his right to move between "pure English" and dialect as appropriate and insists on the relationship between dialect and the authentic lived experience of Jamaicans.[35] At the same time, "Quashie to Buccra" describes the breakdown between signifier and signified in the postslavery agricultural landscape. We hear this breakdown in the slant rhyme in the couplet ending "do'n / tongue," suggesting that language and taste (in both the literal and figurative senses of the word) are inadequate to the task of accounting for labor. Specifically, what Buccra sees and tastes ignores the reality of black labor.

> Aldough de vine is little, it can bear;
> It wantin' not'in' but a little care:
> You see petater tear up groun', you run,
> You laughin', sir, you must be t'ink a fun. (19)

The speaker points to the distinction between the meager appearance of agricultural products and their reproductive potential ("it can bear"), showing how this distinction is parallel to that between Buccra's response ("you laughin'") and the visual reality of the scene ("petater tear up groun'"). Replicating a grammar characteristic of Jamaican patois, the poem's penultimate stanza syntactically renders this break between appearance and reality by omitting the copula that would connect the production of crops for eating with the production of beauty:

> De fiel' pretty? It couldn't less 'an dat,
> We wuk de bes', an' den de lan' is fat;
> We dig de row dem eben in a line,
> An' keep it clean—den so it *mus'* look fine. (19)

The omission of "be" from the first line suggests that the field might *be* less than pretty, in that its fecundity depends on the invisibility of those who "wuk de bes'." By omitting the copula McKay also forces the rhythm of the line to fit into the poem's established pentameter. By keeping the lines thus "eben," he suggests a connection between the violence done to the land under a plantation

system and the potential violence done to language to accommodate fixed prosody. However, even in putting the question "De fiel' pretty?" the speaker cannot
deny the beauty of the scene; indeed, he insists on the significance of labor and
skill in making it so, emphasizing, in the parallel structure of the middle two
lines, the agency of the laborers: "We wuk de bes' . . . / We dig de row dem eben
in a line".

In response to the erasure of black labor that is the precondition of Buccra's
"tas'," the poem makes visible the beauty of that labor and at the same time critiques the ugliness of a system in which one man's hard labor makes another
man's taste. The speaker ultimately celebrates the virtues of labor only in relation to its economic value, for "yet still de hardship always melt away / Wheneber
it come roun' to reapin' day" (20). This conclusion deflates both the significance of "hardship" and the extraeconomic possibilities for contextualizing
the "value" of agricultural work. That is, in taking recourse to economy in the
poem's final lines, the speaker stops short of fully acknowledging the aesthetic
or cultural value of work (even though the poem itself performs a kind of cultural value). Especially when we remember that McKay raised money for his trip
toward "fuller expression" by growing subsistence crops for trade, "Quashie to
Buccra" reads as a cynical acceptance of the economic value of cultivation, as
well as a critique of the economy of poetic taste. But the poem also crucially emphasizes the process and duration of the peasants' labor, which takes place in
the habitual present, ensuring its own continuity beyond the "day" when it
"melt away." As the peasants "dig de row dem eben in a line," the poem enacts a
literary version of that process by "dig[ing] de row dem eben in a line" of verse,
equating the cultivation of the land and the poetic process, allowing agricultural time to unfold in "eben" measure. The poem delineates an alternative history of taste that foregrounds agricultural labor, even as it bemoans the lack of
value attributed to that history.

THE LYRIC FORM OF LABOR: "FLAME-HEART"

Although many critics argue that McKay's American poems mark the poet's
radical turn away from both folk forms and dialect, and the realities of agricultural labor, the poems in *Harlem Shadows* at times encode the language of the
Jamaican landscape and the temporality of agricultural labor within their lyric
forms. "Flame-Heart," the poem that immediately follows "The Tropics in New
York" in *Harlem Shadows*, is a kind of anti-georgic whose central conceit is the
speaker's failure to remember the seasonal rhythm of his childhood landscape.[36]
Drawing on a classical distinction between representations of landscapes as

sites of leisure, on the one hand, and labor, on the other, Timothy Sweet has defined "georgic" as the literary mode that "treats those aspects of pastoral, broadly construed, that concern not the retreat to nature or the separation of the country from the city, but our cultural engagement with the whole environment" (*American Georgics*, 5). McKay's "Flame-Heart" appears to reverse the conventions of the georgic, echoing the language of Virgil's georgic poems, while the speaker professes to remember only the leisure of his childhood environment.

Georgic poems are known for their didacticism and their specificity about husbandry and agricultural labor, the technical terms that led Sir Phillip Sidney to critique Virgil's *Georgics* as too close to their subject, too close, as it were, to the dirt.[37] "Flame-Heart" simultaneously refuses the technical language that details agricultural work and foregrounds the precise language that describes agricultural beauty. In so doing the poem does not gloss over the function of labor in producing beauty so much as mark the speaker's refusal to perform it. "So much have I forgotten in ten years," the speaker laments. In particular, he has forgotten time itself:

> What time the purple apples come to juice,
>> And what month brings the shy forget-me-not.
> I have forgot the special, startling season
>> Of the pimento's flowering and fruiting;
> What time of year the ground doves brown the fields
>> And fill the noonday with their curious fluting.
> I have forgotten much, but still remember
> The poinsettia's red, blood-red in warm December.

In forgetting "what time," "what month," what season, the speaker suggests that his memory contains the sensory products of Jamaica ("the poinsettia's red, blood-red") but that it fails to retain the processes of "flowering and fruiting." In the second stanza, these forgotten processes expand to include the role of humans in cultivating nature's bounty:

> I still recall the honey-fever grass,
>> But cannot recollect the high days when
> We rooted them out of the ping-wing path
>> To stop the mad bees in the rabbit pen.

What the speaker does remember, he finally tells us, are "the days / Even the sacred moments when we played, / All innocent of passion uncorrupt, At noon and evening in the flame-heart's shade"—leisure rather than labor. The poem would seem, then, to indulge in a pastoral idyll, a nostalgic memory of "feasting upon blackberries in the copse." Indeed, insofar as the poem luxuriates in the naming of Jamaica's flowers and fruits, it is a feast, offering up the "embalmed" memory of "the sacred moments" of youth for readerly consumption. As such, the poem seems at first to echo some others in *Harlem Shadows* which offer up the "sweet . . . tropic lands" as spaces of idyll. One oft-cited example of McKay's more saccharine nostalgic nature lyrics is "North and South," a poem in which "time and life move lazily along. . . .// And swarthy children in the fields at play,/ Look upward laughing at the smiling skies" (159). Unlike "North and South," however, "Flame-Heart" represents the speaker's nostalgia as a limitation and a loss.

The poem both evokes the particularity of the Jamaican landscape and, by naming the very processes that have been forgotten, registers labor as part of the landscape. Even as the speaker laments his distance from home, McKay names that which has been lost: flame-heart (which might refer to the poinsettia or to the flame tree), pimento (the all-spice tree, native to the Caribbean), and the "honey-fever grass" which "we rooted . . . out of the ping-wing path." "Ping-wing," a fruiting plant used as hedging in the Caribbean, comes directly from the lexicon of *Songs of Jamaica*. In the earlier dialect poem "My Mountain Home," for example, the nostalgic speaker laments, "How I did lub my little wul'/ Surrounded by pingwin!" (80). Far from a work of universalizing nostalgia transforming the Jamaican scene into a palatable fruit plate for the American reader, "Flame-Heart" bears the echo of McKay's dialect verse, and its language recalls the particular qualities of the Jamaican landscape.

While lamenting the speaker's gap in memory, "Flame-Heart" ultimately emphasizes process over product. The litany of that which has been forgotten, the repetition of units of time—"What weeks, what months, what time of the mild year"—marks the impossibility of using them to describe, contain, or call up the past. The poem thus thematizes, rather than enacts, the speaker's loss of connection to the agricultural process. That the poem is a kind of lament reminds us that knowing or being able to recall "what time" is the central work of memory.

The rhythm of poetic labor displaces agricultural rhythm, so that the work of memory becomes the work of poetry. The speaker has forgotten time in the calendrical or diurnal sense, time associated with natural processes, as well as with the seasons and with agricultural work. But the very relentlessness of the speaker's memory lapse—the persistent repetition of the phrases "I have forgot," and "I have forgotten"—establishes the poem's rhythm and its form, a cat-alogue. The "ten years" elapsed from the past become the form of the poem, whose stanzas have ten lines each. The poetic process unfolds the landscape of memory. While the speaker declares his distance from agricultural process and laments the loss of his childhood in Jamaica, the poem formally enacts the re-petitive processes of agricultural labor and takes on the catalogue structure of georgic poetry. Thus the poem evokes the speaker's connection to the Jamai-can agricultural landscape both through the particularity of its language and by instantiating the time of agricultural labor within poetic form. So, too, to the extent that the poem does celebrate leisure, it is not so much to deny the rela-tionship of human labor to natural beauty as to posit freedom from work as a form of artistic freedom.

THE SONNET AS PROVISION GROUND

Here it makes sense to return to Gikandi's insistence on the extraeconomic value of the provision grounds, in particular his assertion that the enslaved laborers made use of the provision grounds in ways that transgressed the very economy they were supposed to serve. If Quashie remains bound by his eco-nomic relationship to Buccra, he nonetheless controls his provision ground and creates its beauty. In "Quashie to Buccra," McKay deals in tubers, making visi-ble the labor of that underground production. In "The Tropics in New York" he takes us above ground, more fully imagining what Gikandi calls a "counter-aesthetic" that transgresses the economy of the residual landscape of slavery (*Slavery and the Culture of Taste*, 239). Accounts by Jamaican planters, as Gikandi points out, lament the amount of time and effort the slaves applied "to plantain-groves, corn and other vegetables, that are liable to be destroyed by storms" as opposed to root vegetables, "which are out of the reach of hurricanes," in other words, to visible rather than invisible cultivation (242). I understand both the provision ground itself and its lyric counterpart, the sonnet, against the grain of criticism that misreads "nature poetry" (and McKay's nature poetry in par-ticular) as nostalgic, provincial, or antimodern. McKay re-creates the dialectic between freedom and constraint that defines the provision ground, yoking to-gether the apparently "rooted" local landscape of the plot and the transnational literary routes of the modern sonnet within what I call a lyric ecology.

Like "Quashie" and "Flame-Heart," "The Tropics in New York" draws our attention to the labor involved in the production of environmental beauty, re-imagining the relationship between sustenance, economy, and the aesthetic for the twentieth century. The poem features objects of trade as the central figure for the speaker's nostalgia. These objects evoke the Jamaican landscape of slavery—specifically the provision ground, but in "Tropics" (unlike in "Quashie") the commodity is beauty rather than sustenance. With one exception, all of the fruit listed in the first stanza of "The Tropics in New York" grows on trees and falls into the category of crops subject to the vicissitudes of extreme weather:

> Bananas ripe and green, and ginger-root,
>> Cocoa in pods and alligator pears,
> And tangerines and mangoes and grape fruit,
>> Fit for the highest prize at parish fairs.

Through the imagery of ripe fruit, the lengthy catalogue, and the precise, exotic visual of "alligator pears," a fruit (avocado) whose name suggests not only the rough skin of an animal but also the luxury fashion products made from its skin, McKay's poem emphasizes the excess of these crops "fit for highest prize" rather than for consumption. The commodity here is beauty (and perhaps exoticism) rather than sustenance. In her critique of "the imperial georgic," Beth Fowkes Tobin describes this kind of catalogue, as it manifests itself in Thomson's eighteenth-century poem *The Seasons*, as "an abstract, universalizing register" that "erases geographical and cultural specificity, and . . . transforms agricultural production into commodities for circulation in the world economy" (*Colonizing Nature*, 55). Michael North makes a similar argument about "The Tropics in New York" (*The Dialect of Modernism*, 112). Given how the Jamaican patois of McKay's early work yields the vocabulary of his later work, however, we can read McKay's detailed catalogue in the tradition of the provision ground, which creates a space for beauty that exceeds the land's use value and resists the legacy of the plantation economy.

Indeed, it is the profound impracticality of the fruit—that it is "fit for prize" rather than consumption—that makes it beautiful. In *Banana Bottom*, McKay's novel depicting his childhood home, a dramatic hurricane lays waste to the community of the protagonist, the appropriately named "Bita Plant." While McKay describes the hurricane's destruction in lyrical prose, he also attends to the economic devastation left in its wake; the loss of the banana crop is particularly "sweeping and paralyzing," for, "since the decade of the boom in the banana many peasants had taken to cultivating that plant only, to the exclusion of other crops" (280–81). Only the farm of Jordan Plant (Bita's father) survives the hurricane, because Jordan "had been a shrewed cultivator" and avoided the dangers of monoculture.[38] The hurricane in *Banana Bottom* knocks the banana to the ground and elevates the sweet potato; it demonstrates the foolishness of the peasants and the wisdom of men like Jordan Plant who think not only of export but also of sustaining their families and communities. The novel celebrates the economic and social potential of the postslavery provision ground, primarily in relation to the utility of its below-ground crops. Banana and other fruit trees subject to the winds, by contrast, turn out to be impractical and foolish investments. Nonetheless, celebrating the taste of foolishness, the novel concludes with a scene of lush indulgence in Banana Bottom's tree-fruit abundance: Bita's son "little Jordan" "overstuffing" himself with ripe mangos from the tree in his yard.

The speaker of "The Tropics in New York" evokes just such a scene through the list of tropical fruits, only to avert his glance from a childhood among mango trees. The fruits are far from the parish,

> Set in the window, bringing memories
>> Of fruit-trees laden by slow-singing rills,
> And dewy dawns, and mystical blue skies
>> In benediction over nun-like hills.

That the fruit is in a shop window in New York suggests its commoditization, and the transition from the richness and particularity of the opening stanza's imagery to the abstract "mystical" language of the second stanza's recollection underscores the speaker's sense of loss and detachment from the "fruit" of his homeland. Thus it has been argued that the detachment between fruit and tree in the poem signifies McKay's dispossession from the Jamaican landscape and language and his transformation into a purely American poet.[39]

Read in light of the provision ground we can understand the poem instead as the production of a diasporic consciousness, indicative of McKay's status as what Brent Edwards calls a "bad nationalist," to the extent that his vagabondage constitutes a refusal to "perform nationalism" or citizenship (*The Practice of Diaspora*, 239–40). McKay dislocates the provision ground's status as a particular, local space, putting into motion what is already part of a global economy. Ground provisions (particularly the tuberous kind) can be evoked as sources of local pride, as in *Banana Bottom*, but they also always represent the cultivation of transnational products by transnational people: yams, of course, came to the Caribbean from Africa with enslaved African people, although sweet potatoes were indeed native to the Caribbean, and bananas came from Asia, Mexico, and South America in the hands of European travelers.[40] Likewise, the fruits listed in "The Tropics in New York" are not purely particular to the colony, as some have suggested, but have long been part of a global economy, as a basic study of the history of the banana trade bears out.[41] Given that these fruits have always been suspended between local identity and global commodity, the poem is not a simple narrative of dispossession.[42]

Instead the fruit situates the American vernacular of McKay's agricultural imagination in relationship to the Jamaican landscape. Until the final stanza, when the speaker's "eyes grew dim" on a New York sidewalk, the poem has no tense, and therefore consigns neither the fruit nor the memory of the Jamaican landscape to history or to any time in particular.

> My eyes grew dim, and I could no more gaze;
>   A wave of longing through my body swept,
> And, hungry for the old, familiar ways,
>   I turned aside and bowed my head and wept.

The ending of the poem is marked by its openness, and this openness invites reading and rereading, as we experience the speaker's unfulfilled craving.[43] McKay withholds the final couplet that would relieve the speaker's longing or firmly unify the movements—and locations—of the poem. The fruit, the memory, and the tropics remain inassimilable by American commerce, and the question of how to resolve the relationship between past and present remains open.

At different points, McKay's ground provisions—both tubers and tree fruits —symbolize, on the one hand, black submission to European and American economic constraints and, on the other hand, cultural autonomy. So too, McKay's use of the colonial form of the sonnet formally mirrors the dialectic between the confines of racialized agricultural economy and the freedom of autonomous agricultural production. As Peter Howarth has put it, for many modernists the sonnet had itself become a sign of "production line thinking," formal stiffness, and tradition; in William Carlos Williams's words it is "fascistic" ("The Modern Sonnet," 225, 226). The Anglo-American high modernist aversion to the sonnet is well known, but, as Howarth and others have begun to unearth, a robust tradition of modernist innovation with the sonnet form arose nevertheless. For McKay, to write sonnets was not only to reject the modernist prescription for newness of white American writers like Ezra Pound, Wallace Stevens, and Williams but also to differentiate his poetry from the free verse and vernacular forms that would become iconically associated with his generation of black American poets (even as a robust formal practice persisted among black poets in the United States throughout the century).[44] Building on Elizabeth Alexander's brilliant insistence that the sonnet is a space for experimentation in African American poetry, indeed a formal "tradition" that "is marked with innovation from its roots" ("New Ideas about Black Experimental Poetry," 614), I wish to suggest that in McKay's hands this experimental space derives even greater power from its entanglement with colonial history and colonial environment.

In a Jamaican context, McKay would have associated the sonnet with European mimesis, his education as a British subject (or, as he puts it in "Boyhood in Jamaica," a "little black Briton" [137]), and the genteel poetry societies that ostracized him. In his memoir of early life McKay recalls,

> We had poetry societies for the nice people. There were "Browning Clubs" where the poetry of Robert Browning was studied but not understood. I had read my poems before many of these societies and the members used to say: "Well, he's very nice and pretty you know, but he's not a real poet as Browning and Byron and Tennyson are poets." I used to think I would show them something. Someday I would write poetry in straight English and amaze and confound them because they thought I was not serious, simply because I wrote poems in the dialect which they did not consider profound. (*My Green Hills of Jamaica*, 86–87)

McKay does not specifically cite the sonnet as a restrictive form imposed by "the nice people" who thought him inferior (and the Browning Clubs may well have been more interested in dramatic monologues, the form most closely associated with their namesake), but given that he eventually turns to sonnets just as he returns to "straight English," we can understand "sonnet" and "restrictive form" to be associated in McKay's thinking. The layering of an international assortment of associations between the sonnet form and rigidity, containment, repetition, and mimesis would seem at first to render it unavailable to McKay as a space for innovation and experimentation. Indeed, early in his career he opted instead to write ballads, which in British poetry were more closely associated with the folk forms in which McKay was interested (and specifically with Scottish poet Robert Burns, with whom McKay is frequently compared). However, in his autographical writing McKay critiques not the British forms themselves but the Jamaican mimicry of them: "Most of the poems that were published in Jamaica at that time were repetitious and not very good. Our poets thought it was an excellent thing if they could imitate the English poets" (*My Green Hills of Jamaica*, 86)

We can understand McKay to have been dogged by two versions of what Gillian White calls "lyric shame." White's book traces the development of 1970s avant-garde critiques of the lyric as insufficiently modern and bound to romantic notions of subjectivity. Modernist critiques of the sonnet's strictures are an earlier instantiation of a similar sort of shame, for the sonnet was associated with a heightened form of bourgeois individuality. For West Indian poets the sonnet also indexed what I might think of as colonial lyric shame—the shame of European mimicry. Poets and critics of West Indian poetry have in turn associated borrowing and imitating British lyric forms with what Lloyd Brown calls the "old-fashioned Caribbean pastoral" (*West Indian Poetry*, 65).[45] Thus there is an implicit connection between colonial lyric shame and environmental poetry. For Caribbean poets and readers, the conception of the romantic self as related to nature is also tied to the colonial history of the plantation. Romantic selfhood betrays the potential for black collectivity and betrays the land itself. McKay's shame about indulging in pastoral nostalgia is not, then, shame over egotism but over mimicry, not the fear of an inflated subjectivity but of a false subjectivity. Eventually Brathwaite would crystalize the connection between the sonnet's prosody, the shameful Caribbean pastoral, and the challenge of representing environmental experience in his assertion that "the hurricane does not roar in pentameters," but as we can see McKay was already alert to the dangers of colonial mimicry (Brathwaite's critique of his poetry notwithstanding).[46] In choosing to write sonnets, McKay both marks the accompanying shame of that imitative tradition and transforms it.[47]

McKay's confinement within the form of "Tropics" mirrors the setting of an array of fruit within a shop window. The division of the poem into quatrains sequesters the image of the fruit "set in the window" in New York from the image of the homeland that produces it ("dewy dawns and mystical blue skies / In benediction over nun-like hills") and from the speaker's emotional experience of these detached landscapes ("a wave of longing through my body swept,") evoking the constraints of the imperfect trade relationships in which the fruit circulates (154). At the same time, the poem insists on the right to "memories / Of fruit-trees laden by low-singing rills" within these constraints and lays claim to the displaced landscape of the speaker's past. Withholding the final couplet, the twelve-line poem (which we can nonetheless recognize as an English sonnet because of the *abab* rhyming quatrains of iambic pentameter) resists an aesthetics of remembering that would valorize continuity or history in a progressive, continuous sense.

But lest we consign the vision of the fruit to universal history, the speaker claims the fragmented sensory experience as his own and as the trigger for a process of remembering that "through my body swept." Given the absence of a linking verb "are" or "were," the first two quatrains constitute a sentence fragment. These are floating moments, suspended in the speaker's consciousness, experienced sensorially. This is particularly significant when we consider how enslaved laborers used the space of the provision ground to assert cultural autonomy in the face of historical fragmentation. That is, the past and the present are temporally suspended but the poem is not atemporal or ahistorical. Elided between these stanzas are the history of the actual cultivation of the fruit and the history of displacement (of the fruit from Jamaica, of the speaker from Jamaica, and perhaps of the speaker's ancestors from Africa) that have led to this moment of diasporic subjectivity; in other words, the very history to which "Quashie to Buccra" gives voice. We can read the conclusion of McKay's poem, the glance averted from the particular scene of childhood, the turn away from a painful history, the missing couplet, as a kind of negative capability that creates what Gikandi describes as a "space for maneuver" (*Slavery and the Culture of Taste*, 246): a flourishing grove within and apart from the slavery and postslavery landscape.

Undercutting the continuity between past and present, McKay uses the form of "The Tropics in New York" to exhibit control over memory. The original publication of the poem in the *Liberator* in 1920, however, featured a significantly different conclusion:

> A wave of longing overwhelmed my soul,
> My heart grew faint ceasing its furious throbbing;
> And in the thronged street, losing self control,
> Like a child lost and lone, I fell to sobbing.

In this ending, the past unhinges the speaker to the point of bodily and spiritual dysfunction: "my heart grew faint" and "a wave of longing overwhelmed my soul." After the caesura in line ten (between "my heart grew faint" and "ceasing its furious throbbing") the heart of the poem skips a beat, and the iambic meter is compromised, both within the lines and in the feminine end rhyme ("throbbing/ sobbing") that concludes the poem. The sense of being "overwhelmed" by longing and by personal history is palpable here.

The final version of the poem, which McKay selected for publication in *Harlem Shadows* and *Spring in New Hampshire* and which was subsequently included in *Survey Graphic* and *The New Negro*, emphasizes instead the speaker's agency in relationship to the past. Although "I could no more gaze" suggests the speaker is beholden to some outside force, the longing is at least limited to the body: "A wave of longing through my body swept" (154). Whereas in the earlier version the speaker "fell to sobbing," here, the speaker acts on his own body: "I turned aside and bowed my head and wept." The iambic meter underscores the speaker's control, the sense that the traumatic break from the homeland need not define the future. Thus, even if the sonnet is the very sign of that break and that trauma, its measure enables McKay's measure in relationship to the experience of displacement. To paraphrase Édouard Glissant, the "boundary" of the plantation, "its structural weakness," becomes the poet's advantage: "The place was closed, but the word derived from it remains open" (*Poetics of Relation*, 75).

The form of the English sonnet, transformed by its historical contact with Jamaica and the United States, mediates the relationship between the poem's two colonial environments. But if landscape is form as Glissant has suggested, it is not so in an easily mimetic sense. That is, a poem does not mimic a single landscape, a national landscape. Recall from the introduction to this book that Glissant frames his discussion of organic forms in *Caribbean Discourse* in terms of *"our* quest for the dimension of time" and *"our* genres" as opposed to "alien" traditions because he is calling for the emergence of a "national literature" (106, 106n1, emphasis mine). Suggesting that the structure of the sonnet derives from the structure of European seasons, Glissant asserts equivalence between nature and nation:

> The pattern of the seasons has perhaps shaped, in the works of Western literature, a balanced rhythm between neutral zones of narrative that are periodically crossed by explosive flashes that arouse the emotions and bring "revelation." A conclusive illustration of this technique is the European sonnet, with its final thrust that both summarizes and transcends the clear meaning of the poem. It appears that the forms of expression in black cultures do not follow this clever shifting from neutral to strong moments in the structure of a work. The unvarying season (the absence of a seasonal rhythm) leads to a monotony, a plainsong whose obsessive rhythm creates a new economy of the expressive forms. (106)

Glissant's use of the term "European sonnet" erases the differences among uses of the form within Europe and also ignores the climatic variations within that geographical region. The sonnet emerged first in the Mediterranean climate of Italy and then was exported to England, France, and elsewhere in Europe. Thus, we cannot reduce the "European" sonnet to a single climatic or cultural environment; neither can we limit the landscape of the colonial counterform or, for that matter, the colonial sonnet as counterform. As William J. Maxwell aptly puts it in his introduction to the *Complete Poems*, the sonnet offers McKay "an exceptionally transnational design" (xxxv–xxxvi).[48] As I have discussed in the introduction, Glissant's distinction between "national" and "alien" would break down considerably by the time he wrote *Poetics of Relation*, in which he argues for new forms of identity that exceed the nation, forms that instead articulate the relation among cultures. One such form, for Glissant, is errantry, a kind of wandering through multiple particular landscapes rather than identifying with a singular "root" (*Poetics of Relation*, 11–22).[49] My interest in Glissant's understanding of the relationship between "the pattern of the seasons" and Western literary form lies not so much in environmental essence, as in his search for "a new economy of expressive form" that might express and generate relational identities and in his positioning of the Caribbean landscape as a potential laboratory for that search (*Caribbean Discourse*, 106).

In this way, even Glissant's discussion of landscape in *Caribbean Discourse* can be seen as emphasizing the need for new forms of discourse beyond rootedness. As McKay's sonnet juxtaposes disparate landscapes and literary forms, it also juxtaposes disparate temporal episodes in order to assemble a collective memory. We perceive a turn in the final quatrain of the poem from neutral description to reflection, as the lush list of the first stanza gives way to the nostalgia of the second and finally to the action of the last:

> My eyes grew dim, and I could no more gaze;
> A wave of longing through my body swept,
> And, hungry for the old, familiar ways,
> I turned aside and bowed my head and wept.

The final gesture is one of aversion, and the bland iambic meter of the last line (consisting almost entirely of monosyllabic words) is far from "explosive." By withholding a final couplet, McKay withholds the revelation and harmony that Glissant defines as characteristic of European literary tradition. Should we conclude, as Glissant's analysis might suggest, that McKay is mistakenly "aim[ing] for spectacular moments, or twists in the narrative, for 'brainwaves'" and failing to achieve that kind of closure because of his alienation from the landscape," that "he "perpetrate[s] at the technical level an unconscious and unjustified submissiveness to literary traditions alien to [his] own" (*Caribbean Discourse*, 106)? On the contrary, McKay's sonnet exposes the gap between the progressive, compartmentalized structure of the form and a landscape that circulates within and beyond its boundaries.

How do individuals, communities, and the land collectively produce history? "The Tropics in New York" frames an episodic relationship to the past, layering discrete moments (the memory of Jamaica, the scene in the shop window) that do not develop continuously. The poem yokes together the locally identified space of the enslaved laborers' garden and the dramatically other space of New York City within the transnationally imagined English sonnet. Thus it can neither emerge precisely from "the pattern of the seasons" nor, on the other hand, take the shape of "a monotony, a plainsong." If Glissant imagines a counterform to the European sonnet—a form that, in Kamau Brathwaite's words, "approximates the natural experience, the environmental experience" (*History of the Voice*, 10)—then he imagines it as yet to come: "Neither poem nor novel," he argues, "are for that matter our genres. Something else will perhaps emerge" (*Caribbean Discourse*, 106n1). In the meantime, the sonnet as provision ground affords McKay both the space for the Jamaican yard on the margins of the colonial plantation and the "space for maneuver" beyond.

In the special issue of *Survey Graphic* magazine, another near-sonnet by McKay was printed on the facing page of Domingo's essay: "Subway Wind." Situated as a pair, these poems force us to reckon with the sonnet as a transnational space for poetic experimentation rooted in and routed through colonial discourse. "Subway Wind," in which an urban experience evokes memories of tropical breezes, at first seems to underscore the prevalent critical contention that McKay's "Harlem" sonnets represent Jamaica as an idealized, pastoral landscape.[50] But the evocation of natural phenomena in the poem ironizes that nostalgia.[51] Where "Tropics" refers explicitly to the products of Jamaica's agricultural economy, "Subway Wind" refers only obliquely to New York City as sharing a geography with the Caribbean. The opening lines describe the bleak, stifling air of the urban wind:

> Far down, down through the city's great, gaunt gut
>   The gray train rushing bears the weary wind;
> In the packed cars the fans the crowd's breath cut,
>   Leaving the sick and heavy air behind.

The heavy alliteration in the first two lines emphasizes the "gray" and "gaunt" quality of the city and contrasts with the "dew drenched night" of the tropics. Rhyming quatrains progress from the "sick and heavy" captivity of the subway to the possibility of nostalgia, creating the expectation that the "weary wind" of the subways will give way to the trades winds of the tropics, and finally "lie idle." However, the movement from quatrain to quatrain undermines the concrete distinction between locales. The two winds blow into each other's worlds, as the poem attributes the "deafening roar" of the subway to "captive wind that moans for fields and seas."

We must attribute the captivity of the wind not only to the subway cars, but to the sonnet itself and the colonial history it embodies. The end of the poem offers a vision of freedom, "Where fields lie idle in the dew drenched night." However, freedom in the poem is unfinished, for the sonnet is elongated (unlike the truncated "Tropics"): sixteen lines without a resolving couplet. Only the literary "moan" of the poem exceeds the boundaries of the subway's boxed cars and the sonnet's boxy quatrains. Calling the winds finally "trades," McKay compromises the sense of winds as "freedom" or inspiration, evoking the possibility of commerce (economic and poetic) between New York and the "islands of lofty palm trees," as well as the slave trade.[52] The last lines of the poem thus read as a kind of ironic haunting, reminding us that the "tropic sea"—site of the middle passage—enabled captivity, and that the fields did not "lie idle" but were the site of enslaved labor: "Where fields lie idle in the dew drenched night / And the Trades float above them fresh and free." The cultural memory of captivity thus haunts the experience of technological freedom just as it haunts the modern poetic form of the New Negro poet.

CULTIVATING *THE NEW NEGRO*

I began this chapter with the scene of McKay leaving behind agronomy to pursue poetry in part because that departure, that movement, mirrors a larger story of migration in the diaspora. McKay's journey is distinct from but parallel to U.S.-based narratives of migration that foreground the movement of black Americans from the U.S. South to northern cities. Nineteen-twelve—the year McKay sailed from Kingston, as well as the year his first two books, *Constab Ballads* and *Songs of Jamaica*, were published in Jamaica—is not typically cited as a significant date in black cultural history (whereas the radicalizing summer of 1919 and the year of *The New Negro*'s publication, 1925, are). But 1912 comes during a wave of Caribbean emigration from Jamaica, Barbados, and other British colonies in the West Indies to Panama and the United States, as agrarianism in the West Indies waned. The year also marks the beginning of a large exodus of Jamaicans to Cuba.[53] I have begun this study then (in the prewar period) and there (in a port of Jamaica) in part to remind readers of the difficulty of any periodization or spatialization that would neatly separate the New Negro poets, often identified with the interwar period and with Harlem, from the longer histories and geographies of migration and immigration that in part produced their art, including West Indian immigration to the United States. Emphasis on how diaspora shapes McKay's poetics in turn sheds light on Locke's *New Negro* anthology (1925). The anthology's diasporic consciousness is located not only in the urban cosmopolitanism previous critics have emphasized but in the way the volume evokes the transnational geography of plantation society as an enduring feature of modern life.

Among many New Negro writers there was a hopeful turning away from the poverty, barrenness, and violence that in part defined the Black Belt, and the anthology highlights how northern urban culture was produced by this turning away, also known as the "great migration." In his prefatory essays, Locke foregrounds mass migration from the U.S. South to the North, along with the "spiritual emancipation" in art that accompanies that movement. In Locke's account the modern promises of urban life displace landscapes of enslavement. In the title essay of the anthology, Locke defines the transformation of black cultural expression in terms of northward movement, emphasizing the city as the center of the New Negro's "newness." He downplays the material conditions of black lives in the South ("labor demand, the boll-weevil," and "the Ku Klux Klan"), insisting that "the wash and rush of this human tide on the beach line of the northern city centers is to be explained primarily in terms of a new vision of opportunity, of social and economic freedom, of a spirit to seize" (6). The movement of bodies, it seems, is a mere figure for the movement of "a spirit," emphasizing Locke's concern with "consciousness" rather than "condition" (7). Describing the "wave[s]" of migration and change as "a deliberate flight not only from countryside to city, but from medieval America to modern" (6), Locke all but equates modern culture with the city.

Locke's emphasis on the overwhelming significance of migration draws our attention to agricultural production as a historical fact, something that the poems in the anthology (including McKay's poems) bring into further relief. At the same time, Locke's formulation of black urbanization and modernization as "natural" processes frequently undoes the linearity of the metropolitan progress he wishes to trace. While celebrating a modern transformation he defines as urban, he takes recourse to the language of agriculture. For it is "in the very process of being transplanted" that "the Negro is becoming transformed" (6). In spite of Locke's explicit framing of this transformation as a movement from the body to the spirit and thus as an abstraction of the "material" contributions of African bodies, his choice of metaphors also evokes the actual tide that carried Africans to the "beach lines" of the country and the labor—the literal planting and transplanting—those Africans and their descendants were forced to perform. As Locke elides the material and the cultural, his references to artistic production as "crop" produced in "fields" appear to be purely metaphorical. Agricultural production is a vehicle representing the tenor of artistic production in the urban North; cultivation is a metaphor for culture. And yet we are forced to acknowledge the landscapes that produce both kinds of "crops" as part of a history of enforced labor and enforced migration, far from the universal, romanticized "racy peasant undersoil" Locke celebrates elsewhere in the anthology ("Negro Youth Speaks," 51).

The New Negro anthology collects a diverse, complex, and mobile public within its pages but nonetheless has often been read within a national framework. Critical and laudatory scholars alike have positioned Locke's anthology as definitive not only of a particular racial culture but of American culture. *"The New Negro,"* Houston Baker writes, "is perhaps our first *national* book" (*Modernism and the Harlem Renaissance*, 85). If for Baker this coalition of national culture, which he names "radical marronage" (76–77), is rooted in racial identity, for George Hutchinson a reading of Locke's investment in the nation requires attention to the anthology's interracial pluralism (*The Harlem Renaissance in Black and White*, 25).[54] Nathan Huggins and Walter Benn Michaels, who critique the failure of Locke's pluralism, nonetheless share the assumption that the function of the anthology is to articulate black identity in terms of United States citizenship and belonging.[55] Their claims about Locke's editorial mission extend broader claims about anthologies in general as nation-building tools of Andersonian "imagined community."[56] But here we can see how Locke's investments in an "American" anthology are compromised by the diasporic geography and consciousness of the black thought he assembles within it.[57]

There is undoubtedly a tension between Locke's evocation of Harlem as a "race capital" and his formulation of U.S. nationalism. This conflict, while inherent in what Barbara Foley calls the anthology's "metonymic nationalism," ultimately undermines Locke's claims for *The New Negro* as a founding document of a precisely American identity.[58] Foley argues that a crucial link in Locke's metonymic chain is the conflation of race and place—that is, the naturalization of Negro cultural identity as rooted in the soil of the United States (*Spectres of 1919*, 237). According to Foley, tropes of "soilness" and "rootedness" are the conduit for the shift in New Negro discourse from radicalism to "culture-based" nationalism. These tropes are pervasive in Locke's rhetoric and across the contributions to the anthology. For example, in his essay "The Negro Spirituals," which introduces the volume's section on music, Locke conflates "race genius" and national representativeness through the metaphor of "soil": "But the very elements which make [spirituals] uniquely expressive of the Negro make them at the same time deeply representative of the soil that produced them. Thus, as unique spiritual products of American life, they become nationally as well as racially characteristic" (199).

Locke enlists the "soil" in his formulation of racialized nationalism to under-score the geographic particularity of a musical form that might otherwise be easily abstracted. His essay goes on to fret over the songs' removal from "their original religious settings" (201) while also celebrating their transition from "peculiar conditions," most certainly a reference to their status as a product of plantation slavery, to "formal music," a transformation that "only classics sur-vive" (199). However, Foley's account of organic tropes in *The New Negro* and other critics' praise and critique of the anthology's nationalist ideology over-look the diverse international presences in the volume. While images of the U.S. rural South in the anthology are crucial to Locke's formulation of black identity, this is just one group of sites in which "the New Negro" is cultivated.

Locke concerns himself explicitly with the cultivation of Negro "crop" as a contribution to "American civilization." In the title essay of the anthology, Locke describes two "constructive channels" through which the "social feel-ings" of the "American Negro" flow: "One is the consciousness of acting as the advance-guard of the African peoples in their contact with Twentieth Century civilization; the other, the sense of a mission of rehabilitating the race in world esteem" (13–14). "The pulse of the Negro world," according to Locke, "has begun to beat in Harlem" (14). Locke ultimately sees "more immediate hope" in the "artistic endowments" of the "American Negro" than in this "new interna-tionalism" (15). Here and elsewhere in his introduction to *The New Negro* Locke explicitly emphasizes the formation of modern America as a product of geo-graphic migration from the U.S. South to the U.S. North.

Yet Locke repeatedly draws analogies between the New Negro Movement and cultural renaissances emerging in the context of anticolonial resistance in Ireland and elsewhere. His racialism depends on transnational connections. In-deed, recent critics have complicated the picture of Locke's cultural national-ism. In "What Was Africa to Him?," John C. Charles excavates the prominence of Africa and Africanism within Locke's formulation of national culture, while Brent Edwards foregrounds translation and collaboration as the means through which Locke embodies diasporic consciousness in *The Practice of Diaspora* (16–21, 69–118). Jeremy Braddock, while conceding to Locke's "nativist" tendencies in the framing essays, emphasizes the reciprocal shaping between the anthology and the texts and collecting practices of European modernism (*Collecting as Modernist Practice*, 156–206).[59] I, too, stress the anthology's transnationalism, as opposed to Foley's metonymic nationalism, not least because of McKay's prom-inent place within its pages.

The anthology's heterogeneous evocations of ecological space invite us to read *The New Negro* as the grounds of more wide-ranging geographies. In some of the anthology's creative works, descriptions and figures of the natural world are abstracted from the specific spaces of black life; in others, they are very precisely imagined. Taken together, the writers in the collection imagine a broader range of such spaces than Locke's narrative of geographic and spiritual migration affords. In some poems in the volume images of flowering, roots, and growing things function as abstracted metaphors for family relationships (Countee Cullen's "Fruit of the Flower": "Who plants a seed begets a bud, / Extract of that same root" [132]), creative imagination (McKay's "Like a Strong Tree": "So would I live in rich imperial growth / Touching the surface and the depth of things" [134]) and (implicitly) emergent racial consciousness (Langston Hughes's "An Earth Song": "I have been waiting long for this spring song" [142]). Some poems, perhaps most famously Langston Hughes's "The Negro Speaks of Rivers" [141]), evoke geographic features as an expression of African diasporic belonging, conjuring an abstracted continental "source" for New World rivers in a way that echoes Locke's sense of the Harlem "Negro" as the "advance-garde of the African peoples" (13).

But other materials in the anthology evoke more specific geographies, histories, and agricultural processes. One striking example of this phenomenon is Eric Walrond's story "The Palm Porch," which portrays the city of Colón during the building of the Panama Canal as a cultural Babylon of modernity. Walrond's story is an example of the complex outernational presences within Locke's volume and significantly complicates the U.S. South to U.S. North migration path that Locke's framing documents so often trace by depicting a community at the edge of the Caribbean Sea that is also a gateway to the Pacific.[60] The story focuses on the cosmopolitan canal city, but it establishes its setting as "a black, evil forest-swamp" transformed by American technological innovation ("saw and spear, tar and Lysol") into "a broad expanse of red, arid land." (115). The dredging of the canal is a sort of cultivation that produces nothing but regurgitation, waste, and excess. The canal itself is at once the process and product of the trade in cultivated goods. Jennifer Brittan argues compellingly that this excess is the point of connection between different locations in the black diaspora, a "geographical *communicate*" (her emphasis) within and beyond the region.[61] The experience of excess on both geographic and human levels in the story also manifests in Walrond's prose style and in the story's structure, replete with lists and catalogues, accumulations of sentence fragments, and ellipses, in such a way that "the idea of surfeit" (as Walrond writes in relationship to the central character's body) indeed "[takes] on the magic of reality." (117).[62]

I dwell momentarily in Walrond's representation of this space of excessive (and yet barren) production to underscore how the processes of culture and agriculture collide in *The New Negro*. The dredging and building of the canal extends and contrasts with the farming that took place on West Indian plantations, insofar as this new industrial form of labor replaced postslavery agricultural labor on plantations for the thousands of laborers who went to Panama for work while also replicating some of the working conditions. As a hub for trade, the canal and the canal cities served to extend the reach of the Atlantic and its agricultural products beyond itself. Walrond's story voices the American "New Negro" in a West Indian space conscribed by old European colonialism and new American imperialism. Walrond's focus on the particular details of Colón continuously underscores the relationship between "the Palm Porch" and other sites in the diaspora. If Harlem represents the "Mecca of the New Negro," the inclusion of "The Palm Porch" in the anthology (as well as in the issue of *Survey Graphic*) offers Colón as a sort of distortion mirror of Harlem's global diversity, one which lays bare the interconnections among modern industry and agricultural production.[63]

Through the diverse contents of the volume he collected, we can understand Locke as inheriting his sense of culture not only from W. E. B. Du Bois, who defined the black man's striving at the beginning of the twentieth century as the desire "to be a co-worker in the kingdom of culture" (*The Souls of Black Folk*, 9), but also from Booker T. Washington who called, though not in so many words, for black Americans to continue working in the kingdom of agriculture. The elision between the metaphorical and the material senses of cultivation pervading the volume of *The New Negro* brings to the fore the complicated historical sense of culture that Raymond Williams lays out both in *Culture and Society* and in *Keywords*. Williams historicizes the process by which the associations of culture shift away from their primarily agricultural connotations to abstracted social meanings, but he also reminds us that we need to keep the material sense of "culture" always in view so as to remain alert to the processes through which abstract notions of cultural superiority gain and maintain traction. Williams insists that "the relations between 'material' and 'symbolic' production . . . have always to be related rather than contrasted" (*Keywords*, 91). In the case of *The New Negro*, attending to cultivation as both abstract and material process also underscores the ways in which the geography of slavery is global. That is, the transnational ecology of the plantation and its postslavery afterlife, and not the progressive ideology of migration which Locke attempts to celebrate here, become the diasporic frame through which we understand black mobility and immobility. I make this point not to undermine Locke's claims to the possibilities of modern "spiritual emancipation" (that is, I don't refer to the geographies of enslavement to insist on that geography as pure conscription) but to question the connection Locke draws between urbanization and emancipation and to enlarge the map through which we perceive the routes of black modern culture.

LOOKING FOR LYRIC

The turn to anthologies and print culture in American studies has emphasized both the formal and the literary historical functions of these texts as forms. In his excellent analysis of *The New Negro* as not only a collection for different forms of black modernism but also in and of itself one of those forms of modernism, for example, Jeremy Braddock stresses that Locke's curation of poems alongside less traditionally literary materials in the shared spaces of the anthology is the heart of the volume's modernist aesthetic: "The bibliographic code of *The New Negro*—at the level of the individual page but above all in the terms of the many forms and media that constitute the collection as such—is pointedly one that does not isolate its poems, but rather persistently articulates its disparate materials together" (*Collecting as Modernist Practice*, 182). For Braddock the inclusion of poems, visual and graphic materials, and essays on the same page constitutes "an instrumentalization of the aesthetic, in the most affirmative possible register" (182). This instrumentalization allows individual works to affirm the stated aims of the anthology in some cases and to challenge in others, as in the case of Countee Cullen's "Heritage," the central focus of Braddock's analysis (182).

The graphic organization and reorganization of "The Tropics in New York" and "Subway Wind" in Locke's anthology, however, tells a different story. As I have described, in *Survey Graphic* Locke arranges these poems in the instrumental (but not merely illustrative) way that Braddock describes as characteristic of the anthology by placing them on the first two pages of W. A. Domingo's essay (figs. 1.1 and 1.2). But in his reorganization of the volume for the purposes of the anthology, he moves "The Tropics in New York" to the poetry section, omits "Subway Wind," and changes the title of Domingo's essay to "The Gift of the Black Tropics," disaggregating the sociological from the poetic. This alternative organization does not negate Braddock's larger claim about Locke's practice of modernist collecting; however, it suggests a simultaneous investment on Locke's part in what we might describe as an uninstrumentalized aesthetic. By removing the poem from the particular context of the West Indian immigrant in New York, Locke dislocates the "tropics" while also abstracting the lyric poem.

The Tropics in New York

By W. A. DOMINGO

ITHIN Harlem's seventy or eighty blocks, for the first time in their lives, colored people of Spanish, French, Dutch, Arabian, Danish, Portuguese, British and native African ancestry or nationality meet and move together.

A dusky tribe of destiny seekers, these brown and black and yellow folk, eyes filled with visions of their heritage—palm fringed sea shores, murmuring streams, luxuriant hills and vales—have made their epical march from the far corners of the earth to Harlem. They bring with them vestiges of their folk life—their lean, sunburnt faces, their quiet, halting speech, fortified by a graceful insouciance, their light, loose-fitting clothes of ancient cut telling the story of a dogged, romantic pilgrimage to the El Dorado of their dreams.

Here they have their first contact with each other, with large numbers of American Negroes, and with the American brand of race prejudice. Divided by tradition, culture, historical background and group perspective, these diverse peoples are gradually hammered into a loose unit by the impersonal force of congested residential segregation. Unlike others of the foreign-born, black immigrants find it impossible to segregate themselves into colonies; too dark of complexion to pose as Cubans or some other Negroid but alien-tongued foreigners, they are inevitably swallowed up in black Harlem. Their situation requires an adjustment unlike that of any other class of the immigrant population; and but for the assistance of their kinsfolk they would be capsized almost on the very shores of their haven.

According to the census for 1920 there were in the United States 73,803 foreign-born Negroes; of that number 36,613, or approximately 50 per cent lived in New York City, 28,184 of them in the Borough of Manhattan. They formed slightly less than 20 per cent of the total Negro population of New York.

From 1920 to 1923 the foreign-born Negro population of the United States was increased nearly 40 per cent through the entry of 30,849 Africans (black). In 1921 the high-water mark of 9,873 was registered. This increase was not permanent, for in 1923 there was an exit of 1,525 against an entry of 7,554. If the 20 per cent that left that year is an index of the proportion leaving annually, it is safe to estimate a net increase of about 24,000 between 1920 and 1923. If the newcomers are distributed throughout the country in the same proportion as their predecessors, the present foreign-born Negro population of Harlem is about 35,000. These people are, therefore, a formidable minority whose presence cannot be ignored or discounted. It is this large body of foreign born who contribute those qualities that make New York so unlike Pittsburgh, Washington, Chicago and other cities with large aggregations of American Negroes.

The largest number came from the British West Indies and were attracted to New York by purely economic reasons. The next largest group consists of Spanish-speaking Negroes from Latin America. Distinct because of their language, and sufficiently numerous to maintain themselves as a cultural unit, the Spanish element has but little contact with the English speaking majority. For the most part they keep to themselves and follow in the main certain definite occupational lines. A smaller group, French-speaking, have emigrated from Haiti and the French West Indies. There are also a few Africans, a batch of voluntary pilgrims over the old track of the slave-traders.

Among the English-speaking West Indian population of Harlem are some 8,000 natives of the American Virgin Islands. A considerable part of these people were forced to migrate to the mainland as a consequence of the operation of the Volstead Act which destroyed the lucrative rum industry and helped to reduce the number of foreign vessels that used to call at the former free port of Charlotte Amelia for various stores. Despite their long Danish connection these people are culturally and linguistically English, rather than Danish. Unlike the British Negroes in New York, the Virgin Islanders take an intelligent and aggressive interest in the affairs of their former home and are organized to cooperate with their brothers there who are valiantly struggling to substitute civil government for the present naval administration of the islands.

To the average American Negro all English-speaking black foreigners are West Indians, and by that is usually meant British subjects. There is a general assumption that there is everything in common among West Indians, though nothing can be further from the truth. West Indians regard themselves as Antiguans or Jamaicans as the case might be, and a glance at the map will quickly reveal the physical obstacles that militate against homogeneity of population; separations of many sorts, geographical, political and cultural tend everywhere to make and crystallize local characteristics.

The Tropics in New York

By CLAUDE McKAY

Bananas ripe and green, and ginger root,
Cocoa in pods and alligator pears,
And tangerines and mangoes and grape fruit,
Fit for the highest prize at parish fairs.

Set in the window, bringing memories
Of fruit-trees laden by low-singing rills,
And dewy dawns, and mystical blue skies
In benediction over nun-like hills.

My eyes grew dim, and I could no more gaze;
A wave of longing through my body swept,
And, hungry for the old familiar ways,
I turned aside and bowed my head and wept.

—From *Harlem Shadows*, Harcourt, Brace & Co.

648

Fig. 1.1. Facing pages from *Survey Graphic*'s special issue, "Harlem: Mecca of the New Negro," published in March 1925. Reprinted courtesy of Social Welfare History Archives, University of Minnesota Libraries.

In the context of black literary history (as opposed to the Anglo-European frame of modernist literary history—such as Pound's collecting and curating practices—that drives Braddock's analysis), this dual strategy for framing lyric poetry constitutes a complex entry into black modern debates about the status of art in the social realm.

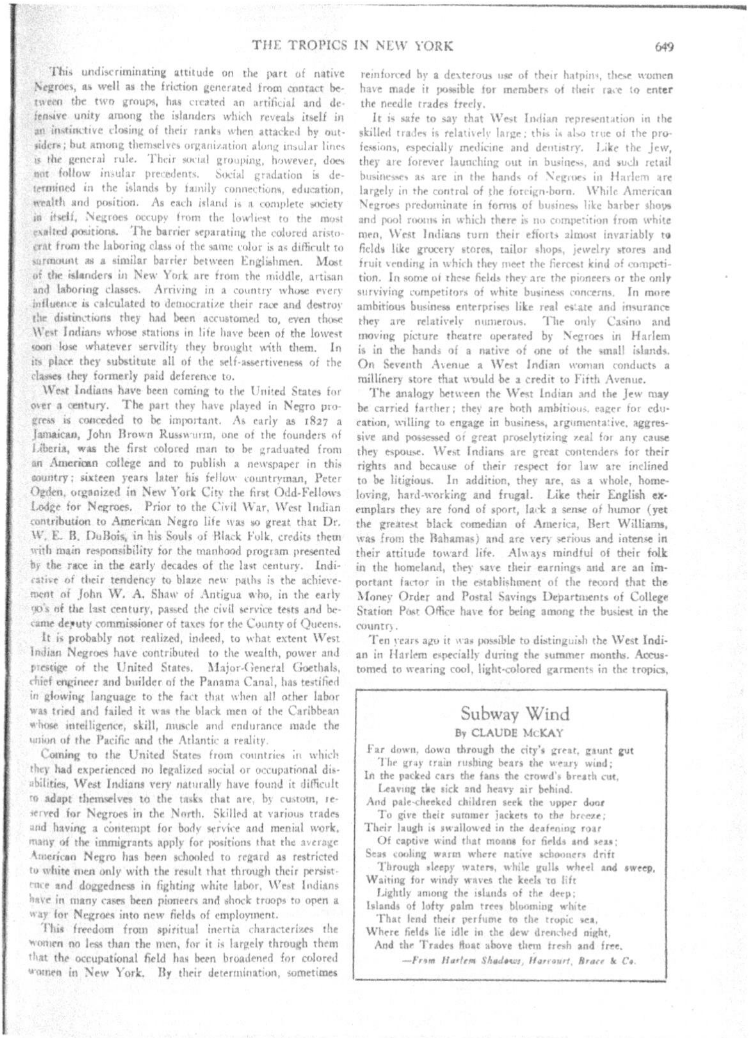

This undiscriminating attitude on the part of native Negroes, as well as the friction generated from contact between the two groups, has created an artificial and defensive unity among the islanders which reveals itself in an instinctive closing of their ranks when attacked by outsiders; but among themselves organization along insular lines is the general rule. Their social grouping, however, does not follow insular precedents. Social gradation is determined in the islands by family connections, education, wealth and position. As each island is a complete society in itself, Negroes occupy from the lowliest to the most exalted positions. The barrier separating the colored aristocrat from the laboring class of the same color is as difficult to surmount as a similar barrier between Englishmen. Most of the islanders in New York are from the middle, artisan and laboring classes. Arriving in a country whose every influence is calculated to democratize their race and destroy the distinctions they had been accustomed to, even those West Indians whose stations in life have been of the lowest soon lose whatever servility they brought with them. In its place they substitute all of the self-assertiveness of the classes they formerly paid deference to.

West Indians have been coming to the United States for over a century. The part they have played in Negro progress is conceded to be important. As early as 1827 a Jamaican, John Brown Russwurm, one of the founders of Liberia, was the first colored man to be graduated from an American college and to publish a newspaper in this country; sixteen years later his fellow countryman, Peter Ogden, organized in New York City the first Odd-Fellows Lodge for Negroes. Prior to the Civil War, West Indian contribution to American Negro life was so great that Dr. W. E. B. DuBois, in his Souls of Black Folk, credits them with main responsibility for the manhood program presented by the race in the early decades of the last century. Indicative of their tendency to blaze new paths is the achievement of John W. A. Shaw of Antigua who, in the early 90's of the last century, passed the civil service tests and became deputy commissioner of taxes for the County of Queens.

It is probably not realized, indeed, to what extent West Indian Negroes have contributed to the wealth, power and prestige of the United States. Major-General Goethals, chief engineer and builder of the Panama Canal, has testified in glowing language to the fact that when all other labor was tried and failed it was the black men of the Caribbean whose intelligence, skill, muscle and endurance made the union of the Pacific and the Atlantic a reality.

Coming to the United States from countries in which they had experienced no legalized social or occupational disabilities, West Indians very naturally have found it difficult to adapt themselves to the tasks that are, by custom, reserved for Negroes in the North. Skilled at various trades and having a contempt for body service and menial work, many of the immigrants apply for positions that the average American Negro has been schooled to regard as restricted to white men only with the result that through their persistence and doggedness in fighting white labor, West Indians have in many cases been pioneers and shock troops to open a way for Negroes into new fields of employment.

This freedom from spiritual inertia characterizes the women no less than the men, for it is largely through them that the occupational field has been broadened for colored women in New York. By their determination, sometimes reinforced by a dexterous use of their hatpins, these women have made it possible for members of their race to enter the needle trades freely.

It is safe to say that West Indian representation in the skilled trades is relatively large; this is also true of the professions, especially medicine and dentistry. Like the Jew, they are forever launching out in business, and such retail businesses as are in the hands of Negroes in Harlem are largely in the control of the foreign-born. While American Negroes predominate in forms of business like barber shops and pool rooms in which there is no competition from white men, West Indians turn their efforts almost invariably to fields like grocery stores, tailor shops, jewelry stores and fruit vending in which they meet the fiercest kind of competition. In some of these fields they are the pioneers or the only surviving competitors of white business concerns. In more ambitious business enterprises like real estate and insurance they are relatively numerous. The only Casino and moving picture theatre operated by Negroes in Harlem is in the hands of a native of one of the small islands. On Seventh Avenue a West Indian woman conducts a millinery store that would be a credit to Fifth Avenue.

The analogy between the West Indian and the Jew may be carried farther; they are both ambitious, eager for education, willing to engage in business, argumentative, aggressive and possessed of great proselytizing zeal for any cause they espouse. West Indians are great contenders for their rights and because of their respect for law are inclined to be litigious. In addition, they are, as a whole, home-loving, hard-working and frugal. Like their English exemplars they are fond of sport, lack a sense of humor (yet the greatest black comedian of America, Bert Williams, was from the Bahamas) and are very serious and intense in their attitude toward life. Always mindful of their folk in the homeland, they save their earnings and are an important factor in the establishment of the record that the Money Order and Postal Savings Departments of College Station Post Office have for being among the busiest in the country.

Ten years ago it was possible to distinguish the West Indian in Harlem especially during the summer months. Accustomed to wearing cool, light-colored garments in the tropics,

Subway Wind
By CLAUDE McKAY

Far down, down through the city's great, gaunt gut
The gray train rushing bears the weary wind;
In the packed cars the fans the crowd's breath cut,
Leaving the sick and heavy air behind.
And pale-cheeked children seek the upper door
To give their summer jackets to the breeze;
Their laugh is swallowed in the deafening roar
Of captive wind that moans for fields and seas;
Seas cooling warm where native schooners drift
Through sleepy waters, while gulls wheel and sweep,
Waiting for windy waves the keels to lift
Lightly among the islands of the deep;
Islands of lofty palm trees blooming white
That lend their perfume to the tropic sea,
Where fields lie idle in the dew drenched night,
And the Trades float above them fresh and free.

—From Harlem Shadows, Harcourt, Brace & Co.

Fig. 1.2.

Viewing the collection itself as literary form has been a crucial turn for histories of the book, for Americanist literary scholarship, and for the study of poetry, which for some time was dominated by ahistorical approaches such as the New Criticism.[64] In some cases, as with some of the postwar periodicals I consider in chapter 2, the study of generation-shaping collections enables us to develop a more lateral literary history than author-based or genre-based study. However, it is equally important to address the poem's formal qualities and its transgression of the frame of the anthology. Addressing McKay's poetry both inside and outside of its publication in *The New Negro* requires that we understand the deterritorialization of his lyric forms (that is, their extraction from the specific geographies of Clarendon Parish or Kingston, Jamaica, or even from Harlem), much as we might understand the fruits they contain, namely, as produced by and exceeding the bounds of colonial history.

By attending to McKay's poems as lyric ecologies, I mean to have evoked the group of formal and historical associations that have accrued to lyric poetry in (and prior to) the twentieth century: the primacy of a fictive first-person speaker; the sense of a poem as a compressed, contained, organic whole; lyric time (the arrest or suspension of temporal progression); and the intimate relations between textual poetry and aural forms such as music and speech. Each of these characteristics is particularly vexed within McKay's oeuvre and in the reception of his work: the tension, for example, between a lyric "I" and a collective "we" animates his most famous poem "If We Must Die"; his shift from writing dialect verse in Jamaica to (apparently) standard verse in England and the United States underscores the artificiality of conceptions of lyric utterance as overheard speech; and, as this chapter has demonstrated, the circulation of McKay's poems in a range of historical and social contexts more broadly raises the question of the relationship between transcendent or universal history and the particular histories and geographies of black social and economic life. In placing McKay's poetics in a black Atlantic context, in the break between colonial and modern subjectivity, I provide an alternative geographic frame for theorizing lyric (and lyric reading) but also a longer temporal view that accounts for the legacy of Atlantic slavery and colonial education. That is, I have taken Virginia Jackson and Yopie Prins up on the invitation to ask "where, when, how and why do we discover theories of lyric" (*The Lyric Theory Reader*, 6), rather than assuming those theories to be universal, by turning to the unlikely chronotope of the plantation.

Given the simultaneous "autarky" and interdependence of plantation spaces, how can we imagine a poetics that reaches beyond the enclosed "little rooms" of the lyric poem?[65] After World War II, West Indian and U.S. writers were increasingly living in urban environments, abstracted and alienated from agricultural landscapes. Whereas U.S. writers reframed their collective sense of purpose in terms of integration into intercultural radical and mainstream literary venues, in the Caribbean the provision ground would assume new political meaning in the decolonial context of a search for a national or regional literary voice. As U.S. writers looked to racial integration and literary citizenship and

Anglophone Caribbean poets expressed regional and national alliances in the hope (and after the failure) of West Indian federation, what aesthetic forms would the provision ground take? Following Sylvia Wynter's theory of the "plot" into the pages of the little magazines that created a space for such a theory, the next chapter begins by testing the idea that the collective form of the journal itself might constitute a postindependence ecological poetics.

two

Cultivating the Nation
The Reterritorialization of Black Poetry at Midcentury

THE PERIODICAL PROVISION GROUND:
SAVACOU AND NEW WRITING

In the first special literary issue of *Savacou* magazine (1970–1971), a publication of the Caribbean Artists Movement, Trinidadian writer Gordon Rohlehr frames a problem for writers embroiled in the political violence of new nationhood that to some degree defined his generation. In the anonymously published prose piece that was later attributed to him, "White Fridays in Trinidad," Rohlehr's narrator looks out over the hills brown with drought and laments that "it is hard to reconcile all this beauty with the barbarity of the time" (20).[1] During and after World War II, West Indian writers lived increasingly in urban environments within the Caribbean and abroad, abstracted and alienated from agricultural landscapes. Some writers therefore defined their surroundings in opposition to romanticized visions of the Caribbean landscape, what Lloyd Brown describes as "blandly escapist and derivative word-painting—the Caribbean pastoral" (*West Indian Poetry*, 66), either by renouncing descriptive language altogether in favor of more abstract political rhetoric or by evoking an ecology of streets instead of seeds. And yet in the wake of the war and the slow process of decolonization, writers from within and without the West Indies also sought ways of defining the Caribbean environment as the site of literary imagination of burgeoning national and regional identities.[2]

Rohlehr connects reparative politics with the need to account poetically for the environment. The piece is structured as a diary, divided into sections that are subtitled with consecutive dates. By the end, turning sharply from a descriptive chronicle of events to literary criticism, Rohlehr praises especially Kamau Brathwaite, *Savacou*'s editor, for being able to align "the glowing burning beauty of these islands, with a constant history of exile and rootless travel" (24). Against reading nature poetry as alien to politics, Rohlehr surprisingly suggests that this alignment is the striving of all "conscious artists" (24). Unraveling the narrative coherence of his own chronicle of events and landing on poetry, he emphasizes the capacity of poetry to undertake the project of national consciousness.

The publication of this special issue of *Savacou* was a watershed moment in Caribbean literary history. Building on the strength of the earlier "little magazines" from the region, *Savacou* represented itself as a more self-consciously regional and generational mouthpiece. The editors, John La Rose, Andrew Salkey, and Kamau Brathwaite had formed the Caribbean Artists Movement in London five years earlier and began *Savacou* (published in Kingston) in 1970 as a quarterly collection of essays, poetry, fiction, drama, and reviews. The special issue was the magazine's first attempt to bring together a collection of creative writing from the region, an effort to consolidate a reading public for Caribbean literature.[3] Thus, we might expect its contents to exemplify what Jamaican novelist and critic Sylvia Wynter would describe, in the same year *Savacou* was founded, as a literary culture that represents "the rooting of the African in the New World; and therefore the process of *indigenization*" ("Jonkonnu in Jamaica," 36, emphasis in original).

For Wynter, the "double relation" between enslaved laborers and the land they cultivate ("Jonkonnu and Jamaica," 36), which I have described in the introduction to this book, was central to the development of a regional literature after emancipation. Wynter published her writings on the provision ground in the early 1970s, both in *Jamaica Journal* in 1970 and in *Savacou* itself in 1971. But in contrast to this pivotal ecological theory of narrative, the poems in the special issue of *Savacou* engage in a more bifurcated relationship to ecological discourse. On the level of content, some eschew the language of cultivation to create different sites of political solidarity. In "Notes Toward a Final Belief," for example, Roger McTair calls for urban progress, celebrating the crumbling cathedrals of European colonialism, and bemoaning the appropriation of carnival by Western audiences: "We need blue-prints for a city. We need all time and energy/talent, thought, art and voice to build this city/This is the new ideal. We must build this city" (95). Similarly, Bruce St. John mocks the artistic fixation on "landscape" as out of touch with the political focus of his generation in a short poem entitled "Art," in which he names various sightings of the painter: "pon de sidewalk," "at de Hilton," and so forth ("West Indian Litany," 82). St. John draws our attention to the artifice of ecomimetic pastoral painting through the dull repetition of "beach, beach, beach" and "tree, tree, tree," the objects of the painter's study. In each case the "landscape" is merely that—an object or commodity that is replicable and has no agency. "Beach" and "tree" can never be anything other than part of the plantation/tourist economy, never part of its critique, or "studyation . . . worryation . . . nation" (82). By contrast, other poets do draw on site-specific environmental language to evoke processes of "indigenization." In "Guyana not Ghana" Mark Matthews explores the links between the African country and the Caribbean one, but he begins and ends with an assertion of difference, insisting on Guyana's "nativeness" by reclaiming its agricultural and culinary products: "Black puddin', corn pone, swank, cuss-cuss an' sugar / Jinghi seeds, black-dam mettagee" (153).

Given these diverse instances of renunciation of and engagement with agricultural and natural discourse, it is hard to generalize about the formal ecology of the poetry of this foundational *Savacou* volume. But perhaps this collection of disparate voices—emerging from and in turn informing the Rastafari communities of West Kingston, the early Caribbean Artists Movement readings in London, political protests, or the Association for Commonwealth Literature and Language Study in Kingston meeting in 1971—is the more significant for bringing to the fore the radical aesthetic and political differences within black diasporic poetry.[4] This model for reading diasporic poetry affords a way to understand the other texts I consider in this chapter and the relationships among them, from midcentury periodicals in Barbados and Atlanta (that emerged on the scene in advance of the Caribbean Artists Movement and the Black Arts Movement, respectively) to Gwendolyn Brooks's "In the Mecca," a poem that constitutes a collection unto itself.

In the second half of the twentieth century, regional diversity (of culture, language, and land) became a central problem for writers and editors. In this context the provision ground on the edge of the plantation retained its imaginative currency for some West Indian writers, who reterritorialized the landscape of plantation slavery—by which I mean, claimed landscape or territory as one fundamental basis of Caribbean identities—in nationalist discourse.[5] But in the waning days of colonial rule, the editors of periodicals sought new geographic metaphors to describe their attempts at literary consolidation in their periodical pages. I focus on one such example in reading *BIM*, a foundational West Indian literary journal edited by Frank Collymore in Barbados that was founded in 1942, in whose pages the bestiary and the archipelago join the plantation and the plot as grounds of geographic belonging. By contrast, in the United States, postwar writers striving for full participation in integrated American literary culture often *deterritorialized* their work from the historical territories of enslavement, as exemplified in the the abstraction and universalizing of black themes in a significant 1950 issue of *Phylon*. As a hinge between this abstracted sense of black literary "movement" characteristic of the 1950s and the new sense of concerted political movement of the 1960s, Gwendolyn Brooks's poetry helps us see how black writing in the United States abstracts and meta-phorizes the material history of the plantation, writing new forms of black social consciousness in urban spaces. In my reading of her long poem "In the Mecca," I identify "the ghetto" and the apartment building as part of the reterri-torialized ecology of black literature in the second half of the twentieth century.

The texts I have collected here do not (individually or collectively) turn to the geographies of enslavement and freedom as signs of a shared transnational modern identification; rather, they occupy various lyric ecologies (the provi-sion ground, the bestiary, the ghetto, the apartment building) in a way that marks the distance between the land (or the nation, or the region) and the dif-ferent kinds of poems and periodicals that work to embody it. What these works share is their antimimetic properties in relationship to the history and land-scapes of cultivation. These diverse poetic instantiations of black diasporic fu-turity invite us to understand "provision" as a verb—an action of material and spiritual sustenance that is always under way in poetics, diffuse and partially expressed, never quite planted in one place or the other.

THE MINOR POEM AND ARCHIPELAGIC READING:
BIM'S EARLY YEARS

In the Trinidad *Guardian*, Eric Roach famously critiqued the poetic heterogene-ity of the *Savacou* special issue in regard to vernacular usage, Rasta traditions, and the rendering of the Caribbean environment, defining a split between what he called the "clap trap" born of the "whirlwind and whirlpool of race and co-lour," on the one hand, and poems that acknowledge the inheritance of Euro-pean literatures and display a "delicate and cunning use of language" and "cool detachment and control," on the other ("A Type Not Found in All Genera-tions," 8). Singling out the baldly political poems of younger (and specifically Jamaican) contributors for critique, he distinguishes the "ranting" of Rasta poets like Bongo Jerry from what he calls the more authentically "native" ren-derings of the West Indies by Walcott and others. Roach's critique of *Savacou*'s "split mind" is itself rife with environmental, geographic, and architectural metaphor, reminding us how central the West Indian's reckoning with place is for his poetics.[6] In Roach's harsh rhetoric, the geography of land ("the stinking dunghills of slavery," "the plantation of extinction") is one of pure constraint juxtaposed against the expansive possibility of the sea, where "one must erect one's own cottage" (8). The plantation is the site of mass death not only in the historical past but in the imaginative future. Published in the issue of *Savacou* following the special issue, Sylvia Wynter's critical reterritorialization of black literature in "Novel and History, Plot and Plantation," her instance on the plot as "the roots of culture" (100), thus functions as a defense of using "geography and circumstance" (and specifically the geography and circumstance of the plantation) as the basis of aesthetics.[7] Coming to the *Savacou* issue with Wynter in mind (that is, thinking about her insistence on the intimacy between nature and culture) I see *Savacou* as the very form of a provision ground. It is an example of what Katherine McKittrick has called "plot-*life*," a space of semiautonomous creative production that emerges within, but in opposition to, plantation logic ("Plantation Futures," 11).[8] The periodical, the collaborative social context for West Indian place-making, *is* (with all of its limitations) "the plot."[9]

The very heterogeneity that is the condition of possibility for the periodical provision ground presents methodological problems for readers of poetry in West Indian periodicals, particularly when the poetry cannot be consolidated into the aims of resisting capital or nation-building. The unevenness of periodical publication indicates that the project of "indigenization" that Wynter advocated was not (and perhaps could never be) complete. It is perhaps helpful, then, to turn to an earlier instance of periodical collection, before independence, federation and its failure, and the full emergence of sovereign nations. The more peripheral or marginal works published in this transitional period at times serve and at times undermine holistic readings of the movements that eventually came out of the journals, including political efforts at federation and decolonization and the artistic and cultural union that would yield the Caribbean Artists Movement. *BIM*, the literary journal from Barbados founded in 1942 (almost thirty years before the first issue of *Savacou* was published) and often thought of as the first major journal devoted primarily to the publication of Caribbean literature in English, is touted in part because of its championing of the early careers of Walcott, Brathwaite, George Lamming, Sam Selvon, and others. But in addition to essentially generating the canon of the "boom" generation of West Indian writing, *BIM* published a broad spectrum of other writing that is hard to reconcile with the aesthetic or political ideals of the moment.

Reading the minor poems that immediately precede the West Indian literary boom of the 1950s and 1960s reveals a moment in which classifications are challenged by the tensions between the thematic and formal concerns of individual poems, the structure and generic organization of journal volumes, and the idea of West Indian literature as national, regional, and racial political formation. While many scholars, particularly within the Caribbean, have noted the legacy of *BIM* to Caribbean literary history, few have read the poems in its pages (particularly the smallest or most minor work) with particular attention. To do so is to attend to what Raphael Dalleo has termed *BIM*'s "ideology of the literary," an ideology grounded in the local, while also questioning the extent to which this ideology is consistent or consistently contributes to "a national project" (*Caribbean Literature and the Public Sphere*, 109). Reading *BIM* requires us to oscillate between an aesthetics of the local represented in individual poems and the striving for regional and transnational identification embodied in the journal's tables of contents and organization. I do so here to highlight the value of a diasporic frame for black ecological thought.

The broad amorphous designation of "minor poetry" seems to encompass two other categories of poetry that are important to the larger argument of *Cultivation and Catastrophe*: explicitly political verse and nature poetry. Strangely, scholars often oppose these two categories, as Evie Shockley has observed in her work on African American poetry: "From the perspective of the literary establishment, the former is typically seen as a lesser, degraded type of work in comparison to poetry taking up the time-honored theme of nature; at the same time, from the perspective an embattled African American community (literary and otherwise), greatly influenced by the aesthetics privileged by the Black Arts Movement, poetry that is not political is often seen as not relevant to the needs of the people" (*Renegade Poetics*, 145). In the Caribbean, too, both categories (the political and the natural) could be deemed "minor" or "bad," and they were often viewed as mutually exclusive. By the time of the special issue of *Savacou*, the problem of how to separate the wheat from the chaff had come to a head in the arguments among Roach, Syl Lohar, Rohlehr and others over the quality of the volume's poetry. By 1971, Roach's postcolonial version of the "raw and the cooked," which had everything to do with the poets' relationships to their landscapes, had taken firm hold of Caribbean literary discourse about poetry and poetic form. But the desire to distinguish between "good" and "bad," and to do so in part based on how poets express their territorial affiliations, extended back to the previous generation, who wrote during a period of transition from colonial to nationalist politics.

Deleuze and Guattari in their work on Kafka refer to minor literature as literature that has been "deterritorialized from its language"—in the case of Kafka, written in German outside of Germany—in a literal sense but also that in other ways distorts, transforms, breaks, and reveals the insufficiency of the (dominant) language in which it is written. According to Deleuze and Guattari "minor literatures" share two other characteristics: they are necessarily political, and they are "collective enunciation[s]" rather than products of individual talent

(*Kafka*, 17). Either a literal or abstract alienation between writers and the landscape of their language can produce a "minor" response. To be deterritorialized (minor) is to escape from the territory rather than to bring the language closer to the ground (the provisioning ground or any other). (Significantly, Deleuze and Guattari see literature as a "line of abolition," a "line of escape.")[10] How, then, can a "minor literature" also be a "nature literature"?[11] Paradoxically, early issues of *BIM* invite reading the minor in the context of Caribbean writers' nascent attempts to reimagine forms of geographic belonging during this period of nationalist formation. I have suggested that we might read a periodical as a partially closed system, a self-sustaining provision ground affording a small degree of freedom within the constraints of the plantation, but looking for a line of escape, we might need to read instead with a broader geography in mind: the archipelago that connects but does not contain the diffuse regional geographies and literary styles.

The most obviously minor poems in *BIM* are Collymore's own. Collymore's major influence on West Indian poetry has been via his role as editor and schoolteacher, not as a poet (he taught both Lamming and Brathwaite and helped to promote both of their careers). His poems have been regularly described as "minor" (although Lloyd Brown would later single out Collymore's "comic talent" and praise his work as "a diversion from the solemnity with which pastoralist and cultural nationalist alike have treated the West Indian landscape"); at the same time, Edward Baugh notes that, like A. J. Seymour (the editor of the contemporaneous Guyanese journal *Kyk-Over-Al*) Collymore's "primary impulse" as editor and poet "is to record as accurately as possible the peculiar life and landscape around them."[12] Collymore's poems evidence a great tonal range, but I turn here to his more playful contributions to *BIM* because of the way they resist this sort of realist impulse. Many of Collymore's poems describe mythical or actual animals, accompanied by illustrations, which he calls "Collybeasts." How can we read these intentionally silly poems in the context of a journal whose volumes would eventually come to stand as one literary mouthpiece for a region? Are they aberrant or central? Do we read them only on their textual surface? How do we understand their relationship to the other poems in the volume and to the institutionalization of West Indian poetry?

Collymore's "The Catt," one of a sequence of his animal poems in *BIM's* first number, thematically, formally, and bibliographically brings to the fore the crises of genre, form, and category that would haunt the formation of West Indian literary culture. The poem comes under the heading "peculiar pets" listed under "verse" in the table of contents. The "verse" section also contains a love poem and an untitled, unlisted war elegy. The second number of BIM features an expanded section of verse and a separate section of "nonsense verse" that includes Collybeasts, along with the illustrated poem "Catmospherics" by Phyllis Evelyn. As more and more poems filled the pages of BIM's issues, its editors further separated the humorous poems from the others. In subsequent numbers, Collymore's poems on fauna, along with other poems, would come under the headings "humorous verse," "humor," "nonsense verse" and "light verse," while the number of poems listed under the serious headings would increase. Which kinds of "verse" should we take seriously, which kinds of moods or affects are produced by or contained within verse, and what even *is* verse or poetry? These were significant questions for BIM's editors at the emergent moment of West Indian national literatures.

If anxiety about genre and classification seems to suffuse the organization of poetry in the early issues of BIM, Collymore's animal poems echo this anxiety thematically and formally, often through reflections on the boundary between the human and the nonhuman. "The Catt" may be a particularly apt focus for this discussion as a mock rumination on speciesism equating speciesism and racialism. The speaker questions the idea of all cats "forming one complete and independent species" and argues for the distinctions between different cats: "For each cat is different / From every other cat" (52). There are, then, two competing allegorical readings. To the extent that the speaker takes issue with declaring one species "independent" from others, the poem critiques the assertion of racial difference between groups. The illustration accompanying the poem, also by "Colly," confirms such a reading (fig. 2.1). The image at once creates hierarchical relationships between lifelike figures (man, cat, statue-like thing) and suggests a likeness among types, or species, or genres. The starkest difference in this image is one of color, suggesting one possibility for the allegorical reading. If the blackness of the cat represents racial blackness and the whiteness of the other figures (or rather clearness, in so far as these are line drawings revealing the color of the page) represents whiteness, then the human/ cat relationship in the image may be an allegory for relationships among the races in which the speaker critiques racial hierarchy and separation.

But the remainder of the poem suggests that the speaker's objection to the species distinction "cat" lies not so much in the problem of distinction *between* species as in the need for greater distinction *within* species. Thus, the racial allegory breaks down or shifts. The speaker wishes not for more *types of cats* (he

Fig. 2.1. F. A. Collymore's "The Catt" first appeared in *BIM* 1.1 (1942). Reprinted courtesy of *BIM: Arts for the 21st Century*.

does not wish, for instance, that we treat tabbies and Siamese as separate species) but for more individual recognition of "each and every cat." On another allegorical level, we might understand "The Catt" as a celebration of individuation against racialism.

But as the modes of perceiving difference within the poem come into crisis, it becomes difficult to read the poem as a celebration of individualism. The speaker instructs the reader in how to read beyond classifications, but following these instructions yields no clear perception.

> Take this cat, for instance:
> My Catt.
> I say nothing of his habits
> Which are, to say the least, peculiar,
> I say nothing of his ways,

> But I ask you: Look at him,
>
> Look at him now
>
> As I am looking at him (52)

The poem surprisingly seems to uphold empiricism as the mode for perceiving individual difference, through the repeated imperative "look at him." No sooner do we expect to *see* a clear marker of difference, however, than the speaker suggests we need to do more, "cogitating, ruminating / meditating and contemplating here" (52). Looking alone is not enough, and in fact can be deceptive: "I mean, he's different, / Looks different" (52).

In the slippage between *being* different in the first line (a contracted difference, at that) and *looking* different in the second, enacted ironically through the repetition of the same word "different," lies both the allegorical power and the allegorical breakdown of the poem. This moment calls into question the idea that we can know difference empirically. The speaker himself relies on categorical rhetoric even while calling for an alternative: "I speak generically," "for instance," "you know what I mean" are all speech acts that depend on shared knowledge of types or the relationship between types and exemplars. Declaring "My cat is queer," the speaker introduces a more ambiguous descriptor of difference to disrupt phenotypical difference.[13] Further, at any given moment the argument against categorical differences between groups threatens to collapse into an argument against the idea that it is possible to identify any kind of difference at all. Eventually, differentiation takes place within the self:

> Now that I regard him intently
>
> I perceive
>
> That he is quite different from what he looked like yesterday,
>
> Indeed, this morning,
>
> In fact, a moment ago. (52)

This increasingly small micro-differentiation becomes a pathology ("Can it be / That he is not quite well?") as well as the answer to the broad problem of speciesism presented by the line drawing and the premise of the entire series of "peculiar pets," for, "I am feeling a bit queer too / To-day / In the head / Myself" (52). Insofar as the poem's answer to racial differentiation is a kind of hyperdifferentiation, the allegorical critique of racial classification falls to pieces.

If I have wanted to read Collymore's animal poem (this one among others), as a political allegory for racial difference, it is in part out of a desire to make central that which is marginal, to find meaning in the minor and thereby to contaminate the major. And in this sense I am motivated by the desire to make this "nonsense" make sense as "minor," to interpret it as an example of deterritorialized verse engaged in "strange and minor uses" of the English language that are "necessarily political" and that amount to "a common action" (*Kafka*, 17). But what if the major—in this case, the West Indian poets publishing their early works in *BIM*, some of them studying at Cambridge, Oxford, or Sussex, and soon to publish internationally—what if this emerging West Indian literary canon is itself minor, is itself that disorganizing, strange politics, the "little England" contaminating the big? How does poetry designated as "minor" by virtue of its aesthetic categorization as "light" or "nonsense" arrange itself in relationship to this major-minor deterritorialized nationalist tradition?[14] And what happens if we allow Collymore's poem to remain minor through its failure to achieve political significance? We're left with a gap between two senses of the major/minor dyad: as a structure in which West Indian literature articulates its relation to dominant Anglophone discourse and, alternatively, as a structure in which the "peculiar" and "queer" heterogeneity of West Indian writing might articulate itself to itself, might be obscured or revealed through acts of minor reading.

If I began with a question that is a problem for anyone reading in a heterogeneous periodical archive, I'm left with a problem of scale produced in particular ways by the exigencies of articulating a poetics of environmental relation in the Anglophone Caribbean, a region that, as I have suggested in my discussion of *Savacou*, would struggle to reterritorialize itself (and its poetry) in the wake of independence from Britain. We can draw lines between the problems of classification taken up in Collymore's poem "The Catt," in the editorial organization of *genres* within the volume, and in *BIM*'s emerging sense of its place in national, regional and diasporic frameworks. *BIM* originated as a local publication of a group of writers in Barbados, but it grew to articulate its relationship to a broader regional and diasporic readership and community.

The particular environment of Barbados becomes a synecdoche for the region as a whole, as *BIM* begins to announce itself as a *regional* rather than a *local* publication. In the foreword to the ninth issue of volume 3 (1949), the editors, W. Therold Barnes and Collymore, take up the relation of the island state to the broader cadre of writers filling up the journal's pages:

The name "BIM" seems to continue to occasion speculation among our non-Barbadian readers; and to them an explanation is no doubt due.

"Little England and "BIMshire" are names that have applied to our island home from times of remotest antiquity: hence "BIM," according to the Concise Oxford Dictionary, "an inhabitant of Barbados."

But, alas, we are losing our insular self-sufficiency. A glance at the contents of this volume will discover the names of many contributors who dwell beyond these shores, far beyond even our lone dependency, Pelican Island.

Yet despite this blow to our pride, we take very great pleasure in introducing to our readers a group of five writers from Trinidad. . . . There is, however, one ray of consolation here—Mr. Lamming is by birth BIM.

We take very great pleasure also in introducing three other newcomers, . . . all of whom are BIM, although the last mentioned owes his inclusion in this category solely by virtue of the definition given by the C.O.D. (1)

We see here the beginnings of a transition from a local to a regional sensibility, from "insular self-sufficiency" to something "far beyond." As *BIM* transformed itself from a descriptive collection of local literary works into a formative archive of a regional literary future, its insular interdependency would come to shape its literary offerings and their categorization within the volumes. The eleventh issue of volume 3 (1950), in addition to individual poems, stories essays, and a survey on Caribbean painting, features a section of work in progress containing poems by Barnes, Collymore, Seymour, Walcott, Roach, Lamming, Selvon, and others. The editors very deliberately collect the poems (and some brief stories) into a single section. The table of contents lists the poems by nation (Barbados, British Guiana, British Honduras, Dominica, St. Lucia, Tobago, Trinidad), but the pages of poetry do not correspond with this order or grouping. Rather, as the unsigned "Work in Progress" article notes, the section is a "cross section of Caribbean poetry" that "cannot claim in any way to be representative" because of the omission of Jamaica. Nonetheless, the editors offer us this "cross-section" as a "group formation" rather than "separately" (237). The table of contents reflects a tension between local and regional formation, but the overall organization of the volume signals its editors' interest in consolidating, indeed forming, a literary voice for the region.

If Roach would later see the "insular" as a confining plantation and the sea as an expansive geography, *BIM* constructs a version of Caribbean interrelation as archipelagic geography through those readers and contributors "who dwell beyond these shores." On a textual level, the proliferation of "Caribbean samples," of lists and bibliographies foregrounding the geographic diversity of the volumes of *BIM*, invites us to see this insistently local journal in a global context. These bibliographic details, like the "The Catt," also convey the various anxieties that accompany the classification of identities. They rupture our sense of the whole. I have turned to the model of the provision ground as a way of describing the collaborative production of West Indian literary identity in this period, but attention to the problem of "minor poems" within the super-structure of these major periodicals invites alternative models for relating (and failing to relate) the individual work to the holistic "roots of culture" (Wynter, "Novel as Plot," 100).

DETERRITORIALIZING AFRICAN AMERICAN LITERATURE: PHYLON'S SYMPOSIUM ON NEGRO LITERATURE

To the extent that the nation-forming West Indian periodicals *BIM* and *Savacou* reterritorialize black writing in both the enclosure of the provision ground and the more expansive ecological structure of the regional archipelago, they re-mind us of the continued shaping influence of cultivation and geography for Caribbean writers even after the sloughing off of the constraints of colonial pas-toral. But midcentury critics of black poetry in the United States sought radi-cally different ways of contextualizing black literary community and agency in the era of urbanization and industrialization that followed the war.

Twenty-five years after the publication of *The New Negro*, Alain Locke would reflect frankly on the limitations of the New Negro era "like the adolescence it was. . . . Gawky and pimply, indiscreet and over-confident, vainglorious and irresponsible."[15] The context was a 1950 special issue of *Phylon*, a quarterly jour-nal on race and culture published out of Atlanta University featuring essays on contemporary black literature. Locke was a sort of elder statesman of the issue, and his cultural movement was the subject of both veneration and critique by the younger writers featured, many of whom celebrated being free from what they saw as the primitivism, dependence on white patronage, and racial limita-tions of the Harlem Renaissance. Much discussion of *Phylon* and the transitional moment in African American literary history between the Harlem Renaissance and the Black Arts Movement has focused on the shifting relationship between art and politics and the temporary movement after World War II away from a specifically "racial" art as defined either by the previous or the later generations of African American writers. These changes had been in evidence since the spectacular success of Richard Wright's *Native Son* and were epitomized by the awarding of the Pulitzer Prize in 1949 to the young Gwendolyn Brooks.[16]

Whether or not the celebration of a new inclusive era was warranted (even at the time, some writers critiqued *Phylon*'s overly triumphant stance on literary integration), the shift in terms for describing the relationships among African

American literary culture, global blackness, and intercultural collaboration is remarkable.[17] Locke draws on a spatial metaphor to express his desire to transcend racial particularity, but the spatial vehicle he references is not rural. He no longer contends with the "racy peasant undersoil of the race life" ("Negro Youth Speaks," 51) that constituted racial memory for him in 1925 but rather the urban enclave: "When the racial themes are imposed upon the Negro author either from within or without, they become an intolerable and limiting artistic ghetto, but that accepted by choice, either on the ground of best known material or preferred opportunity, they stake off a cultural bonanza" ("Self-Criticism," 391). In adapting his metaphors for a new literary moment, Locke substitutes the "ghetto" for the "racy peasant undersoil." He finds a new language for the relationship between constraint and freedom that McKay had transplanted—via the provision ground—into Locke's Harlem "Mecca" twenty-five years before.

Underlying my claim is the assumption that what Kenneth Warren describes in *What Was African American Literature?* as the literature of Jim Crow was a response not only to the legal and economic circumstances of that period but also to environmental circumstances (and profound environmental changes) that were both local and global. While the political and legal consequences of Jim Crow may have begun to give way during the period leading up to the civil rights era (and this is a matter of considerable debate) the imperative to write in response to various forms of dislocation, relocation, grounding, and uprooting did not. By insisting that both the history and the geography of enslavement have shaped black literary forms of particularity I balance Warren's temporal analysis with a spatial analysis and offer what I hope is a more expansive (and transhistorical) frame for understanding the relationship between art and politics for the *Phylon* generation and their counterparts in the Caribbean. As I attend to the differences among black cultures (the essayists in *Phylon* strive for universalism, for example, while Wynter holds fast to the particularity of Afro-Caribbean culture), I am struck nonetheless by the way the transatlantic geography of enslavement shapes these different poetries, albeit often in reterritorialized, abstracted, or urbanized forms.

The shift in Locke's rhetoric signals not only an explicit shift in thinking about the relationship between art and politics but also a shift in his geographic imagination and perhaps more broadly in the kind of environmental relation imagined in black American print culture. Even when he wishes to describe the racial material of black writing, Locke searches for new metaphors in a different sort of industry: "Negro life and experience contain one of the unworked mines of American dramatic and fictional material, overworked and shabby as their superficial exploitation has been. For both the white and the Negro author in this area, the era of pan-mining is about over or should be; the promising techniques are now deep-mining and better artistic smelting of the crude ore" ("Self-Criticism," 392).

In adapting his metaphor for artistic source material to reflect the moment, Locke substitutes the "crude ore" of the nineteenth-century American West for the "racy peasant undersoil" of the early twentieth-century American South. In *The New Negro*, descriptions of cultivation metaphorically represent "emancipation" from that very labor while at the same time reminding us at every turn of its history. Here, Locke enacts a kind of metaphorical migration in his own prose that mirrors the demographic migration that has yielded his new language. Locke seeks a release from that agricultural history, entry into some broader American story, and in his attempt to escape it he abstracts black labor from its historical context. We can, alternatively, understand Locke's metaphor as connected to the material and economic practices of mining rather than as merely symbolic. For, as noted by Clark Foreman in a subsequent issue of *Phylon*, United Mine Workers was exceptional among unions in the early 1930s as the only such organization in which white and black workers were integrated (efforts by workers to integrate were often blocked in other industries, such as the steel industry). This process of mining itself thus represents racial progress through industry (progress otherwise too slow or entirely unrealized) that Foreman insisted must be linked to agrarian reform, "full political democracy," and "full civil rights" if the economic and social transformation of the South were to be achieved and the "full advantage of [its] natural wealth" was to be used ("The Decade of Hope," 138).[18] The mining metaphor thus gives us two ways to understand the abstraction of African American literature in this *Phylon* issue: as an example of critical deterritorialization accomplished by Locke's removal of black artistic labor from the scenes of black agricultural labor and as a reterritorialization manifest in writing that situates black cultural production in new spaces of black oppression. In order to stake out a place for the black writer as "American" (and, by implication, less "racial"), the essays in *Phylon* at times cut black literature off from the more specific sites of black historical experience. In turn, as the following sections of this chapter suggest, deterritorializing the blackness of African American writing paradoxically severs the ties between those writers and other sites for the cultivation of global blackness.

If in the 1920s Locke described a process whereby African American writers distanced themselves from the agricultural landscapes and labor of the South, and if he had himself attempted to enact the spiritual and creative abstraction he noted, it would seem that by 1950 that process had been completed. The absence of the language of cultivation in this iconic issue of *Phylon* is consistent with the demographic shifts that had taken hold in the United States. By the end of the first great migration (said to have begun roughly with the beginning of the First World War and to have ended with the Second World War), approximately 2.5 million southern-born African Americans had left the South; by 1970 (generally considered to be when the second wave of migration concluded), that number would more than double by most accounts.[19] In the preface to the December 1950 issue, the editors of *Phylon*, Mozell C. Hill and M. Carl Holman, implicitly acknowledge the need to account for these spatial changes as one of the driving forces behind the magazine: "One of the major concerns of PHYLON is that of *orientation*—of 'placing' the elements of race and culture. Since those elements are constantly in flux, the task of necessity becomes one of reexamination and revaluation" (preface, 296, emphasis mine). Over the course of several essays on the current state of African American literature and criticism, including assessments of the New Negro Renaissance and the intervening decades, the familiar tropes of cultivation—of roots and tides and flowers and fruits—receive scarce mention. Nowhere does the volume evoke the plantation, that vexed landscape of enslavement, either as a region of horror still haunting the present or as a birthplace of aesthetic innovation and experimentation. When writers do refer to cultivation, they do so in the mode of the dead metaphor, as when Langston Hughes expresses his pleasure that an increasing number of black writers are working "in the general American field" ("Some Practical Observations," 311). The pivotal *Phylon* December 1950 issue opens a window onto the country's agricultural past as it is becoming historical as the scene or source of black art.

The poetry and sociological prose in various issues of *Phylon* frequently work together to establish a link between the social history of urbanization and the aesthetic abstraction of black art. In "Changing Structure of Negro-White Relations in the South," from the third issue in 1951, Joseph Himes describes the changing shape (and the changing geography) of black labor and social organization: "Change of Southern society is evidenced at the level of power and prestige by transference of the center of control from the rural tidelands and farming areas to the growing industrial centers. Wealth is increasingly concentrated in urban industrial equipment and activity. The population, even that part which remains on farms, is growing steadily more urban-oriented. Social organization is more and more dominated from the urban industrial centers" (233). Himes is perhaps overly optimistic about the positive social changes industrialization might yield, predicting that the rise of a Negro proletariat would generate greater intraclass cooperation among black and white workers and that raising awareness of antiblack violence (in spite of the failure to pass antilynching laws) was changing the hearts and minds of white southerners (although he acknowledges that such a process would not come about "with ease and smoothness" [237–38]). Even such an optimistic account of social change marks the continuity between old and new structures of power and oppression (from slavery to sharecropping to industrialization) and between agrarian and industrial systems of labor (insofar as the latter replaced the former).

The abstraction of black labor in Himes's essay mirrors the abstraction of black poetry from agricultural landscapes in the journal. In 1952 *Phylon* would publish Margaret Walker's stunning poem "A Litany from the Dark People," which describes a process of moving "upward" from the "chains of chattel slavery" to "build a race of leaders and a nation more sublime" (252–53). In its first few verses the poem dwells in the imagery of enslavement, drawing a connection between violence ("bending to the lash" [252]) and the sites of agricultural labor. The repeated word "from," begins nearly all of the lines in this "litany" and is itself an example of language that can be both abstract (it is, after all, a preposition) and spatially concrete. One of the uses of "from" is to indicate geographical or temporal remove. So when the poem describes the life of enslavement in the third stanzaic verse—"From planting of the cotton crop and bending with the hoe; / From pulling the tobacco plants across each wearying row"—the poet evokes a time (the past) and place (the plantation) from which "the dark people" have traveled to the present work of "build[ing]" a race, a time and place now firmly gone. On the one hand, "the soil of wasted hopes" has been fully abstracted into the hope of "the coming of that day when all mankind shall be / United." On the other hand, the preposition "from" points to the originating subject position of the poem's speech act (as in "A Litany *from* the Dark People"). Each line beginning with "from" indicates another place, object, or action informing the poem's voice and its collective subject position. The poem's objects ("crop," "plants," and "backwoods") and actions ("weeping," "planting," and "working") are not in the past but are the starting points for the speakers' present hopes for "a nation more sublime."

Walker's poem performs the process of aesthetic abstraction through a description of the process of urban migration. The poet lays bear the process by which the agricultural past becomes the past. But having evoked Locke's essay at the start of this section, I do not mean to suggest that it is entirely representative of black American writing after 1950. We cannot say that a single periodical or even a group of periodicals defines this generation, and I am not suggesting that writers turned only to the urban landscape for the thematic content of their writing after the war.[20] The bitter legacy of the agricultural south remained alive in many works in the 1940s and 1950s, from Richard Wright's *Twelve Million Black Voices* to Sterling Brown's continued investment in the traditions of African American folklore. Lena, the eldest protagonist of Lorraine Hansberry's 1959 family drama *A Raisin in the Sun*, would fight Chicago's housing segregation practices to seek a piece of ground for her garden. Some of the writers featured in the December 1950 issue themselves lived with and wrote about the legacy and the present of rural environs. Margaret Walker by 1949 had moved to Jackson, Mississippi, where she would remain for her long teaching career. But the 1950 issue of *Phylon* that attempts to announce the state of black literature (and black literary criticism) at midcentury by and large minimizes even a metaphorical focus on spaces of cultivation. As the essays in this and subsequent issues of *Phylon* make agricultural blackness historical, they also in various ways express the desire for black writing to be part of the American whole.

Critical deterritorialization in this December 1950 issue functions, paradoxically, to recircumscribe the African American writer within the United States. In his "Essay in Criticism" Blyden Jackson is clear about his ambitions for black writers: "to integrate our own literature into the national consciousness" (342). Ulysses Lee similarly reflects in "Criticism at Mid-Century" that "the Negro artist is viewed as a man knocking at the door of American publishing houses, of American magazines, of American homes and minds. The great hope is that there will be ever widening opportunities for the writer to produce in freedom from racial bonds" (329). Langston Hughes, in an interview with the editors of *Phylon*, celebrates increasing opportunities and successes for writers, especially novelists and poetry, while calling out for a more fully developed critical apparatus for analyzing this new work. The author of "The Negro Artist and the Racial Mountain" (1926), who years before had celebrated that which was "racial" in art, now opines that "the most heartening thing for me, however, is to see Negroes writing works in the general American field, rather than dwelling on Negro themes solely" ("Some Practical Observations," 311). In her essay "Poets Who Are Negroes" Gwendolyn Brooks in a characteristically acerbic tone warns against the "crouching danger" of feeding a hungry mob of (presumably white) readers with mere "lofty subject," which she describes as uncooked dough (312).

Mixing metaphors liberally, Brooks shifts her attention from "raw materials" that are external, to the poet's own person:

> His mere body, for that matter, is an eloquence. His quiet walk down the street is a speech to the people. Is a rebuke, is a plea, is a school.
>
> But no real artist is going to be content with offering raw materials. The Negro poet's most urgent duty, at present, is to polish his technique, his way of presenting his truths and his beauties, that these may be more insinuating, and, therefore, more overwhelming. (312)

She calls for something beyond the particular eloquence of the racialized body, something more universally available by one's being polished or cooked.[21] In her essential book on the Black Popular Front in the 1950s, *The Other Blacklist*, Mary Helen Washington concludes that "these calls from the symposium contributors to erase blackness and discover the 'universal' subject are not signs of a postmodernist move toward hybridity and multiple subject identities. By minimizing racial identity and racial strife and promoting the image for a democratic and racially progressive United States, the *Phylon* group was offering race invisibility as a bargaining chip for American Citizenship status" (42). What is striking is how these claims to universality involve a concomitant turn away from the landscapes of cultivation. With the exception of Hughes's dead metaphor of the "field," writers turn to the ghetto, to dough, to "raw materials," to the body, and the home to describe the task of seeking American literary citizenship. So whereas in the West Indian periodicals of this period, poets defined national and regional belonging in a decolonial context through an imaginative retrenchment in the land, writers in the *Phylon* group in the United States, warily approaching citizenship and integration, seemed to look away from a geography of transatlantic slavery.

To the extent that writers in *Phylon* did occasionally turn to that geography, it was often in reference to outernational spaces, in particular Africa and the Caribbean. By 1950 *Phylon* was on its way to becoming a venue for discourse among and about writers from the African continent and throughout the African diaspora. However, the scarce references to cultivation, plantation, and climate serve not as metaphors for exchange and mobility among landscapes and nations but rather as markers of diasporic difference among them. In the subsequent decades, the U.S.–based publication featured essays, interviews, and creative works focused on continental and Caribbean culture, politics, and history by both black and white writers who were situated in or had emigrated from African and the Caribbean, such as George Shepperson, Claude McKay,

Leopold Senghor, and René Maran. Not long after the December 1950 issue that focused largely on the relationships among race, politics, and aesthetics within the framework of U.S. "national consciousness," *Phylon* was beginning to "reach out."

The writers of *Phylon* also began to theorize about the limits and possibilities of this reach. In two frequently cited essays from 1953 and 1962 issues of *Phylon*, "Ethiopianism and African Nationalism" and "Pan-Africanism and 'Pan-Africanism,'" George Shepperson partially outlines a theory of pan-Africanism that would eventually lay the groundwork for his championing of "diaspora" as a term that, in Brent Hayes Edwards's analysis, "allows for an account of black transnational formations that attends to their constitutive differences" rather than positing an abstract or ahistorical notion of political or cultural unity ("The Uses of Diaspora," 54). Shepperson would later identify his study and writing of poetry as formative for his work as a historian.[22] Shepperson's war poem "Rain," included in a 1951 issue of *Phylon*, offers one measure of how poems in this period marked diasporic difference.[23] In "Rain," Shepperson ties agricultural growth in Nyasaland to global and local histories. The poem appears in *Phylon* as part of a trio of war poems including "Secret Weapon" by Lindley Williams Hubbell and "Dead Soldiers" by Robert Hayden.[24] Shepperson would much later describe the circumstances of its production (his service in the British military in Burma, alongside soldiers from what would become the independent state of Malawi by 1964). Among the three poems printed in the war poems section of *Phylon*, Shepperson's poem "Rain" is the only one to generate a specific sense of place, using the rain in Burma to mark a contrast between the British soldiers and the Askaris anticipating crops and political change in Nyasaland.[25] The poem posits a potential interracial solidarity (in death) between the two groups of soldiers even as it marks what Shepperson elsewhere calls the "colour bar" in the colonial army.

Shepperson would reprint "Rain" nearly forty years later in his 1990 essay "Malawi and the Poetry of Two World Wars," as part of his inquiry into the scarcity of poetry produced from and about Malawi during the wars.[26] This printing history enlists the poem both in pursuing the travel of black people (black military people in this case) across global sites (in *Phylon*) and, on the other hand, in the much later publication, in excavating a particular local history.[27] If by including his own poem in his essay on Malawi poetry in 1990 Shepperson locates the poem squarely within African colonial history (and the particular history of that nation), submitting the same poem to *Phylon* nearly half a century earlier he enters the poem into a transnational cultural sphere prepared for

U.S. readers. As preparation (witting or unwitting) for Shepperson's 1953 essay "Ethiopianism and African Nationalism," this instantiation of the "crops . . . coming up now in Nysaland" surprisingly anticipates the aim articulated in that essay's closing gesture, namely, "to find a few sparks which may throw some light on the obscure roads into the African future—and also into the byways of the past which make up a significant, if overlooked, section of the 'glory road' of American Negro history" (18).

As in this example, the language of cultivation in *Phylon* often marks outernational spaces, underscoring differences between the spaces for constructing U.S. citizenship and those for emerging black consciousness. In 1953 *Phylon* published a segment of the late Claude McKay's then-unpublished biography, heavily edited and with an introduction by Cedric Dover. In what forms one piece of their shared autobiography (also published posthumously in McKay's case) *East Indian, West Indian*, Dover celebrates "these things we shared," notably, "the smell of good earth after tropical rain; the sap-scent of gardens lined with crotons and cannas; the bright reds splashed on the rich greens of abundant nature; the sting of hail-stones on our palates and naked bodies; the aroma of rose-apples, the fibrous sweetness of sugarcane, and the tangy flavour of squelchy mangoes" ("These Things We Shared," 145). Dover's emphasis on the shared tropical ecologies of Jamaica and India foregrounds a "colored world" (to cite the final words of McKay's "Boyhood in Jamaica" [145]) over and against any affiliation between McKay and the "ugliness" of the United States (to which McKay also refers in this oft-cited critique of American racism). Leon-Francois Hoffmann's 1961 essay "The Climate of Haitian Poetry" historicizes Haitian literary culture in relationship to both the economic and the environmental circumstances (poverty and soil erosion) in which "self-expression" and "rich cultural heritage" emerge (61). In theorizing Haitian poetry and its relationship to the metropole, Hoffman seeks "roots" which he finds in "hills," just as Locke twenty-five years before had sought the "race life" in the "racy peasant undersoil." Connecting landscape and language in this way, Hoffman's essay recalls McKay's "Quashie to Buccra" and anticipates Brathwaite's *History of the Voice*. I do not wish to claim any kind of historical belatedness (of Haitian literary modernity in relationship to African American modernity, for example) here. On the contrary, by featuring such essays on Haitian poetry, on the life and work of Claude McKay, on *négritude*, and on Afro-Brazilian poetry in the decades following the "Negro in Literature" symposium, *Phylon* hosts a diverse range of "territorial" poetries and provides a more vivid context for reading black poetry in U.S. publications. These offerings contrast with the abstract universalism

through which the essayists in 1950 stake a claim to belonging in the national literary sphere. The discrepancies between descriptions of black U.S. literature
and literature from other parts of the black world mark the failure of the *Phylon*
group to, in Mary Helen Washington's words, "imagine[d] African American literature in global terms and race as an international issue" during this period
(*The Other Blacklist*, 45).

Perhaps the only way in which Locke's 1950 essay represents black U.S. experience in terms of concrete and specific geography is in relationship to *urban*
space. Describing the tension between constraint and freedom in black literature, Locke relocates the provision ground in which he sought to "transplant"
the negro youth of 1925 to the "limited artistic ghetto" of 1950 ("Self-Criticism,"
392). While in *The New Negro* Locke draws on natural metaphors to connote the
movement of migrants from south to north and the language of rootedness and
soil to describe the particular blackness of New Negro writing, here the language of cultivation gives way to the language of urbanization. If black writers
are confined, it is within a "ghetto," that urban ethnic enclave of isolation and
segregation that by 1950 had become firmly associated in the American mind
with ethnic immigrant and African American communities, as well as with pred-
atory and discriminatory urban planning processes. In an effort to tout his own
prescient embrace of universalism, Locke praises not Richard Wright's *Native
Son* (although he grudgingly acknowledges that "all would agree that the first
two chapters . . . had such quality" ["Self-Criticism," 392]) but Jean Toomer's
1923 work *Cane*, which he heavily excerpted in *The New Negro*. Where previously
the city was the site of modernity, of "spiritual emancipation," the place where
the New Negro was "becoming transformed" while "in the process of being
transplanted," here Locke paradoxically evokes Toomer's representation of a
Georgia sojourn as a respite from the tedious urban confinement of propaganda
("The New Negro," 6). "For we must remember," Locke writes, "the two ways in
which Russian literature achieved its great era; through the cosmopolitan way
of Turgenev, Tolstoi and Chekov and the nativist way of Dostoievski, Gogol and
Gorgki, each of which produced great writing and universal understanding for
Russian experience."[28] Locke sees the value of cosmopolitan and nativist writ-
ing alike, but rhetorically the ghetto replaces the provision ground.

Blyden Jackson, like Locke, laments the "Negro ghettoes" as spaces of con-
striction. Whereas Locke evokes the term as a metaphor for aesthetic practice,
Jackson reminds us of the relationship between aesthetic and lived experience,
referring instead to ghettoes as urban spaces that restrict black Americans to
lives of poverty. He calls for a greater appreciation for the possibilities of educa-

tion as alternative, not only in the buildings on campuses of black colleges but also in institutional commitments to black literary history ("An Essay in Criticism," 339). It is notable that this essay, while relocating the site of conscription from the plantation to the city, contains some of the volume's rare pastoral tropes: Jackson figures criticism of black literature as a "veritable green pasture" awaiting the labor of intellectual inquiry, citing as one positive example Lorenzo Turner's "barehanded" work in the "field" of linguistics (339–40). In these formulations, fieldwork (briefly resuscitated from its status as dead metaphor) becomes oriented toward the future rather than locked in the past, both through its contrast with the urban ghettoes of the present and through its transformation of historical fields of plantation into fields of study. If the field and pasture contain both the richness of black culture and the possibility of entry into American culture (in a way that curiously echoes Locke's rhetoric from 1925), in 1950 the ghetto is the sign of a limiting racial particularity. Locke's and Jackson's references to the urban scenes of black art and black life, respectively, have not entirely erased the ecology of plantation slavery so much as they have repeated, with a difference, the spatial and temporal structures of constraint that once defined agricultural space.

"IN THE MECCA": BLACK ENVIRONMENTAL ONTOLOGY AFTER THE PLANTATION

Although I have noted that Locke's language is abstracted and deterritorialized, it is perhaps more accurate to say that this and other contributions to the 1950 volume of *Phylon* reterritorialize black writing in the city. The term "ghetto" in *Phylon* may mark a clear shift from one geography to another, but it is neither abstract nor universal.[29] "Ghetto" points to the particular experiences of black urban life while also implicitly comparing those experiences to other experiences of social isolation, segregation, and solidarity in the American city and in Europe (particularly those of immigrant groups in the United States, as well as particular ethnic and religious groups in Europe, such as the Jews in Italy). Locke's use of the term "ghetto" brings to mind his discussion of black folk life in *The New Negro*, where he celebrates the extraction of black culture from rural folk sources as both a localized achievement of blacks in America and parallel to peasant revolutions elsewhere in the world. Thus, while a far less idealized metaphor for constraint and conscription, the literary "ghetto" of Locke's midcentury formulation is a provisional structure of feeling that, like both the Harlem "Mecca" and the unnamed rural space of cultural production in Locke's earlier prose (which I have called the provision ground), mediates between particular and global experience. Just as the urbanization of black life was neither abstract nor universal, it was also, significantly, dynamic rather than complete. Many historians in the 1960s and 1970s subscribed to what Joseph Trotter has called "the ghetto model," pathologizing black urban life and black migrants as "passive objects of external forces beyond their control" (introduction, 13). But Trotter and others have demonstrated how migration was instead an ongoing "social process with deep southern roots" (13).[30] Thus it makes sense to think of the "ghetto" as connected to the past, serving as a reterritorialized ecology of black literature for the second half of the twentieth century.

Gwendolyn Brooks did not, to my knowledge, use the word "ghetto" to describe black urban neighborhoods or communities in her poetry, although she did occasionally use the word in interviews (interview with George Stavros, 7). But she did create imaginative spaces of urban enclosure in her poetry that we can understand in relationship to this geographic designation. Critics and reviewers of Brooks's work have routinely used the word "ghetto" to describe those spaces in a way that captures the dual function of the word. For example, Dan Jaffe in his essay critiquing the category of "black poetry" grudgingly acknowledges that Brooks's poetry is born of "ghetto experience" but is quick to add that such "experience" would be of limited literary value in and of itself (presumably because of its racial specificity).[31] D. H. Melhem, by contrast, describes Brooks's Bronzeville as "the black ghetto that becomes Brooks's microcosm of national life."[32] In Brooks's poetry, the "ghetto" as such is not merely a thematic concern but a problem of poetic form, made visible by reading Brooks's poems as urbanizing an ecological tradition.

It might seem surprising to turn in this final section to the work of Brooks, a single poet, given the argument I have made in this chapter for treating periodicals as ideal venues for transforming the economic, ecological, and social legacies of plantation geographies. Further, by the 1960s and 1970s, while critics like Sylvia Wynter and Kamau Brathwaite sought to "indigenize" black writing by claiming the landscapes and processes of cultivation in the Caribbean, black American writers involved in the Black Arts Movement and its local corollaries engaged in parallel and intersecting projects of cultural nationalism through urban space. On a literary-historical level, it might make more sense to explore the flowering of periodicals associated with the Black Arts Movement and its many offshoots in cities like Detroit and Chicago: *Negro Digest*, *Black World*, *Freedomways*, and Dudley Randall's *Broadside Press*.

Brooks's life and career signify both the demographic changes of the late twentieth century (she migrated from Kansas as an infant with her parents and was raised entirely in Chicago) and the communal literary commitments represented by these publications. Brooks published some of her earliest poems in the newspaper the *Chicago Defender*, wrote for *Negro Digest*, spearheaded the "Gwendolyn Brooks Literary Award" for young writers through the magazine, and was one of the first conztributors to the *Broadside Press* broadside series. Like her contemporaries elsewhere in the United States, Barbados, and Jamaica, she was invested in emergent forms of national and racial consciousness and engaged in collective community-building efforts.[33] She demonstrated her investment in circulation, collection, and community by hosting living room workshops, supporting the Organization of Black American Culture in Chicago, and sponsoring prizes for young writers. But she also did so by collecting and circulating past and present voices within her individual poems. In other words, we can think of Brooks as taking up the material provisioning practices of the black press in her individual poems. Attending to the ways environmental experience shapes Brooks's literary forms, I foreground her transitional role between the New Negro writers who influenced and mentored her and the political energies of a younger generation. In her lyric forms, Brooks both experiments with spatial containment, extending McKay's tradition of the provision ground, and demonstrates an archipelagic reach, mediating the relationship between local and broader environments. Finally, even during this period of various forms of emergent national ideologies, the local "territorial" commitments in Brooks's poems invite reading beyond the national frame.

Brooks shares with her predecessor McKay a reliance on the formal structure of the provision ground, but in her case this structure is devoid of its thematic references to the geography of the plantation. In *Annie Allen* (1949), the Pulitzer Prize–winning book that at least in part inspired *Phylon* editors and contributors to celebrate the shifting intercultural terrain of American literature, Brooks reconfigures the experience of social and artistic constraint of the plantation as architectural, interior, and urban. We might think of Brooks's urban poetics as symptomatic of the sense of alienation from the "outside" or, more neutrally, simply a reflection of the new environment that shaped much black cultural and intellectual life. Or we might view the poems' detachment from history as an assertion of black ontology and epistemology within urban spaces of constraint—one that concerns itself with social rather than ecological relationships.

The first section of *Annie Allen* ("Notes from the Childhood and the Girlhood") initiates the book by going beyond the constraints of interior space and the sonnet. The title of the poem "the birth in a narrow room" signals from the start that Brooks will imagine artistic and social freedom as constricted by environment (broadly understood). I begin my analysis of Brooks's poetry with this most private, subjective experience (birth) in this narrow space so as to establish the relationship between experience writ small in the early poems and Brooks's aesthetic struggle against collective environmental alienation in *In the Mecca*. The sixteen-line poem that closes with a rhyming couplet parallels Annie's reaching beyond the "white venetian blinds" and "prim low fencing pinching" (83) of her domestic sphere. This elongation of the sonnet form resembles the movement of trade winds through subway cars—and beyond fourteen lines—in McKay's sixteen-line "Subway Wind." Although her room is "pinchy," Annie "prances nevertheless with gods and fairies" (83). The closing couplet itself "pinches" whatever movement either Annie or the poem undertakes. Even the fruit of the "grapevines" mentioned in line 13 has been canned by the poem's end, for Annie prances

> By privy foyer, where the screenings stand
> And where the bugs buzz by in private cars
> Across old peach cans and old jelly jars. (83)

Poetic form and domestic space (and, by extension, economy, as Brooks's oeuvre largely represents the pinchy residential circumstances of black life in relationship to economic hardship and discrimination) are the "narrow room" into which this "wanted and unplanned" child is born. But what if, with Claude McKay and even Sylvia Wynter in mind, we understand Brooks's near-sonnet in the tradition of lyric innovation that responds to and exceeds the constraints of plantation geography and the violence of Jim Crow?

In this context Brooks works to redefine the "natural." That is, she seeks to hold the relationship between human and nonhuman productively in suspension within the space of urban blackness in order to foreground the black subject's right to be in place, to "be involved in concern for trees," as she puts it in a 1969 interview with George Stavros, "if only because when he looks at one he thinks of how his ancestors have been lynched thereon" (19). I have in mind the poem "Beverly Hills, Chicago," which is part of a suite of poems, "The Womanhood," making up the last section of *The Anniad*. In this satirical poem about the middle-class (and, in 1949, white) residents of a privileged neighborhood, the speaker (part of a first person plural "we") is in a car "driving by" the neighborhood in autumn, taking in its residents, first in their gardens and then inside their homes (128). The structure of the meditation on place thus figures the passengers inside the car as constrained from accessing the apparently desirable outside. The central conceit of the poem, signaled with its epigraph ("and the people live till they have white hair" [128]), is inquiry into the relative longevity of the wealthier community. The poem juxtaposes the human life cycle against that of the cultivated natural world in Beverly, "their golden gardens" (128). It seems that even nature's seasonal cycles (the way leaves fall) are subject to social hierarchy (or at least to the effects of labor: "the handyman is on his way" to remove the "dry brown coughing" leaves so that only the golden ones remain) (128).

While acknowledging death as a natural leveler of leaves and humans alike, Brooks nonetheless reveals the power of social hierarchy upon something as basic as the life of a body. In a chiastic logic (and with a subversive nod to the corpse-fed flowers in Eliot's *The Waste Land*), the poem eventually turns from the constructed beauty of nature to the inevitability of natural cycles:

> Nobody is saying these people do not ultimately cease
>   to be. And
> Sometimes their passings are even more painful than ours.
> It is just that so often they live till their hair is white.
> They make excellent corpses, among the expensive
>   flowers . . . (129)

While held together in quatrains, the lines of the poem have begun to disintegrate, exceeding the rough (though by no means metrically regular) pentameter and end-stopped lines that begin the poem, introducing abrupt enjambments and prose rhythms. Thematically and formally, the poem disrupts claims to the "natural" status of social superiority ("even the leaves"), setting the stage for a conclusion that puts the adjective "natural" under erasure. Brooks goes on to list a number of things that are "only natural," repeating that phrase three times in the three concluding stanzas: "It is only natural" that "it should occur to us / How much more fortunate they are than we are," that "we should look and look . . . / And think . . . / How different these are from our own," and that "we should think we have not enough" (129). What is "natural," then, are not segregated deaths and expensive flowers, not a long life afforded by leisure, not even difference or economic disparity themselves, but the human perception of those differences and the physical embodiment of that perception in poetic voice: "We drive on, we drive on" the poem concludes, and "when we speak to each other our voices are a little gruff" (129). If "Notes from the Childhood and Girlhood" begins by asking what can be born "in a narrow room," "The Womanhood" takes the poetic speaker beyond the "pinched" constraints of her singularity out onto the streets. Annie finds a collective voice, a "we" with whom to drive and talk, but in "Beverly Hills, Chicago" the garden is no paradise of freedom or futurity. It is a product of human inequity.

Annie Allen therefore sets the stage for Brooks's much later work "In the Mecca," the title poem of her 1968 book of the same name. "In the Mecca" to some degree reflects the departure from the poetics of cultivation common among African American writers who were physically distant from the landscapes of enslavement , a rejection of "plot-*life*" in the search for a "black life" legible in "black urban presence."[34] At the same time, the poem reimagines the lyric in terms of a shared social subjectivity held together in spaces of urban confinement. "In the Mecca" describes a mother, Sallie, searching the halls of her apartment complex for her child, Pepita. The complex is Chicago's famous "Mecca Flats." Designed as a luxury apartment building for the wealthy, the flats became a hotel during the 1893 World's Fair, then apartments for working-class white residents and then, after 1912, for African American migrants from the South. By 1952 the building had fallen into disrepair, was declared by many to be a "slum," and was razed to make room for Mies van der Rohe's building for IIT. Brooks, who as a young girl worked making deliveries in the building, memorializes the heyday of African American life in the Flats, depicting a struggling, vital community within this decidedly urban environment. To read this poem I situate Brooks as an inheritor of McKay's lyric practice, drawing on the claim I make in chapter 1 that poetic structures of containment can produce vibrant spaces of social life. However, here I turn from the more obviously "compressed" lyric forms of Brooks's early work to her longer poem as a collection of and container for an entire community.

"In the Mecca" is a transitional work between what are often viewed as the two periods in Brooks's work. It was the title poem of the last volume of poetry Brooks signed with Harper and Row, which was published in 1968, not long after Brooks attended the Second Black Writers' Conference, to which she attributed her political awakening.[35] After *In the Mecca*, Brooks published her subsequent books with black publishers, namely Broadside Press and Third World Press. By 1968, Brooks was already excited about the possibilities of the black press: She had been publishing in various black periodicals for decades, as I've already noted, and Dudley Randall's new Detroit-based Broadside Press, devoted to making books available inexpensively for broad audiences (compare, for example, the list price of *In the Mecca*, $4.95, and that of *Riot*, her first full book for Randall, which cost $1), had featured her poem "We Real Cool" in its first broadside series. Brooks was participating and would continue to participate in the provisioning, self-determinist work of the black press, even though *In the Mecca* itself was published by the mainstream Harper and Row. This is one sense in which we can understand "In the Mecca" to embody the tension between constraint and freedom that I have argued takes shape in ecological readings of black poetry.

The poem "In the Mecca" establishes a dual relationship between the architecture of the apartment building and the memory of the plantation. That is, Brooks depicts the historical and spatial distance between the plantation and the apartment building while also representing them as part of the same history of violence and conscription. As the family fans through the building knocking on doors in search of Pepita, only one response to the mother's plaintive question, "Where Pepita be?" (415) makes explicit the connection between historical memory and the contemporary violence and despair evoked through Pepita's disappearance. About half way through the poem and Sallie's search, Great-great Gram answers the door:

> Great-great Gram hobbles, fumbles at the knob,
> mumbles, "I ain seen no Pepita. But
> I remember our cabin. The floor was dirt.
> and something crawled in it. That is the thought
> stays in my mind. I do not recollect
> what 'twas. But something. Something creebled in that dirt
> for we wee ones to pop. Kept popping at it,
> Something that squishied. *Then* your heel come down!
> I hear them squishies now. . . ." (417)

In a sense Great-great Gram's non sequitur resembles many of the other residents' responses to Sallie's query: that is, it represents her self-involvement, distraction, and distance from Pepita, laying the groundwork for the speaker's eventual exasperated lament, "How many care, Pepita?" (427). But this is, significantly, the first *voiced* reply in the poem, the first time one of the building's residents answers the question in his or her words in quotation marks (rather than through indirect discourse or interior reflection). We can understand Great-great Gram's words to be a genuine response to the mother's cry that immediately precedes them ("One of my children is missing. One of my children is gone") (417) and to the question "Where Pepita be?" The memory of the cabin with the dirt floor is offered as an alternative location, a place to look. A seed, after all, might be found in the dirt, among crawling things. This, too, is where children may be found:

> We had no beds. Some slaves had beds of hay
> or straw, with cover-cloth. We six-uns curled
> in corners of the dirt, and closed our eyes,
> and went to sleep—or listened to the rain
> fall inside, felt the drops
> big on our noses, bummies and tum-tums. . . . (417)

This brief recollection of life in the plantation cabin goes some distance toward explaining why black writers in the urban North, a century after emancipation, might distance themselves from that very dirt. There is, first of all, the historical fact of migration—that this historical memory is *only* historical for Brooks and her characters who were born and raised in Chicago. There is also the violence and poverty of life lived outdoors, which Brooks references here. In Great-great Gram's world, to live close to nature was at best to sleep on "hay or straw, with cover cloth," at worst on the bare dirt. And it was to be outdoors (subject to the elements, as with the rain falling on the children's bodies) even when indoors.

Pepita's disappearance, what we might think of as her disembodiment for most of the poem, attests to the distance of this urban community from its southern roots, insofar as this "little seed" has been cut off from her fully cultivated (grown) self. After moving up the stairs to her apartment, in the process introducing us to neighbors (St. Julia, Alfred) and children (Yvonne, Melodie Mary, Cap. Caseu, Thomas Earl, Tennessee, Emmett, Briggs), Mrs. Sallie discovers that one of her children is missing. This revelation visually interrupts the poem, printed as it is in all capital letters: "SUDDENLY, COUNTING NOSES, MRS. SALLIE / SEES NO PEPITA. 'WHERE PEPITA BE?'" (415). This is the urgent question driving the rest of the poem, posed to the Mecca's other inhabitants and evoking a range of responses, all variations on the theme of "*Ain seen her I ain sine her I ain seen er* / Ain seen er I ain seen her I ain seen er" (416).

This is also, several pages into the poem, the first mention of Pepita's name or her existence. Pepita means "pumpkin seed" in Spanish (and in English through Spanish) but can also mean "gold nugget." It is the diminutive form of the Hebrew name Joseph (Pepe), meaning "God will add." In some Spanish-speaking countries "pepita" is also slang for female genitalia. Thus the name signifies regeneration, population, and reproduction in various senses, and it does so through the association between the female body and agricultural production. Although the poem ends with her curiously naturalized body in the "dust" with the "roaches," Brooks does not mine Pepita's name explicitly for its metaphorical value. This is the most profoundly antipastoral move the poem could make—to deny not only the growth of Pepita's body in a place so antithetical to growth but even the imaginative growth of the sustaining squash or pumpkin within the poem.

Through the name of the poem's missing protagonist (if the poem has a protagonist it is the dead child rather than the living mother who searches for her), Brooks establishes a rough contrast between Pepita's agricultural origin and her urban setting. Early on, describing one of Pepita's brothers, the poem reminds us that it is hard to grow:

> In the midst
> Of hells and gruels and little halloweens
> Tense Thomas Earl loves Johnny Appleseed.
> "I, Johnny Appleseed."
> It is hard to be Johnny Appleseed.
> The ground shudders.
> The ground springs up;
> Hits you with gnarls and rust,
> Derangement and fever, or blare and clerical treasons. (414)

Or, rather, this passage reminds us that it is hard to be an "appleseed" also because it is hard to "cultivate" anything in this landscape. It is hard because "the ground shudders. / The ground springs up; / Hits you with gnarls and rust, / Derangement and fever, or blare and clerical treasons" (414). Brooks personifies "the ground" even as she conflates the person and the "seed." If it is already hard to be a seed, it is especially hard to be a female seed, the diminutive (female) form of the prophet through whom the people will replicate. Brooks describes "The Mecca" as a place where

> many flowers start, choke, reach up,
> want help, get it, do not get it,
> rally, bloom, or die on the wasting vine. (417)

Here, in stark contrast to the poetry of Claude McKay in which the references to cultivation have a material, economic function, flowering is a metaphor for personal growth, for the fulfillment of potential. Pepita is not a singular seed but one of many potential "flowers" in the housing complex. It is perhaps the contrast between seed and setting that renders Pepita nearly invisible, apparently literally out of place (in the sense that she is not present for most of the poem), symbolically suggesting, in turn, the distance between city and country.

However, by the end of the poem we recognize that the built environment of the plantation and the Mecca are not so very far apart. Sallie's discovery of her daughter in the dust brings to mind Great-great Gram's recollection. "That is the thought," Great-great-Gram insists, when recalling life on the ground, "stays in my mind." Earlier in the poem, Brooks establishes the connection to history in a different way, creating a sense of a surrounding space as both separate from and integral to the way "people live." In other words, the Mecca comes to resemble the plantation not through the poem's antipastoral references to cultivation (which constitute a refusal of that historical space) but through Brooks's use and transformation of the language of social death to describe the apartment complex.

"In the Mecca" is perhaps most obviously "environmental" in relationship to the built environment. The structure of the poem is the architecture and the environment of the Mecca, one in which every body is visible, including Pepita's body, although it is also unhinged from the social body of the community. Here, I am referring to the architecture of the Mecca Flats, but insofar as the poem draws a connection between the urban present and rural history, the walls and rooms of the Mecca juxtaposed against the plantation interior of Great-gram's memory remind us that the enclosure of the plantation was itself "built" (that is, it was a space of human-made divisions). The first of four epigraphs that precedes Brooks's poem is a quotation from journalist and diplomat John Bartlow Martin describing the apartment complex, the Mecca Flats, into which the poem takes us, as "a great gray hulk of brick, four stories high, topped by an ungainly smokestack, ancient and enormous, filling half the block north of Thirty-fourth Street between State and Dearborn . . . The Mecca building" (*Blacks*, 404).

Brooks seems to write directly against Martin's description, in which human growth and life are excessive, indicative of an Eliotic scene of waste.[36] The building is not empty; rather, it replaces the plantation as the space of black life. The subsequent epigraphs read "How many people live there? . . . Two thousand? Oh, more than that. There's 176 apartments and some of 'em's got seven rooms and they're all full," signed "A MECCAN," ". . . there's danger in my neighborhood . . . ," signed "RICHARD "Peanut" Washington," and "There comes a time when what has been can never be again," from Russ Meeks (404). The Mecca is both a space of death ("there's danger") and a space of elaborate sensory detail, as suggested by John Bartlow Martin's description: "The dirt courtyard is littered with newspapers and tin cans, milk cartons and broken glass." The effect of such details in the sociological and journalistic discourse of the period was often to dehumanize and / or desensitize black life.[37] Martin's 1950 article juxtaposed the "ragged patches" and "naked brick and mortar" (87) of the Mecca against the "new-turned earth" and "new trees and new grass" (86) of a newer housing project, depicting the abundant sounds, smells, and sights of human life—"the powerful odor," "always the sound of distant human voices . . . no words distinguishable," excessive numbers of "small human figures in a vast place" (87)—as signs of social death. For, Martin notes, each entrance is a "grey stone threshold" (87), as if opening onto a grave. Brooks's transformation of such descriptions in the imaginative world—emphasized by her attention to sensory detail in the poem—returns the sensory experience of the environment not so much to the individual black subject but to the collective forms of life within the walls of the Mecca.

The Mecca is an alternative space to the cabin (the very title "Mecca" contrasting with the humility of "cabin"), an inside to contrast with history's outside, and, on the other hand, a repetition and replication of that history, insofar as the memory of children sleeping in the dirt and getting rained on immediately follows the metaphorical reference to children as flowers waiting for help (rain?) to bloom. The poem thus reminds me of the link Joseph Himes identified in the 1951 issue of *Phylon* between agricultural and industrial racism, all the while hoping nonetheless that with relocation might come progress.

I want to return for a moment to the speaker's sense of distance from nature in "Beverly Hills, Chicago": if the cabins of Great-great-Gram's memory produce an uncomfortable and violent intimacy with nature, urban housing segregation violently reasserts black subjects' alienation from nature and denaturalizes their perceptions and feelings. Both poems strive against that alienation. Great-great Gram's assertion that "I hear them squishies now" is performative, conjuring the sound into being: "*Pop*, Pernie May! / That's sister Pernie. That's my sister Pernie. / Squish"; the sounds of the cabin echo in "the Mecca" that is the poem, just as the poverty and depravation of the cabin echo in the apartment building. The alliteration and repetition of "Something that squishied" associates the encounter between the children and the "something" that "crawled" and "creebled" with a childlike pleasure. The sound is nearly onomatopoetic but not quite, so that we are aware always of the work of poesis in producing the sonic environment. Brooks's poetic rendering of the richness of Great-great Gram's memory and the pleasure she takes in it exemplifies the particular capacity of lyric poetry to render the break between sonic and textual sense. It is in this break that Brooks asserts a subjective, sensory alternative to a desensitizing sociological description like John Bartlow Martin's.

I have written in this chapter about two different ideas of lyric poetry. In the case of the West Indian provision ground in the second half of the twentieth century, I am interested in how poets situate lyric poetry in public formations—that is, in how lyric forms (and collections of them) mediate between sonic, graphic, and textual forms of expression of a people. In the case of Brooks's oeuvre I evoke lyric as a sensory space that counters forms of violence that work against individuation. But of course these two senses of lyric are connected; sensory environmental memory links public and private history in Brooks's poems. Referring to *Annie Allen* (as well as Derek Walcott's *Omeros*), Susan Stewart describes lyric in terms of subjectivity. According to Stewart, "lyric is only possible given conditions of individuation of persons in culture and a certain breakup of forms of identification available to the audience" (*Poetry and the Fate of the Senses*, 325). Here Stewart is drawing on the familiar association between lyric poetry and individual subjectivity to argue for the necessity of sensory poetic experience as a counter to "the destructive capabilities of war" (325) associated with epic. Stewart frames lyric in relationship to the traumatic histories of war, but the traumatic desensitization and environmental alienation brought about by enslavement and migration similarly call for a lyric subjectivity. "In the Mecca" responds to that call, recreating the sensory environmental experiences of individuals (the characters in the poem), experiences otherwise lost to the building that was destroyed in 1952, but evoking them through the many voices of the collective. The poem becomes the container for these multiple experiences in the present because the building, the historical environment that contained them in the past, is gone. If, as Stewart argues, lyric emerges when individuals on the margins rupture the totalizing (nationalizing) effects of epic, what happens to lyric (or to poetry) when "forms of identification" (often nationalist identification) again became necessary, poetically and politically, as they did for black Americans by the end of the 1960s?

By the time of "In the Mecca" Brooks is also interested in speaking "for my people" (to borrow the title of Margaret Walker's well-known poem), in this sense practicing the kind of nation-building rhetoric associated with epic. Elizabeth Alexander identifies *In the Mecca* as a moment of outward turning for Brooks, her shift from an "I" to a "we," with all the challenges such a shift entails. While Alexander describes the poem as an "epic" (in order to draw on the public, nation-building, large-scale qualities of epic poetry), and Cheryl Clark identifies Brooks's turn to more overtly political and less formal work as "the loss of lyric," I'm interested in the ways this public, plural poem maintains an investment in lyric expression in its attention to detail, specificity, and subjectivity.[38] That Brooks remains undoubtedly a poet of the senses in the title poem "In the Mecca" reminds us of the continuity between Brooks's earlier and later poetry.[39] This continuity in turn underscores the relationship between the public and the private, the interior and the exterior, in all of her writing. The poem engages with the sensory environment both formally and thematically in a way that binds the imperatives of individuation and collectivity, thereby affording a more expansive view of Brooks's lyricism.

We might view "lyric individuation" in "In the Mecca" as part and parcel of (rather than distinct from) Brooks's ongoing investment in community building through the black press. Describing the poem as "a text of texts," Clarke sees it also as "a post-modern elegy on the place of the lyric in African-American poetry" (138). However, it is precisely as a genre containing other voices, texts, and media that Brooks reinvents and idea of black lyric subjectivity as *collection*. The collecting and collective impulse within "In the Mecca" takes several forms in the poem. There is, first of all, the architectural structure of the poem itself, opening doors onto many different lives, voices, and narratives, from the poet Alfred to "Great-great Gram." These stories themselves often resemble literary genres (as in Great-great Gram's "slave narrative") and are part of the Mecca's collection of literary genres and literary works. This free-verse poem varies not only its voices and conventions but in its prosodic form to tell stories of different residents; there are moments, for example, when the poem temporarily moves into ballad quatrains, as in "The Ballad of Edie Barrow," (425) a story of disappointed love. When the police finally arrive and (after some delay) take up the search for the missing girl, the resident poet Alfred ("who might have been a poet king") cannot offer any information but instead holds forth on Leopold Senghor, Senegal's poet-president (422). Brooks interrupts the residential interviews with a digression on the poet and publisher Don Lee (Lee would eventually become Brooks's publisher at Third World Press). "Don Lee wants / not a various America. / Don Lee wants / a new nation / under nothing" (425). In both of these episodes Brooks evokes the nationalist aims of epic but contains those epic aims within the lyric poem. In addition to supplanting the poet Alfred's reading list of "Shakespeare . . . Joyce / or James or Horace, Huxley, Hemmingway" (409) with an anthology of nationalist ideologies—Lee and Senghor—Brooks also takes a range of other media into poetry's environment: "headlines," *Vogue* magazine, couplets, and hymns. As we shall see in part 2 of this book, lyric poetry can often function as an archive of black culture, a way of preserving sonic, visual, textual, and kinesthetic forms in response to the material destructions of extreme environmental catastrophe. Like the periodical collections I discuss in the earlier part of this chapter, Brooks's "In the Mecca" exemplifies the vitality of poetry as an intermedial genre in the face of another sort of catastrophe: radical alienation from the agricultural and cultural past.

PILGRIMAGE

It's easy to think of Brooks in a U.S. context as a poet who "stayed home" and reimagined ecological and social relation in the private sphere of the domicile, particularly in her early work. But the very title of "In the Mecca" evokes the global reach of her imagination by 1968. Nor should we associate this reach with an escape from the "narrow room" of her earlier poetry. Although there is undoubtedly a greater focus on global blackness in the later poems, Margaret Walker, in the 1950 special *Phylon* issue, had already praised the "global outlook" Brooks achieves in writing about the war in *Annie Allen*.[40] In "In the Mecca" Brooks continues to concern herself with the potential of environmental constraint as the basis for art making. The mecca to which Brooks refers is not only the Islamic holy site of pilgrimage but the name of a Chicago apartment complex, and it also brings to mind Locke's description of Harlem in the title of the special *Survey Graphic* issue that became *The New Negro*: "Harlem, Mecca of the New Negro." In other words, Brooks turns to the idea of a global capital in the most local terms. In contrast to Wynter, who would imagine the provision ground as "indigenous" within a few years of Brooks's transitional book, Brooks instead imagines black environmental ontology as pilgrimage. Rootedness does not so much establish our nativity to our place and time as provide the networks through which we move in place and time.

In the next chapter, I travel to the watersheds and shorelines of the Atlantic, where the problem of roots animates Derek Walcott's postcolonial poetics. Like Gwendolyn Brooks's, Walcott's career spans from the 1940s to the twenty-first century. And although he is a major international literary figure, his poems, like the range of texts I have assembled in this chapter, require attention to local environmental, political, and literary contexts. His work confronts not only the legacy of the colonial plantation but also the violence of a property-based relationship to the environment in the Caribbean present.

three

Cultivating the Caribbean
"The Star-Apple Kingdom," Property, and the Plantation

40 ACRES: TWO FANTASIES OF RETURN

In May 1929, just before the dramatic transformation of the Great Depression, the American writer and ethnographer Zora Neale Hurston wrote to Langston Hughes to ask his opinion about an opportunity to buy a "plat" (a plot of land) in southeastern Florida, on the Indian River. The land, she writes, "parallels the ocean all the way with the merest strip of land between so that one has the river and the ocean together." She went on to detail her plans for the fifteen lots: "A Negro art colony" (*Zora Neale Hurston*, 145).

What would it have meant for Hurston to have realized this dream, to have raised the money—perhaps, as she suggested to Hughes, by soliciting funds from the wealthy daughter of black cosmetics entrepreneur Madam C. J. Walker—for the $1500 down payment, and become the first black American to buy land on the Dixie highway or the Indian River? For Hurston herself, the chance to build "a little town of our own" must have evoked memories of her childhood in Eatonville, the first all-black town to be incorporated after the end of slavery. Land ownership might also have meant financial security and independence from her wealthy white patron, Charlotte Osgood Mason, also known to Hurston and Hughes as "Godmother."

The realization of Hurston's fantasy would have had implications not only for her personal economic stability but also for the legacy of black modernism. In dreaming of the Indian River colony, Hurston imagined a geographic repositioning of the literary and artistic center of black culture. Her vision placed quintessential Harlemites (Bruce Nugent, Wallace Thurman, Langston Hughes, and others) not only in the South but at the edge of the Atlantic. As a geopolitical region, this "plat" would situate Hurston and other artists along the intracoastal waterway connecting the Atlantic to the Gulf of Mexico, and put them in closer contact with the Atlantic communities whose folk culture Hurston studied: the Bahamas, Haiti, Jamaica, and of course Florida.

Hurston also envisioned a self-sufficient black community tied to black land ownership; it is no coincidence that she mentions A'Lelia Walker, not Mason, as a potential patron for this particular venture. In proposing to shift the geography of black modern artistic cultivation, Hurston reimagined the relationship between black culture, land, and property. Rather than turn to the northern city as the site of possibility, Hurston proposed black ownership of southern land. Further, she dreamed of an isthmus between "the most beautiful river in the world" and the Atlantic—that is, a space that would allow black writers a local identity and, at the same time, access to that very culture and geography from which they had been dispossessed. In this sense, Hurston's imaginary, collaboratively owned "plat" anticipates Sylvia Wynter's mapping of the "roots of culture" in the plot.

But Hurston's dream was never realized, whether for lack funds or interest among her counterparts, on account of the impending Great Depression, or because of the collapse of her friendship with Hughes. The fantasy of redefining black intimacy with the landscape of the rural South continued to pervade Hurston's consciousness, most notably in her 1937 novel *Their Eyes Were Watching God*, which is the focus of chapter 5, but so too did the failure of this fantasy. In fact, with no property to call her own, near the end of her life Hurston was evicted from her beloved rented home in Eau Gallie, a mere three miles from the projected site for her colony.

In his 2008 poem "Forty Acres," written on the occasion of the inauguration of Barack Obama, Derek Walcott similarly projects new possibility onto the southern scene of slavery. In this poem Walcott figures the American president as a ploughman—"a young negro at dawn in straw hat and overalls"—making his way through a landscape marred by the violence of history: "beyond the moaning ground, the lynching tree, the tornado's / black vengeance" (75). Referring to the false promise of Reconstruction-era democracy, Walcott stops short of claiming Obama's inauguration as a belated fulfillment of this promise. The plough "continues" past these violent scenes but leaves us waiting "for the sower." It is not necessarily in the political realm, the poem suggests, but "on this lined page" that it might be possible to uncouple the metonymic association between the natural world and the human violence of slavery, segregation, and social oppression.

Hurston's letter and Walcott's poem alike affiliate power and possibility with property. Whether the forty acres never given to U.S. blacks during Reconstruction or the "merest strip of land" in Florida citrus country, Walcott and Hurston suggest both the power and the danger of attempting to reinhabit such spaces after slavery. Hurston also goes to great lengths to reassure Hughes that they would be "safe" and "isolated" even though "they have never allowed a Negro to buy on the Dixie or the Indian river" in the past (*Zora Neale Hurston*, 146). Walcott's poem, too, marks the violence of the landscape's history, even as it imagines an open field of possibility. To inhabit or transform the agricultural landscape is to navigate between that danger and that future, to live and write conscripted by a modernity that enslaves.

If "Forty Acres" indulges in the fantasy of political transcendence through the fantasy of reclaiming (and reworking) the land, "The Star-Apple Kingdom" (1978), Walcott's much earlier poem about political leadership, suggests the need for an alternative logic of modernity, one in which neither "a negro art colony" nor an ecological mandate would depend on property. While turning the racialized history of slavery on its head, Walcott reimagines the Caribbean as a space of dwelling rather than ownership. Walcott is now especially well known for *Omeros*, his epic narrative of St. Lucia, a poem whose length and scope references the urge toward wholeness and teleology that defines the epic genre. "The Star-Apple Kingdom" by contrast concerns itself both formally and thematically with that which is shrunken, fragmentary, and compressed. To read the poem is in part to assemble its "specks" and "shards," to experience the poem's geography—the Caribbean archipelago—through the senses, to engage in a mode of poetic relation other than claiming or ownership.

"The Star-Apple Kingdom" plunges into the meditations of a great political leader, Michael Manley, who was Walcott's friend and the prime minister of Jamaica from 1972 to 1980 and then again from 1989 to 1992. Opening with a description of "that ancient pastoral" of the plantation, the poem circumscribes its hero within the plantation, looking out "from the Great House windows" (383). The view from those windows reveals both the counterpastoral qualities of the landscape and the failures of Manley's political career. From that vantage point the poem traces a broader geography of Jamaica and the Caribbean, shifting in and out of Manley's consciousness. Unfolding Manley's dream (and nightmare) of revolution, the poem is dense with both political allusions ("CIA, PNP, OPEC" [389]) and environmental details. In 1979, the year the volume in which "The Star-Apple Kingdom," its title poem, was published, Manley's popularity was dwindling, in part because of his affiliations with Castro's Cuba and also because of the perceived failures of his agricultural reform. Most accounts of the poem describe it as a political allegory or cautionary tale about the dangers of socialism, but "The Star-Apple Kingdom" concerns itself with the agricultural

landscape as more than a metaphor and accounts for the lived connection between social and environmental experience.[1]

Walcott critiques the logic of private property within the colonial system, but
he does not stop there. The image of Manley, the descendent of both Africans
and Europeans, within the plantation Great House undoubtedly bears much
of the symbolic power of Barack Obama reclaiming the forty acres due to black
Americans. However, Walcott's poem also critiques property as reconceived
within the nationalist postcolonial state under Manley's leadership. Challenging both colonial and nationalist models for civic and environmental belonging,
the narrative of political failure the "The Star-Apple Kingdom" relates brings to
mind Michael Hardt and Antonio Negri's critique of "the republic of property."
Property, Hardt and Negri contend, is the recurring obstacle to social democratic reform (of the sort which Manley attempted), not least because of the intimacy between slavery and the republic of property (*Commonwealth*, 71–77).
Having begun this chapter within the landscapes of the U.S. south, it seems
important to mark the significance of Caribbean geography for Walcott's alternative mode of dwelling. Like many Caribbean writers Walcott turns to the
archipelago, rather than the nation, to describe the geography of Caribbean
belonging. Against the emergent national reconception of property, he posits the
transnational archipelago's overarching and fragmentary curve as the primary
structure for relating to the land.

This is not to say that the oceanic setting of the Caribbean geography inherently suggests a critique of property, any more than the plantation of the U.S.
south is inherently defined by its economic and geographic enclosure. Glissant
usefully unlocks the paradox of plantation geography when he asks, "If each
Plantation is considered as a closed entity, what is the principle inclining them
to function in a similar manner" (*Poetics of Relation*, 64)? Glissant argues that
even as the economic structure of the plantation, "a pyramid organization"
(64), repeated itself from one plantation to the next, enslaved Africans and their
descendants established modes of relation—economically and culturally—"on
the edges of the system" (65) in order to survive. For Glissant these modes of
material survival were the basis of a literature: "first as an act of survival, then as
a dead end or a delusion, finally as an effort of passion or memory" (68). Glissant
wrestles with the plantation's enclosure only to discover that "the word derived
from it remains open" (75). For Walcott the shape of the archipelago describes
that openness of one plantation to another, of one word to another. It is by embracing the fragmentary and oceanic as aesthetic forms (but not necessarily as

political formations) that Walcott suggests an alternative politics of environmental belonging. Antonio Benítez-Rojo is especially attentive to how the structure of the "meta-archipelago" underscores the uneven development of the plantation across islands (and, accordingly, the differences in acculturation of African and European cultures to one another in the plantation region).[2] It is with this sort of differential repetition in mind that I approach *The Star-Apple Kingdom*. The title poem is the heart of my analysis, but the shape of the archipelago, which the book as a whole traces, invites us to read Walcott's geographic imagination from a range of scalar perspectives, attending to the sea, the island, and the garden as spaces where Walcott rejects and revises the tropes of cultivation and their relationship to history. Such reading also requires shifts in the scale of my attention to the political and historical contexts of Walcott's poems, to the literary historical modes and genres with which he engages (such as epic, lyric, and pastoral), and to such poetic details as prosody, diction, and voice, to Jamaica in the 1970s, to the Caribbean archipelago that includes both Jamaica and St. Lucia (Walcott's home), and to the curve in the imagination that might include as well Hurston's isthmus of black modern art.[3]

ROOTS

In the waning days and aftermath of British colonialism, Caribbean poets of Walcott's generation faced the task not only of evoking discrete local environments in order to define transnational racial identities, but also of defining their poetics against the colonial order and within the context of emerging nation-states. As the West Indian periodicals I discussed in chapter 2 demonstrate, even after independence the language of cultivation provided some of the most powerful, and problematic, metaphors for anticolonial nationalist sentiment in the Caribbean and beyond. *Roots*, for instance, was the title of Kamau Brathwaite's 1986 volume of essays. No figure more accurately encompasses how critics often distinguish Brathwaite from Walcott, his supposed ideological adversary. According to this school of thought, whereas Brathwaite seeks out African "roots" and acknowledges their foundational role for Caribbean culture, Walcott is skeptical of the black power movement among his contemporaries, arguing in many of his prose essays for a poetics that begins from a place of "amnesia" in relationship to the past.[4] And yet tropes of cultivation pervade Walcott's work as they do Brathwaite's.[5]

In spite of his reputation as an international literary figure, a poet associated more closely with routes than roots, Walcott dwells in the local. Here, I am borrowing anthropologist James Clifford's evocative and by-now familiar pun to name the relationship between travel and dwelling that we might argue does not divide Caribbean poets but rather defines modern Caribbean poetics. Clifford posits "travel" as a corrective to "the field" as the key mode for studying culture (*Routes*, 2).[6] The anthropological turn to travel has undergirded corresponding shifts in literary and cultural study from nationalist frames for reading black culture to the diasporic ones which are a basic premise of this book. In this chapter I take seriously Clifford's corollary claim that "once traveling is foregrounded as a cultural practice, then dwelling, too, needs to be reconceived" (44). Thus, even in the context of Walcott's internationalism, his conception of the archipelago as poetic form continually produces what I call the Caribbean detail.

Although the much-noted tension between Walcott and Brathwaite has hinged in part on their differing politics and poetics in relationship to Africa as a potential homeland, equally important for both poets and for their generation more broadly is the idea of a return to the Caribbean itself. What can it mean, in life and in language, to dwell in a landscape now defined by colonialism and its postcolonial aftermath? In the Caribbean context, resistance to poetry of the land emerges as resistance to the landscape traditions of English verse—that is, to poetic attempts to represent the landscape in the mode of classical pastorals, idylls, and georgics.[7] Brathwaite, for instance, describes James Grainger's 1764 georgic *The Sugar-Cane* as an example of "Tropical English" (*Roots*, 13): "At once the 'Caribbean' disappears and we find ourselves in English autumn, anticipating Keats" (140). Even more problematically, as Brathwaite goes on to argue, Grainger imposes his "picturesque and sylvan" view of nature onto enslaved people and ignores "the harsher realities of his society," namely, the brutality of slavery (142). The problem with Grainger's poem is not merely that it ignores the brutality of slavery but that it enacts some of that violence through its use of the georgic. That is, Grainger categorizes humans (specifically, enslaved Africans) within the taxonomic mode of the georgic alongside soil, nectar, and cattle (bk. 1.1–6). He places the "Afric's sable progeny" (bk. 1.4) in the category of Virgil's sheep, oxen, and kine, relaying an unsettling sense of the enslaved worker as an animal and product, something to count, categorize, and own. The idea of humans *as* property troubles the form of Grainger's poem, even as it demonstrates the inextricability of poetry, property, and plantation within colonial logic.[8]

In the generations preceding Brathwaite and Walcott's, Caribbean poets struggled with the legacy of poems such as Grainger's and the pervasive tradition of imitative pastoral verse. The turn against pastoral, however, is not necessarily a turn from the "countryside" to the city (notwithstanding Walcott's celebration of Port of Spain as the place where culture is made) but a return from English, European, or Europeanized landscapes to Caribbean ones.[9] Walcott claims specific geographies—imagined and real—as the cornerstone of his resistance to colonial impositions on the land and as the source of his dwelling in poetic form.

"THE SEA IS HISTORY" AND "THE SCHOONER FLIGHT": AGAINST CULTIVATION

If many Caribbean poets negatively associate cultivation and its poetic representation in pastoral with the brutal history of enforced agricultural labor, Walcott embraces the sea as one site of imaginative possibility unmoored from that history. The sea, as an environment that "does not have anything on it that is a memento of man" (interview with J. P. White, 158), seems an ideal geography for imagination. The poles of migratory and rooted Caribbean sensibilities thus emerge not only in the distinction between the city and the country but in the distinction between agricultural and marine environments. To the extent that Walcott claims the sea as site of oblivion and amnesia, he turns away from the metonymnic relationship between land and slavery. If the sea can exist in a metaphorical relationship to human experience, suffering, and culture, it can represent something other than the history of slavery over which Walcott's contemporaries obsess:

> Nothing can be put down in the sea. You can't plant on it, you can't live on it, you can't walk on it. Therefore, the strength of the sea gives you an idea of time that makes history absurd. Because history is an intrusion on that immensity. History is a very, very minor statement; it is not even an intrusion, it is an insignificant speck on the rim of that horizon. And by history I mean a direction that is progressive and linear. (interview with J. P. White, 158)

In order to position the immensity of the sea against history "that is progressive and linear," Walcott at the same time opposes the sea to cultivation: "You can't plant on it." Of course it is not the case that nothing grows on or in the sea; Walcott's distinction emphasizes the role of human labor in land-based agriculture and associates cultivation with an "intrusive," "progressive and linear" history. I return in the penultimate section of this chapter to the significance of the "speck" in Walcott's conception of history, but first it is important to consider the alternative temporality of the sea.

The "idea of time" Walcott finds in the sea does not merely oppose growth; it also opposes ruin. Walcott acknowledges the self-canceling quality of a place where "nothing can be put down": "You feel that first of all, that if you weren't there you wouldn't be missed. If you are on land looking at ruins, the ruins commemorate you. . . . And that's what the ruins of any great cultures do. In a way they commemorate decay. . . . The sea is not elegiac in any way. The sea does not have anything on it that is a memento of man" (interview with J. P. White, 158). To long for ruins is to long not for formlessness but for a form that can express loss. Anita Patterson understands Walcott's comments in this interview as evidence of his "yearning for monuments" and "his awareness of the historical absence of ruins in the Americas," which, according to Patterson, drew Walcott to the modernist model of the craftsman as someone who builds "durable monuments" (*Race, American Literature and Transnational Modernisms*, 175). But Patterson elides a crucial difference between monuments and ruins. What the sea does not have (and, by contrast, what the land produces) is ruin, decay, remnants. In the slip from "you" to "decay" there is a sense that "you" are "decay." Thus, to the extent that Walcott embraces the sea's self-annihilating quality, he embraces the annihilation of what he describes as an already-decayed or decaying self.

Walcott frames this annihilation as an opportunity; the absence of literal cultivation ("you can't plant on it") is, perhaps paradoxically, the occasion for creative possibility. That is, to the extent that they "reject this sense of history," namely, history as shipwreck, New World poets have the privileged opportunity to create something new, to name the world as they see it in the mode of Adam ("The Muse of History," 47). "It is this awe of the numinous," writes Walcott, "this elemental privilege of naming the New World which annihilates history in our great poets" (40). Thus Walcott turns on its head James Anthony Froude's assertion that there is "no people" in the Caribbean (qtd. in "The Antilles," 67), as well as Hegel's claim that Africans had no history and no culture. As Paul Breslin has argued, "even the sense of being without a history turns out to be historically produced" and poetically productive (*Nobody's Nation*, 5).[10]

The title "The Sea Is History," which is the title of a poem that appears in the same volume as "The Star-Apple Kingdom," is an epigrammatic, quotable metaphor whose power rests in its uncanny yoking of history and oblivion. If the sea is the site of amnesia—of forgetting the past—it seems paradoxical to equate it with a new "idea of time" (interview with J. P. White, 158). The title invites us to ask how this metaphor will work, how these two radically unlike things will become alike. If Walcott elsewhere equates the sea with the necessary amnesia that is the starting point of West Indian art, the native speaker of "The Sea Is History" performs a kind of submarine archeology, diving into the wreck of the past to describe the very history the sea apparently cannot contain. Structured in the form of a dialogue, "The Sea Is History" juxtaposes Hegelian doubts about African (or in this case African diasporic) history against the response of another speaker who replies in the mode of an ethnographic native informant. Against the European critique of diasporic culture, this speaker describes the middle passage, slavery, and emancipation as historical developments parallel to biblical narrative.

> Where are your monuments, your battles, martyrs?
> Where is your tribal memory? Sirs,
> in that grey vault. The sea. The sea
> has locked them up. The sea is History. (364)

The declarative speaker's assured assertion that "the sea is History" becomes the poem's question. From the opening stanza, the poem refuses to distinguish clearly between the dismissive Hegelian voice and the defensive responding voice. The enjambment after "sirs" in the second line emphasizes the interpenetration of these voices rather than their discreteness. The separation further breaks down as the European speaker's questions vanish; it becomes impossible to determine who asserts that "that was just Lamentations,/it was not History" (366).

The poem depends on the uncomfortable intersection of unlike things—that is, on the uncomfortable work of metaphor. Consider, for example, the poem's brief description of the middle passage:

> Then there were the packed cries,
> the shit, the moaning:
>
> Exodus. (364)

The extended metaphor's progress depends upon a narrative reversal: the poem compares the passage of Africans into slavery with the biblical passage out of slavery. The stanza break between the two terms of the comparison, and the harsh brevity of the single-word line "exodus," underscore the incommensurability of the two narratives. Rather than equating the history of African slavery with the unfolding of biblical narrative so as to justify or memorialize Caribbean history against European claims of its nonexistence, the poem points out the difficulty of such comparisons. The comparison of the title (the sea is history) and the comparison of the poem (African diasporic history is as important and meaningful as biblical history) taken together equate the West with history and Africa with "the sea," recapitulating Hegel's assertion that Africa is "still involved in the conditions of mere nature" (*The Philosophy of History*, 115).

This is not to say that Walcott's poem repeats Hegel's dismissal of black history. On the contrary, once the voice of the poem seems to accept or at least repeat the notion that "it was not history" the poem posits an alternative starting point for culture, one that challenges not only the West Indian claim to the "wreck" as origin but also the insistent direction of European teleology. By the end the ocean sounds "like a rumour without any echo / of History" (367). The sea in Walcott's poetry exemplifies nature's status as at once freighted with history and independent of it, existing in both metaphoric and metonymic relationship to human experience. That is, the sea does not merely contain history on a metaphorical level, as "that grey vault," but also literally contains "the packed cries, / the shit, the moaning" (364) in the cargo holds of slave ships "all subtle and submarine" (365). Turning away from the sea as a metaphor toward the sea as a natural space through which humans have moved (and in which humans have died and drowned), Walcott's poem produces "the sound" (367) that indeed has a history.

Walcott's wish to move beyond linear, time-based models of history that describe either progress or decay is a wish whose fulfillment rests specifically in the possibilities of poetry as a genre. For Walcott, the absence of history is the condition for the creation of *poetic* culture: "this elemental privilege of naming the New World" ("The Muse of History," 37). Walcott longs for a form that can express not only the history of loss but the loss of history. In the opening stanzas of Walcott's mini-epic "The Schooner Flight," the protagonist Shabine represents his cultural hybridity as a contest between nationality and annihilation.

> I'm just a red nigger who love the sea,
> I had a sound colonial education,
> I have Dutch, nigger, and English in me,
> And either I'm nobody, or I'm a nation. (346)

The list of first-person declarations reads at first like a series of comma-spliced independent clauses, each upending the claims of the last as the speaker shifts among his various voices, the stodgily earnest "I had a sound colonial education" canceling out the mockingly self-deprecating "I'm just a red nigger who love the sea." The final two lines of the stanza reconcile these conflicting claims and tones, but suggest yet another potential erasure. A "nation" can exist only if it can account for the diversity of its individuals. The line also suggests that without nationhood, "I'm nobody"—that individuals cannot exist without the possibility of a hybrid nation. To be a "bad nationalist," then, might cost existence.[11] However, whether it is the nation, the individual, or both, whose ontology is threatened here remains ambiguous, suggesting at once the inextricability and the irreconcilability of these two forms of subjectivity.

Walcott also posits belonging to the poetic imagination as an alternative to national identification. In "The Schooner Flight," the idiomatic present tense opens the poem: although the narrative unfolds in the past, Shabine's story begins by recollecting that "in idle August . . . I blow out the light" (345). Thus, Caribbean idiomatic syntax formally bridges past ("I stood like a stone and nothing else move") (345) with present ("either I'm nobody or I'm a nation"). Shabine draws an apparently stark divide between nation and annihilation, a divide that raises important questions for our thinking about the relationship between nature and culture in black poetry: if hybridity both defines national belonging and threatens existence, then what lies between nation and annihilation? The answer may be poetic language itself, which mediates the relationship between the present and the past through the shifting verb forms in the passage. Later in the poem, the process of Shabine's expatriation appears complete as he departs from "the Republic" and stages an encounter with "History" in the form of his white grandfather: "I had no nation now but the imagination" (350). This formulation is equal parts foreboding and promising. Here the poem goes beyond annihilation (with "no nation," "I'm nobody"). It might be possible to imagine an ideal nation as an alternative to existing ones; imagination might provide an alternative form of belonging.

IN THE GREAT HOUSE: "THE STAR-APPLE KINGDOM"

"The Sea Is History" and "The Schooner Flight" offer the sea as an alternative space for rethinking nation, imagination, and the relationship between past and present. But the landscape of slavery haunts the volume of *The Star-Apple Kingdom*, in which both "The Sea Is History" and "The Schooner Flight" appear. If the sea functions metaphorically to articulate how the loss of history enables Caribbean artistic practice, what does Walcott make of the detritus of history on shore? What kind of relationship to nature and nation is possible within the confines of the plantation?

Following Walcott into the circumscribed territory of the plantation yields insight into the ways in which that space has produced and continually produces the conditions of modernity. David Scott has argued we need new "story-forms" to account for modern conscription within the plantation. We might productively think about Walcott's move into the space of the plantation, however, as something other than a transformation of "the problem of *narrative*" (*Conscripts of Modernity*, 7, emphasis in original). Given that narrative is the problem, how might poetic and specifically lyric forms allow us to reconceptualize the relationships among past, present, and future in the postcolonial moment? Walcott's representation of the encounter with the colonial logic of property occasions a specifically poetic response: it is the lyric scope of the senses in "The Star-Apple Kingdom" that allows the poem to redefine dwelling in the Caribbean.

"The Schooner Flight" has received more critical attention than "The Star-Apple Kingdom" perhaps because it predicts the epic ambitions of *Omeros*.[12] Those critics who have attended to "The Star-Apple Kingdom" do so largely because of its political message.[13] To evaluate "The Star-Apple Kingdom" (or any Walcott poem for that matter) exclusively according to its political "statement" is inadequate precisely because the poem makes multiple political readings available: while Paul Breslin calls the poem "a mordantly satirical account of the disintegration of the West Indies Federation" (*Nobody's Nation*, 217), for instance, Patricia Ismond sees Walcott's Michael Manley (the central figure of the poem) as the object of great sympathy (*Abandoning Dead Metaphors*, 253). This is not to say that the poem's political explorations are irrelevant; the poem is remarkable within Walcott's oeuvre for its direct confrontation with political reality. Walcott's formal choices and engagement with lyric modes, however, are irreducible to what Ismond describes as a "conclusive statement"; instead Walcott engages the pastoral so as to highlight the incommensurability between European poetic forms and Caribbean landscape, history, and politics.

Walcott depicts the period of Jamaican nationalism through the transformation of the literary and artistic modes of pastoralism—that is, poetic and painterly attempts to represent the landscape. For Caribbean writers, the English pastoral tradition was often associated with historical erasures: lush paintings or descriptions of the plantation landscape, for example, often obscured the violent labor of that landscape's production. Walcott explicitly unites antipastoralism with political resistance, but only to reclaim and reframe pastoral poetry for different purposes. Walcott reappropriates the mode to critique a colonial system in which people and place alike were private property. The opening section of the poem conflates the idea of "ancient pastoral" as a form of painting, as a literary mode, and as the form of the land itself.

> There were still shards of an ancient pastoral
> in those shires of an island where the cattle drank
> their pools of shadow from an older sky. (383)

From the outset, the poem formally replaces what Ismond calls the "picture-perfect of the ancient pastoral" (*Abandoning Dead Metaphors*, 253) with fragmentary glimpses of history and environment. As ekphrasis, this description of broken porcelain shards asserts a measure of poetic distance from the supposed subject (the landscape.) Walcott also reverses the usual mimetic presupposition. That is, while we usually understand pastoral poetry or painting as artistic modes that copy the landscape, here, "the landscape" of the star-apple kingdom "copied such subjects as / 'Herefords at Sunset in the Valley of the Wye'" (383). The very title of the poem, referring to a characteristic West Indian fruit tree, already throws into question the nature of this reverse mimesis (and, in turn, the realist claims of conventional mimetic art): how can the land of the "star-apple kingdom" resemble this generic English subject of pastoral? The colonial landscape necessarily reveals a crisis at the heart of representation.

It would be possible to read Walcott's remaking of the pastoral mode on the postcolonial plantation as revolutionary, something like the romance narratives David Scott associates with the legacy of the anticolonial struggle in *Conscripts of Modernity*. Such a reading might unfold in the following way: The poem opens in the mode of poetic idyll, describing a Jamaican landscape that mirrors the idealized landscape of English pastoral "Herefords at Sunset in the Valley of the Wye." The introduction of political discourse in the second stanza disrupts the pastoral description by revealing the bitterness, violence, and rage of colonialism itself. The painting at the center of the first stanza represents pastoral and the remainder of the poem the rejection of pastoral, its values, exclusions, and omissions. The overturning would thus function as a political allegory: to expunge "shards of an ancient pastoral" from the image of Jamaica is to overthrow the yoke of colonialism and the property relationship that pastoral records and hides of master over both slave and scene.

We might also be tempted to read as allegorical the narrative that surrounds the poem's central character, Michael Manley. Indeed, one thing that might lead us to this reading is Walcott's reluctance to describe his apparent protagonist with any specificity. The poem is otherwise precise with names, evoking, for example, "Parish Trelawny" over and over again (384, 385, 394) and repeating

the title of the pastoral painting "Herefords at Sunset in the Valley of the Wye."
Why, then, in a poem that takes care with names, would Walcott omit the name
of its hero? The poem is apparently about Manley and Jamaica, but neither the
title nor the opening lines explicitly identifies the place, time, or the particular
political context. While many poems in *The Star-Apple Kingdom* carry a dedication to a particular figure (Joseph Brodsky, for instance, and Kenneth Ram-
chand), the title poem does not identify Manley in this way, either. The poem
does not in fact introduce its "hero" until the third stanza of the poem, placing
the land and its history ahead of the man and his history, and when Manley does
emerge, he is unnamed. In an interview with Carrol Fleming, Walcott unequivo-
cally identifies Manley as the historical subject of the poem ("The Star-Apple
Kingdom is a constant place—Jamaica. 'He' is Manley, my friend. . . . You know
Michael Manley, a young person in charge of a country") but he does not name
Manley in the poem itself.[14]

Withholding the name of its historical protagonist, the poem would at first
seem to enact a version of "national allegory." In this way of reading, reversing
Ismond's psychologizing interpretation of the figure of Manley, we would understand the poem's protagonist as representative (of all Caribbean nationals,
or all Caribbean leaders or Jamaica) and his struggle as representative of the national struggle. But the poem refuses to be writ large on political terms, and
Walcott thus renounces the romance plot *and* the trap of third-world allegory.[15]

The central obstacle to an allegorical reading is Manley's participation, as a
leader and as a character, in conflicting discourses: visionary and populist, literary and political, historical and prophetic. We first meet Manley in the interior
of the landscape, looking out "from the Great House windows" across history
and its present manifestations.

> he saw the Botanical Gardens officially drown
> in a formal dusk, where governors had strolled
> and black gardeners had smiled over glinting shears
> and the lilies of parasols on the floating lawns (385)

This portrayal immediately introduces Manley's conflict: the history of destruction and revolution that is his inheritance. Although the Great House of Mona
plantation was considered as a potential site for the prime minister's residence
after independence, Manley's actual residences during his first period of leadership were Jamaica House, which was built specifically for the purpose of housing prime ministers, and other unofficial homes in Kingston. Walcott thus fictionalizes Manley's physical surroundings in the poem.[16] Positioned within the

"Great House," Walcott's Manley occupies the seat of power, but he is able to see both the center and the margin, both "black gardeners" and "governors," the smiles of those gardeners and the "glinting shears"—the good and the terrifying remains of history.

Rather than standing in for a larger story, place names in the kingdom draw us into the particular geography of colonialism. Manley's position in the "Great House" circumscribes him within the plantation geography, which the poem relates to twentieth-century English and American power. Walcott now makes visible those who have been "innocently excluded" from the scene of agricultural production: the "black gardeners" who "had smiled over glinting shears." The gardeners voice the "silent scream"—the critique—that the pastoral painting and family photo suppress in the poem's opening stanzas but that will later take over the poem:

> What was the Caribbean? A green pond mantling
> behind the Great House columns of Whitehall,
> behind the Greek facades of Washington. (393)

In this analogy Walcott compares the Caribbean to the physical landscape of the plantation and the plantation "Great House" to sources of colonial and contemporary power. The metaphor itself ("the Caribbean" was "a green pond mantling") is unstable insofar as it describes an impossible spatial relationship (is the pond behind the columns and facades or behind Whitehall? Or is the pond behind Whitehall, which is behind Washington?) The unstable comparison foregrounds the metonymic relationships between place names, architecture, and power: Whitehall, a palace only part of which remains in the present day, gives its name and monarchial power to all of English government; Walcott layers on this the metonymic association between the Great House and the brutality of planters' power on the plantation and the suggestion that "Whitehall" might be connected to the White House (in Washington).[17] At stake is more than a process of writing the gardener back in in order to empower him. In addition, in giving Manley power over the reclaimed landscape of slavery, the poem critiques even the emancipated version of power, calling for a different ecological relationship to the land than one based on property ownership. The landscape, rather than Manley, becomes the "character" through which Walcott evokes the Caribbean particular. The natural world yields the ideal set of tropes for Walcott's critique of Caribbean nationalism because of its double function as metonymy and metaphor—it is the site of economic and physical oppression, and it is also representative of imaginative labors.

PUBLIC PROPERTY

We might expect Walcott's placement of Manley within the plantation geography to mirror the powerful symbolism of the black and brown Jamaican state taking control of the sugar plantations. In this version of what Scott would call a "romantic emplotment," the Great House of colonialism and slavery, diminished by revolution, is now the site of that revolutionary power. However, just as the sugar cooperatives failed to uplift the poor or shore up the ailing Jamaican economy, Manley fails to create social change through environmental power in Walcott's fictionalized landscape. We might read the poem instead as unfolding a tragic narrative, the kind that Scott sees as definitive of postcolonial modernity: Manley remains trapped within the plantation, and the ethos of the plantation marked by excessive agricultural and social control is essentially flawed, even in transformative postcolonial hands.[18] To some extent, then, Walcott represents Manley's state control of plantations as a repetition of the logic of colonial power, however much the view from the Great House windows has changed. But tragic emplotment proves an equally problematic model for understanding the poem because of the way Walcott uncouples social power from environmental power.

Rather than metaphorically representing his social power, Manley's environmental mandates produce a tension between his agrarian reform schemes—designed to increase the nation's agricultural production and give economic, political, and social power to small land owners and peasants—and the poverty and social inequities that persisted in spite of those efforts. Looking out from the Great House windows, Manley seems to regard both governors and gardeners from a temporal and emotional distance, "in a formal dusk, where governors *had* strolled / and black gardeners *had* smiled." Walcott portrays Manley as an agriculturalist—that is, someone who attempts to cultivate or control the land (and nature more broadly); he governs and gardens. Where there had been governors in the center and black gardeners on the margins, gardening and governing become one act. The earth, apparently, responds to Manley's commands: "The flame trees obeyed his will and lowered their wicks, / the flowers tightened their fists in the name of thrift" (385). Manley's environmental power stands in contrast to his social power, for he cannot control persistent poverty:

> his hand could not dam that ceaseless torrent of dust
> that carried the shacks of the poor, to their root-rock music,
> down the gullies of Yallahs and August Town. (385)

Although his powers over nature are limited (his "mandate" does not extend to the sky, "that ceiling / of star-apple candelabra"), Manley's environmental power "from tangerine daybreaks to star-apple dusks" nonetheless exceeds his ability to control the poverty and destitution of his people. Walcott emphasizes the distinction between Manley's "given mandate" over the earth and his inability to effect social change.

We can understand Manley's agricultural development projects as attempts at cultivation in a double sense insofar as the prime minister intended the initiatives to create and preserve the culture and agriculture of the island. This dual cultivation was crucial to the nationalist project of defining an independent Jamaican economy and society. Manley, the son of Norman Manley, a former prime minister and leader of the People's Nationalist Party, rose to power in the wake of his father's resignation with a combined platform of democratic socialism and a call for Jamaica's participation in an international economic order. According to James Phillips, his policies thus constituted "an attempt to defend and preserve localism and the preservation of local culture and historical memory while functioning in a global economy" ("Democratic Socialism, the New International Economic Order, and Globalization," 188). The sugar cooperatives in particular were at once Manley's most ambitious reorganization and his most disappointing project. On the one hand, Manley's transformation of the sugar plantations into worker-owned cooperatives—which the previous government purchased at low cost from corporations—must have seemed a powerful historical transformation: the independent state taking control of an industry that for centuries had been integral to the oppression of the black majority and handing that control over, at least in part, to the cane workers themselves. On the other hand, as Michaeline Chrichlow has argued, Manley's projects enlisted workers in the service of state development projects without creating significant social or economic change. While the sugar cooperatives undoubtedly restructured the economy of the plantation, they failed to restructure the economic lives of the sugar workers. Arguably, the cooperatives functioned to consolidate state power over the land rather than empower small farmers (*Negotiating Caribbean Freedom*, 105–42).

By depicting Manley's agricultural power as the sign of Jamaica's economic decline, the poem implicates state property in the same destructive pattern as private property. Further, the poem begins to suggest that the division and commodification of land and communities corresponds with the organization of poetic language. Where Walcott elsewhere celebrates the "numinous" ("The Muse of History," 40) as the essence of poetic creation, here he represents Manley as a kind of apocalyptic Adam whose urge to name and control the environment is overly circumscribed by history.[19] From its opening lines, the poem represents the act of naming the landscape as an act of violence rather than creation. After evoking the "shards of pastoral" the poem describes the process by which "the landscape copied" this fragmentary art. The sound of water

> on the treadmill of Monday to Monday would repeat
> in tongues of water and wind and fire, in tongues
> of Mission School pickaninnies, like rivers remembering
> their source, Parish Trelawny, Parish St. David, Parish
> St. Andrew, the names afflicting the pastures. (383)

These place names are a sign of human social control, "afflicting the pastures." The colonizing language divides the landscape according to the English missionary system. These names contrast sharply with the name the poem gives the landscape, an expansive (albeit monarchial) title that emerges from the landscape itself: star-apple kingdom. This reminder of the formation (and naming) of parishes (particularly Trelawny, which was named for Edward Trelawny, who was governor of Jamaica from 1738 to 1758) marks the English governance of Jamaica as an affliction. Naming thus claims as property that which cannot belong.

Lest we read the newly empowered inhabitance of the plantation by the descendants of Africans as an allegory for political resistance, "The Star-Apple Kingdom" also suggests the dangers of poetic comparison. In a sense, comparison is the poem's singular obsession. The comparative word "like" occurs three times in the first stanza, and even more direct comparisons are in abundance. However, Walcott represents such comparisons as violent yoking of unlike things. At the end of the poem's second stanza, the poem describes the function of art as the simultaneous representation of two things. The work of the "ancient pastoral / of dusk" is "making both epochs one" (385)—bringing together through artistic comparison the colonial era of English pastoral and the rage of postcolonial politics. Jahan Ramazani has suggested that *Omeros* uses metaphor as a way of bringing together dissimilar things across boundaries of class, race, gender, and power, rendering the Caribbean legacy of suffering a condition of woundedness that can be understood globally (*The Hybrid Muse*, 71).[20] But in "The Star-Apple Kingdom" Walcott suggests that such transnational, intercultural comparisons are far from transcendent. Instead, the process of "making both epochs one" enacts artistic violence towards history and environment alike. The "scorching wind of a scream"—the voice of nationalist revolution— blew all without bending anything" (384), shrinking reality into readable forms, so that Nanny, the monumental foremother of Caribbean marronage, is rendered a "chimerical, chemical pin speck" and live Herefords are transformed to "brown porcelain cows" (384): souvenirs, consumable commodities.

Walcott represents the failure of the West Indian Federation, Manley's environmental policies, and poetic methods of comparison as parallel and related processes of disintegration. In one of the poem's most interior moments, Manley reflects on the inadequacies of both his human and his environmental mandates: "aerial," "marine," "terrestrial," and "paradisal" (389–90). The transformation of bauxite from the "bled hills" of earth into "angels sheathed in aluminum" (390) suggests the exploitation of Jamaica's natural resources. In this section of the poem the linear structure breaks down, enjambments overtaking the previously end-stopped lines. The stanza listing Manley's mandates has the quality of a bulleted to-do list, whose items from "aerial" to "paradisal" become increasingly brief and abstract. The reflections also begin in first person ("I should have foreseen those seraphs with barbed-wire hair") but shift to third, suggesting the increasing exteriority of Manley's power. Again the poem contrasts different kinds of power, emphasizing Manley's control over Jamaica's *commodities* (not only the "bled hills" but the chimneys of paradise are sheathed in "aluminum"—which was, by 1978, the predominate, yet faltering, industry in Jamaica) but not, fundamentally, its economy.

The rhythmic repetition of the environmental mandates reduces the air, sea, land, and even heavens to partial representations. This poetic gesture enacts in advance the division and commoditization of the Caribbean itself, which Walcott describes two stanzas later: "One morning the Caribbean was cut up/by seven prime ministers who bought the sea in bolts" (390). As Manley's power grows too great, human error and violent revolution corrupt the possibilities of the landscape, for, "now a tree of grenades was his star-apple kingdom" (391). In spite of Manley's democratic socialism and ideological commitment to the uplift of the poor, he is in Walcott's poem ultimately subject to the notions of property inherent in the topos of the plantation. The excessive urge to environmental ownership, the poem suggests, turns hills rich with aluminum "leaden under martial law" (391).

DWELLING IN THE ARCHIPELAGO:
SENSING THE "SPECK" AS HISTORY

Against the sweeping proportions of the plantation, Walcott's details, specks, and fragments constitute an alternative scale for dwelling in the environment. These shrunken details render the violence of poetic representation, but they also suggest a way of perceiving without possessing our environment, of making meaning in the process of poetic assemblage. In this sense Walcott's poetry plots neither a romantic story nor a tragic one. It does not plot at all. Rather, "The Star-Apple Kingdom" assembles the plantation's fragments into a lyric form. Even in Walcott's Nobel Prize acceptance speech, "The Antilles," whose subtitle is "fragments of *epic* memory" (emphasis mine), and even in the middle-length poems of *The Star-Apple Kingdom*, which many critics regard as some of Walcott's "rehearsals" for *Omeros*, Walcott dwells in the possibilities of the particular for defining individual and collective Caribbean identities. In fact, it is not until the wind of history blows through the poem, shrinking, shriveling, and extinguishing scenes of past and present, that we learn of the poem's particular national geography: the pastoral and the scream alike are "in Jamaica." Being "in Jamaica" thus foregrounds a crisis of representation with regard to the landscape, but it also produces the "specks" and "shards," the Caribbean details that themselves make up the landscape of New World poetry.

As particular details of the landscape, the "shard" and the "speck" are remnants of a sensory experience of the environment. In her reading of Walcott's *Omeros*, Susan Stewart has argued that lyric poems afford a sensory experience we need in the aftermath of the violent desensitization of war (*Poetry and the Fate of the Senses*, 293–325). Walcott, according to Stewart, embraces the first-person subjectivity of lyric as an alternative to war, in a "counterepic" that works against the generalizing, allegorizing, nationalist aims of epic by way of the particularity of place and the consciousness of first-person lyric (320). As I have already suggested in chapter 2, by invoking at the start Marx's critique of the desensitizing effects of the "trade in human bodies," Stewart's reading implicitly suggests it might be profitable to think about lyric as a necessary counter not only to the violence of war but to the desensitizing effects of racial violence (294).[21] If *Omeros* functions as a "counterepic" by engaging epic's traditions, "The Star-Apple Kingdom" demonstrates the possibilities of lyric poetry by transforming the pastoral so as to revivify the details of the landscape of slavery. In spite of Walcott's claims to historylessness, this lyric subjectivity constitutes a response to the particular legacy of slavery, insofar as "The Star-Apple Kingdom" emerges from plantation geography. The loss of history, rather than the absence of history, motivates the rhythm of the poem.

Extending Stewart's claims, I want to suggest further that "lyric's role as the continuing form of [sensory] expression" (325) emerges in Walcott from his preoccupation with environmental detail as sensory experience. If art "shrinks" both nature and history, lyric compression affords access to the particular, the distinct. Within the structure of the book *The Star-Apple Kingdom*, each individual poem constitutes a fragment of history. The geographic movement of the book from Trinidad to Jamaica, with stops in places as diverse as Tobago and Joseph Brodsky's Russia, mirrors the shape of the archipelago in a way that emphasizes both the interconnection and the integrity of the "speck"—which is, in Walcott's poetry, perhaps another word for "island viewed from above."

Walcott figures the relationship between the universal and the particular through the topography of the Caribbean archipelago. While "archipelago" literally refers to the Aegean Sea, the word also by extension refers to any sea that contains a group of islands or the group of islands itself, according to the OED. Walcott evokes the archipelago to refer to the whole of the sea and the group and likewise describes "the Caribbean" and "the Antilles" as having this dual archipelagic structure. "The Star-Apple Kingdom" laments that "one morning the Caribbean was cut up / by seven prime ministers who bought the sea in bolts," transforming "the Caribbean" from what Walcott depicts as "natural" and originary ("the sea") into an economic commodity, from "archipelago" into "this chain store of islands" (391). Thus even as Walcott celebrates the particular, he embraces the unity offered by the archipelago. This is not to say that Walcott champions West Indian unity "in the necessarily reductionist and romanticized terms of a collective epic" that Antonio Benítez-Rojo ascribes to his dramatic work *Drums and Colours* (*The Repeating Island*, 300). On the contrary, dwelling in the environment, the poem renders a coalition of specks as an alternative to nationalist paradigms of that epic unity.

Walcott has elsewhere questioned the construct of discrete Caribbean (or any American) nationhood: "We have broken up the archipelago into nations," he remarks in in his prose essay "The Caribbean: Culture or Mimicry?," "and in each nation we attempt to assert characteristics of the national identity. Everyone knows that these are pretexts of power if such power is seen as political. This is what the politician would describe as reality, but the reality is absurd" (51). In this essay Walcott's notion of the archipelago is so expansive that it includes "America" (by which Walcott means alternately the United States of America and "the Americas"). The flexibility of the term testifies to Walcott's suspicion of the "pretexts of power" that accrue to individual nations within the Caribbean and contributes to his interest in defining alternative social and political formations. The archipelago also offers a compelling geography for revising the kind of black unity Hurston sought in building an "African king's mélange" on an isthmus still connected to and bound by the political and social realities of the United States.[22]

On the political level, then, Walcott bemoans the collapse of the West Indian Federation—the division of the Caribbean into fragmentary entities with national interests. On the aesthetic level, however, he accepts the fragmentary and partial nature of his environmental experience. The archipelago relates both metaphorically and metonymically to human history. Its shape encompasses the detail, the "speck," even as it draws a partial curve around Caribbeanness, establishing belonging. Just as Walcott associates the archipelago with the totalizing whole of the sea in "Culture or Mimicry?," in his Nobel Prize lecture "The Antilles" he celebrates the small-scale of the fragment: "Our archipelago is becoming a synonym for pieces broken off from the original continent," which, Walcott insists "is the exact process of the making of poetry" (69). And if the division of the archipelago is at times the figure for its commodification, Walcott also views wholeness as a threat. In "The Antilles" he critiques the representation of the Caribbean in tourist brochures as "a blue pool": "This is how the islands from the shame of necessity sell themselves; this is the seasonal erosion of their identity, that high-pitched repetition of the same images of service that cannot distinguish one island from the other" (81). Walcott's reference to "seasonal erosion" to describe the degradation or disappearance of local Caribbean identities underscores the link between environmental and sociopolitical survival.

Walcott's persistent interest in the process of reduction reflects his concern with "distinguish[ing] one island from the other." The nature of the "speck" emphasizes the process of distinction, a process that for Walcott is grounded in the ecology and agriculture of the island. A speck, according to the *OED*, is "a small spot of a different colour or substance to that of the material or surface upon which it appears," a term that is "applied to things rendered extremely small by distance or by comparison with their surroundings," or "a small piece, portion, etc., of ground or land,." If Nanny rendered into a "speck" becomes "chimerical," Walcott nonetheless renders "small piece[s] of land" as part of the task of "distinguish[ing]" his own poem so that it is "certainly West Indian." Against "the empires of tobacco, sugar, and bananas" (387) that constitute the economic basis of the island, Walcott juxtaposes a "kingdom" of star apples, bay trees, ginger lilies and magnolias, plants whose origins and histories suggest both the indigenous and the transplanted quality of Jamaican culture. As Elaine Savory has observed, "Plant names that are sonorous, like frangipani or ginger lily, are often key to Walcott's use of heightened patterns of sound" ("Toward a Caribbean Ecopoetics," 90). Whereas Savory goes on to argue that Walcott's plant references are metapoetic representations of Caribbean literary history, I believe the Caribbean details of Walcott's poetry resist representation and allow us to sense and dwell in the small scale of the fragment.

Walcott frequently describes the making of poetry as a process of assembling those fragments. In "The Antilles," he also qualifies (even as he rehearses) his description of Caribbean writing as Adamic:

> Antillean art is this restoration of our shattered histories, our shards of vocabulary, our archipelago becoming a synonym for pieces broken off from the original continent.
>
> And this is the exact process of the making of poetry, or what should be called not its "making" but its remaking, the fragmented memory, the armature that frames the god, even the rite that surrenders it to a final pyre; the god assembled cane by cane, reed by weaving reed, line by plaited line. (69)

In the shift from "making" to "remaking" Walcott acknowledges the inescapability of, if not history, then the material past. If "the muse of history" is tyrannical, "fragmented memory" is generative. And it is generative in particular in and through the landscape: the "cane" and "reed," materials of agriculture, are woven into the basis for cultural ritual and performance. Assembling natural fragments in a poem that is itself necessarily partial and fragmentary constitutes an aesthetic alternative to property ownership. If "our archipelago" is "a synonym for pieces broken off from the original continent," and if "The Star-Apple Kingdom" assembles those pieces, it stops short of making them whole. Rather, the poetry of the archipelago demands and models a way of dwelling through the senses.

The archipelago, whose geography is traced by *The Star-Apple Kingdom*, is the site of a collective ritual of redemption. But Walcott challenges our sense of the words "national," "collective," and "allegory." In a stanza in "The Star-Apple Kingdom" that traces the history of the Caribbean, Walcott stages a double baptism. This scene unfolding "before the coruscating façades of cathedrals" (387) suggests the glittering, reflective surface of the water and also history's unreliability (the poem does not describe the cathedrals so much as their "facades"). The first baptism takes place in "a parenthetical moment / that made the Caribbean a baptismal font" (387) and the second, in a moment "before" this one, in which "the Caribbean was borne like an elliptical basin / in the hands of acolytes, and a people were absolved / of a history which they did not commit" (387). The repetition of the image displaces a static sense of time; the Caribbean is a "baptismal font" both in the "parenthetical moment" and in that which supposedly precedes it. The pun on borne/born suggests that the Caribbean is not only the "font" or "basin" in which "a people were absolved" but also an infant awaiting his or her own baptism "in the hands of acolytes." Walcott proposes the Caribbean as a site of nationalist solidarity, but he also imagines another kind of entity altogether, a basin in which the "shards" of culture float and define themselves.

READING THE ARCHIPELAGO: A NEGRO ART COLONY

From the floating islands of the Caribbean basin we might glimpse again Zora Neale Hurston's imaginary isthmus of black art. Describing it, she imagines a utopic space for black diasporic creation apart from both the violent history of the plantation and the harsh realities of urban life. But she also describes the particular conditions that produced and continue to produce inter- and intra-racial fragmentation, displacement, and isolation (geographic and otherwise). In her letter to Hughes about the plots of land on Indian River, she painfully acquiesces to the hierarchies of race and class that shape the fantasy of property ownership: "They say they do not mind Negroes having the plat, but NO niggers. They do not want the property to lose its value" (*Zora Neale Hurston*, 145).

In his essay "Archipelagic Diaspora, Geographical Form, and Hurston's *Their Eyes Were Watching God*," Brian Russell Roberts has proposed that more attention be paid to geographical materialism as a way of understanding the relationship between Hurston's writing and the Caribbean. He argues that attention to the "formal geography" of Hurston's writing—meaning the material features of the island geographies that shape Hurston's ethnographic and fictional works—can bring to light "cultural geography" as a rubric for understanding and theorizing diaspora (123). It is in part in this same spirit that I return us to the creative "plats" of Hurston's geographic imagination. What is most compelling in Roberts's recovery of the "insular" as something other than an American exceptionalist form is his insistence that archipelagic geography necessitates a way of reading.

Roberts suggests that while heightened attention to geographical form, on one hand, facilitates the close reading of specific literary texts, it also calls for a concomitant mode of far reading that asks critics to look toward cultural geographies (nation-state, global South, diaspora) and recognize the formal geographies (mountain, river, archipelago) that through their planetary repetitions forge interlinkings of the planet's disparate cultural regions and literary traditions (144). In the first three chapters of this book, I have been motivated in part by a methodological imperative similar to that which Roberts outlines here. I have read individual lyric poems as provision grounds that are contained, isolated, and at times autonomous yet also connected through the network of the historical plantation, as well as through literary circulation. This method for figuring autonomy and interdependence is not unlike traversing islands in the sea. Hence, too, by focusing on periodicals in chapter 2 and evoking Hurston's isthmus community in this chapter I seek to disrupt what Roberts calls the "desert-island" status of single authors in favor of the kind of far reading that he calls for and that Walcott's poem formally enacts.

But the archive I've assembled here is an archive of racial diaspora, by which I mean an archive attentive to the history of the black Atlantic produced by race (and racism) and through which race has been produced. By placing the "planetary" in contradistinction to the "identitarian" as heuristics for reading Hurston (and, by implication, reading African American and American literature more broadly), Roberts usefully challenges both Caribbean and American exceptionalism, revising in one gesture Benitez-Rojo's figure of the "repeating island" as a mark of the Caribbean's particular access to global culture and decades of Americanist scholarship that remained constrained by national borders, as well as more recent scholars' "postexceptionalist" correction of that nationalist framing (123–24). But I hesitate to embrace the idea of "planetary archipelago" as an alternative to "racial diaspora" because to do so risks erasure of the economic and political flows (the transatlantic slave trade, the trade in sugar, rum, cotton, and tourism) that have produced other regional and transnational formations. As Nikhil Singh reminds us in *Black Is a Country*, "What if the political lesson of the long civil rights era is that we advance equality only by continually passing through a politics of race and by refusing the notion of a definitive 'beyond race'?" (218). Singh frames this particular question in relationship to historicizing the present of racism in the United States, but it is just as useful a caution in relationship to the embrace of planetary geography as a way of thinking human interrelation. I have categorized Walcott's and Hurston's black aesthetics as being part of a common Atlantic archipelago not because they insist on identitarian politics (they do not) or because they reach "beyond race" through planetary forms of geography but rather because they differently remind us that "property" *must* "lose its value" in any poetics of environmental relation after the plantation.

Hurston's letter to Hughes describes the social and political vulnerability of the watershed, the land that feeds and lives off of rivers and the oceans. She evokes the human violence characteristic of the landscapes of enforced cultivation and enforced migration that have been the subject of part 1. As Hurston's and Walcott's oeuvres equally attest, islands, isthmuses, and peninsulas in the global South are vulnerable as well to the violence of events sometimes understood as "natural": earthquakes, hurricanes, and floods. In fact, environmental catastrophe may have produced the collective land ownership opportunity Hurston sought, since the resulting economic downturn suppressed land prices.[23] But if the hurricane produced an unrealized opportunity for black artistic cultivation (and economic self-determination), on a broader scale it disproportionately destroyed the lives and economic security of African Americans. These intersecting literary histories of imaginative cultivation and economic, social, and environmental destruction—as taken up in the work of Hurston as well as Sterling Brown, Bessie Smith, Lloyd Lovindeer, Kamau Brathwaite and NourbeSe Philip—are the focus of the second half of this book. Part 1 has focused on how the geography of plantation enslavement—as enclosure and escape, particularity and repetition, rootedness and transplantation—shapes modern literary form. In part 2, I explore the sonic and textual archive of diaspora that black writers have generated in response to environmental catastrophe.

part 2   catastrophe

four

Continuing Catastrophe

The Flood Blues of Sterling Brown and Bessie Smith

NO MUSIC

The flooding originated in heavy rains along the Ohio, the Mississippi, and their tributaries in the fall and winter of 1926, followed by months of heavy rain in early 1927. By spring, the Mississippi water levels were so high that backwater had accumulated, preventing the tributaries from emptying into the river. Waters at several key points in the delta reached flood levels in early 1927, with flooding and storms alike causing structural damage and deaths. In spite of months of attempts to inspect and reinforce the levees (labor performed largely by black workers), the levees began to break in mid-April in Missouri, Arkansas, and most famously Greenville, Mississippi, with disastrous results. Black sharecroppers were displaced, forced into work on the levees, and relocated to refugee camps (called "concentration camps").[1]

Reporting the following winter on the NAACP's investigation into the aftermath of the Mississippi floods of 1927, W. E. B. Du Bois used the pages of *The Crisis* to offer a powerful critique of the Red Cross and the National Guard, arguing that they not only neglected the black refugees but perpetuated the violent, repressive, racist system of sharecropping that dominated much of the affected areas:

> The most impressive thing about these camps was the incredible melancholy of the colored refugees. There was no laughter, no music, no negro lightheartedness. They sat in silent apathy, or talked in low tones. They had come from scenes of horror, many of them greater than any white refugees knew, as the helplessness of the Negro in Mississippi exceeds anything known to whites. One woman stood all night waist-deep in rising water. A few rods away, but out of sight, her husband screamed for help. He could not be reached. After a while his screams stopped. In the morning there was no sign of him. Two young girls went to the Red Cross tent day after day to ask for news of their brother who had been taken to work on the levee at Greenville. At last the news

came: he had been found drowned near the levee. The girls turned without a word and went in silence to their own tent, tears streaming down their faces. There was no sound of mourning, no lamentation in the camp. The calamity of all was too great for that easy expression. ("The Flood, the Red Cross, and the National Guard," 1:5)[2]

The reports in *The Crisis* echo earlier newspaper reporting on conditions in the camps, in particular accounts of conscripted, unpaid labor after the levees broke in April 1927.[3] In the opening of this first installment of his report, Du Bois draws a contrast between the relatively humane conditions of the camps for white refugees (who were nonetheless, Du Bois acknowledges, as impoverished as their black counterparts), and the resource-deprived, overcrowded, and un-safe conditions of the camps for the blacks. But perhaps most striking in Du Bois's comparison is his description of the "colored camps" as silent spaces. The author of "The Sorrow Songs," the man who heard at the beginning of the twentieth century "the most beautiful expression of human experience born this side of the seas" in the voices of the formerly enslaved and their descendants (*The Souls of Black Folks*, 168) here describes instead a place with "no laughter, no music, no negro lightheartedness[,] . . . no mourning, no lamentation" ("The Flood, the Red Cross, and the National Guard," 1:5). It was Du Bois who had in-structed readers that the sorrow songs themselves, as evidence of the very de-humanization against which they strove, were no "easy expression," inviting us to listen to black music and black poetry as a complex representation of beauty and horror. But in the refugee camps, which Du Bois elsewhere calls "the slave camps" and which the magazine represents visually as "the slave ship" (fig. 4.1), "the calamity of all was too great" for song.[4]

The pages of *The Crisis* themselves are one counterpoint—though perhaps not the antidote—to the silence Du Bois evokes in the report. Along with the NAACP report, the January 1928 issue contains drawings, poems, a play, reports of awards and successes among prominent black artists, writers, and academ-ics, a list of favorite spirituals, advertisements for, among other things, colleges and universities, "pictures of distinguished negroes," and "race records"—all entreaties to the rising black bourgeoisie to keep rising or, as Du Bois would put it, to keep striving. To identify this contrast between silence and striving is to acknowledge, to a certain degree, the Lockian narrative of migration from South to North as a narrative of progress, to embrace the conventional wisdom that to cultivate the negro's artistic gifts it is necessary to move away—physically and through time—from the work of cultivation.[5] The floods themselves were an agent in this narrative. In "Panel 8" of his 1941 *Migration Series*, which is the cover

The Flood, the Red Cross and the National Guard

"No One Has Gone Hungry, Unclothed, Unprotected," Herbert Hoover

MISSISSIPPI

The Situation

Second Installment Based on an Investigation Made by the N. A. A. C. P. in October, 1927

EACH large plantation is farmed by a number of tenants, or share-croppers, who are furnished with houses and living through the year by the planter. That is, they are given credit at the plantation store and "Christmas money" for the holidays. In the fall when the crop is in, the amount of the tenant's indebtedness is, theoretically, subtracted from the amount coming to him as his share of year on cotton. One successful year will make him rich. For five or six years he has been losing steadily. The price of cotton went down until last year it reached a point so low that a few planters refused to sell. Those who happened to store their crop in a high place sold this year at a high planter must show that he has a tenant family to every twenty acres. The loan is used for all the year's expenses—seed, feed for the stock and food, clothing, etc., for the tenants. The planter is thus dependent on his tenants and obliged for his existence to hold them on his land by fair means or foul.

There is an understanding to the effect that a disaster which destroys the year's crop automatically cancels the contract. Therefore after a serious overflow, if a share-cropper wishes to leave a plantation he feels free to do so. At such times the planter often resorts to any pressure

The Slave Ship, 1927

the crop and the balance is paid to him. The planter, of course, keeps the amount of indebtedness higher than the value of the crop, and by this method can hold the tenant to work for another year under the same contract. Practically all such tenants are Negroes and in some cases there are several hundred families held in this kind of peonage on one plantation.

The Yazoo-Mississippi Delta is a one-crop country. The planter is a gambler, who stakes all he has each profit. With the exception of these the entire Delta, bankrupt before the flood, was left in a hopeless condition by the disaster. Practically all of the plantations were already mortgaged for more than their actual value. The mortgages are, for the most part, held by insurance companies. Plantations are financed each year by a "furnish loan" from a local bank. This is actually a mortgage on a potential crop. The amount of the loan is based on the amount of land and labor. The possible to keep his tenants from leaving him. The unwritten law in Mississippi is that no plantation owner will try to entice labor away from another plantation. Anyone who is suspected of this crime is despised and outcast. Therefore the labor agent, whose business it is to do this, is considered the most contemptible of men. He must carry on his work in secrecy, for if it were definitely known, he would certainly be treated with violence, if not lynched.

Fig. 4.1. First page of part 2 of W. E. B. Du Bois's "The Flood, the Red Cross, and the National Guard," published in *The Crisis* in February 1928. Photo: Department of Special Collections and University Archives, W. E. B. Du Bois Library, University of Massachusetts Amherst.

image of this book, the painter Jacob Lawrence famously depicts the floods as one of the poor conditions that prompted northward migration. As *The Crisis* articles report, mobility within the affected areas was limited for the black evacuees, both before and after the floods; as sharecroppers, they were eternally in debt to plantation owners. According to *The Crisis* this debt was canceled in the event of a disaster so severe as to destroy the crop. However, by refusing to transport the refugees anywhere other than back to the plantation, the Red Cross reinstated the ongoing system of peonage while also using a pass system to curtail movement within and beyond the camps. Thus, those refugees who were able to escape the camps without being transported back to their "home" plantations as sharecroppers left the region in large numbers and travelled to cities. *The Crisis* enjoined them to do so:

> We hope that every Negro that can escape from the slave camps guarded by the National Red Cross for the benefit of the big planters of Mississippi and Louisiana and the lynchers of Arkansas will leave the land of deviltry at the first opportunity. Let them ride, run and crawl out of this hell. There is no hope for the black man there today. . . . We do not know where the refugees from the Mississippi bottoms can go, but we are frank to say it would be better for them to starve in Memphis and Chicago than to be slaves in Arkansas and Mississippi. (Du Bois, "Flood")

As a factor in the ongoing migration of sharecroppers from the rural South to the urban North, the floods assured that a future black culture would take root in urban environments. This chapter makes audible the sound of the floods and serves as a bridge between the literary history of cultivation that has been my focus in the first half of this book and the lyrics of catastrophe that preoccupy its remaining chapters.

It turns out there *was* music in the Mississippi delta after the floods: an outpouring of it that famously evoked the landscape of the flood and at the same time shaped the modern blues. As David Evans has usefully documented in "High Water Everywhere," an essay on African American musical response to the floods, there was music in the camps and throughout the Mississippi delta, not to mention the hit records that were released in the months after the floods. In this chapter I inquire into the surprising persistence of songs and words after catastrophe. I look first at how Bessie Smith's blues account for the storm as a figuration of pervasive problems of social injustice, violence, and homelessness in the south and as a sensory environmental experience. The recursiveness of blues lyrics and performance, coupled with the rise of the classic blues vocalist, yield a formal structure that embodies the collective experience of catastrophe and the historical repetition of structural violence.

By representing the flood zone as a space of pure social death juxtaposed against the liveness of black urban art, *The Crisis* reinforces the boundary between nature and culture, a boundary that sonic and literary responses to the floods push against, ignore, and blur. In attempting to record, convey, or fill the melancholic silence Du Bois overheard, the flood blues also generate lyrical forms that have crucially informed the way history—by which I mean the relationship between past and present, as well as the idea of history as that which must be retained, preserved, and recounted—unfolds in modern black poetry.

As print recordings of both the music and the floods, Sterling Brown's poems "Cabaret (1927, Black & Tan Chicago)" and "Ma Rainey" suggest that the movements among song, storm, and text are necessarily ruptured by the experiences of catastrophe, marked by both textual and temporal discontinuity, even as catastrophe itself repeats and continues. In lieu of the silence Du Bois heard (perhaps erroneously) in the camps, how can poetry sound this continuing catastrophe? The basis of Brown's poetics lies in the approximate relationship between poetry and the blues themselves, what Brent Edwards describes as "the fuzzy area between the song lyric and the literary lyric" ("The Seemingly Eclipsed Window of Form," 583). Rather than attempting a faithful transcription of the events of the flooding or Smith's musical renditions, Brown's poems approximate the relation between poetic language and the objects of historical memory (including both storms and songs) it contains. In claiming Kamau Brathwaite's use of "approximate" (as a verb) as a theoretical alternative to mimesis for reading Brown, I situate Brown (often understood as a regional U.S. poet) in a tradition of diasporic writing. The floods themselves reproduce the conditions of diaspora—the alienation of a people from their land—and Brown participates in a poetic process of collecting, arranging, and cultivating art in response to that catastrophic rupture.

As I have discussed in the introduction, Brathwaite turns away from traditional European representational forms in describing the problem of black (and specifically Caribbean) poetry. He asks, "how do you get a rhythm which approximates the *natural* experience, the *environmental* experience" (*History of the Voice*, 10)? Seeking poetic language that will "approximate" a particular "natural" or "environmental experience"—hurricanes, not snow—Brathwaite acknowledges the difference between approximation and representation. The verb "approximates"—this action of bringing near that which is far, of bringing dis-

parate entities close to but not into union—describes both the relationship between nature and culture in diasporic poetry and the task of poetic form in articulating that relationship. Even in staking a claim to a potential authentic
rhythm in his definition of "nation language," Brathwaite assumes a distance
between "the natural" and the rhythm that would give voice to or transcribe the
experience of the natural. The identity of the rhythm remains open to experience and change, defined by simile: "*like* a howl, or a shout or a machine-gun or
the wind or a wave" and, perhaps most importantly for our purposes, "*like* the
blues" (13, emphasis mine).[6] If we think of the poetics of disaster as a poetics of
approximation, in other words, we can begin to see how black diasporic poetry
potentially avoids the trap of colonial mimesis. Brown does not so much "preserve and transmit" a source from the past as much as he reveals the approximation of musical and environmental sources alike to be a hallmark of black
modern poetry.[7]

Brown's poems further suggest that we can read and listen to the flood songs
as something other than a chronicle or narrative. In contrast to scholarship that
holds blues performances of black historical experience under the "conceptual
umbrella" of narrative, I turn to Smith's flood recordings, as lyrics in and of
themselves and as quotations within Sterling Brown's flood poems, to highlight
poetry's capacity to account for different kinds of organic time simultaneously.[8]
Many of our salient metaphors for diaspora have to do with movement through
space—the "ships in motion," for example, that anchor Paul Gilroy's reorienta-
tion to the black Atlantic (*The Black Atlantic*, 4), railroads, or even the "Southern
Road" that gives its title to Brown's 1932 volume of poems. In part 1 of this book
I have attended to how agricultural metaphors figure both rooted and scattered
representations of black historical experience. If a certain alienation from geography is a precondition of diaspora, so, too, imaginative responses to that alienation must account for the historical and temporal ruptures that have shaped
black diasporic experience. Modern narratives can provide diasporic communities with one such way to do so: in the absence of a homeland, these narratives
inscribe cultural and national identity within genealogies, linear histories, and
progressions in time. Hence, for instance, the persistent concern with genealogy that pervades the genre of the slave narrative and the popularity and significance of this form in the foundation of African American literary canons. But
poetic time can also account for the discontinuity of those histories and genealogies. The blues song and the blues poem structurally mediate between the
temporality of everyday violence and the radical rupture of disaster brought
about by the floods.

OUT OF MUDDY WATER:
CATASTROPHE'S ARTISTIC AFTERMATH

Why, given the excessive violence wrought by the floods, the tornadoes, and deeply ingrained institutional racism in the affected areas, was there music after the storms? Du Bois was perhaps reluctant to describe the music for fear of reinforcing stereotypes of "negro lightheartedness." In Vicksburg, according to John Barry, "one group of black refugees, before being allowed off a barge onto dry land, was ordered to sing Negro Spirituals" (*Rising Tide*, facing page 127). They refused, thereby insisting on the insurmountable horror of events. But for others music rendered an alternative history of the present in the South. In this way, catastrophe brought to the fore a tension between testifying silence and testifying sound that has defined black cultural expression for the last century. Blues music in particular afforded a way for the sounds of the storm to travel and for a singular voice to collect the experiences of a people.

By the 1960s Ralph Ellison would write that "as a form, the blues is an autobiographical chronicle of personal catastrophe expressed lyrically" ("Richard Wright's Blues," 78–79). In the context of the floods that in part precipitated both the blues and the great migration, we must understand the meaning of "personal" to be something more than individual; for catastrophe in the blues does not merely stand in for the experiences of unrequited love and individual loss that are the signatures of the genre but also signals a history of man-made and natural disaster, experienced collectively. Ellison describes this history as "all those blasting pressures which in a scant eighty years have sent the Negro people hurtling, without clearly defined trajectory, from slavery to emancipation . . . and which, between the two wars, have shattered the wholeness of its folk consciousness into a thousand writhing pieces" (80). As the "personal catastrophe" is what "sent the Negro people hurtling," Ellison suggests the need for something beyond a solution at the level of the individual, the need for a collective response that would bring the "thousand writhing pieces" together.[9] The unusual mobility afforded to the blues singer, her ability to collect people's experiences and perform them back, gave her the capacity to voice that response.

At the same time, even as Smith's blues narrate the circumstances of migration —from the threat of violence to the floods themselves—they also signal the representational crisis Du Bois evokes in his description of the camps. How can there be song in the midst of such melancholy? What words can go there? How can the blues genre, whose signature feature might be the transformation of collective experience into a singular voice, effectively represent the geographic and temporal rupture of community brought about by the floods? And how can a genre of music we have often understood as a narrative of black Americans' cultural progress account for the recursive, sometimes circular historical and environmental experience of catastrophe? In Smith's blues these questions emerge in the interplay between lyrics and performance, as well as in the circulation history of the songs.

The catastrophic in Bessie Smith's flood blues names at once the suffering of an individual and the suffering of a community. The catastrophic blues challenge our sense that individual consciousness dominates lyric form. Smith wrote and performed several songs associated with the 1927 Mississippi River floods: "Muddy Water," a Tin Pan Alley hit written by an interracial team of composers that does not directly refer to flooding, "Homeless Blues," written by Smith's pianist Porter Grainger, and Smith's "Back-Water Blues." Of these, "Homeless Blues" was the only one penned, performed, and recorded after the floods and in direct response to them. The apostrophic mode of address in "Homeless Blues" unifies the personal suffering of a lyric speaker, the demographic suffering of the people in the face of environmental disaster, and the racial suffering of the people in the Jim Crow South. The speaker directly addresses the river as if a lover: "Mississippi River, what a fix you left me in." The speaker's emotional and spiritual distance from the Mississippi are all the more palpable in this cry to which no one responds, even as she claims a deep link to her "home sweet home" beside the river. The accusation—"what a fix you left me in"—could just as easily address a lover as a body of water; thus, the lyrics construct the relationship with the natural world through the blues tradition of the abandoned woman's lament.[10] As Farah Griffin has noted, the song also draws on associations between the river and southern violence during and after slavery. In Griffin's analysis, coded references to the violent history of the South exemplify the artistic representation of causes for northward migration (*"Who Set You Flowin'?,"* 19–20). Although Smith did not write this song, her choice to record and perform it is consistent with her practice of writing and revising (through performance) lyric accounts of catastrophic suffering.

In "Back-Water Blues," Smith's representation of the bind of forced migration after the floods unmistakably brings to mind the forced displacements of slavery, evoking past and present in a single breath. Her telling renders the "home sweet home" of "Homeless Blues" as "no place." In the "backwater" Smith describes, the very title conflating economic and social stasis with the ecological circumstance of tributary waters accumulating in flood conditions, the "Southern Road" of Brown's poems is far from the open road. The final verses of the song fuse the experiences of "thousands" with those of the speaker, "a poor old girl" who substitutes an impersonal description of herself for the personal pronoun "me":

Then I went an' stood up on some high ol' lonesome hill,
Then I went an' stood up on some high ol' lonesome hill,
Then looked down on the house where I used to live.

Backwater blues done cause me to pack my things and go,
Backwater blues done cause me to pack my things and go,
'cause my house fell down and I can't live there no more.

Mmmmmmmm I can't move no more,
Mmmmmmmm I can't move no more,
There ain't no place for a poor old girl to go.

The specific condition of the speaker's mobility—"my house fell down and I can't live there no more"—becomes the broad category of "Back-Water Blues," a conglomeration of personal, environmental, economic, and social conditions endemic to the "backwater."

Following the discussion of cultivation in the first half of this book, we might consider Smith's recordings as part of an antipastoral tradition in black poetry and song that recasts the agricultural landscapes of the South in light of historical violence while also reimagining those spaces as artistically generative. This transformation is evident in her recasting of a Tin Pan Alley hit not originally written as a record of the floods at all titled "Muddy Water," which was composed by Peter DeRose, Harry Richman, and Jo Trent (an interracial team) and released in late 1926.[11] While Smith did not write this song, her recording of it manifests the tension between personal longing and collective loss precisely in the gap between the text of the lyrics and her voicing of them. In March 1927, as the Mississippi rose throughout the delta, not yet overreaching its banks in Arkansas, Louisiana, or Mississippi, a young Bing Crosby made his first solo recording, singing this tune with the Paul Whiteman orchestra. Crosby's abbreviated version of the song fully voices its longing for "Dixie," which begins with a lengthy, swingy instrumental intro featuring brass and string sections. Crosby's voice and the lyrics enter for the last chorus and verse, shortly thereafter yielding to the atmospheric rhythms of the orchestra:

Muddy water, round my feet,
Muddy water, in the street.

Just God's own shelter,
Down on the delta.

. . . .

They live in ease and comfort down there, I do declare.

Even in advance of the immense havoc the Mississippi River would soon wreak "down on the delta," the Crosby/Whiteman recording evinces a characteristically naïve (and historically racist) portrait of easy life in the South.[12]

The same week in another studio in New York, Bessie Smith recorded her version of "Muddy Water (a Mississippi Moan)," giving the lie to the line "They live in ease and comfort down there, I do declare." Whereas the same declaration comes across as earnest—indeed easy—in Crosby's contemporaneous version of the same song, and in composer Harry Richman's 1926 version, Smith's performance renders the (perhaps unintentional) irony in the lyrics unmistakable. Smith recorded the song as part of a session including largely popular or "commercial" music.[13] Some blues critics have written off "Muddy Water," unlike "Back-Water Blues" and "Homeless Blues," as a nostalgic, idealized fantasy of southern life, but Smith's performance mediates between the nostalgic lyrics and the catastrophic experience—the violence of the southern landscape—to which the song only obliquely refers. In "The Blues as Folk Poetry," Sterling Brown himself describes "Muddy Water" as insufficiently authentic, "stereotyped," and "sentimentalizing." In contrast, he praises "the gain in vividness, in feeling" achieved in such songs as 'Backwater Blues,' or the 'Mississippi Water Blues',"which "substitute[s] the thing seen for the bookish dressing up" (330–31). It is true that the lyrics, as Angela Davis points out, "reflect the banality of Tin Pan Alley assembly-line musical products" (*Blues Legacies and Black Feminism*, 88) and that, as Chris Albertson concedes, "there is barely a trace of blues in this 'moan'" (*Bessie*, 150). At the same time, Albertson goes on to contend that Smith's performance is marked by "conviction" in which "we have to believe." Davis takes Albertson's argument a step further by emphasizing the "contemplative and complicated" tone of Smith's performance, "as if she is summoning her audience toward a critical reading of the lyrics" (*Blues Legacies and Black Feminism*, 89).

As Brown's poetic interpretation of the song will show us, we can understand Smith's critique in relationship to the collision of the southern environment and its cultural representation. Accompanied by traditional New Orleans jazz orchestration sans Whiteman's drum kit and strings, Smith slows the tempo way down, singing "Muddy Water" as something like a dirge rather than a swing tune, so that when the speaker is "headed homebound *just once more*" (emphasis mine), we imagine her headed toward her final resting place. The very contention that "Southland has got its grand garden spots / although you believe or not" seems to elide the history of plantation slavery and indulge in pastoral fantasy, but this claim is followed by a particularly powerful example of Smith's performative irony: "I hear those trees a-whispering, 'Come on back to me,'" a line that, as Davis notes, would inevitably evoke a traumatic association with lynching for some black listeners (88). Following these lines Smith introduces the refrain with increasing intensity and volume, her voice taking on the quality of vibrato, as if holding steady beneath a wail. The "muddy water 'round my feet / muddy water in the street" does not merely evoke life on the river but threatens death by drowning. If Smith's voice has a singular capacity to transform the Tin Pan Alley lyrics into a critique of southern violence, she also brings to life the tension between performance and lyrics that is part of the structure of the blues. It has not been my intention to suggest that no black southern artist can express nostalgia and critique simultaneously in regard to the "muddy water." On the contrary, Smith's performance voices both the beckoning voice of the "Southland" and its violence. We might think of Smith's dual representation of irony and nostalgia as an example of what Anthony Reed—developing a theory of postmodern experimental poetics rather than modern lyric poetry—calls "affirmative blues irony," that is, "a horizontal play of heterogeneous differences" that refuses to resolve (*Freedom Time*, 136). The complex "affirmation" of Smith's performance lays the groundwork for Brown's poetic representation of the floods' migratory effects.

The different recordings of "Muddy Water" bring to the fore the challenge of making "muddy water" signify one way or the other. Does the landscape of the poem evoke southern belonging ("come on back to me") or southern violence ("trees-a-whispering")? How does the context of the song's production—having been written and recorded before the great flood of the Mississippi but circulated and promoted in the context of that disaster—make audible the devastating silence Du Bois heard? I have described these two renditions of "Muddy Water" because they highlight how the flood blues reimagine the southern landscape and because it seems that Sterling Brown had heard both and went on to play them back in his 1932 poem "Cabaret (1927, Black & Tan Chicago)." Through his citation of the song and description of its performance, Brown reveals the movements of migrants and dancers to be something other than a "one-way ticket" to freedom.[14]

HOW DOES THE FLOOD ROAR?
STERLING BROWN'S CABARET

Unlike "Muddy Water," Sterling Brown's poem "Cabaret" was written after the levee break and resulting destruction, written, in fact, at a point well into the Great Depression. By drawing on the song lyrics and their various recordings, Brown evokes both the social death of the refugee camps and the possibility of social life in black art. He does so not by faithfully representing the event of "the great flood" *or* by faithfully representing any single performance of "Muddy Water" but rather by rendering the rough seams between environmental experience and its representation, between lyric and performance, between song and text. "Cabaret," along with "Ma Rainey," Brown's other effort to make sounds and storm audible, thus puts us in mind of Kamau Brathwaite's call for a new Caribbean poetics, his assertion that "the hurricane does not roar in pentameters, and that's the problem: how do you get a rhythm which approximates the *natural* experience, the *environmental* experience?" (*History of the Voice*, 10). That is, the poems remind us of the impossibility of "get[ing] a rhythm" that is commensurable with song or storm.

There's no evidence in the poem that Brown had Smith's version exclusively in mind when he wrote "Cabaret"—indeed, the poem seems explicitly to reference and parody a nostalgic Tin Pan Alley rendition. But elsewhere he describes his "zeal for Bessie Smith" (*A Negro Looks at the South*, 38). Further, the date in the subtitle of the poem unmistakably places the poem in relation to the Mississippi flood and to Smith's more well-known "Back-Water Blues." Brown's poem indexes the power of Smith's transformative performance of "Muddy Water," even as it critiques the Tin Pan Alley versions. To some extent Brown emphasizes the banality of the "Muddy Water" lyrics: the "home" the speaker longs for becomes "home sweet home," apparently calling on the tone of Bing Crosby's version. But he also makes room for Bessie Smith's voice in the "moans" from the "lovely throats" of the chorus dancers, which echo the subtitle of Smith's recording, "a Mississippi moan." Smith's performance emphasizes the power of vocalization and the capacity of a singular voice to "moan"; Brown's indirect citation of her suggests the difficulty of conveying the horrors of the floods through words alone and through a singular speaker.

If the accounts of the flood in *The Crisis* draw a sharp line between the silent suffering of the refugees and the generative art of modernist urban dwellers, Brown's poem understands both to be the basis of black modern poetry, collecting the "easy" and the frenzied expression within the same space. The poem does not merely undermine the white fantasy of "life upon the river"; rather, it reveals that fantasy—as a projection of urban art—to be deeply intertwined with, indeed dependent on, the reality of black "life upon the river." The migrations of black people (of which the floods in Mississippi and racial oppression were twin causes), after all, make the cabaret scene possible. The chorus, for instance arrives "from New Orleans" by way of "Atlanta, Louisville, Washington, Yonkers,/With stop-overs they've used nearly all their lives" (111).

The genealogy of suffering in the poem unmoors any visions of a liberatory northern metropolis, even as the object of its satire is southern nostalgia, and it unmoors at the same time the narrative of progress "up from slavery." The power imbalance between sprawling "overlords" and the "deaf-mute waiters" (111) and performers who variously serve the "overlords" corrupts the space of cultural production. The poem draws an odd parallel between the condition of the performers in the chorus ("Their shapely bodies naked save/For tattered pink silk bodices, short velvet tights") and sharecroppers forced into relief work in Arkansas following the floods, "poor half-naked fools, tagged with identification numbers,/Worn out upon the levees" (112), as well as peoples for sale on the auction block: "*A prime filly, seh/What am I offered gentlemen, gentlemen.*" These parallels—between urban black performers and rural black laborers and between both groups and their enslaved ancestors—defy the idea that time or northward migration has brought progress.

To some extent the poem bemoans the lack of power and agency in the music—or at least the lyrics—of the song "Muddy Water." Shifting voices, Brown juxtaposes the fantasy of the lyrics—"There's peace and happiness there/I declare"—against the economic and social reality of those affected by the floods:

> (*In Arkansas,*
> *Poor half-naked fools, tagged with identification numbers,*
> *Worn out upon the levees,*
> *Are carted back to serfdom*
> *They had never left before*
> *And may never leave again*) (112)

Brown is referring here to the fact that black sharecroppers were conscripted to shore up the levees against the encroaching waters, and forced to wear visible tags that would prevent migration, while whites were rescued and evacuated from the floodplains.[15] This historical atrocity, which Du Bois, Walter White, and others recount in their critiques of the Hoover administration's response to the flood and which Richard Wright fictionalizes in the short story "Down by the Riverside," renders the song's claim to the "peace and happiness" of the river unmistakably ironic. The voice of "reality" and the voice of the song (which is also the voice of a lyric speaker) therefore seem to be "antithetical," as Brown's biographer Joanne Gabbin has suggested (*Sterling A. Brown*, 121).

The poem foregrounds movement and performance as a way of countering the destructive nostalgia of the song. Diverse bodies inhabit the space of the cabaret: the white overlords and "their glittering darlings," the musicians and chorus, and the "deaf-mute waiters." The waiters above all are—in the most literal sense—without voice. Their appearance in the first stanza signals the poem's reach for modes of communication and resistance beyond vocality. The waiters move "surreptitiously"; "going easily," they are "wary"; they seem to submit to the degradation of the club, but at the same time they engage in deliberately strategic behavior, "flattering the grandees." Against this "easy" movement,

The jazzband unleashes its frenzy.

> *Now, now,*
> *To it, Roger; that's a nice doggie,*
> *Show your tricks to the gentlemen.*

The trombone belches, and the saxaphone
Wails curdlingly, the cymbals clash,
The drummer twitches in an epileptic fit. (111)

The stanza in italics ironizes even the alarming "frenzy" of the musicians; this, too, it seems, is a servile "trick" to please the master. In his near-scientific reading of the poem, Stephen Henderson argues that "the band is depicted in pathological images" ("The Heavy Blues of Sterling Brown," 45). While this may be the case, I maintain that Brown assigns a kind of agency to the "fit." In a pun that pits musicality against semiotics, he renders the musicians' frenzy inassimilable to the club goers' fantasy: "the cymbals clash." The "epileptic" twitching of the drummer is jarring against the steady, clipped rhythm of the song lyrics:

Muddy water
Round my feet
Muddy water (111)

The performers resist the easy, "banal" nostalgia of the song and the sound "wails curdlingly" around the "feet" of the poem. The chorus of "Creole Beauties" initially "sways in" to "bring to mind . . . / Life upon the river" for the club goers fantasizing about the "river sweet." But the overlords are not the only ones with a "mind" about the river. In evoking the Arkansas levee workers and the auction block ("show your tricks to the gentlemen"), the poem represents black consciousness and memory alongside that of the white overlords.

Brown makes audible the suffering of refugee labor through the tension between lyric and performance. He renders the memory of catastrophic trauma visible in the bodies of the performers:

> The band goes mad, the drummer throws his sticks
> At the moon, a *papier-mâché* moon,
> The chorus leaps into weird posturings,
> The firm-fleshed arms plucking at grapes to stain
> Their corralled mouths; seductive bodies weaving
> Bending, writhing, turning (113)

The "creamy skin" of the "quarterounes" or "creole" chorus (presumably a product of illegal and forced interracial unions) testifies to the objectification of black female bodies under slavery. The bodies that "twist and rock" in the cabaret bring to mind the speaker of the song "Muddy Water," who is "reeling and rocking to them low down blues" with "muddy water in my shoes." Drowned or drowning bodies performing this dance resonate with all the associations of black bodies sold downriver, black bodies drowned by rain and violence alike. The labor of the dancers parallels that of the workers in the refugee camps. But the Chicago performers, like Bessie Smith, perform beyond the constraints of the song's lyrics, in opposition to drowning: they are seductive, active; they hurl their music against the "papier-mâché" fantasy of the scene. The "weird posturings" of the dancers, alongside the "mad" movements of the band, exceed the pathologizing gaze of the club goers and achieve a dynamic, sculptural grace. If the "black folk" in Mississippi "huddle, mute, uncomprehending," and wonder quietly about their condition, then the collective performance of bodies "weaving/Bending, writhing, turning," leads to their "huddling," evoking both the devastating image of bodies drowned in the river and the creative possibility of "weaving" something beautiful out of that catastrophe. In Brown's poem the two groups of bodies and voices are ever adjacent, the waters of the Mississippi ever encroaching on the Chicago cabaret. The representation of the cabaret itself as a site of pain is one way in which the poem resists a celebratory, linear narrative of migration.

The voice that insists "still it's my home, sweet home" also "cries out," signaling the ways in which migration is an experience of loss and rupture. Reminding us of the human consequences of social and environmental catastrophe and creatively sounding out a response to that catastrophe, this cry is what Fred Moten would call "blackness," that is, "testament to the fact that objects can and do resist" (*In the Break*, 1). At the end of the poem

> My heart cries out for
> MUDDY WATER
>
> (*Down in the valleys*
> *The stench of the drying mud*
> *Is a bitter reminder of death.*)
>
> Dee da dee DAAAAH (113)

The "moans and deep cries for home" that issue from the "lovely throats" of the dancers are deep not only because of the richness of their longing—whether for "Nashville" or for "Boston"—but because of the pain accompanying their itinerancy and experience of displacement.

The juxtaposition of different voices (nostalgic song lyrics against the dehumanizing voices of history, a voice that mourns the destruction of the floods against another describing the scene in the club) brings into relief the seams between different forms of discourse. The scribal scat that closes the poem draws our attention to the gap between music and voice, voice and page. Even in recorded or performed music, the scat simultaneously marks and attempts to bridge the difference between instrumentality and vocality in that it is a vocalization of instrumental sound. Brown's "Cabaret" maps this tension onto the problem of recording music with the *written* word, drawing attention to the difficulty of transcription with the capital letters of the poem's extended wail: "Dee da dee D A A A A H" (113). Striving and failing to articulate death, the voices in the poem do not harmonize, but death makes itself audible in what we might call a scribal scat—the printed representation of the song's musical improvisation. We cannot read the scatting in the poem as the trifling nostalgia of this banal blues; rather, the scat—if only in its inability to communicate the sound it represents or to find the soft, final consonant "th" of death—sounds the "bitter reminder" of the floods' human effects.

What is perhaps most striking about Brown's representation of music, his homage to the blues "as folk poetry," is not so much his rendering of sound but his incomplete approximation of it. Describing the anthropological "allegory of salvage" that motivated Brown's response to natural disaster, Daphne Lamothe argues that "the almost seamless continuity between the folk culture he observed and the poetry he wrote suggests that Brown's poetry, like an ethnographic narrative, aspired to preserve and transmit the source material" (*Inventing the New Negro*, 92). As Lamothe suggests, there is a sense in which the "natural forces" of catastrophe both literally call for "salvage," and provide the perfect metaphor for the cultural process at work in this moment. Like Lamothe I believe that the floods represent not only a threat to buildings and lives but to culture and community and that poetry constitutes an attempt at preservation.

However, whereas Lamothe turns to the open road as the governing metaphor of the "seamless" relationship between past and present she describes, I maintain that the "cataclysmic change" (92) of catastrophe itself figures both the disruption and the continuity, the aberration and the adaptability, of black cultures.[16] The continuity between folk culture and Brown's poetry is far from "seamless" and far from linear (as the shape of the open road would suggest) but rather bears the marks of its own catastrophic creation. Brown's poetic representation of sound is a process not of transmission or transcription but what Brathwaite calls "approximation," or, as Amiri Baraka (Leroi Jones) puts it in "Look for You Yesterday, Here You Come Today," that "envious blues feeling" (11).

BACKWATER BLUES AND FLOOD TIME

The trope of the hurricane taken up by Brathwaite emphasizes the break, the turn, the interruption of genealogical, agricultural, and social progress, but the 1927 Mississippi River floods to which Bessie Smith and Sterling Brown responded in blues and poetry have a different relationship to time. According to H. C. Frankenfield in the supplement on the floods published by *Monthly Weather Review* in October 1927, rains stretching as far back as the previous year, long-term saturation of the soil, floods of local tributaries, and the unusually high water levels of the Ohio and Mississippi (before the heavy rains of 1927 even began) contributed to the 1927 flood. The "great flood," then, is really a collection of floods, a disaster whose making—cumulative, lengthy, and ongoing— belies its status as an "event" and underscores the continuity of the catastrophic. These two types of meteorological temporality, the continuous and the ruptured, figure the relationship between the pervasive ongoingness of economic disparity and violence in the rural South, on the one hand, and the narrative of social, political, and familial displacement in the black diaspora, on the other. In other words, this ecological structure captures the continuing catastrophe that is the shape of black historical experience.

Continuing catastrophe is close to but not identical with what Rob Nixon, insisting on the ongoing and progressive qualities of environmental violence, describes as "slow violence." Nixon's important work seeks to make visible previously invisible environmental violence and its connections to colonialism, empire, and neoliberalism. He distinguishes this kind of violence from more static "structural violence," emphasizing the "gradual" and slow nature of environmental violence over time, and at the same time posits "slow" ways of living as a kind of antidote. We can confront slow violence, he suggests, only by slowing down. Nixon notices that conversations about gradual environmental violence typically draw on a narrative vocabulary. That is, they expose the absence of narratives to account for slow violence. Nixon concludes:

> To confront slow violence requires, then, that we *plot* and give *figurative shape* to formless threats whose fatal repercussions are dispersed across space and time. The representational challenges are acute, requiring creative ways of drawing public attention to catastrophic acts that are low in instant spectacle but high in long-term effects. To intervene representationally entails devising iconic symbols that embody amorphous calamities as well as narrative forms that infuse those symbols with dramatic urgency. (*Slow Violence and the Environmentalism of the Poor*, 10, emphasis mine)

I agree with Nixon that we can think of the problem of slow violence as a representational one—that is, that our vocabulary for representing the event exceeds our capacity to account for the ordinary. Nixon seeks "narrative forms" to convey "dramatic urgency," and indeed it is possible that emplotment is the most direct method of "drawing public attention." However, by suggesting that what we need is a *story* to "infuse [iconic] symbols with dramatic urgency," Nixon draws on the very narrative structure—linear, climactic, progressive—of the politics of slow violence.[17] Smith's "Back-Water Blues" and Brown's "Ma Rainey" suggest instead that "to intervene representationally" might be to imagine non-narrative forms of experience.

To listen to the flood blues as "the migration narrative of the mass of migrants" or to Brown's poems as an "ethnographic narrative," as Griffin and Lamothe, respectively, invite us to do, is to hear in the story of rain and rising waters another story: of enslavement, disempowerment, lynching, loss, and sometimes escape.[18] It is to recognize environmental catastrophe as linked to social and economic history. But our desire for a story that will hold together "these writhing pieces" in a "chronicle," as Ellison puts it ("Richard Wright's Blues," 79–80), also allows us to elide the extranarrative formal properties of the blues. The central device of the lyrics of "Homeless Blues," for instance, is apostrophe, a characteristically lyric mode of address. And insofar as the addressee—Mississippi River—stands in for the lover only through metaphoric substitution, the lyrics favor poetic equivalence over the narrative causality that would place environmental and social experience in a sequential relationship to one another.

In "Back-Water Blues" the flooding is not an allegory for some other kind of suffering, but the very context and occasion for the story of personal loss. That is, the floods produce both the speaker's homelessness ("'cause my house fell down / and I can't live there no more") and that of the masses, the "thousands of people / Ain't got no place to go."[19] Insofar as the lyrics relate floods and loss through causal sequencing rather than metaphorical substitution, this blues song in particular constitutes a narrative of the masses. However, reading and listening to the song as lyric foregrounds a quality narrative analysis subordinates: the song's attempts at formal mimesis of environmental experience. The lyrics structurally approximate both music and the sensory experience of the floods themselves.

"Back-Water Blues" not only narrates but formally re-creates the experience of the flood, enacting a musical version of what Timothy Morton describes as "ecomimesis," that is, the attempt to bring humans and nature into proximity through writing (*Ecology without Nature*, 31–32). The repetition of the central melodic phrases without break for several verses evokes the relentlessness of the rain, and Smith uses the same phrases to describe environmental and human action: "When it rain five days and the skies turn dark at night" is musically parallel to the start of the next verse, "I woke up this mornin', can't even get out of my door." The voice intersperses personal experience ("I woke up this mornin'") with the description of a catastrophe that affected entire communities so as to equalize, rather than compare, human and nonhuman nature.

One problem with ecomimetic writing according to Morton is its literalism with regard to "nature" and a corresponding anti-aestheticism (60). Another problem he has more recently elaborated is the false "rhetoric of immediacy" of nature writing or ecocritique that assumes a "now" in which we can act authentically (*Hyperobjects*, 92). "Back-Water Blues" instead mediates between the ecological "now" and traumatic events of the past through the vernacular structure of the syntax. As they alternate between general and particular experience, the verses also alternate between a vernacular present tense ("When it rain five days") and a past tense narrative ("I woke up this morning'"). In a particularly powerful gesture, the song shifts its focus from the homelessness of the speaker to that of the community. The speaker describes her experience of displacement in the past tense, having been rescued ("I packed all my clothes"), but the homelessness of "thousands" continues in the present ("There's thousands of people ain't got no place to go"). To the extent that it represents both an individual story of suffering and displacement and the experience of "thousands of people," the song powerfully juxtaposes the loss that can be contained in the past against the collective suffering that persists.

The vernacular grammar of the blues voices the temporality of continuing catastrophe. The lyrics of "Homeless Blues," for example, evoke the social world through the intersection between disruptive and continuous catastrophic time. The second verse underscores that poor living conditions preexist the floods. Describing the speaker's lost home, the stanza emphasizes her poverty ("plain old two-room shanty"), profane existence ("without a steeple") and exposure to the elements ("didn't even have a door"). In light of these conditions, the on-going catastrophe of the speaker's life, how can we understand the repeated, pointed accusation of the next verse: "Mississippi, you to blame"? The speaker's rebuke ("I can't stand to hear your name") ironizes the notion of the blues as a "merely" personal form insofar as the river is more than a lover, the speaker's relationship to it more than romantic. As the repetition of "blame" suggests, Mississippi is at fault in a double sense. The lyrics synecdochally associate the flooded river and the politically and socially restrictive state: the state is "to blame" for the speaker's poverty, the river for her more immediate loss. The AAB blues structure of the repeated line punctured by a singular one under-scores the double temporality of catastrophe as immediate and one-off, on the one hand, and ongoing and repetitive, on the other.

Smith's lyric blues thus cause us to question not just Ellison's formulation of the blues as a narrative of "personal" experience but also as a "chronicle" or narrative of collective experience—to the extent that a chronicle is understood to be an orderly report of events in time.[20] After all, Ellison describes the blues as a *"lyrical"* expression of catastrophe, inviting us to understand the blues as articulating an expanded sense of the lyric subject as collective and as ordering (or disordering) events in time.

CATASTROPHE'S CAESURA: MA RAINEY'S LYRIC TIME

Brown's "Ma Rainey" draws on the rhythm of the floods—their relentless flow-ing coupled with their disruptiveness—to convey the experience of rupture and the ongoing social and environmental forces shaping black culture. Recalling Ma Rainey's performance of her protégé Bessie Smith's "Back-Water Blues," the poem opens with a list of place names along the destructive river's path. Thus the poem would seem to preoccupy itself with movement through southern space that was spurred on by flooding, movement that only underscores the lingering stasis of much of black life in America at the time.[21] But the relationship of the poem "Ma Rainey" to "Back-Water Blues" and its production history invites us to rethink that stasis in relationship to black historicity. The poem depicts catastrophe as a temporal experience that reorganizes the relationships among history, memory and the present.

The flood precipitated a crisis in space, reprising the geographic displacement and immobility that had been imposed by the slave trade and remained characteristic of diasporic experience. The final lines of Bessie Smith's "Back-Water Blues," the song to which Brown refers in "Ma Rainey," bring to the fore this paradox of homelessness and immobility:

'cause my house fell down and I can't live there no more.

Mmmmmmmm I can't move no more,
Mmmmmmmm I can't move no more,
There ain't no place for a poor old girl to go.

The lyrical pause between "I can't live there no more" and "I can't move no more" brings to mind the paradox of constrained mobility that has defined black historical experience in multiple forms across centuries: the enforced, violent transportation of Africans across the middle passage ("I can't live there no more") coupled with imprisonment within the cargo hold ("I can't move"); the sale of enslaved laborers from one plantation to another and attendant separation of families ("I can't live there"), alongside the Fugitive Slave Act designed to keep free and enslaved black people "in their places" ("I can't move"), the rise of industrialism and the need for migrant labor that sent black people on the move for jobs after emancipation ("I can't live there") under the shadow of Jim Crow laws dictating how and where they can sit on a train ("I can't move"), and the homelessness wrought by catastrophe ("I can't live there") up against the planters' control of refugee transportation and labor ("I can't move"). At the same time the hum between these lines, extended in Bessie Smith's recording, constitutes what Nathaniel Mackey calls an "alternate vocality," sounding a "fugitive spirit" (*Paracritical Hinge*, 187, 190). A metrical placeholder, audible when words are not and used to extend the rhythm of the song, the sound voices the tension between enforced mobility and social immobility but also a blues response: the potential for song to *move* and even to *live* where bodies cannot.

The sound of that hum emphasizes the fugitivity of sound in and across time:

across the meter of the song's line, as well as historical time. The song's capacity
to overrun the bounds of its immediate context manifests in its recording history. Like "Muddy Water," the song was recorded before the major flooding of
the Mississippi River and released before the April 1927 levee break in Arkansas
but was heavily marketed by its producers as if a response to the apparently singular event of "the great flood," and became popular as a result of that association.[22] Smith most likely wrote and recorded "Back-Water Blues" in the aftermath of a 1926 Nashville flood of the Cumberland River, which she witnessed
and which likely contributed to the eventual flooding of the Mississippi the following year.[23] Her sister-in-law Maud Smith describes the incident as follows:

> After we left Cincinnati, we came to this little town, which was flooded, so everybody
> had to step off the train into little rowboats that took us to where we were staying.
> It was an undertaker parlor next door to the theater, and we were supposed to stay
> in some rooms they had upstairs there. So after we had put our bags down, Bessie
> looked around and said, "No, no, I can't stay *here* tonight." But there was a lot of other
> people there, and they were trying to get her to stay, so they started hollerin', "Miss
> Bessie, please sing the 'Back Water Blues,' please sing the 'Back Water Blues.'" Well,
> Bessie didn't know anything about any "Back Water Blues," but after we came back
> home to 1926 Christian Street where we were living, Bessie came in the kitchen one
> day, and she had a pencil and paper, and she started singing and writing. That's when
> she wrote the "Back Water Blues"—she got the title from those people down South.
> (qtd. in Alberston, *Bessie*, 146)

In his meticulously researched essay on the origins of the song, musicologist
David Evans clarifies this account and definitively locates the song in the Nashville context. If his motivation is to pin the song down in time and place, the effect of his argument is in fact to demonstrate the song's openness to reuse in
various contexts. Unsurprisingly, for example, the song resurfaced on countless
playlists, news stories, and documentaries in the aftermath of Hurricane Katrina. This recording history indicates the iterability of environmental disaster,
social disaster, and cultural forms alike: the flood is not merely a singular event
with specific individual and historic repercussions. Rather, it has the repetitive,
accumulative structure of the blues. At the same time, the blues have the repetitive, accumulative structure of the floods and of black diasporic experience in
the flood plain. That is to say, as I have argued in chapter 1 with regard to the sonnet, there is no essential relationship between environmental experience, historical experience, and lyrical form. But we can see how varied environmental

experiences shape these forms, their uses, and their circulation in specific historical ways. In the case of the backwater blues, there is a doubly approximate relationship: between the blues and the floods and between the blues poem and the blues. Here I wish to recall the distinction I have made in this chapter between *mimesis* and *approximation*, exemplified in Kamau Brathwaite's description of nation language (poetry that would account for Caribbean environmental experience) not as a blues but as *"like* the blues" (*History of the Voice*, 13).

In Brown's hands, lyric poetry is not a genre apart from history but a genre that disrupts temporal progression even as it "keeps alive the making of the past."[24] Ma's performances take place within an uncertain geography, but they are continuous, as she "hits" like a storm occurring repeatedly along the track of the river. The first two sections of Brown's poem are set in the habitual present; Ma is as unremitting as the floods themselves. A crowd gathers, awaiting a performance by the legendary Ma Rainey:

> Dey stumble in de hall, jes a-laughin' an' a-cacklin',
> Cheerin' lak roarin' water, lak wind in river swamps.

> An' some jokers keeps deir laughs a-goin' in de crowded aisles,
> An' some folks sits dere waitin' wid deir aches an' miseries,
> Till Ma comes out before dem, a-smilin' gold-toofed smiles
> An' Long Boy ripples minors on de black an' yellow keys. (62)

Brown figures the performance as a reenactment of the storm's temporality. The crowd takes on the aural qualities of the storm, "a-cacklin'" and "roarin.'" While ecological disaster detaches folks from the land (the drama of the poem takes place "anywhere's aroun'"), Ma Rainey's performance inspires a different kind of itinerancy. The crowd moves "*when* Ma Rainey / Comes to town," "*when* Ma hits." The *time* of Ma's performance provides the occasion for coming together. The poem establishes Ma's approach and arrival as a performative counterbalance to the "aches an' miseries" of life, a "hit" that borrows the rhythm but transforms the content of the floods. The continuity of black performance in time answers the continuity of black suffering.

Alongside both forms of continuity, Brown's lyric time accounts for their disruption. Brown's necessarily partial transcription of Rainey's performance indicates the significance of discontinuity for a poetics of catastrophe. Kamau Brathwaite calls for a poetry that would *break* the pentameter; we must hear this "break" not only as a geographical departure—from England to the New World—but as a metrical pause, a caesura. In Brown's poem, the lyric voice interrupts the narrative of habitual itinerancy and delays the satisfaction of hearing Ma's song.

> O Ma Rainey
> Sing yo' song;
> Now you's back
> Whah you belong,
> Git way inside us,
> Keep us strong. . . .

> O Ma Rainey,
> Li'l an' low;
> Sing us 'bout de hard luck
> Roun' our do';
> Sing us 'bout de lonesome road
> We mus' go. . . . (62–63)

These brief lines interrupt the rippling abundance of the previous section, leaving behind the historically specific landscape of river settlements for the domain of generalized "hard luck." The three-syllable lines with one or two beats in mostly falling meter indeed "break the pentameter," and the rhymes (song/belong/strong and low/do'/go) decrease the poem's velocity.

We might read the layering of temporalities and voices in "Ma Rainey" as an example of the move toward compression and unity that Sharon Cameron calls the driving impulse of lyric. "The lyric's collective voice," Cameron contends, "or more accurately the voice of its collective moments, bound together as if one, is not equal to a human voice" (*Lyric Time*, 208). But by making the speaking "I" a *self-consciously* plural "we," Brown renders the human audible. The final section of the poem disperses the authority of lyric among Ma Rainey, the singer who voices the experience of the flood, her unnamed protégé, Bessie Smith, who spoke for the people in writing the song, the reporting "fellow" who appears in the final part of the poem, and "de folks" who "bowed dey heads an' cried" (63) at the sound of Ma's blues, creating what Nathaniel Mackey calls a "buzz" of multivocality.[25] We feel the vibration of lyric both in this splitting of voices and in the collection of multiple *moments* "as if" bound, but not entirely bound to one another.

Far from consolidating experience into a "unitary" moment, the narrative structure of the final section, in which we "hear" the lyrics of "Back-Water Blues," draws our attention to the stratifications of time. The poem shifts abruptly from the present tense imperative to a nearly ethnographic narrative in past tense. In this moment, a first-person speaker enters for the first time, then cedes narrative authority to another "source":

> I talked to a fellow an' the fellow say
> "'She jes' catch hold of us, somekindaway.
> She sang Backwater Blues one day." (63)

The temporality of "Ma Rainey" undermines a narrative of cultivation "up from" the past that would seamlessly transform the suffering of slavery into modern literary sensibility. But it does not deny history. When the "fellow" then cites the lyrics of Bessie Smith's "Back-Water Blues," he evokes the collective and personal histories of the floods captured in the present of the performance. The terse final couplet omits the blues repetition of the first line, creating a caesura between the fellow's narrative and the "ethnographer's" conclusion: "Dere wasn't much more de fellow say: / She jes gits hold of us dataway" (62). The fellow's vernacular past tense ("She jes catch hold of us") becomes the present tense of the poem ("She jes' gits hold of us"). Speaker and fellow, past and present, collide within this break from narrative and history. Various pasts—the great flood, the violent history of the Mississippi River, the "one day" in which Ma Rainey "sang," and the moment in which the speaker "talked to a fellow"— hum beneath the present tense of shared cultural experience.

The fugitive temporality of "Ma Rainey" draws on and contributes to the making of a diasporic poetic tradition, which is what invites us to read Brown's poetics of catastrophe alongside Brathwaite's. Although the poem begins with place names, it concludes by pointing "dataway," not toward a place but toward a *memory*. With this closing gesture, the event of Ma's performance—and the long-ago catastrophic memory of slavery it evokes—displaces the particularity of the Greenville floods and invites us to dwell instead in "crisis ordinariness" (Berlant, 10). The poem's answer to the geographic problem of diaspora is to reside in the time of song, in the caesura of lyric time.

When the poem closes, we become privy to a textual recording of Ma Rainey singing her protégé's powerful song. At the same time, we are aware that we have not experienced that which the poem describes; we have not been taken hold of "dataway." There is a missing line that would—but, of course, cannot— convey the meaning and essence of the "Back-Water Blues," and Brown's poem resists that satisfaction. If natural catastrophe has the capacity to destroy communities and cultures, to displace folks from their homes and histories, and to echo the violent displacements *of* history, then Brown's response is not so much to advocate a process of "salvage," in which a dying culture of the past is pre-served and categorized, as to write into being a process of memory.

CATASTROPHIC MEMORY

Joseph Roach compellingly depicts catastrophe (and here he means not neces-sarily environmental disaster but any form of destruction, calamity, or "down-ward turning" in dramatic performance) as a structure of memory holding the past and the future in relation. "The choreography of catastrophic closure," he writes, "offers a way of imagining what must come next, as well as what has al-ready happened. Under the seductive linearity of its influence, memory oper-ates as an alternation between retrospection and anticipation that is itself, for better or worse, a work of art" (*Cities of the Dead*, 33). Roach offers an appealing model for understanding how memory in "Ma Rainey" negotiates the relation-ship between past and future. But must this relationship always be defined by its linearity and inevitability? Can catastrophe offer a way of imagining not "what *must* come next" but what *might* come next?

Roach draws a strong contrast between what he calls "the linear narrative of catastrophe" characteristic of Western tragic drama, on the one hand, and, on the other, spirit-world rituals that "tend to place catastrophe in the past, as a grief to be expiated, and not necessarily in the future, as a singular fate yet to be endured." In the future, in the circumatlantic performances Roach describes, celebration and affirmation may replace violent closure owing to the sense of continuity with the ancestors, the sense of dynamic relation to the dead. "In such circumstances, memory circulates and migrates like gossip from location to location as well as from generation to generation, growing or attenuating as it passes through the hands of those who possess it and those whom it pos-sesses" (35). Roach describes a kind of memory exempt from the "seductive lin-earity" of fate (which Roach seems to regard as the same as "the choreography of catastrophic closure"), a kind of memory in which the past is transformed or even transcended through processes of circulation, allowing for the agency not of catastrophe itself but of the people who experience and survive it and in whose hands it is transformed.

Memory operates in just this way in Sterling Brown's "Ma Rainey," but not because the grief of catastrophe has been safely compartmentalized in the past. On the contrary, the catastrophic floods are an experience defined in part by their continuity. At the same time, however, the catastrophic is not *fate* in Brown's poems; the past does not determine or enclose the future in quite the linear way that Roach attributes to Western tragedy. Rather, the structure of environmental catastrophe—repetitive, migratory, circulatory, transformative, dispersive, and connecting—itself provides the aesthetic alternative to teleological narrative.

Sterling Brown has often been understood as a poet particularly rooted in the idiom of the U.S. South. The title *Southern Road* is the most explicit indication of Brown's self-conscious artistic identification with a particular geography, an identification he underscores in his commitment to representing the South—and particularly the black South—in the prose writings he undertook during his time at Atlanta University.[26] Unlike his contemporaries Claude McKay, Langston Hughes, and Zora Neale Hurston, he did not travel beyond the borders of the United States in his search for folk materials, and he is often understood as a "rooted" poet rather than a diasporic one. It should come as no surprise, then, that "Ma Rainey" was first published in B. A. Botkin's anthology *Folk-Say: A Regional Miscellany*. By positioning Brown's flood poems in the context of Roach's theory of circumatlantic cultural production and Brathwaite's theory of diasporic poetic language, however, I hope to have displaced these poems at least partially from the theory and practice of what B. A. Botkin describes as American folk culture. In the following chapter I turn to Brown's contemporary Zora Neale Hurston, whose account of environmental catastrophe more explicitly disrupts the U.S.-based North-South axis of the "Southern Road" and who assembles a dynamic sonic archive through her ethnographic writings and in the pages of her novel *Their Eyes Were Watching God*.

five

Collecting Catastrophe
How the Hurricane Roars in Zora Neale Hurston's
Their Eyes Were Watching God

THE REELS OF CULTURE

Having traveled to the Bahamas to collect stories, song, and dance, a body of artistic production she describes as especially varied and vital, novelist, playwright, folklorist, and anthropologist Zora Neale Hurston lived through a hurricane, which hit Nassau in 1929 and killed a relatively small number of Bahamians but devastated the industry and agriculture of the island.[1] In her memoir *Dust Tracks on the Road* Hurston remarks that the Nassau hurricane lasted five days and was "horrible in its intensity and duration" (690).

Her experiences of the hurricane and of her musical work are inextricable in her accounts. A few weeks after returning to Florida from the Bahamas in the fall of 1929, she described the Bahamian hurricane in a letter to her friend Langston Hughes. She worried not only that she might not survive but also that she might lose the work she had been doing, "for I had just collected 20 marvelous Bahamian songs and learned the two native folk dances, and gotten a Congo drum (called GimBAY, accent on the last syllable) for us. That would be terrible to miss bringing back now wouldn't it. I got 3 reels of the dancing too" (*Zora Neale Hurston*, 148). Hurston perceived the storm as a potential threat to the circulation of cultural materials in a way that anticipates, for instance, the tremendous anxiety about literary and cultural archives in Haiti after the 2010 earthquake. In Hurston's formulation, nature is a purely menacing force threatening to overtake culture. Hurston would later dramatize this menace in her novel *Their Eyes Were Watching God* (1937), in which she describes a different hurricane as a "senseless monster" (158) threatening the lives and livelihood of the people.

What is striking, however, in Hurston's recollection of the Nassau hurricane, is the way she describes her experience of the storm and her musical collection in a single breath, suggesting a greater intimacy between nature and culture than at first appears. As much as she values her own life and mobility, she values equally the materials of a black folk culture she alternately describes as vanishing or as robust and dynamic. Further, her representations and transformations of that culture are part and parcel of the intensity and duration of a five-day hurricane. In what follows I contend that Hurston's musical recordings (as well as those collected by her counterparts and sometime-traveling companions, Alan Lomax and Mary Elizabeth Barnicle) illuminate the interconnection between environmental and social catastrophe in Hurston's most well-known novel.

Storms and sounds alike, informed by Hurston's practice of collecting and recording music, transform the narrative structure of *Their Eyes Were Watching God.* The need to account for the extreme environmental experience of a hurricane leads to the irruption of lyric within the novel and also points to the immense challenge of transcribing, recording, and finally responding to nature. If Sterling Brown's poetic responses to disaster collect and juxtapose multiple voices and performances that remain unassimilated within the form of the poem, the presence of music in Hurston's novel enacts a transformative response to racial violence. As we shall see, the hurricane causes the environmental violence at stake in the novel, but at times it also figures and continues the violences of enslavement and Jim Crow—that is, the catastrophic consequences of enforced cultivation.

In Hurston's hands environmental catastrophe does not parallel the south-north migrations of U.S. blacks but rather figures diasporic movement and diasporic consciousness. Hurston's engagement with transnational, circumatlantic black musical folk culture lends its shape to her fictionalized representation of the Florida hurricane of 1928. We might read Hurston's novel as a collection rather than an historical narrative. Specifically, we might hear the storm sequence in *Their Eyes* as a *reel,* a collection of aural and lyrical experiences, alternately mimetic and fractured in relation to the environmental experience of the hurricanes.

GETTING A RHYTHM

As chapter 4 suggests, destructive environmental experiences may have threatened black culture, but they also occasioned its production. The floods were not unique in this respect, and the hurricanes that inspired *Their Eyes Were Watching God* likewise produced a musical response. While the 1929 Bahamas hurricane is one historical precursor to the literary storm in *Their Eyes Were Watching God,* we can draw a more obvious connection with the massive Florida hurricane of 1928, one of the deadliest Atlantic hurricanes in history, which left approximately three thousand people dead in Puerto Rico and Florida. Although

the reporter for the *Monthly Weather Review* for September 1928 called the hurricane the "West Indian Hurricane of September 10–20, 1928," reminding us of its
archipelagic path, its greatest damage to lives and property was along the Florida coast, where waters from the storm flooded Lake Okeechobee, resulting in
massive destruction.[2] In 1935, in the field with Alan Lomax and Mary Elizabeth
Barnicle, Hurston collected a song recounting the experience of the Florida hurricane, "God Rode on a Mighty Storm," performed in 1935 by Lila Mae Atkinson
in Georgia. This recording is part of a body of music responding to the Florida
hurricane, songs that collectively extend the time of the hurricane, creating a
sense of what in chapter 4 I call "continuing catastrophe."[3]

"God Rode on a Mighty Storm" structures catastrophe not so much as an
event as a repetition. As is fairly standard among the folk ballads recorded by
Hurston and others during this period, alternating verses unfold a narrative
while the chorus interrupts the narrative and repeats a lament. In this case, the
song's first gesture is to establish the date of the hurricane:

> Sixteenth day of September,
> Nineteen twenty-eight,
> God started to riding early,
> And He rode until very late.

> [Chorus:] Oh, in that storm,
> Ohhhh, in that storm,
> Lord, somebody got drownd-ed
> In that storm.

The first verse establishes a characteristic tension between the nonspecific
divine temporality of "early" and "late" and the precise time of the event, mir-
roring a similar juxtaposition between the general dead "somebody" and the
deictically defined "that storm" of the chorus. Fixing the date of the hurricane is
a common feature among other folk musical responses to the storm recorded
during the same period, held in the archives at the Library of Congress American Folklife Center: "In That Storm," attributed to "George Washington and
group of Negro convicts" (collected by John A. Lomax), and "The West Palm
Beach Storm," sung by Viola Jenkins (whose lyrics are almost identical to those
of "God Rode on a Mighty Storm"). The precision of the dating within all of the
songs (and the precision and slow pace with which the singers unfold the dates
within the rhythm) establishes the significance of the single moment, the static
event within history.

These songs thus differ in two important respects from the blues responses to the Mississippi river floods. First, whereas Bessie Smith's blues circulated widely and popularly through both performance and media, recorded by Columbia, a major record label, the spirituals and other songs discussed in this chapter at least initially circulated informally in the mode of what Amiri Baraka (LeRoi Jones) would later describe as "primitive or country blues," through the increased mobility afforded (and made necessary for) black laborers after emancipation (*Blues People*, 69, 61–65). With one notable exception, folklorists rather than record producers recorded these songs. Second, whereas the popularity and profitability of "Muddy Water" and "Back-Water Blues" depended in part on the temporal ambiguity and situational interchangeability of historical context, the Florida hurricane songs make a point of situating themselves in a particular time and place. Even though they were written and performed in the late 1920s, the hurricane songs that influenced Hurston embody what Jones describes as the remarkably "personal nature" that characterized the early blues, a product of "what can be called the Negro's 'American Experience.'" (66). The circulation of these two different musical archives of disaster suggest two different ways of understanding catastrophic environmental experience: as specific, local, and regionally produced and as flexible, dynamic, and abstracted. Taken together, these methods of listening to disaster music also describe the central tension in defining diaspora that has shaped this book, that between the desire for rootedness and growth (cultivation), on the one hand, and the fact of rupture and discrepancy (catastrophe), on the other. Listening to the storm reel requires us to attend to and compare particular regional and local differences among different parts of the black world while also noticing the ways that diasporic cultural experience is shared, iterative, and dynamic.

Even though these songs were seemingly local Florida hurricane songs, for almost a decade after the hurricane they appeared in different locales in Florida and Georgia, where they were sung in male and female voices and in solo and ensemble performances and transmitted through oral repetition and recording as well as print transcription and notation. Their utility in and resonance through a variety of contexts and over time underscores their expression of a collective experience. In Washington's version, the date of the hurricane "On the sixteenth day of September / In nineteen twenty-eight" echoes the rhythm of an earlier date in a previous verse "in nineteen hundred and fourteen / That World War begun." God's motion on the water thus echoes "a awful battle" in which "no nations won." Washington's voice rises up in the penultimate stanza of the song, just as the quartet accompanying him seems to be drawing the melody to a close, pushing toward the final verse as if to emphasize the relentlessness of the storm beyond its time and place, into the era of "this mighty depression," which, of course, began a year after the storm and would continue beyond the moment of the song's recording. Washington's recording thus crucially connects war, environmental destruction, and poverty, destabilizing the hurricane's status as a singular catastrophe. Recorded in 1936, eight years after the Florida hurricane, the performance is a work of memory but at the same time a reflection on contemporary struggles. The tension produced between the repetitive forward motion of Washington's lead voice and the impulse toward closure conveyed by the chorus accounts for the particularity and the universality of the storm and suggests more broadly the need for simultaneous methods of relating, musically, to history.

It is not only on the level of lyric and performance but on the level of technology that the sounds of the hurricane remain suspended between catastrophe's historical particularity, on the one hand, and its availability to the present, on the other. Listening to the Lila Mae Atkinson rendition of the song, recorded by Hurston and stored on reels at the Library of Congress, I hear a similar historical process unfolding in a different register. The poor condition of the recording renders some of the lyrics inaudible and also yields skips where already there is repetition; the shifts between the harmonizing chorus and Lila Mae's voice are thus often unduly abrupt, and one is hard pressed to determine when the chorus comes to a close. Half way through the recording one such skip indefinitely delays the closing of the chorus. The chorus repeats twice, with increasing volume and urgency, the second time beginning with a call and response structure, but it sticks on the final line.

Ohh in that storm,
Ohh in that storm,
Lord somebody got drownded
In that storm.

[LMA:] Ohh in that storm,
[CHORUS:] Ohh in that storm,
Ohh in that storm,
[Together:] Ohhh somebody got drownded
In that, in that, in that, in that, in that—

The recording cuts abruptly to Lila Mae Atkinson's solo voice in the next verse. Time and material deterioration prevent the chorus from arriving home, from repeating or concluding the storm, from pointing to the "that" which is the song's referent. The remaining two minutes of the recording are similarly fuzzy, inaccessible und unintentionally repetitive.

These songs raise the question not only of how to account for and respond to extreme environmental experience in words and music but also of how to account for historical disjunction and distance in attempts to preserve and record the sounds of continuing catastrophe. If, as I have already contended in my reading of Sterling Brown's poetry and as Alexander G. Weheliye has more broadly suggested, "African American literature bridges the divide between the sonic and the graphic in the realm of textuality" (*Phonographies*, 39), then its recordings of history are catastrophic. In his essay on the work of transcription in James Weldon Johnson's poetic preferences, Brent Hayes Edwards briefly asks what would happen if we listened to the "unheard or inaccessible music" in *Their Eyes Were Watching God*, referring to the singing of nature in an early lyrical scene describing the novel's protagonist, Janie, beneath a pear tree ("The Seemingly Eclipsed Window of Form," 581). In taking Edwards up on this as-yet unrealized invitation, I want to suggest further that we must ask how the "new form of sonic blackness" (*Phonographies*, 39) made possible by the recording technology Hurston used formally shapes her fictional narrative of environmental catastrophe.

Given Hurston's attention to Bahamian music making within the Floridian context in *Their Eyes*, it should come as no surprise that the tradition of musical response to catastrophe, too, circulated among the locations affected by catastrophic weather. There is a marked formal likeness, for instance, between "God Rode on a Mighty Storm" and "Pytoria," a musical account of the 1929 storm that Hurston herself lived through in the Bahamas. Thought to have been composed by John Roberts, a singer from Andros, most likely in the aftermath of the 1929 Bahamian hurricane, "Pytoria" was made popular as "Run, Come See Jerusalem" in the Bahamas by Nassau tourist entertainer "Blind Blake" Higgs and in the United States by the Weavers, the Highwaymen, Odetta and Larry Mohr, and Arlo Guthrie.[4] Like "God Rode on a Mighty Storm" and the other Florida hurricane songs recorded in the 1930s, "Pytoria" begins by spelling out the date of the event it recounts: "It was nineteen hundred and twenty-nine / run come see." Odetta and Mohr's version underscores the significance of the year by adding the refrain: "It was nineteen hundred and twenty-nine / Run Come See, I remember that day pretty well." Notably, however, the song was recorded and performed at least into the 1960s, transformed from a mournful folk tune into a curiously jolly tourist calypso and eventually (in both John Roberts's and Odetta's versions) back again. The song traveled across both time and space, speaking beyond the local context of its composition.

In "Run, Come See Jerusalem" the 1929 storm becomes a figure for the displacements of the slave trade and their afterlife in twentieth-century diasporic consciousness. The song's concluding narrative of bodies drowning at sea powerfully evokes the earlier history of the middle passage, especially in the context of the prolonged, mournful recording of American civil rights icon Odetta: "There were thirty-three souls on the water (run come see, run come see) / Swimming and praying to their Daniel, God." As Larry Mohr intones the refrain ("run come see"), Odetta sings the second line of the verse simultaneously, building the intensity of the song in preparation for the increased tempo of the next repetition of the chorus. Whether the souls are in the water or on the water remains ambiguous in this rendition, but the overlapping voices attest to the vitality of the souls in the moment of the bodies' drowning. The number "thirty-three" suggests a spiritual context for understanding both death and survival, that being the age of Jesus when he was crucified, even as Odetta's recording in other ways secularizes the message of theological hope emphasized in earlier versions. In this case, as with the Florida storm songs, catastrophe demands to be historicized even as it resists temporal and geographic compartmentalization. "The horrible . . . intensity and duration" (*Dust on the Tracks*, 690) of that storm through which Hurston lived stretches both forward to the civil rights movement and backward to the middle passage and calls for a poetics that can contain and give shape to that long moment.

WRITING THE HURRICANE

Their Eyes Were Watching God embodies the tension between the historical experience of violence and disruption and expressive possibilities for containing and countering that experience. The novel establishes itself as a coming-of-age narrative, unfolding the sexual and social development of its protagonist, Janie, as "a great tree in leaf" (8). After following Janie through two miserable marriages, we find her finally more or less happy with her third husband Tea Cake, with whom she has made a life as part of a community of workers picking beans in the Florida Everglades. But just as that community has begun to take shape, their lives are dramatically altered by a forceful hurricane. The hurricane marks a shift in the narrative structure, evoking both the physical horrors of the middle passage and the indignities of Jim Crow racism. After the storm, "Corpses were not just found in wrecked houses. They were under houses, tangled in shrubbery, floating in water, hanging in trees, drifting under wreckage. . . . Some bodies fully dressed, some naked and some in all degrees of dishevelment" (162). In a novel famously condemned by Richard Wright as having "no theme, no message, no thought" ("Between Laughter and Tears," 25–26), Hurston's words perhaps surprisingly bring to mind the cargo holds of slavers, the waters of the middle passage, Jim Crow lynchings, and the range of physical and social deaths befalling slaves and their descendants. Indeed, these images also deeply resonate with Wright's own symbolic landscape of corpses in another flood story, his "Down By the Riverside." But the storm is not merely an allegory for history; Hurston further reveals how the human practices around the storm emerge from and continue that history. The most obvious example of this continuity between environmental and human violence are the Jim Crow burials that famously took place after the 1928 Florida hurricane, to which Hurston refers when Tea Cake, conscripted into labor after the storm, is instructed to bury the black dead in mass graves and the white dead in coffins (and to distinguish the bodies by their hair): "'They's mighty particular how dese dead folks goes tuh judgement,' Tea Cake observed to the man working next to him. 'Look lak dey think God don't know nothin' 'bout de Jim Crow law'" (171). Tea Cake's remark is ironic, given that both propositions at stake—that people need to be identified racially to God or that God *knows* race—are ridiculous. But his words also resonate with his more earnest expressions of the unshakeability of the racial social order. Before the hurricane, for example, he rejects the Seminoles' departure as a sign that a storm is coming, on the grounds that "de White folks ain't gone nowhere. Dey oughta know if it's dangerous" (156). The scene of the Jim Crow burials, which more closely resembles Wright's social realism than anything else in Hurston's novel, demonstrates the pervasiveness of Jim Crow in the white supremacy of the guards and the strength of the racist social order even after death.

This twentieth-century experience of destruction and displacement, rather than a mimetic claim to a particular meteorological phenomenon, constitutes "environmental experience" in *Their Eyes*. Hurston's depiction of the relationships between American and Bahamian workers, alongside the historical reference to the hurricane, brings into relief the reality of workers' lives.[5] Hurston also represents the flood's environmental damage as a product of ongoing "anthropogenic disturbance," as Susan Scott Parrish has brilliantly demonstrated by drawing our attention to the history of Lake Okeechobee drainage (for the purposes of establishing a ground for monocultural production) that preceded the hurricane ("Zora Neale Hurston and the Environmental Ethic of Risk," 35). By foregrounding "disturbance," Parrish emphasizes the context of risk and violence for black ecological thought, arguing that blacks' agricultural labor actu-

ally makes them the *means* of environmental catastrophe as well as the dispro-
portionate sufferers of its consequences. Parrish rightly insists on the necessity
of a material, historical framework for understanding the way physical and anthropogenic "risk" are connected in *Their Eyes Were Watching God.* But I am
equally interested in the resources Hurston finds for countering or reimagining
that disturbance which I have been calling "catastrophe." To reconcile the destructive aspects of cultivation with the novel's emphasis on love, community,
and continuity it is necessary to recognize the way the novel moves between
symbolic and historical frameworks. By understanding cultivation and catastrophe in both senses—the metaphorical and the metonymic—we can lay claim to
Hurston's environmental ethos for the present. Through the hurricane sequence,
Hurston's novel offers a twentieth-century rehearsal of slavery's destruction
of individual bodies, social organization, culture, and the environment.[6] But
the novel also attempts—in words I'm borrowing from Brathwaite—to "get a
rhythm," creating a reimagined poetics to account for "ourselves, the networks
of us" (*History of the Voice*, 10).

Hurston's sound recordings and performances are the basis for the novel's
dramatic shift from narrative to lyric time. In chapter 4 I describe the caesura
in Brown's poetry as marking one characteristic temporality of lyric poetry, allowing for the compression of history within the poetic imagination. Listening
"in the break" to Hurston's novel we hear a different catastrophic sound: the
catastrophic chronotope in which description of violence emerges.[7] The events
that unfold after the hurricane—Tea Cake's forced conscription into labor, Jim
Crow funerals, and the subsequent violent end of Janie and Tea Cake's love and
marriage—link the terror of environmental disaster to the racial terror of the
southern United States. But in its aural presence as diasporic sound the hurricane also occasions a rhythmic, transformative response to that terror. By "description" I mean something other than representation or that which can be reduced to an account of events. Following Fred Moten, I mean rather description
in the sense of improvisation, that which allows us to hear the diasporic ensemble that plays, listens to, and watches the storm in *Their Eyes Were Watching God,*
interrupting the novel's progress toward catastrophic closure.[8]

The structure of the novel parallels cultivation, the growth of individual subjectivity, and ideas of linear progress, insofar as the development of productive
agricultural labor and of Janie's romantic life are its twin narrative arcs. Janie's
cultivation, from her sexual awakening "under a blossoming pear tree" where
"the inaudible voice of it all came to her" (10) to her love-filled married life in
which she engages in productive agricultural labor beside her husband among

"big beans, big cane, big weeds, big everything" (123), parallels the novel's traversing of generic boundaries from romance to realism.[9]

The hurricane interrupts the temporal economy of cultivation and of narrative by suspending the main story of Janie's romantic and subjective development, as well as the agricultural production of the laborers in the muck. As Tea Cake puts it, "You couldn't have a hurricane when you're making seven and eight dollars a day picking beans" (155). But quickly, "the time of dying was over. It was time to bury the dead" (168). Dispersal and death displace the economy of the laborers. In this sense the hurricane is like the drumming that Janie first comes upon during a break in the agricultural season:

> The season closed and people went away like they had come—in droves. Tea Cake and Janie decided to stay since they wanted to make another season on the muck. There was nothing to do, after they had gathered several bushels of dried beans to save over and sell to be planted in the fall. So Janie began to look around and see people and things she hadn't noticed during the season.
>
> For instance, during the summer when she heard the subtle but compelling rhythms of the Bahaman drummers, she'd walk over and watch the dances. She did not laugh the "Saws" to scorn as she had heard people doing in the season. (139)

The hurricane simultaneously disrupts this rhythm and the economy of human labor on the muck and figures the already erratic lives of the workers. Its narration demands a rethinking of time that the copresence of sound and lyric make possible.

The hurricane and music enter the novel not merely diegetically but as interdependent formal presences that shape its structure. Hurston depicts the hurricane as an event to be interpreted aurally. When Janie sees the Seminoles "headed toward the Palm Beach Road," she inquires as to their direction. They reply, "Going to high ground. Saw-grass bloom. Hurricane coming" (150). These lines have the compressed rhythmic economy of a poem, linking the present progressive movement of the people ("going") and the storm ("coming") with the natural sign of the impending catastrophe ("saw-grass bloom"). The temporality of the Seminole "poem," then, is suspended, lyric, and yet signals the grand historic proportions that juxtapose progressive natural time and human history. We can understand *people going* and *storms coming* as a re-creation of diasporic experience, especially when we consider the path of an Atlantic hurricane, forming off the cost of West Africa and making land fall in the Caribbean and the United States.

This scene of transnational cultural production sets the stage for the impending disaster and, more importantly, establishes its beat. On the night of Janie's encounter with the Seminoles, "the fire dance kept up till nearly dawn. The next day, more Indians moved east, unhurried but steady. . . . Another night of Stew Beef making dynamic subtleties with his drum and living, sculptural grotesques in the dance" (147). The scene juxtaposes the "unhurried but steady" movements of both people and storm against a description of Stew Beef, one of the Bahamian workers, playing his drum for the community. Bahamian music and dance is the continuous, "unhurried but steady" rhythm of daily life on the muck, keeping "dynamic . . . living" time, against which, it seems, the hurricane's "time of dying" will emerge.

While the beginning of the chapter moves through three days in a page and a half, the rest of the chapter simultaneously constitutes a single day and a lifetime: "It was the next day by the sun and the clock when they reached Palm Beach. It was years later by their bodies. Winters and winters of hardship and suffering" (158). Here, in what Homi Bhabha might call "a temporal break or caesura effected in the continuist, progressivist myth of Man" (*The Location of Culture*, 340), narrative time departs from natural time, disjoining the suffering of the storm from any possible claims to "natural" or essential experience. This caesura, this new thinking of history, is embodied in the lyric.

By emphasizing how the hurricane "stops time" I do not mean to suggest, as Hazel Carby and others have, that the novel creates an ahistorical community.[10] Leigh Anne Duck calls the novel "allotemporal" (*The Nation's Region*, 123), that is, constructed in private chronotopes removed from national and economic frameworks, and Hortense Spillers emphasizes the "notion of eternal order" rooted "in the organic, metaphorical structure through which Hurston manipulates her characters" (*Black, White, and in Color*, 104). For Spillers, the first half of the novel compensates for its "ahistorical, specifically rustic, image clusters," its "timeless current" through "psychic specificity," a specificity, Spillers argues, that Hurston fails to pursue after the flood, passing on the opportunity to represent a "postdiluvial" "crack in the mental surface of character" (108) The crack in the novel is, I would argue, narrative and structural rather than characterological (109). Indeed, it is precisely through the shift away from "self-realization" or interior development that the novel engages the communal and the historical. I agree with Martyn Bone that the Bahamian workers and the hurricane sequence alike signify the presence of "history" in an expanded sense in *Their Eyes*.[11] I wish to move beyond rehistoricizing the novel, however, and to identify its poetics within a diasporic tradition. The hurricane's stopped time formally disrupts the romantic narrative that highlights the development of individual consciousness, foregrounding instead the connections among narrative, history, and violence. To what extent, the novel invites us to ask in that pause, might it be possible to read "stopped time" as engaged with the past even as it fractures and disrupts history?

A SOUND PROPOSAL

Hurston's work as a collector and producer of sound offers one approach to this question. Listening to the music Hurston recorded, performed, and transcribed invites us to revise existing theories of her literary vernacular to take into account not only the preoccupation with oral narration that has dominated Hurston scholarship for two decades, "the emulation of the phonetic, grammatical, and lexical structures of mimetic speech" famously described by Henry Louis Gates Jr. as "the speakerly text" (*The Signifying Monkey*, 196), but also those rhythms in Hurston that exceed speech.[12] An increasingly significant body of research explores the relationship between Hurston's ethnography and her literary imagination, but none explains in depth how Hurston's work as a performer and collector of music in particular might inform our understanding of the rhythms, structure, and language of her most famous novel.[13]

Hurston herself proposed listening to music as one particularly rich way of gaining access to the diverse cultures of Florida, Hurston's home state, the "field" for much of her anthropological research, and the landscape in which *Their Eyes Were Watching God* unfolds. In the waning days of the Federal Writers' Project, Hurston submitted a grant application for musical research in Florida to Carita Corse, the state director for Florida, who in turn submitted the proposal to Henry G. Alsberg (Federal Writers' Project director) and B. A. Botkin (director of the state guides project). A generically heterogenous document, "Proposed Recording Expedition into the Floridas" (1939) simultaneously undertakes and proposes the recording of sound and geography. The document is itself a kind of "recording" insofar as it collects that which has been produced, heard, witnessed, and recorded in other forms and saves the lyrics of Florida songs for posterity, even as it "proposes" doing so more extensively in the future. By the time Hurston wrote "Proposed Recording Expedition" she had been collecting music and dance for over a decade, so much of what is "proposed" here was already under way. Hurston grew up in Eatonville, Florida, and went to school in Jacksonville. The places of her childhood figure significantly in her literary and anthropological work, so we might think of her as having been on this expedition from the beginning. As a teenager she toured as a maid with a Gilbert and Sullivan troupe and as a Barnard undergraduate under the tutelage of mentor Franz Boas she conducted anthropological research in her native Eatonville, and later the Bahamas in 1929. In 1935 Hurston traveled throughout the U.S. South with Alan Lomax and Mary Elizabeth Barnicle recording for the Library of Congress, and by the late thirties she was working for the Federal Writers' Project state guides project in Florida and conducting extensive research in both Jamaica and Haiti through a Guggenheim grant. "Proposed Recording Expedition" thus not only charts out a path for work to be done but signals the literal and literary reels Hurston has already recorded, reminding us of the interplay between the forms of recording that make up Hurston's oeuvre.

"Proposed Recording Expedition" borrows from the lexicons and rhetoric of a range of discourses and genres, mingling song lyrics and geographic descriptions with ethnographic analysis. The proposal also structurally reflects the hurricane sequence in *Their Eyes*; in both cases, musical and lyrical forms interrupt the prose form. Each section of the proposal is devoted to a specific region of Florida and begins with a song lyric as an epigraph, evoking but not repeating the doubleness of the musical and lyrical epigraphs of Du Bois's *Souls of Black Folk*. Following the epigraph, the prose describes the region's borders and offers an overview of its agricultural products and industry. Additionally, Hurston outlines the cultural characteristics of each region and the types of music and stories likely to be found there. In her description of west Florida, for example, she observes that it "is the cotton-corn-tobacco region. Here people live under the patriarchal agrarian system. The old rules of life hold here. Down the Gulf Coast of this section are large fishing and oyster settlements with their songs and traditions. West Florida is a very rich and little touched area. It is worth an expedition in itself. In addition to the purely cultural material to be found it is possible to make recordings that bear on the economic and sociological set-up of the area" (1–2). The geographical, economic, sociological, and cultural seem impossible to disentangle. Sometimes lyrics also emerge not only as epigraphs but in the middle of a section, as when Hurston offers a chant in the second section. To some extent, then, "Proposed Recording Expedition" is a kind of musical baedeker, suggesting the deep intimacy between place and recording for Hurston's work. But it is a baedeker that is likely to get you lost, switchbacking as it does through a dense geographical and cultural landscape.

If the narrative prose of *Their Eyes Were Watching God* cannot contain the hurricane, the argumentative prose of Hurston's grant proposal cannot contain the racial violence and terror that haunts it from the outset. We hear this violence in the opening epigraph, an excerpt from a rhythmically awkward ballad lyric spoken in the voice of a rifle-toting man hunter in search of a black victim:

"Got my knap-sack on my back
My rifle on my shoulder
Kill me a nigger 'fore Saturday Night
If I have to hunt Flordy over." (1)

Without overstating the link between environmental and human violence, I want to suggest that for Hurston these two types of terror engender similar methodological problems. In a proposal that apparently celebrates Florida's cultural richness, what can we make of the violent image offered in the first lyric epigraph? We are aware, at the very least, that the expedition Hurston proposes here is far from sound—in the sense of "safe"—for her to undertake.

Nonetheless, through the epigraphs and other lyric insertions in the document Hurston transforms the depiction of southern racial violence into lyric prayer. In the last sentence of each of the first three area descriptions, Hurston offers the same piece of advice to Florida's would-be ethnographers: she recommends "a serious study of blank verse in the form of traditional sermons and prayers" in the first section (2), and reiterates the suggestion twice as a command to "look for the roots of traditional sermons and prayers" (4) in the second and to "look for fine examples of those folk poems in blank verse known as sermons and prayers" (4) in the third.

Throughout the proposal, however, Hurston frustrates this order. She tells us to look for "folk poems in blank verse known as sermons and prayers," evoking three generic categories whose boundaries are already difficult to draw, but produces instead railroad songs, chants, and blues. For instance, following her second suggestion to "look for the roots of traditional sermons and prayers" at the end of the second section (4), she opens the third with two blues epigraphs (from two different songs attributed to the same singer, Richard Jenkins of Mulberry, Florida). The first are lines from a highly sexualized blues lyric:

I got a woman, she shake like jelly all over
I got a woman, she shake like jelly all over
Her hips so broad, Lawd, Lawd her hips so broad. (4)

The second epigraph comes from a different song. It describes an indeterminate scene of grief and loss that comes from hearing the song "Po' Lazaraus" about a levy worker who disrupts the camp, steals money, and is chased by the sheriffs. Out of context this second epigraph reads as a scene of crucifixion, or lynching, or both.

> And they found him, found him in between two mountains,
> And they found him, found him in between two mountains,
> With head hung down, Lawd, Lawd, with head hung down.

The epigraphs share a parallel blues structure, down to the shared apostrophe "Lawd, Lawd." Together, they invite us to hear a range of emotional and physical experiences in the song form as something Hurston's topographical prose, even as it describes the geography that produces this poetics, cannot contain or express.

The journey Hurston takes us on, then, is not only a geographic journey from area to area, but a call for a reparative poetry that can encompass the diffuse experiences of violence, sexual longing, and prayer. The tangled path by which Hurston guides us underscores the great difficulty of this task. The summary section finally answers the call for prayer, for the proposal ends with a "sanctified anthem" that is followed by Hurston's closing, "respectfully submitted":

> O Lord, O Lord
> Let the words of my mouth, O Lord
> Let the words of my mouth, meditations of my heart
> Be accepted in Thy sight, O Lord. (7)

Here, those other lyrics—terrifying, lusty, hard-working, and heavy with grief—become "the words of *my* mouth." That is, they emanate from the voice of the writing subject who is Zora Neale Hurston. The anthem is Psalm 19, which Hurston curiously attributes to a particular singer, Mrs. Orrie Jones of Palm Beach, Florida. The attribution marks the status of the lyrics as a mere synecdoche for the performance of the song. At the same time, the lyrics function independently. That is, the speaker within the song lyric prays to God for the acceptance of her words, while Hurston, signifying, prays that her federal benefactors accept her words, insofar as these are the closing words of the proposal she has "respectfully submitted." Hurston has not only recorded a miscellaneous collection of sound but transformed the sonic realm of "the Floridas" from the racial violence indicated by the epigraph to the first section to a meditative prayer in her own voice. In doing so, Hurston suggests a purpose to the work of "expedition" beyond scientific observation. A "serious study" of sound, for Hurston, involves an ethical transformation from racial terror to lyric prayer. What enables this transformation in Hurston's sound proposal and in *Their Eyes Were Watching God?*

LISTENING TO DIASPORA

Paradoxically, through her rhythmic contributions to a state guide, Hurston enacts the ethical transformation of American racial violence by slipping the bounds of the United States. Hurston hears in black music—not only the "folk poems, sermons and prayers" but the blues and jumping dances and ringshouts —an expression of and response to violence. Before the closing anthem, Hurston's proposal offers a summary of the Floridas in the form of a genealogy of diaspora:

> No where else is there such a variety of materials. Florida is still a frontier with its varying elements still unassimilated. . . . The drums throb; Africa by way of Cuba; Africa by way of the British West Indies; Africa by way of Haiti and Martinique; Africa by way of Central and South America. Old Spain speaks through many interpreters. Old England speaks through black, white and intermediate lips. Florida, the inner melting pot of the great melting pot—America. (6)

In this panoply of mixed metaphors Florida is at once exceptional and representative, a laboratory for unassimilated diasporic culture and a melting pot. What do we make of the juxtaposition between the sound of Africa manifest in the form of diasporic drumming and the "sanctified anthem" that are Zora's last words of prayer? After announcing that "the drums throb," Hurston enacts their throbbing, repeating the phrase "Africa by way of" four times, so that Africa becomes the beat against which Hurston describes the diaspora. We can easily imagine these lines as a poem from the Black Arts Movement thirty years hence; indeed, they may call to mind the late Langston Hughes poem "Drums" (1964), in which the speaker dreams of the sounds of percussion and recalls a generalized version of the middle passage that transports both enslaved people and sounds from Africa to New Orleans's Congo Square. A repeated refrain—"remember, remember, remember!"—emphasizes the work of memory rather than geographically based racial ontology, interrupting what otherwise appears to be a seamless narrative connecting the originating moment of enslavement with what some have called the most original art form in America: jazz. The speaker recalls at a temporal remove from both moments, relegating the middle passage and the scene at Congo Square alike to history and to dreams. Whereas Hughes's poem describes a national origin story rooted in Africa, Hurston's proposal maps a more disjunctive geography insofar as Haiti, Martinique, South America, the

West Indies, "Old Spain," and "Old England" all mediate the relationship between Africa and the "sanctified anthem." The throbbing diasporic drum enables Hurston to venture the lyric petition that closes the document.

Likewise, Hurston draws on her vast collection of diasporic music in order to transform both racial and environmental destruction via suspended lyric time in *Their Eyes Were Watching God.* In the epigraph to the fourth section of the "Proposed Recording Expedition," Hurston cites the lyrics of a song she has recorded: "Evalina, Evalina, you know the baby don't favor me, Eh, / Eh, you know the baby don't favor me" (4). Hurston notes not only the singer of the lyrics (Lias Strawn, Miami, Florida) but the drummer (Stew Beef), as if the quotation she has offered can in some way transcribe not only the words but the beats. In light of her claim elsewhere that "the words do not count" when it comes to her ability to identify the coherence of a particular song (*Dust Tracks on a Road,* 706), this moment draws our attention to the incongruity between the textual form of this document and the record of performance it both creates and calls for. Readers of *Their Eyes Were Watching God* will recall that Stew Beef is the Bahamian musician who keeps the rhythm at the camp, "making dynamic subtleties with his drum and living, sculptural grotesques in the dance" (147). What does it mean to have established Stew Beef's Bahamian drumming as the beat against which catastrophe breaks in *Their Eyes Were Watching God*? Listening to two recordings of "Evalina" (recorded again here through written description) can help us to hear that sound in the novel as well.

In 1935 Alan Lomax and Mary Elizabeth Barnicle, with whom Hurston had traveled on other expeditions that same year, recorded a version of "Evalina" in the Bahamas. The song, over two minutes long, features a chorus of voices accompanied by steady drumming. The voices harmonize and build as the drums intensify. Toward the end of the song, the voices and drums together peter out. Following a silence of a few seconds, two drumming sounds return, one hand beating while the other chafes against the side of the drum. The drum becomes the sound that counts at the end, a solo instrumental commentary on the collective vocal experience.

Hurston strives to re-create this process not only in text but in her own voice. One month after submitting her proposal, on June 18, 1939, Hurston herself recorded "Evalina," attempting to replicate in solo vocal performance what we know from her descriptions and from the Lomax and Barnicle recording to be a collective mode of production.[14] In Hurston's mouth "Evalina" undergoes a process analogous to that of the song lyrics in "Proposed Recording Expedition," in which multiple first-person speakers become "the words of my mouth."

The song is followed by a brief interview between Hurston and Carita Corse, the Florida state director for the Federal Writers' Project state guides project. In response to a question from Corse about whether the songs are sung in the United States as well as the West Indies, Hurston replies by enumerating the Florida locations through which the songs circulate, "where a great number of Nassaus are working in the bean fields and what not. There're a great number of them in Florida. They hold jumping dances every week." Corse finds it "very interesting" that southern United States and West Indian culture coexist in Florida. The dialogue between Corse and Hurston draws our attention to the ways in which the "Proposed Recording Expedition" and indeed *Their Eyes* demand to be read in the diasporic context of the movement of music, dance, and people among the locations Hurston lists. In spite of its collection under the heading of the state guides project of the Federal Writers' Project, we cannot understand Florida's cultural production in a rigidly regional or even national sense.

In the exchange with Carita Corse, Hurston's Floridian body and voice are the media for assimilating the diaspora into this American collecting project, but even after her performance the scene requires further translation and explication, suggesting the inassimilable quality of the work. Hurston wrote to Corse in June 1938 noting that she had found many folk songs "of the type that you discussed with me in the office, but the difficulty in collecting them is that it is hard to set them down correctly at one sitting." According to Hurston, "The answer is a recording machine," and she asks Corse if it might be possible to acquire one (*Zora Neale Hurston*, 415). It seems reasonable to conclude, in fact, that Hurston wrote the grant proposal for the express purpose of procuring a machine.[15] Listening to Hurston's recordings of the songs in her own voice, one becomes aware of Hurston's double role as informant and ethnographer, as well as, in the absence of "a recording machine" in the field, as performer and "recorder." One hears what Daphne Brooks has described as Zora's "ability to, like Edison's queer little late-Victorian instrument, both record and playback the sound around her" (" 'Sister, Can You Line It Out?,' " 263). One also hears in the elongated, vibrating "eh" of Hurston's voice and in the strange brevity of the performance a sense of that which is lost: namely, the collective scene of production and collection. Given Hurston's production of collectively made music in a singular voice, we need to understand her innovative "speakerly text" not only in relationship to vernacular speech but also in relationship to vernacular music.

What happens when we return to *Their Eyes* with this music in our ear? I have suggested already that the presence of lyric interrupts both the prose argument of her "Proposed Recording Expedition" and the prose narrative of *Their Eyes Were Watching God*. The collective scene of diasporic musical performance also enables Hurston's lyric response to the disruptions and displacements of environmental catastrophe. After a night of storytelling, guitar playing, chanting, and dancing, the eve of the hurricane finds Tea Cake and his friends playing dice (artfully) while the weather deteriorates.

> Sometime that night the winds came back. Everything in the world had a strong rattle, sharp and short like Stew Beef vibrating the drum head near the edge with his fingers. By morning Gabriel was playing the deep tones in the center of the drum. So when Janie looked out of her door she saw the drifting mists gathered in the west— that cloud field of the sky—to arm themselves with thunders and march forth against the world. Louder and higher and lower and wider the sound and motion spread, mounting, sinking, darking. (184–85)

Hurston represents the storm as a rhythmic interruption to the narrative structure of the novel. The "motion" Hurston describes in this passage resembles the sonic motion of Lomax and Barnicle's recording of "Evalina." The simile comparing the sounds of the storm to Stew Beef's drum makes explicit the connection between human artistic creation and "natural expression." The description draws a contrast between the singular, erratic, and dramatic beat of the storm, "sharp and short," then "louder and higher and lower and wider[,] . . . mounting, sinking, darking," and the literal drumming it interrupts: the monotonous "another night of Stew Beef." At the same time the progressive verbs, including the neologism, "darking," suggest the profound continuity of the condition of catastrophe. It is precisely the need to account for these two kinds of temporality— the continuous and the catastrophic—that occasions the narrative suspension in the novel. The gap between the "dynamic subtleties" of Stew Beef's percussive music and its representation in words *is* lyric time.

If we look back at the summary paragraph of Hurston's "Proposed Recording Expedition," we recall that Hurston's description and mimesis of drumbeats emphasizes Africa and its relationship to the diaspora as the beat: "The drums throb; Africa by way of Cuba; Africa by way of the British West Indies; Africa by way of Haiti and Martinique; Africa by way of Central and South America" (6). To evoke God's message in the form of Gabriel drumming is therefore to suggest that God's will is manifest beyond the framework of the nation-state. Such is the form of kinship that not only produces the parallel music of the hurricane (for it was the "Saws'" music and dancing that attracted Janie to them) but also the relationships among the migrant workers on the muck. When Janie and Tea

Cake's friend Lias evacuates in his uncle's car he promises his friends that "if Ah never see you no mo' on earth, Ah'll meet you in Africa" (156), echoing a familiar conflation of Africa with heaven. Later, when Tea Cake and Janie finally flee the storm, leaving behind their reluctant friend Motor Boat to sleep through the storm in the top floor of the house, the friends again promise to reunite elsewhere. Tea Cake says, "Goodbye, then, Motor. Ah wish you all de luck. Goin' over tuh Nassau fuh dat visit widja when all dis is over." Motor replies, "Definitely, Tea Cake. Mah mama's house is yours" (164). These exchanges suggest that while the hurricane has replicated the displacement and homelessness of various enforced diasporas and migrations, beginning with the slave trade and continuing through labor migrations, it might also—in the imaginative realm, at least—have the power to reverse them, to bring people "home" to each other.

Brian Russell Roberts has recently suggested that attention to geographical form in Hurston's novel—and particularly the form of the archipelago as represented both discursively and structurally in *Their Eyes*—foregrounds "planetary archipelago" rather than race-based diasporic thinking (which Roberts associates primarily with Tea Cake's "American exceptionalist" perspective). Roberts's "geoformalist" reading of Hurston's writings is especially compelling insofar as it offers us a method for reading diasporic literature with both distance and proximity in mind. Having addressed his reading of the planetary in relationship to literary methodology in chapter 3, I return to it here to think through its implications for Hurston's work more specifically. Like a growing group of scholars including Ian Baucom, Dipesh Chakrabarty, and Ursula Heise, Roberts suggests that we need a different scale for understanding natural and "cultural geographies" together.[16] As he does, I see in Hurston's writing an important and often-neglected environmental consciousness, indeed, to borrow Rob Nixon's expression, an "environmental double-consciousness" (*Slow Violence and the Environmentalism of the Poor*, 245). But I would be reluctant to accede to Roberts's minimization of race consciousness within *Their Eyes* or rather to the opposition he posits between race consciousness and planetary thinking. If we not only read but hear Hurston's representation of catastrophe, it is hard not to hear cultural linkages concomitant to geographic ones.

Hurston's evocation of African drumming evokes multiple sources rather than a single thread of influence. This is not pan-Africanism; it is rather what Brent Edwards describes as a diasporic consciousness that is not obsessed with "origin" but that "forces us to consider discourses of cultural and political linkage only through and across difference" ("The Uses of Diaspora," 64). Hurston's diasporic genealogy of Floridian music manifests on a geographic scale

the challenge of accounting for collective experience and collective cultural production with a single artistic voice, a challenge that animates much of Hurston's
work. Hurston herself writes in her 1934 essay on Negro spirituals that "Negro
songs to be heard truly must be sung by a group, and a group bent on expression
of feelings and not on sound effects" (*Folklore, Memoirs, and Other Writings*,
870). And yet in concluding the same essay she leaves open the possibility of
"unaccompanied" prayer, which she describes as "an obligato over and above
the harmony of the assembly" (874). An obligato here resonates as a sound that
is at once "over and above" and absolutely essential insofar as it responds to
or extends the "jagged harmony" of the group.

Like "Proposed Recording Expedition," *Their Eyes* transforms terror into the
occasion for lyric prayer through the recording and replaying, textually and aurally, of diasporic sound. Although Hurston was a writer of prose fiction, both
of the documents I've read in this section, novel and proposal, enter lyric modes
as one way of finding such a voice. If catastrophe causes a breakdown in narrative structure, it finds its form in a lyric poetry that mediates between "the
words of my mouth" and the diffuse sounds of diaspora. Collective experiences
of catastrophe require the continuous reinvention of lyric subjectivity as a way
of containing or at least rendering this collectivity. Hurston's novel invites us to
imagine not only how sounds become the words of her mouth but also how the
words of her mouth are never hers alone.

DE PARTY BOOK BEYOND

In a 1928 letter to Langston Hughes written from Magazine, Alabama, where
Hurston was collecting materials for her anthropological research, she describes reading aloud from Hughes's *Fine Clothes to the Jew* as a way of starting
off the storytelling contests she held among the community of men she was
studying. She tells Hughes, "You are being quoted in R.R. camps, phosphate
mines, and Turpentine stills, etc." (*Zora Neale Hurston*, 122). The workers, then,
are not simply a source for Hurston's and Hughes's modern material or a passive audience for Hughes's work (although Hurston frequently encouraged
Hughes to go on "reading tours" through the South, which he eventually did)
but are themselves modern artists. Hurston goes on to describe the process by
which the workers respond to and adapt Hughes's poems:

> So you see they are making it so much a part of themselves they go to improvising on
> it. . . . They sing the poems right off, and July 1, two men came over with guitars and
> sang the whole book. Everybody joined in. It was the strangest and most *thrilling*

thing. They played it well too. You'd be surprised. One man was giving the words out-lining them out as the preacher does a hymn and the others would take it up and sing. It was glorious! (122)

Hurston does not just provide a classic example of the participant-observer but also reminds us that the music and stories she collects are always already products of modern literary culture. While many critics have proposed that Hughes's poems (along with Sterling Brown's) are influenced by folk musical forms, Hurston's letter suggests that these poems are "more than mere transcriptions," to cite James Weldon Johnson's description of Brown's poems (introduction, 17), and also that the path of influence is far more circular than we often account for, so that the musical inspirations for *Fine Clothes*, the print publication and distribution of that book (and *The Weary Blues*, which Hurston also eventually distributed in her travels), the recitation aloud by Hurston of the poems, the "improvising on it," the chanting in games and singing, and the form of church hymns all contribute to the making of black modern culture.

This kind of circulation further expands our sense of the geographical boundaries of cultural production during this period. For if Alain Locke famously describes the northward migration of blacks as a "deliberate flight not only from countryside to city but from medieval America to modern" ("The New Negro," 6), then Hurston's letter to Hughes dislocates the temporal-spatial relationship Locke's influential formulation inscribes, uncoupling modernity from such a northward "flight" and identifying multiple sites of cultural production.

Hurston's practice as a cultural collector, of course, also uncouples "modern" from "America." Edwards's observation that there is "a hint of a move afield" ("The Seemingly Eclipsed Window of Form," 594) in James Weldon Johnson's celebration of black vernacular music in the *Book of American Negro Poetry* suggests an inherent relationship between a poetics of vernacular transcription and black diasporic collecting practices. Recent work by Alexandra Vazquez extends these claims further by noting the presence of the "far beyond" in Johnson's preface. Vazquez draws our attention to Johnson's evocation of tango and the Cuban poet Placido as foundational for Johnson's anthology and his theories of African American music, even as he names Cuba as that which is "far beyond" the limits of his own project. The "far beyond" is not merely "out there" in the diaspora but a precedent for "extranational and protointerdisciplinary work" (*Listening in Detail*, 62). In chapters 4 and 5 I hope have suggested something similar about the collecting work of Sterling Brown and Zora Neale Hurston.

Brown's and Hurston's literary responses to natural disaster can be understood as anthological, both in the textual sense of Edwards's reading of Johnson and in the extratextual sense at the heart of Vazquez's intervention. That is, *Their Eyes Were Watching God* and *Southern Road* collect the lyric and the sonic. To approach the presence of the musical in these texts is to hear in them that which may travel "far beyond" the geographic and political constraints of the national. Having already summoned Kamau Brathwaite's theory of hurricane poetics as "nation language" throughout this book, I turn in chapter 6 to the real-life hurricane that threatened Brathwaite's home in Jamaica and to the musical and poetic responses it engendered, including Brathwaite's own. In doing so I shift my focus from lyric interruptions of narrative to lyric as a transmedial genre that contains culture against the threats to its survival.

six

Collecting Culture
Hurricane Gilbert's Lyric Archive

"AT THE EDGES"

In the week that the Beach Boys' "Kokomo" reached the top of the U.S. charts, a very different song, imagining a very different tropical space, entered the "shots to watch" slot in the top ten list of the Jamaican newspaper the *Gleaner*.[1] While the Beach Boys invited listeners to a mysterious island associated with a list of international destinations, Lloyd Lovindeer's massive hit "Wild Gilbert" freshly reported the hurricane that had all too recently devastated the agriculture and infrastructure of Jamaica—not to mention the delights of its tourist industry.[2]

The coincidental juxtaposition of these tropical hits on the U.S. and Jamaican music charts (both reported in the *Gleaner* every week) points to the contrast between touring and dwelling in the Jamaican environment. Tour companies were told to halt the iconic "Come Back to Jamaica" ads in the immediate aftermath of the hurricane, but it was not long before the country had launched a promotional campaign geared at reviving the Jamaican tourist industry, reassuring prospective visitors that the island was still safe and beautiful, still one of the tropical paradises described in "Kokomo."[3] While the Jamaica Tourist Board quickly devoted its resources to restoring the image of Jamaica's coastlines as hospitable to tourists enjoying the atmosphere, Jamaicans faced the continued challenges of dwelling in this landscape, in many cases without electricity, clean water, or telephone service. Gilbert also caused long-term damage to the island's agriculture and ecology. As Betsy Wade, a travel writer for the *New York Times* reported in December, three months after the storm, the country was still "on the mend at the edges": there were still downed trees and power lines, broken up coral reef, tent communities, and homeless people. However, she pointed out, "the things that most tourists go to the Caribbean for—warm weather, swimming, golf, tennis, fresh food, pampering hotels—[were] in place" ("Practical Traveler").

Lloyd Lovindeer's "Wild Gilbert" and Kamau Brathwaite's long poem *Shar/*

Hurricane Poem, both composed in the immediate aftermath of Gilbert, dwell in another Jamaica, one "at the edges" of the tourist destination evoked in such a description. In different ways they describe and respond to the "absence from the *landscapes* of Jamaica" (emphasis mine) that poet Kwame Dawes evokes in his book on reggae aesthetics:

> While I live with this absence from the landscapes of Jamaica—physical, political, and social—I think my position as a writer outside Jamaica is quite different from that of the generation of writers who left the region in the 1950s and 1960s. And the difference is reggae, which gives me the sense of being part of some global, electronic Caribbean community, from whose sounds and lyrical concerns I can still get some sense of 'home' and its changing sensibilities. (*Natural Mysticism*, 264)

Dawes describes this absence as a symptom of migration, but it is also, as Glissant has contended, a more long term effect of "a brutal dislocation, the slave trade" (*Caribbean Discourse*, 61).[4] According to Glissant, the catastrophic imagination in the Caribbean can be symptomatic of this dislocation and its attendant "nonhistory." Referring to the lack of continuous resistance to colonial oppression in Martinique, Glissant writes that "nature and culture have not formed a dialectical whole that informs a people's consciousness. So much so that obscured history was often reduced for us to a chronology of natural events, retaining only their 'explosive' emotional meanings. We would say: 'the year of the great earthquake,' or: 'the year of the hurricane that flattened M. Celeste's house,' or: 'the year of the fire on Main street'" (*Caribbean Discourse*, 63). Glissant calls on Caribbean writers to reestablish "the creative link between nature and culture" (63). The "explosive" structure of catastrophe, according to his formulation, stands in the way of the formation of such a link. How can we reconcile Glissant's critique of catastrophic historiography with Brathwaite's embrace of the hurricane as a figure for Caribbeanness? And to what extent might it be possible for catastrophe itself to produce that link, to bring nature and culture into proximity, all the while marking the brutal history of their alienation? Brathwaite has stated it clearly: "Art must come from catastrophe."[5] Dawes describes music—and reggae in particular—as uniquely capable of mediating environmental distance. However, Lovindeer's is an urban music, performing absence from the natural and agricultural worlds. By contrast, Brathwaite's *Shar/Hurricane Poem* suggests the profound interconnectedness of environmental and cultural experience. In his hands, the lyric poem performs a fugitive Caribbean archival practice, a material form of "nonhistory." Catastrophe yields to the cultivation—and the collection—of art.

In turning from music to poetry over the course of this chapter, I do not suggest that the latter is a kind of supplement to or inadequate transcription of the former. On the contrary, Brathwaite's range of responses to Hurricane Gilbert—in poetry, in published interviews, and in informally distributed letters —demonstrates the interconnectedness of oral and scribal forms within lyric poetry. The problem of environmental approximation draws our attention to lyric poetry's special status as a textual embodiment of song, that is, a form that is always an approximation of another form. The hurricane appears to cause a crisis in Brathwaite's genres, insofar as the line between his poetry and his poetics is blurry. But the proximity between poetry and other genres and media in Brathwaite's oeuvre establishes lyric as an intermedial genre. Diasporic lyric is catastrophic insofar as it is always bound up in the disjunctive poetics of transcription, but it is also generative insofar as the sonic, visual, textual and performative properties of the poem do more than merely preserve nature.

WILD GILBERT'S ELECTRONIC COMMUNITY

Hurricane Gilbert traversed the entire island of Jamaica as a category 4 hurricane, causing forty-five deaths, massively damaging agriculture, livestock, schools, houses, and the tourist trade, and transforming the political landscape of Jamaica.[6] "Wild Gilbert" hit the streets of Kingston in the fall of 1988, three weeks after the massive Hurricane Gilbert blew through, providing Jamaicans with a bit of reprieve from the enormous physical, emotional, and social loss brought about by the flooding and winds. The abundant outpouring of topical music on the radio waves after Gilbert memorialized and recorded the experience of the hurricane and its relationship to social issues and national identity. From Banana Man's mournful and devout "Gilbert Attack Us" to Yellowman's hopeful "Starting All over Again," these songs were broadly performed, circulated, and compiled, constituting an archive of the nation's response to disaster. The *Gleaner* was right to watch Lovindeer's "Wild Gilbert," by far the most popular of the post-Gilbert songs primarily because of its humor and its relevance across class lines. The song climbed its way up the charts and soon became (and remained) Jamaica's best-selling single, selling over fifty-five thousand copies and launching Lovindeer's success as a solo dancehall artist.[7]

Lovindeer's account of the hurricane unfolds in the urban space of the street and the neighborhood. The song aired in the context of curtailed and unequal mobility, a kind of involuntary urban rootedness, but "Wild Gilbert" itself had the capacity to spread like wildfire, to borrow another catastrophic metaphor. People turned to music in part because without power and generators, other forms of entertainment were not available, while music could be played and heard on radios both in cars or on the street—all factors Lovindeer dramatizes in the music video for "Wild Gilbert." One Jamaican survivor of Gilbert, DJ Culture Norm, recalls how his adolescent awakening into music took place:

> After the 1988 hurricane Gilbert hit Jamaica head-on, leaving the island in total darkness, Discovery Bay, the north coast town I lived in at the time[,] experienced damage to plantations, homes, churches, schools and so on. The island was left without electricity in most places for over a year and that meant amplified car stereos were the only source of entertainment.
>
> When the electricity was finally restored in December 1989, I walked by a record shop and heard the sweet melody of fully amplified reggae music and that moment has been stuck in my head ever since. I purchased a dozen new records[,] went home and pulled out my dad's old Pee Vee tube amp, a pair of 15" midrange speakers and a single turn table and spent the weekend mixing my new tunes with my dad's old ones. ("Lake Shady Reggae")[8]

DJ Culture Norm is not a major musical figure, but he describes a major narrative in which the material deprivations of Hurricane Gilbert give rise to a musical culture. Indeed, in their popular history *Reggae Routes*, Kevin Chang and Wayne Chen go so far as to contend that "Hurricane Gilbert was indirectly responsible for blowing the dancehall scene uptown and upmarket" (193). Almost twenty-five years later and an ocean away in Minnesota, Culture Norm's sound system is called "Wild Gilbert." Even as an urban music form, however, dancehall emerges from black diasporic practices of performance tied to the agricultural spaces and economy of the plantation.[9] Geographer Sonjah Stanley-Niaah explains that the genre not only has roots in the reggae of the sixties and seventies but, following Gilroy, in a transnational black Atlantic tradition extending to the plantation and the slave ship. Stanley-Niahh productively excavates the connection between the need for surreptitious, resistant, and nomadic celebration in the constrained space of the plantation and "the needs of the disenfranchised to ease the tension, to give praise, to survive and to entertain" in the city. Posthurricane environmental conditions thus reproduce and magnify the nomadic social conditions that are the basis and shape of dancehall. Lovindeer takes up the hurricane's dispersals and displacements "as a culmination of New World history and imagination, today centered in the urban space" ("Negotiating a Common Transnational Space," 764).

Gilbert exacerbated conditions that some geographers have contended emerged as part of a plantation economy, conditions that have implications not only for human social survival but also for the long-term survival of the land-scape. Yet Lovindeer's song makes no reference, even mockingly, to agricultural and environmental damage; instead, it underscores the continuous sociality of the street as an alternative to the disruptive disaster, depicting natural disaster as "social disaster," to borrow a phrase from Neil Smith ("There's No Such Thing as a Natural Disaster"). In the song and video, Lovindeer chastises urban looters, walks through the streets with the admiring chorus members, and represents American cultural imperialism and related class divisions through the figure of the satellite dish. While roots may be a metaphor for national identity, the human plight unfolds in an urban geography. The song personifies Gilbert from the start ("Wa wa wild Gilbert! Well Gilbert yuh gone ha ha / Now wi can chat behind yuh back"), incorporating the natural phenomenon into the human world, confronting disaster by putting it on a social scale.[10]

Lovindeer's song brings what Dawes calls a "global, electronic Caribbean community" into existence not only through its massive appeal but also because it gives voice to collective social experience.[11] Rendering this collectivity, the song ironically mitigates the destructiveness of Gilbert and depicts the storm as creatively generative, drawing attention to the song's own survival. Parody in Lovindeer's song at first seems to make light of disaster. "Wild Gilbert" in no way signifies on the Beach Boys' touristic tropics—in fact, another notable feature of this song is its lack of musical or textual repetition of North American music—but it does in a very different way insist on making the Caribbean landscape "danceable."[12] The chorus, borrowing a common trope of Jamaican music, quotes a popular nursery rhyme: "De likkle dog laugh to see such fun/ And di dish run away with the spoon." The song continues to mock the storm's destructive powers in its first verse, which contains both the song's most hilarious pun and its most somber voice. Here, the "dish" of the song's opening domestic scene becomes a different type of dish:

> Unno si mi dish unno si mi dish,
> Anybody unna si mi satellite d-d-dish
> Unno si mi dish unno si mi—fiahhh!
> Rough! We would like to express our sympathies
> To those affected by gilbert
> Wa wa wild gilbert

Lovindeer stages class and value difference in the pun, which unites the common domestic "dish" with its more aspirational counterpart, the satellite dish. Mid-verse the speaker shifts from the desperate, comic, materialist "mi" to the institutional, funereal, radio voice "we" and dramatically shifts his tone from silly to serious, foregrounding the irony of collective "sympathies." After all, the mock-serious tone implies, how "rough" can it be when you mourn not lives, housing, income, or agriculture, but satellite dishes—when you can sweep the water away with a broom?

Lovindeer's parody of a range of social classes—from the aspirational middle class to the poor youths who engage in looting after the storm—gives voice to the populace and brings them together under the umbrella of the storm. Chang and Chen attest to the song's transformative influence across classes in Jamaica:

> The direct social impact of "Wild Gilbert" is often overlooked. There was a time when rich uptowners scorned deejay music as "dibbi dibbi" rubbish, completely ignoring dancehall in favour of soca, Bob Marley and North American pop. Hurricane Gilbert, however, was an experience every Jamaican—rich or poor, white, black, yellow, or brown—went through, so "Wild Gilbert" was a song with which everyone could identify. Indeed it was the first deejay song many of the upper-class had ever bothered to listen to. . . . Of course "Wild Gilbert" was not solely responsible for changes like this, but it did more than any single song to establish dancehall as the universal sound of Jamaica today. (*Reggae Routes*, 193)

This account echoes the surprisingly nostalgic descriptions of Hurricane Gilbert's leveling effects offered by many, including Lovindeer himself. Chang and Chen attribute these effects not only to the storm but to the song, describing "Wild Gilbert" and Hurricane Gilbert in similar terms as agents of cultural change.

As destructive as Hurricane Gilbert was, many noted that it also equalized communities and brought people together. As evidence of this theory, David Barker and David Miller cite public opinion represented in the *Gleaner* in the days immediately following the storm: "Gilbert, in his violence, wrote on the chalkboard of the Jamaican countryside the lesson that affluence and poverty have common cause when it comes to nature" and "Gilbert, as destructive as he was, will be seen as a catalyst in energizing the national spirit of togetherness" ("Hurricane Gilbert," 114).[13]

The song "Wild Gilbert" celebrates this aspect of the storm and draws attention to music's ability to do the same. Asked to account for the song's popularity, Lovindeer recalls, "It was a feel-good song in the midst of disaster. After you go through that and survive, you want to celebrate. It's not 'woe, woe.' . . . It was danceable and everybody could relate. It was fun for everybody. You find the man from uptown couldn't get ice either. The man from ghetto couldn't get no ice. Everybody was one at the time until the light come back and everybody go them separate ways."[14] While celebrating the moment when "everybody was one," Lovindeer's tune also humorously points out the ongoing reality in which "everybody go them separate ways." The Rasta character "Natty Dreadlocks" might be the song's quintessential symbol of the storm's equalizing force. He proclaims the destruction of other spaces, as the "breeze lick dung mr chin restaurant" and "two sheet a zinc blow off a joe house," justifying the storm's violence in relationship to his theology. For in destroying their homes but keeping them alive, Jah will "show dem seh a we run tings." The Rasta speaker identifies himself with the divine, for "it's through I merciful why dem alive." But Lovindeer, repeating a trope of Jamaican popular music, gives the pious man a taste of his own medicine. No sooner does the caricatured Rasta take pleasure in the storm's wrath, than

> Likkle after that Gilbert turn back
> Lift off di roof of a natty dread shack
> Him seh, blouse and skirt, Jah must never know
> Seh I & I live right ya so

In blowing off the roof, the hurricane challenges the Rastafari theology of retribution, but Natty quickly adjusts his theology to the change in circumstances: the roof has blown off because the "I" who is divine is unaware of the presence of the "I" who is human in that shack. In spite of his rationalization of the storm, the destruction of his own roof suggests both the randomness and the equality of violence. Indeed, as Barker and Miller have noted, the leveling of the Rasta's house seems to reflect the prevalent notion that disasters function as social levelers. Without questioning the accuracy of the claim that Gilbert "brought together" the nation, Barker and Miller note the power of representing Gilbert as "personifying nature, an omnipotent social leveller, a humbler of the mighty in the context of a nation with such stark social and economic differences" (114).

But Lovindeer's song draws our attention equally to the continuing catastrophe of rigid social class structures. Lovindeer transforms the dish of the nursery rhyme into a synecdoche for loss and destruction on a larger scale. In the second verse the storm intensifies:

> Come! dish tek off like flying saucer
> Mi roof migrate without a visa
> Bedroom full up a water

Mi in a di dark nuh light nuh on you

And true mi nuh have no generator mi she

The reference to migration signals unequal access to interstate travel. By the 1980s, Jamaican emigration to the United Kingdom and the United States had declined, most likely as a result of increasing immigrations restrictions in both countries: the 1988 Immigration Act in the UK and the 1986 Immigration Reform and Control Act signed by President Reagan. While emigration continued to offer opportunities, these opportunities were radically limited by class and gender. The migrating roof ignores national boundaries in a potentially resistant way, but at the same time it signals the inequalities revealed by the need for a visa in the first place. These inequalities would have been particularly apparent after a hurricane, when those who had access to international wealth and who could afford to migrate would were able to obtain to imported generators that others had to do without.[15] Getting Lovindeer's joke depends on knowledge of the broader political and economic context in which Jamaicans often must seek global identities against the pull of national pride and the push of international restriction.

Lovindeer at once critiques a society in which class corresponds to curtailed mobility and enacts the mobility of his own music. As the size of the dish increases through the comparison to a flying saucer, so too does the scale of the disaster's consequences: water, previously swept away with a broom, now floods the bedroom, and the electricity has gone out. The increase in the physical scale and intensity of the storm corresponds to social concerns, for the speaker "mi nuh have no generator" nor a visa with which to obtain one. Unlike the speaker, Gilbert's destruction migrates. In the context of Lovindeer's upbeat dancehall, however, the storm's movements create a sense of possibility—what Alexandra Vazquez has called "instrumental migrations," the capacity for music and musical culture to transcend political boundaries.[16] Now the dish, too, is "like a flying saucer." Rather than being swept away by the wind, it has agency; it "tek off," presumably for more exotic (or at least safer) parts of the galaxy. Brian Heap interprets the dish as "the means by which information and North American culture bombard the region" and contends that Lovindeer evokes this sense of "dish" as a way of mocking the middle classes ("Songs of a Surrogate Mother," 32). The dish also signifies the loss of connection to outside entertainments, which in turn enables a turn toward locally produced, more readily available culture that makes audible the particular shared experience of Jamaicans.

"Wild Gilbert" had the capacity to move even in the aftermath of disaster.

Lovindeer produced the song a few weeks after the hurricane, at Dynamic Sounds studio, which had reopened after being flooded, and then distributed the single on his own label, the Sounds of Jamaica. Although it was slow to enter the charts, it remained in the top one hundred for two years, the first song from Jamaica to have done so.[17] Perhaps more interestingly, the song's popularity has persisted long beyond the event it records. Especially when he performs overseas, Lovindeer says, audiences continue to request the song.[18] In other words, Lovindeer's song evoked and continues to evoke for Jamaican expatriates their sense of belonging to a digital Caribbean community. If this is what all reggae does for Kwame Dawes, the experience of Hurricane Gilbert undoubtedly heightened the need for such belonging insofar as it exacerbated the sense of displacement from and destruction of the Jamaican landscapes.

Lovindeer's impulse, like that of Zora Neale Hurston and Sterling Brown in the United States, is anthological in that he seeks to bring together other voices. "Wild Gilbert's" multivoiced critique of Jamaican class structure unites people across the class boundaries it mocks and maligns. The terror of disaster—of loss, displacement, mortality—engenders this collecting of culture. In an interview with the *Sunday Gleaner* nearly twenty years after the storm, he recalls his process when asked about inspiration: "I had to write something about it. It is not just my experience, but everybody's. I would go into the different communities after it happened and talk to the people and some of the experiences were other people's."[19] The narrative of creating "Wild Gilbert" out of "other people's" experiences recalls the ethnographic voice of Sterling Brown's "Ma Rainey": "I talked to a fellow an' the fellow say." Lovindeer does not equalize "other people"; rather, he listens to the diverse and disjunctive voices of an urban public.

Foregrounding reportage as a mode of witness, Lovindeer creates a song with which people from various strata of society can identify, not so much through a universal voice but through "Wild Gilbert's" playful, polyvocal acknowledgment of contrasts. The lyrics shift between plural and singular pronouns and in and out of character. After describing how the storm encroaches on him ever further with "water wet up mi shoes and ah wet up mi hat," the speaker "a look somewhere safe dry and warm." In this moment the song enters yet another plural voice and draws a contrast between pious church culture and youth culture:

> *We* thank di lord we never get hurt
> *Dem* seh thank yuh lord for mr gilbert
> Cause! yuh si mi fridge! a gilbert gimme

Yuh si mi colour tv! a gilbert gimme

Yuh si mi new stereo! a gilbert gimme

Yuh si mi new video! a gilbert gimme come now (emphasis mine)

The song draws a contrast between "we"—those who "thank di lord" they are safe—and "dem"—those who take advantage of the storm for personal gain. At the same time, Lovindeer's song ventriloquizes "di youth," giving voice to their jubilation in the context of disaster.

Against the global mobility of the runaway dinner dish turned satellite dish turned "flying saucer," Lovindeer juxtaposes the local fugitivity of a rebellious youth culture he alternately mocks and celebrates. Disaster transforms the looters by giving them access to a new kind of property: luxury consumer items. The looters' joyous chant replays the dish-deprived speaker's request that we "si" what has abandoned him, transforming his question to a command. Thus, although Lovindeer mocks the youth by distancing "we" from "dem," the looters' gain signifies on the middle-class loss. The repetition reinforcing the command to look at what "a gilbert gimme" has the rhythmic effect of commanding the listener to transform sorrow over what Gilbert took into joy at what "a gilbert gimme." The last two items on the list: "mi new stereo" and "mi new video" in particular suggest that the gift is not only material but cultural: "a gilbert gimme" music.

The song and video depict the looting as morally suspect, but also full of fugitive, resistant potential, insofar as the act of theft claims the means of production for music. "Mi new stereo" and "me new video" describe both the electronic devices used for consuming music and, in a more abstract sense, the sounds and performances themselves. Since "mi stereo" was required as part of the sound system for dancehall during this period, the work of deejays like Lovindeer also uniquely blurs the boundary between devices of consumption and devices of production. The video of "Wild Gilbert" emphasizes the double-voiced nature of the song's relationship to looting. Lovindeer's voice amplifies when he expresses the gratitude of the looting youth who "thank de lord for mister Gilbert," and in the video we see a young man reaching into crawl spaces in the rain to claim stolen goods, then raising his arms and lip-syncing in praise. The video cuts quickly from the looting youth to scenes of women indoors showboating their new electronic acquisitions, presumably purchased from or gifted by the boys. The women are also mouthing, awkwardly, Lovindeer's words. The sloppy ventriloquism, far from deepening the distance between the speaker and these figures, instead draws our attention to Lovindeer as the real speaker of these words and underscores our sense that he shares in the celebration of the boys and women. The song thus invites us to think of looting in connection with, though not quite as equal to, the collective cultural work of song in the aftermath of disaster. Even as it makes fun, democratically, of the middle class's subordination to North American bourgeois values and the looters' opportunism, "Wild Gilbert" unearths both the devastations and the opportunities of catastrophe. Most importantly it suggests to us that song itself, with its speedy and inexpensive circulation, its immediacy, and its wide appeal, is one such opportunity.

"A DIARY OF WATER": KAMAU BRATHWAITE'S POETRY OF APPROXIMATION

If the technologies of music enable its dispersal and distribution even at times when whole communities are literally without power, the harsh conditions of floods and winds might seem to threaten print culture in a more material sense. Thus, while under normal circumstances we might associate text with greater permanence, in the face of a hurricane, song can be more durable, indeed more possible.[20] When Hurricane Gilbert destroyed Brathwaite's house in Irish Town, Jamaica in 1988, it destroyed his library of poetry and music, which was, in his words, "one of the largest & most important archives of Caribbean literature & culture in the world. . . . It contains a record—since I keep almost everything— of many of our writers' progress (drafts unpublished manuscripts letters diaries artifacts books books books thousands of miles of tapes LPs)— possibly one of the largest collections of Caribbean poetry in the world" (*Shar*). The winds and flood waters gave meteorological shape to what was already a major question in Brathwaite's engagement with Caribbean culture and history: how does one capture the form, the rhythm of the hurricane on the page, when its very precondition is that of dispersal, displacement, and loss?

Although the elision between his personal library and Caribbean literary history may seem surprising, Brathwaite details, in his published interview *conVERSations with Nathaniel Mackey*, the immense resources lost and the broader context in which their loss resonates. In newly born nations with minimal infrastructure for collecting and preserving regional literary heritage, private libraries are often essential repositories of public culture. In the aftermath of Gilbert, Brathwaite issued an extensive list of what was damaged in Irish Town, which included not only books but recordings from radio and TV broadcasts, the paper archives of the Caribbean Artists Movement, interviews and readings from poets all over the world, field recordings from Ghana, Haiti, and elsewhere, and videos of theatrical presentations. Brathwaite structures much of the list geographically, listing place names followed by the figures represented in his archive, for example: "Cuba (inc Carifesta 79, inc Retamar, Nancy Morejon, Guillén, Iliana Sanz)" (*conVERSations with Nathaniel Mackey*, 300). In this way, Brathwaite's list constitutes a kind of literary map of the diaspora. The list also echoes the bibliography, titled *Our Ancestral Heritage*, that Brathwaite composed in connection with Carifesta in 1976, at the time that he was writing the early versions of *History of the Voice*, reminding us of the *longue durée* of Brathwaite's bibliographic project. Even as he emphasizes the singularity of his own collection— referring to "a very rare recording" of a particular worship service in Ghana and "several recordings (that xist nowhere else) of Yard Theatre grounnation" (*conVERSations with Nathaniel Mackey*, 300–301)—he insists on the archive's representative status and its broader significance for Caribbean scholarship. As one example of the latter he cites his inability to compose a chapter on folk culture of the Caribbean for the UNESCO *History of the Caribbean* because of the loss of his library. Although he acknowledges that he would have been able to access some resources at university and national libraries, he also identifies the special status of private collections: "Not mine only, but all collections such as mine: private, like personal, even somewhat idiosyncratic collections, which, unlike official collections, have the value and virtue of this very personal element— the conscious/unselfconscious dedication of collecting, storing & tryin(g) to preserve, over a long period of years, a kind of *timehri* of one's livin(g), one's culture (*conVERSations with Nathaniel Mackey*, 299)."[21] Brathwaite goes on to cite the collections of major Caribbean writers that were partially damaged or destroyed during Hurricane Gilbert, including those of Lorna Goodison, Louise Bennett, and John Hearne (306–307). He connects these losses to a larger uncertainty about where and how Caribbean literary culture is preserved, warning that "if we don't create archives of our culture in a land of drought, roaches, rodents, fire, damp, termites, volcanoes, earthquakes and hurricanes—we might have very little 'culture' left by the year 2000, okay?" (308).

In *History of the Voice* Brathwaite demonstrates the difficulty of transcription and preservation through references to the oral presentations from which the text is derived. For example, in the essay text, discussing Jamaican poet/ performer Louise Bennett's (Miss Lou's) use of the "language of her people," Brathwaite notes that "I couldn't satisfactorily reproduce in print Miss Lou's 'Street cries' played for the lecture from her LP *Miss Lou's Views*" and goes on to cite instead "her more 'formal' verse" (*History of the Voice*, 28). Referring to the sound of Don Drummond's trombone in Walcott's poem "Blues," Brathwaite laments that "the print/text can't reveal these things"; a footnote refers to the audio recordings played for Brathwaite's lecture (*History of the Voice*, 40). In both of these instances, Brathwaite identifies the aural/oral as the limit of textuality, as that which must be (but cannot be) preserved.

In Brathwaite's writing, the gap between vernacular performance and text is not a problem of the technology of transcription, nor is it a statement of the inherent superiority of oral forms. Rather, it is a question of the proper relation of poetry to history. In a recording of the question and answer period following the original presentation of *History of the Voice* at Carifesta in Kingston, Jamaica, in 1976, Brathwaite responds archly to a question about his characterization of Miss Lou in relation to nation language. "I hope this is recorded on the tape," he begins, "but my point was . . ."[22] It is not on the tape; the case labeled "History of the Voice" in the archives of the Library of the Spoken Word at UWI Mona, where the Carifesta literature symposium took place, contains only the question and answer session, not Brathwaite's presentation itself. Further, in *conVersations with Nathaniel Mackey* Brathwaite lists a recording of "History of the Voice" as one of the literary and musical works threatened or damaged by the flooding after Gilbert (300). Brathwaite's remark signals his persistent concern with the preservation not only of his own voice but of Caribbean literary history more broadly. The impossibility of hearing Brathwaite's archive of diasporic sound—from Claude McKay's reading voice to Derek Walcott's to Brathwaite's own to Don Drummond's trombone—is a defining feature of the text. The "blips" Brathwaite acknowledges between his own text and the rich aural performances that gave rise to it constitute the very form of poetry for which Brathwaite is calling.

In *History of the Voice* the hurricane functions in part as a metaphor for a sought-after poetic break from the past. How can we reconcile this future-oriented call for national poetics with Brathwaite's interest in preserving and restoring the history of Caribbean culture, an interest that also defines the themes and forms of his first two poetic trilogies? His fragmentary experimental poetic style might invite us to call into question what critics commonly take to be his investment in repairing a sense of wholeness and continuity, particularly in relationship to Africa. But Brathwaite's poetic response to Hurricane Gilbert undermines any overly mimetic reading.

Shar represents not only the destruction and displacement caused by Gilbert but also its figuration of the earlier human catastrophe of slavery. *Shar* begins with an echo of Brathwaite's earliest work, *The Arrivants*. This trilogy narrates both early migrations across the Sahara and the forced displacements of transatlantic enslavement as points of origin for Caribbean culture. In the opening poem of *The Arrivants*, "Prelude," the speaker under the whip of slavery dreams of African villages. The voice of the poem commands,

Build now
the new
villages, you
must mix spittle
with dirt, dug
to saliva and sweat (5)

These villages in the imagination of an enslaved person who has become disconnected from the past under the master's "whip/lash" become the starting point for a narrative of loss that also seeks to reclaim a connection to Africa. In its opening stanzas, *Shar* echoes the call to build, but in a way that frustrates that connection from the start. In the wake of the hurricane, the poetic style is fragmented as the landscape:

wood
has become so useless. stripped. wet .
fragile . broken . totally uninhabitable
with   what we must still build

a half-a-million shaved off from the auction block
curled & cut off from their stock
without even that sweet scent of resin on a good day

The reference to the auction block relates the hurricane to the slave trade's destructive effects on continuity within families, communities, and cultures. Natural disasters have the effect of deepening and revealing existing racial and social hierarchies, and Brathwaite returns to the scene of slavery several times throughout the poem. But Brathwaite does not actually liken the storm to the forced migrations of slavery. Instead, he depicts the former as an interruption of the latter. Hurricane Gilbert disrupts a culture that is already unbuilt. Referring to another Brathwaite poem, Nathaniel Mackey has described these kinds of connections as "historical rhymes," by which events and people "separated in time and space" come together in poetry ("An Interview with Kamau Brathwaite," 22). Mackey's term, unlike other forms of comparison such as "analogy" or "allegory," emphasizes the poetics of Brathwaite's historicism and describes the sonic process by which we can experience disparate historical moments as interconnected but not continuous.

Lamenting history's disjunctiveness, *Shar* nonetheless creates a history through sound and geography. As do many of Brathwaite's earlier poems, *Shar* begins by taking us through time and space to West Africa, but the poem reneges on the hopeful possibility of remaking the African village in poetic memory. The speaker laments that after being "bombed" by the storm, all is "wasted wasted wasted all all all wasted wasted wasted / the five hundred years of Columbus dragging us here / and the four thousand three hundred years before that / across valley & dune . dry river bed . gully & waddi . slip." The poem goes on to contrast the eroded history of the landscape with an abundant "grove" of West African environment and culture:

> scream of sandstorm . salt . mineral . glint . quartz
> cutting the soles of my feet . gold
> in the harrowed face of the rock . gold
> in what will become leaf . branch . gilt . eucalyptus . cocoa
>
> pod . odoum . tweneduru . chikichiki even the evening man.
> grove
> at Golokwati Krachi & Pong
>
> &
> the spider arachne Ananse
> the sweet of your arms hollowed out at Anum

Interspersing the names of trees in English, French, and West African languages within the geography of Ghana, Brathwaite creates a hybrid linguistic environment, at the same time using the stanzaic structure of the poem to suggest the distinct "shores" from which those languages come.

The storm does not interrupt this environment, however, so much as it interrupts the forced removal of "us" from that environment. "All" is "wasted" since Columbus. The storm interrupts wasting, a process Brathwaite describes in relationship to soil erosion. The substitution of "gully & waddi" for "valley & dune" poetically re-creates an environmental process whereby the valley, or wet riverbed, gives way to a gully, part of the process of soil erosion, and finally a wadi—the Arabic word used in English to describe valleys only intermittently inhabited by water, in the form, for example, of flash floods. The storm wastes what is already an experience of erosion and reduction.

> And all this. all this. reduced to all this
>
> to so little. this

to so almost nothing like this in the shattered cess of the storm . to this

nothinglessness in the thistle & cease. less like cease. less

Brathwaite describes a culture of ruin reduced to ruin: that which the slave trade has "shaved off," the storm has now "reduced." The repetition of the pronoun "this" within a tautological equation suggests that there is no distinction between the two processes, that there was no "this" to reduce. The premise of the poem, then, is the *end* of genealogy, the end of rootedness, a people "curled & cut off from their stock." The material work of the hurricane makes palpable the break from the history of colonialism that Brathwaite had long ago imagined, which in turn becomes the occasion for poetry. "This" becomes not only "cease" but "thistle," something that grows.

Under these circumstances, the poem asks us, in what form can culture reside and survive? *Shar*'s proximity to generically different texts in which Brathwaite describes the same events, sometimes in the same words, invites us to understand the poem as part of Brathwaite's archival project. The prefatory material in *Shar* consists of prose remarks by Carolivia Herron, who introduced Brathwaite's reading of the poem at Harvard's Center for the Study of Epic Poetry (or "Epicenter"). Herron's introduction reminds us of the poem's provenance as oral even as it also draws our attention to its interconnectedness with prose. Specifically, the bulk of the introduction is a quotation from "a small [prose] piece" Brathwaite "wrote when he heard of the hurricane," beginning "What can I say? What can I do?," a refrain that gets picked up in the repeated "What more can I tell you?" of the poem. The line between Brathwaite's prose and poetic responses to Gilbert is permeable. For example, Brathwaite reprints his prose descriptions of the destruction of his library not only in *Shar* but in his later interview with Mackey.

Just as in *History of the Voice* poetry is haunted by its supplemental status in relationship to music, in *Shar* poetry is both defined and threatened by its relationship to an informal and private form of writing: the diary.[23] The speaker recalls his flooded mementos:

all those scares that I have hidden in my closet . in this diary of water for
my daughter where I have placed a fern or fan or withered birthday rose .
poor croton leaf or yam shoot mark to mark some special page or love .

one of time's arrogant adornments.

The "diary of water" evokes the material reality of books flooded with water during the hurricane, especially in the context of Brathwaite's personal reflections on his flooded archive of Caribbean culture in Irish Town, reflections that frame *Shar*. The form of a diary defines the text of *Shar* in its opening sections in two important ways. First, for the first several pages the poem indeed proceeds as a narrative, a personal account of a public event in the immediate aftermath of its unfolding. The poem describes the scene of destruction ("it was like this all over the island"), then the storm's escalation ("and that more wind . rip . gust"), its effects ("this one Third World world of flickering rubbish"), and finally its resolution into song ("un / til at last"). Second, the lines of the poem in these sections visually approximate prose. One of Brathwaite's many accumulative descriptions of the winds, to take one example, extends close to the right margin, approaching and receding from the prose line:

And what. what. what . what more. what more can I tell you
on this afternoon of electric bronze
But that the winds . winds . winds . winds came straight on
& that there was no step . no stop . there was no stopp.
ing them & they begin to reel . in circles . scream. ing like Ezekiel's wheel

This is not to say that Brathwaite is actually writing prose here. These lines are undoubtedly poetic, attentive as they are to the break of the line and the tension between the line and the sentence, between syntactical structures and rhythmic ones. Brathwaite draws our attention to the approximate relationship between poetry and prose through excessive punctuation, fragmentation of prose syntax, and repetition. Like the winds it describes, the poem moves "in circles," returning again and again to the same phrases. In spite of the poem's impulse to narrate an event, the process of environmental approximation creates what Brathwaite would call a "tidalectic" pattern of circular motion. Brathwaite uses this environmental metaphor to describe how the shape of his writing has evolved over time. Describing his earlier trilogies he told Nathaniel Mackey that "it's not a linear movement, except in the sense of thesis-antithesis-synthesis. That is an overall idea. But since I started that it has been superseded with the idea of tidalectics, which is dialectics with my difference. In other words, instead of the notion of one-two-three, Hegelian, I am now more interested in the movement of the water backwards and forwards as a kind of cyclic, I suppose, motion, rather than linear" ("An Interview with Kamau Brathwaite," 14). The tidalectic motion between poetry and prose draws our attention to both the poem and the diary as physical objects. The poem is a "diary of water" that tells the story of flooding because it is itself flooded.

To imagine the poem *Shar* as a diary, indeed as one of Brathwaite's "sodden books," is to consider the status of poetry as both a print object and an extension of an oral tradition (song) with the capacity to circulate beyond the print archive. One of the poem's challenges is to describe or evoke the sounds of environmental experience. Throughout the opening sections, which narrate the direct environmental experience of the storm, Brathwaite emphasizes environmental and poetic noise:

And that more wind . rip . gust . scissors-howl

copper kettle boiling . boiling . boiling
over into your years
would wait. wait. wait like a snap or a flat rat trap in the streets
to freeze freeze frizzle

The alliteration sonically reproduces the sound of the wind, and the odd punctuation, coupled with occasionally pixelated letters, visually renders the "noise" of the hurricane's destruction. Even in the most narrative-like section of the poem, disaster's noise lays the groundwork for a more fragmented poetic form. *Shar* emerges as a lyric poem in part because of the way it transmutes sound into song.[24]

At the same time, we are aware of the poem we are reading as a physical object, one of those things drying out or lost. The "diary of water" might describe one of the books in Brathwaite's lost library, but also the poem itself, which contains "a fern or fan or withered birthday rose ./poor/croton leaf or yam shoot." The poem can contain "one of time's arrogant adornments," contain history even as it marks its loss. Brathwaite celebrates continuity here in the context of "my daughter," suggesting the continuity of both cultivation and writing intergenerationally and beyond the life of the poem. But the double status of the "diary of water" as the poetic page that survives, on the one hand, and the flooded archive, on the other, suggests the profound difficulty of this kind of continuity. The poem at once evokes the lost archive of sound and text and recreates that archive.[25]

Brathwaite's reference to the poem as a "diary of water" that preserves disjunctive history raises the crucial question of how the private, individual poem can account for a public or collective experience. Referring to the poem as "all those scares" and "this diary," the speaker describes poetry's albatross (to account for "time's arrogant adornments") and its instability as a genre. *Shar* also traverses the literary terrain between the diary of the private "I" who lived through the hurricane and speaks the poem and the history of the public "us"

Columbus dragged to the New World at the beginning of the poem. Brathwaite does not introduce a first-person speaker until the third section of the poem, and this speaker has a self-conscious authorial voice, as if burdened with the narrative of the storm: "And what. what. what more can I tell you," he asks, and then asks again two pages later, reminding us of the difficulty of narrating disaster. But if this speaker is removed from the experience, the "I" who speaks of the diary has a particular history: "all those scares that I have hidden in my closet."

The publication context of *Shar* underscores the relationship between Brathwaite's lyric "I" and a broader literary archive. Like many of his books from the eighties and early nineties, Brathwaite published *Shar* through Savacou Publications, which allowed artistic control over the visual form of the text. Having this control likely mitigated the difficulty of ensuring correct typesetting of his poems.[26] Connected in name with Brathwaite's influential *Savacou* journal, the press is at once culturally foundational and personal, idiosyncratic, Brathwaite's own. Many of its publications (including *Shar*) are limited editions, circulating mostly through academic libraries and private collections. In other words, the poem is a kind of public diary, embodying all of the contradictions of that oxymoronic phrase. Put differently: the poem becomes the private library of public culture whose loss Brathwaite laments.

When the poem moves beyond narrating the events of the storm, song functions thematically as a collective art form. After its meditation on the loss of the "diary of water" the poem interrupts its own formal continuity. Up until this point, the poem has proceeded more or less by offering a narrative of the storm. Brathwaite marks each section with a space, as well as the word "and," with the initial A enlarged and elaborate in the manner of an illustrated manuscript. After describing the diary of water, however, the poem moves from A to X, from the beginning of a sentence to its transgressive, criss-crossed middle.

one of time's arrogant adornments
X.
posed now & like a kicked up coin in the sun.

Unlike the A that begins a word, X stands alone on a line as if a Roman numeral. A compressed form of the prefix *ex-* (in the word "exposed," which is completed on the line below), X appears in the middle of the sentence, enlarged and pixelated, exemplifying the exposure it describes. We can think of X as the visual form of the approximation Brathwaite calls for in *History of the Voice*: both a connective and a marker of difference in relationship to the extreme environmental experience of the hurricane as well as the sonic experience "Xpressed" within the poem.

This moment marks the narrative break in the account of the hurricane. In her introduction, Herron calls on the poem to do the work of epic, which she defines as "a long narrative describing the origin & nature & destiny of a race, group, tribe, nation or gender, depicting a hero or heroic ideal and incorporating the cultural world-view of that hero and his/her people." Herron voices her desire to "save" such songs from their potential erasure. But having begun *Shar* with a kind of origin story, Brathwaite goes on to portray that origin as an historical rupture. Catastrophe is the starting point of poetic cultivation and collection. *Shar* must preserve a song that accounts for "the long narrative" of culture as well as its cycles and breaks, a song that reflects not just "the cultural world-view" of a "hero and his people" but a collective culture. After evoking the material losses suffered by those in the community in the form of hunger and thirst ("widows'/faces that must eat . that must eat . that must drink . that must sleep/beside these water ."), *Shar* turns to lyric as both its subject and its method. The widows "will open their doves again & again to a wet/leaf tomorrow . despite any sodden/or sorrow":

Un/til
at last
Stone
lone/ly
at first
& Slow/ly

out of the valleys. smoke. trail. trial. song

Approaching or approximating song, the poem shifts abruptly from phrases and sentences strung together in long lines with periods to a narrow column of text in enlarged (and varying) fonts, beginning with the pixelated, "illustrated" letter *U*. Even as the poem revels in sonic play, as in the internal rhymes taking us from "stone" to "lone/ly" to "slow/ly," it increasingly relies on visual play on the page, and self-consciously reminds us of the computer's creation of that play.

Whereas *History of the Voice* describes the challenge of accounting for environmental experience as a struggle to re-create sonic experience, "the actual rhythm and the syllables" (8), *Shar* and much of Brathwaite's later work reimagines its poetics of salvage in relationship to visuality, textuality, and print media.

In the nineties Brathwaite began to experiment with computer fonts, in particular, the font he would eventually name "Sycorax Video Style" after Sycorax, the witch who was Caliban's mother in *The Tempest*; we see the beginnings of this turn in *Shar*.[27] Insofar as Sycorax Video Style (given its excessive pixelation) is "dated" almost as soon as it is produced, it marks its own status as an archive. What are the implications of this deep engagement with the textual archive for a poetic language that seeks to transcend English print culture?

A textual or scribal poetry that foregrounds its own material form might seem to contravene the aims of nation language (the theory of poetic vernacular that Brathwaite develops in *History of the Voice*) insofar as such a language emphasizes the primacy of oral cultural forms. While celebrating Brathwaite's turn to Sycorax Video Style as an extension of nation language, Elaine Savory nonetheless describes written English language text in terms of its "strictures," against which the "freedoms" of orality are juxtaposed or within which the "freedoms" of orality are transposed ("Returning To Sycorax/Prospero's Response," 217–18).[28] But Brathwaite makes use of the visual properties of the text in a way that breaks down these binaries. As Anthony Reed puts it, "SVS's ensemble of techniques undoes the hierarchy between orality and visuality while, in a different register, illustrating orality to be a function of visuality insofar as it serves as an aural racial marker" (*Freedom Time*, 60). Brathwaite identifies textual experimentation as continuous with the project of an orally based nation language. Whereas Savory portrays video style as the bridge between an authentic or folk orality aligned with Caliban and a commercial print culture aligned with Prospero, maintaining the definitional divide between the two, Brathwaite imagines print culture in more expansive terms.[29] In *conVERSations*, Mackey asks him, "Are you no longer an oral poet?" (211). Brathwaite reassures him. "Have no fear!," he replies "Is more than oral—if we can put it this way—rather more than *conventionally* oral—because I think 'oral' in the conventional sense can only be part of what the 'Oral Tradition' is about. I mean, is never only 'voice' or 'sound' or 'narrative' or 'rap' or what have you. I mean what's *song* for goodness slake?" [*sic*] (211). For Brathwaite, a sense of "oral tradition" that includes the visual ("*timehri*/mural/graffiti") is especially crucial "in a world of *electronic* (s)" (215–16). It is not the task of written poetry alone to transcribe or even approximate performance; rather, performance embodies the visual and the oral at once.

To translate nation language into video style, Brathwaite evokes the experience of witnessing performance. Not surprisingly, this transformation takes

place both discursively and performatively. Brathwaite responds to Mackey in a
lengthy column of text:

> What we have to remem
> ber—get to know—about
> the   'Oral   Tradition,'
> is   that   it's   never
> only   *heard*,   it's   *seen*
> —is   *part*   of   a   total
> kinesis,   right?   is   n-
> ot simply that we he-
> ar it but we watch an
> (d)   we   *witness*   the   *gr*
> *iots*   as   they   go   thru
> the   sweat   of   their   me
> mory   to   their   memory
> (224)

By referring to "the sweat of the me/mory" that the audience witnesses,
Brathwaite draws attention to the body of a poet, the force mediating between
the visual witnessing and the oral recitation of the poem. He goes on to describe
the crucial role of the audience, addressing his audience at the Poet's House
event at which he and Mackey spoke "as watchful breath-/ing witness and
parti/cipants" (225). "Orality" in this rendition is more than sound or noise; it is
performance that relies on all of the senses. It relies, too, on reading and on perceiving the page visually. In *History of the Voice* Brathwaite draws our attention
to the lost sound, the inadequacy of the text in relationship to what is "on the
tape." In the "transcription" of *conVERSations*, however, he foregrounds a kind
of textual excess, augmenting and building around the original conversations
with large sections of poems in Sycorax Video Style, scribbles and shapes, boxes
and asides, font alterations. The published work, part of Brathwaite's library of
responses to Gilbert, visually insists on the textuality of sound and the sound
of text. Here Brathwaite's theory and practice of poetry anticipate Harryette
Mullen's important essay "African Signs and Spirit Writing," in which the black
American poet reverses the privileging of orality that has been common in African American literary criticism. Unearthing a spiritual and folk tradition of
writing (one separate from the imposed European tradition that equated literacy with freedom and humanity), Mullen reminds us "that African American
literacy might be continuous rather than discontinuous with African ways of

knowing, and with traditional systems of oral and visual communication that
represent natural and supernatural forces as participants in an extralinguistic
dialogue with human beings" ("African Signs and Spirit Writing," 679–680).
With Mullen in mind, Brathwaite's investments in the scribal emerge not as a
necessary evil in an age of print but as a visionary practice.

We might infer that Brathwaite's avant-garde motion from roots (the title of
his 1986 collection of essays) to software constitutes a move away from the ecological to the technological and, in turn, a transformation of the particular into
the universal. However, even in *History of the Voice* Brathwaite evokes "software" as a metaphor for the language that would allow us to evoke the hurricane
(8). In the second half of *Shar*, song takes the form of image and artifact, self-
consciously enlarged, punctuated, at times pixelated. Part 2 opens with a command: "So / sing / sing / clatter of ashes / collapses of coal." If the poem begins
with a capture narrative evoking the flora of West Africa—"leaf . branch . gilt .
eucalyptus . cocoa / pod . odoum / tweneduru"—its concluding song brings us
into a more generalized landscape: "what's left of the / stone of the / mourn. /
ing / the mount. ain / black." But by emphasizing the materiality of language
through pixelation and enlargement, Brathwaite reminds us that pages contain
the particular materials of place and of culture: "poor croton leaf or yam shoot."
Throughout part 2 the words "sing" and "song" punctuate the song itself. "Sing"
is often a command that interrupts storytelling in the poem. To take one example, a first-person speaker begins to tell the story of his interaction with the
weather:

> but
> looka me borrow a
> cloud from de rain
> wid it rain. bow
> still wet when a
> shine. when a
> shine. in wid. out
> com. pen. sation
> or. as I say. sorrow

These lines take up an entire page, and are the wordiest passage in part 2. Most
of the lines have at least two stresses, distinguishing the meter of this passage as
fluid and fast. These qualities, along with the visual approximation of colloquial
speech (the conventional "de" for "the"), create the sense of a storytelling "I."
In its particularity, this moment contrasts sharply with the abstract "Stone of

the / mourn. ing" to follow. The very next page interrupts the story of the cloud borrower:

but

Sing.

ing

&

Sing.

ing

The syllabic arrangement of the page undermines the narrative cohesion of the previous one. This moment disrupts one kind of particularity while generating another: the song "from the throats of the five hundred thousand" is its own cultural artifact, made palpable in its visual presentation on the page (see figs. 6.1–6.4). Enlargements, pixelations, and repetition of the letter S and the word "song" emphasize the song's visual materiality over its sonic qualities. Paradoxically, then, the storm gives literal shape to the presence of that cultivation or culture which it has destroyed.

In "Another 'Our America,'" Raphael Dalleo argues that Brathwaite's work in this period crucially challenges the framework of genealogical continuity as the basis for Caribbean culture. In particular, Dalleo cites Brathwaite's experimentations with visual form made possible by computer typography as a discourse of identity that constitutes an alternative to "rootedness" (7). But if his turn to technology is a turn away from rootedness in a metaphorical sense—insofar as disjunctive visual forms disrupt continuity with either Europe or Africa—Brathwaite nonetheless remains interested in the language and forms of cultivation as markers of culture.

If Brathwaite maintains his focus on the material world (necessarily) as a place for housing the material archives of culture, the emphasis on song in *Shar* nonetheless suggests that poetry functions and endures beyond the printed page, beyond, that is, that which can be stored—and lost—in the archive. The catastrophe forces us to imagine an enduring archive that would not be subject to the destructive forces of hurricane winds. I am reminded here of the songs that traveled in the aftermath of Gilbert, in the streets and on the radio. The aural experience of those songs has remained part of the Jamaican imagination for almost thirty years, outliving the sonic technology of the LP and resurfacing on CDs and MP3s and online in bootleg YouTube videos that allow the music to migrate that much more easily. While celebrating such "instrumental migrations," to use Vazquez's term again, Brathwaite is not quite content to turn the

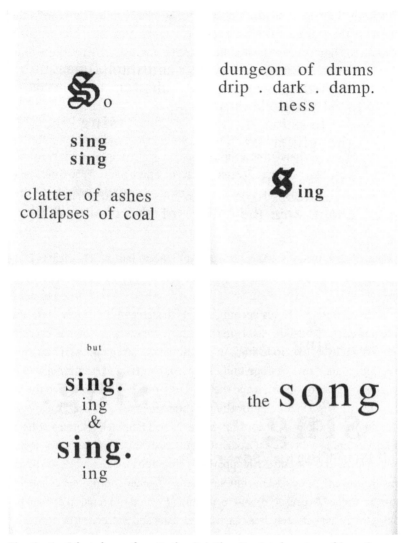

Figs. 6.1–6.4. Selected pages from Brathwaite's *Shar*. Reprinted courtesy of the author.

page on the duration of the written word; for him, then, "software" is one potential form of that duration, not the end of cultivation but its future.

THE LIBRARY AND THE MOUNTAIN

Throughout his reflections on Gilbert, Brathwaite makes visible the intimacy between cultural and environmental experience. In *conVERSations with Nathaniel Mackey*, he describes the conditions of what Herron calls, in her introduction to *Shar,* his "Library of Alexandria" in Jamaica. After coming into conflict with officials at the University of West Indies, who failed to help him rescue and maintain the library after the flooding, Brathwaite responded in these lines to officials' accusation that Brathwaite had not cared for his own library:

> that the house at IT
> is built on an older structure or "Dump"
> which we find & buy there—a structure, as I say, like build into the
> mountain, the main back wall being right up against the breathing
> bulk of the massif itself, which, since the library occupied the whole
> space of this wall, means that we find damp coming in thru the
> wall & into that whole line of books on the shelves along there
>
> (148)

In spite of Brathwaite's efforts to stave off the moisture, Hurricane Gilbert brought "water coming onto the floor of the library," which resulted in "sodden books," and left "the road & most of the roofless house itself buried under this landslide mountain." In his account of this disaster in *conVERSations*, Brathwaite makes the landslide visible in the right-justified text, which is eventually overwrought by its own long lines. In describing the mountain, as if human, as a "breathing bulk," this passage unifies environmental and literary space, suggesting their shared condition and their interconnected histories. Even the word "massif," used as a synonym for the mountain, evokes the "massive"—which in reggae terminology is, according to the *OED*, a noun describing a collective (often a listening collective at a party or musical event). The boundary between the landscape and the culture it apparently threatens is permeable. At the same time, Brathwaite opposes continuous "damp" against continuous culture (the books he wishes to preserve) and in so doing highlights a tension central to all of his works: that between breaking from the past and preserving it.

The conditions Brathwaite describes were not unique to his house or his archive, as he points out in *conVERSations*. Photos of Hurricane Gilbert's damage in the archives of the National Library of Jamaica (see figs. 6.5–6.8) draw attention to the bloated, roofless remains of culture and education elsewhere in and around Kingston. These images of the University of West Indies campus besieged by water, "sodden books" left out to dry, and of a parish library's migrated roof draw our attention not only to the personal and economic consequences of the hurricane but also to the institutional and cultural ones.[30] Likewise, Brathwaite's description of his damp library invites us to consider the special challenges of preserving cultural materials in light of the climatic alternation between drought and flood. The image also evokes the particular intimacy (albeit

Fig. 6.5. Books being placed outside to dry at Norman Manley Law School. Photo: Courtesy of the National Library of Jamaica, Kingston, Jamaica.

Fig. 6.6. University of West Indies grounds after Hurricane Gilbert. Photo: Courtesy of the National Library of Jamaica, Kingston, Jamaica.

Fig. 6.7. St. Ann's Parish Library. Photo: Courtesy of the National Library of Jamaica, Kingston, Jamaica.

a threatening and destructive one) between the library and its environment. Brathwaite's books cannot exclude the water of the world. Although Gilbert exacerbates the problem, Brathwaite's account of the library's fate in *conVERSations* underscores the universality and the continuity of the "damp" that threatened his collection of Caribbean culture. That is, Gilbert extended and exacerbated a preexisting dampness that poses a challenge to preserving not only Brathwaite's archive but also Caribbean archives more broadly.

The environmental condition of Brathwaite's library mirrors the environmental condition of Jamaica's agriculture and ecology after Gilbert: devastated by the event but also by continuing catastrophe, that is, a gradual overturning whose results have the effect of disaster. As Barker and Miller have noted, Gilbert intensified the preexisting problem of soil erosion "as a consequence of both historical and agricultural malpractice" ("Hurricane Gilbert," 109). While there is some debate as to the extent and cause of deforestation in Jamaica's Blue

Mountains, at the time of Gilbert it was believed that Jamaica had a high rate of deforestation and attendant problems with water supply, agricultural productivity, biological diversity, soil erosion and landslides.[31] This environmental degradation was caused both by logging and by small-scale farming practices, particularly the production of coffee for international export, which extended the destructive agricultural economy of the plantation.[32] If it is true, as Jamaican economist Michael Witter has claimed, that "no problem, and particularly the environmental one, can be seen clearly except through the lens of our colonial history" (qtd. in Weis, "Beyond Peasant Deforestation"), then Brathwaite's lost library, in its intimacy with the mountain, also indexes that environmental history. Thus, it is not only the case that the natural world—in the form of a hurricane—is a menace from without that threatens cultural progress. Rather, in Brathwaite's account, Jamaican culture and ecology share a colonial history, in the face of which both struggle to survive.

Like Lovindeer's "Wild Gilbert," Brathwaite's poem sets itself up within the urban geography of Kingston (although Irish Town itself is outside of the city limits). The cover of the volume depicts a street sign that reads "Stanton Terr,"

Fig. 6.8. St. Thomas Parish Library. Photo: Courtesy of the National Library of Jamaica, Kingston, Jamaica.

indicating a street in the northern part of the city, and the opening lines establish Kingston as a kind of synecdoche for Jamaica:

For the stone of this island to be bombed
by this wind & all this. all this. water
O longshore late light duppy Kingston nights

However, whereas "Wild Gilbert" emphasizes the hurricane's costs only within that urban environment and specifically in the realm of material culture, Brathwaite's poem draws our attention to the interconnectedness of nature and culture. Alongside the detritus of human habitats—"zinc sheets crippled to the earth," "wrecked homes" and of course sodden books—he describes

all over this island of the dead Arawaks

craters of outflung cherry & guinep & guava like they never knew
what hit them

the sacred lignum vitae stunned into a sudden sullenness of olive
grey
banana windmills broken

Here the "duppies" of "Kingston nights" get named: "dead Arawaks" haunt the landscape; their death is in fact the precondition for the cultivated landscape. And yet the indeterminacy of the pronoun "they" in the second line seems to equate the flinging of "cherry & guinep & guava" with the near extermination of the indigenous population, elevating those fruit trees and even the "banana windmills" to the status of the island's lost ancestors, equating the violent erasures of history with the violence of the storm, and imbuing trees with the capacity to know and be "stunned." Evoking the intimacy between his diary and the island's agricultural products, between his familial and creative genealogy and the cultivation of land, between ancestry and ecology, Brathwaite writes against the alienation between land and community that Glissant has described in *Caribbean Discourse*.

SCATTA ARCHIVES

Having evoked the hurricane as the sign of Caribbean poetics in *History of the Voice* Brathwaite transforms the meteorological formulation of the hurricane into more than a metaphor for poetry in his writings on Gilbert. Almost thirty years after Gilbert, Brathwaite still strives to find a home for his archive, as development projects in Barbados threaten his homestead "Cow Pastor," where, he has written, he dreams of establishing a cultural center, with "enough peace & space & beauty" ("The Lass Days of KB and CowPastor Vandal"). Much of the discourse around this continued displacement—including Brathwaite's poems as well as letters to and from editors and friends—has taken place using new "software": on websites and online discussion boards, which, as Joyelle McSweeney points out in an interview with Brathwaite, we might understand as continuous with the intersection of technology and catastrophe that produced Sycorax Video Style. In this context Brathwaite not only makes the case for the preservation of his archive but for the environment of Cow Pastor itself. In these electronically circulated pleas, he laments the loss of cattle, of a water catchment that would prevent future flooding, and of a bearded fig tree that he describes as "cruelly unethically soon to gone" ("The Lass Days of KB and CowPastor Vandal"). The bearded fig tree (a type of *Ficus* native to the Caribbean, South America, and some southern states in North America) is a visual metonym for the bearded poet Brathwaite and a cultural metonym for Barbados. In an early poem, "The Emigrants" (*The Arrivants*, 55), Brathwaite alludes to the popular theory that these trees were Europeans' first observation upon sighting the island (and, some say, the source of the island's name, which means "the bearded ones" in Portuguese).[33] Brathwaite thus laments both the diminishment of nature and the loss of the home where he had hoped "to in-gather the scatta archives" of Caribbean culture. Brathwaite's reference to "my nation here—my maroon town" does not evoke nation in a genealogically and geographically bound sense but rather as a place (in a poem) where it is possible "to keep alive the making of the past."[34]

Brathwaite's essential claim that the hurricane does not roar in pentameter has resonated throughout this book because it provokes a crucial question about the relationship between organic and literary forms. His account of Irish Town suggests that the local and global exigencies of environmental disaster require a way of understanding both rupture and continuity as formal qualities in literature. As Ursula Heise has argued, the study of environmental literature in particular requires "formal countermodels to ecolocalism" as an antidote to the way environmental discourse and American nationalism have developed in tandem (*Sense of Place and Sense of Planet*, 7).[35] My starting point has not been a historical moment in American environmentalism so much as a series of moments in the development of black modern consciousness. But like Heise I believe that the intersections of environmental and social history in these moments have produced a transnational body of literature. Brathwaite is a key figure because the hurricane sweeps through his writings in both theory and practice, uniting our concerns with literary form and our understanding of Caribbean environmental experience.

Rob Nixon has cautioned against "historically indifferent formalism that treats the study of aesthetics as the literary scholar's definitive calling," particularly in the context of literary environmentalism (*Slow Violence and the Environmentalism of the Poor*, 31). Nixon is concerned about what Anne McClintock has called a "fetishism of form" (*Imperial Leather*, 63), the process through which certain kinds of formal practices become invested with too much political or social meaning. Nixon and McClintock rightly worry that we run the risk of attributing too much agency to discourse or form and not enough to people. In the realm of environmental change, Nixon contends, writers must engage and affiliate with "nonliterary forces for social change" or risk irrelevance (32). By condemning both "indifferent" criticism and politically engaged formalism, however, he leaves little room for aesthetic attention in literary criticism, or at least literary criticism concerned with environmentalism. Nixon's project crucially aims to generate more complex, intersectional identities, but writing off the power of literary forms eliminates a foundational element of anticolonial and postcolonial literary development. We need to ask instead what a historically *attentive* formalism would look like. That is, how can we attend to poetic form without turning our backs on the real world or, on the other hand, falling prey to anthropomorphism and abstraction?

We can augment Nixon's crucial rethinking of catastrophic time by attending to "nonhistory" as a poetic practice and historical method articulated by black diasporic writers.[36] Critical attention to the *forms* of poetic language in Brathwaite's poetry, interviews, and missives in response to Hurricane Gilbert allows us to approach the poet's representations of historical time. While a poetics of rupture may not be inherently progressive or revolutionary (and here is where Nixon's caution is well-taken), it is the case that for many poets in the African diaspora, poetic forms (such as the sonnet), meters (such as iambic pentameter), images (the daffodil, snow) and languages (nation language) have been intimately linked with the histories of colonialism, slavery, and resistance. For Brathwaite, lyric poetry, as a visual and aural medium, encompasses both continuous and disjunctive cultural and environmental histories, creating a place in the poetic imagination of the future capacious enough for the "scatta archives" of land and language alike.[37]

coda

Unnatural Catastrophe
The Ecology of Black Optimism in M. NourbeSe Philip's *Zong!*

NO SUCH THING AS A NATURAL DISASTER

Edwidge Danticat's book of essays *Create Dangerously* opens with an image of a political execution during the 1960s and concludes with one of the rubble of the 2010 earthquake in Port-au-Prince. In between, the collection meditates on the collective losses of our times—from AIDS to 9/11. Danticat started writing the collection in 2008, two years before the earthquake, but the published volume elegizes the "two hundred thousand and more" lost in the earthquake, to whom Danticat dedicates the book. "And more" not only refers to the difficulty of counting those lost in the earthquake but of counting losses that extend beyond this singular event. The earthquake animates Danticat's poetics of grief, giving physical form to a catastrophe in the making that was already the subject of the book. My concluding inquiry pauses in the space between the "two hundred thousand" and the "more" of Danticat's collection, between what we would typically describe as "natural disaster" and the continuing catastrophes of poverty, political upheaval, and illness that are at least partially the subjects of Danticat's book.

Popular contemporary discourse on contemporary disasters, such as Spike Lee's documentary *When the Levees Broke* (2006) and the HBO series *Treme* (2010–13), exposes the connection between racial and environmental experience. But as we have seen, the intersection between race and nature has a long tradition in black diasporic writing that derives not only from catastrophic experience but from a persistent interest in the labor, processes, and spaces of cultivation. This tradition has remained surprisingly robust in the United States and the Caribbean throughout the twentieth century in spite of urban migration, metropolitan immigration, and the vexed legacy of enforced agricultural labor. In my discussions of environmental disaster, I have restricted my study so far to catastrophes that nature causes (or at least seems to cause): floods and hurricanes as opposed to acts of terror, holocausts, oil spills, or nuclear accidents. But as Danticat's book suggests and as Junot Díaz makes explicit in his 2011 essay "Apocalypse" in the *Boston Review*, the Haiti earthquake and Hurricane Katrina were "social disasters" insofar as they revealed and intensified racial, economic, and global inequities, blurring the boundary between human and natural agency. After Katrina, geographer Neil Smith went so far as to say that for environmental geographers, "there is no such thing as natural disaster," but Smith clarified that, "the denial of the naturalness of disasters is in no way a denial of natural process" ("There's No Such Thing as a Natural Disaster"). Elsewhere, he has identified the central problem in trying to disentangle "natural" and human agency: "the attempt to distinguish social" from "natural contributions to climate change . . . leaves sacrosanct the chasm between nature and society" (*Uneven Development*, 244). Disasters like Katrina and the Haiti earthquake require us to think of ecology in a broader sense, to wade into this chasm, as the temporality of the event gives way to continuing catastrophes of everyday life. Can the mutual formation of the social and the natural likewise help us to understand disasters we have more commonly understood as "human"?

That is, what happens when we think of a political execution, a massacre, or a bombing as environmental experience? In this coda I turn to another text that has been haunting my definitions of disaster, indeed, my definition of nature: *Zong!* a 2009 book-length sequence of poems by Tobagan and Canadian poet M. Nourbese Philip that recounts the well-known story of the 1781 massacre aboard the *Zong* slave ship. Traversing the boundary between human and natural catastrophe, Philip engages in the kind of dangerous creation for which Danticat calls.

Although Philip's book is not about a hurricane, an earthquake, a flood, or a drought, I have been unable to shake the sense that it belongs in a project that considers the intersection of race studies and environmental experience. *Zong!* does not respond to environmental disaster so much as it writes the continuing catastrophe of black diasporic experience. Representing the middle passage as such a continuing catastrophe, Philip encourages us to rethink the natural in natural disaster. It is in this sense that we can think of *Zong!* as ecological—that is, not only as a poem that seeks to exhume black bodies from the confines of history but also as one attempt to articulate a model for interrelation among and between humans and their nonhuman environments.

The story of the *Zong* ship has been told not only in Philip's poem but in J. M. W. Turner's 1840 painting *The Slave Ship*, originally titled *Slavers Throwing Overboard the Dead and Dying—Typhoon Coming On*, in Ian Baucom's 2008 critical historiography *Specters of the Atlantic*, which approaches the *Zong* massacre and ensuing legal case as a test case for unearthing the flows of Enlightenment capital, and in a number of creative works by Caribbean writers, notably *Feeding the Ghosts* by Fred D'Aguiar. Turner's painting anticipates the entanglement of natural and human violence that would later concern Danticat. The original title syntactically links "slavers throwing overboard" to "typhoon coming on," and the painting itself seems to bring together the two kinds of violence. One could argue that Turner's painting therefore naturalizes the murder of the Africans, first, by making invisible any sense of human agency and, second, by depicting an environment whose very danger rests in the proximity, near indistinguish-ability, of the waves and the body parts.[1] Philip's poem similarly immerses us in this danger but toward a different end: the poem invites us to hover between experiences of racial violence as natural and as human, between the curse and the promise of black subjectivity, between the confinement and the movement of the middle passage.

Bound for Jamaica with a fully insured cargo of approximately 470 people from the west coast of Africa, the ship *Zong* was delayed by a series of naviga-tional errors; provisions ran low, people died of thirst, others threw themselves overboard. Finally, the captain ordered 150 African captives to be thrown over-board in order to keep the rest of them alive. After making landfall, the captain attempted to collect insurance for the economic loss of the drowned "cargo." The insurance company denied the claim, and a series of legal court cases en-sued. Of the legal archive, what remains is a single transcription of the *Gregson v. Gilbert* appellate court's decision (which decision Philip includes as the final pages of her book) in which insurers appealed an earlier verdict awarding dam-ages to the ship's owners. The justices ruled for a new trial, but it is unclear whether it took place. In spite of abolitionist Granville Sharpe's attempts to shift the terms of the conversation from economic to human loss, the case re-mained an insurance case—not a murder case.[2]

Philip's *Zong!* draws our attention to the suspension of the terms "natural" and "human" in the face of the massacre (and the violence of the legal language that is our only written record of the story). Philip's poem is divided into five sec-tions and is accompanied by a glossary, a ship's manifest, "Notanda" (Philip's essay on the writing process), and the legal transcript. The surrounding docu-ments are as much a part of the books' ecology as the poems themselves. I dwell on the legal language before getting to the poems because we need to untangle the vexed category of the "natural" in the legal case and because the texts con-stitute one environment in *Zong*'s poetics.

The legal decisions hinged on whether the enslaved had died "by the perils of the seas," in which case the insurers were liable, or whether their deaths were a mere matter of "mortality," in which case the insurers were not liable (*Zong!*, 210–11). According to a digest of insurance law published in the same year as the *Zong* massacre took place, in maritime law,

> the insurer takes upon him the risk of the loss, capture, and death of slaves, or any other unavoidable accident to them: but natural death is always understood to be excepted: —by natural death is meant, not only when it happens by disease or sickness, but also when the captive destroys himself through despair, which often happens: but when slaves are killed or thrown into the sea in order to quell an insurrection on their part, then the insurers must answer.[3]

The digest contends, reasonably, it seems, that throwing the Africans overboard is "unnatural" but it also naturalizes the ongoing conditions of the slave trade: if enslaved captives die of hunger, thirst, or illness or kill themselves because of the inhumane conditions of the human trade in human bodies, then that is "natural." This kind of logic motivated the ship company's lawyers to insist that the enslaved passengers died not from mortality but from "the perils of the seas and of enemies." Embracing the unnaturalness of these deaths, the company did not, however, acknowledge human agency. So, the system of slavery depends on a false and violent differentiation between the human and the nonhuman—one justice siding with the plaintiffs refers to his "fellow-creatures" as "goods" and "residue"—but at the same time on a blurring of the boundary between natural and human dangers, between "the perils of the sea" and murder.

In the context of environmental study, it might be thought desirable to blur the line between humanity and its other, nature, as a way of invoking a new kind of care and responsibility for the nonhuman world. In *Ecology without Nature* Timothy Morton writes with and against this grain of environmental criticism, drawing a connection between works ordinarily read under the sign of "nature poetry" and self-consciously experimental or "ambient poetry," which, he argues, depends on the idea of a "surrounding atmosphere" even when it doesn't explicitly refer to "nature" (22). He doesn't necessarily celebrate one kind of environmental writing over the other, but he finds ambience a useful category for understanding both our desire for intimacy with nature and the obstacles to the fulfillment of that desire. This expansive way of reading ecologically invites us to think of ecological writing as concerned with "the environment" not just in terms of content but also in its form.

Along these lines I'm asking what it means to think of *Zong!* as an ecology rather than as descriptive of ecology. But given that the category confusion be-

tween human and nonhuman worlds might be desirable as one way of reimagining our relationship to the environment, the poem whose "surrounding atmosphere" is the slave ship and its accompanying dehumanizing discourse also
marks the violence of ambience itself. Philip's manipulation of legal language
at the most basic level draws our attention to the consequences of this category
confusion for the survival of black subjects. In "Zong #9" she describes

            slaves

        to the order in

destroyed

          the circumstance in

fact

          the property in

subject

         the subject in

creature

           the loss in

underwriter

        the fellow in

negro (17)

Situating herself within the legal language of the case, Philip to some extent enacts what Morton calls "ecomimesis," that is, writing which draws our attention
to a surrounding world. She limits herself, in the cycle of poems that makes up
the first section of *Zong!*, to what she calls the "word store" of the legal decision
Gregson v. Gilbert. The first word prison in which we find ourselves is "water,"
which in "Zong #1" acts as a *pharmakon*—both deadly and desirable. The speaker
of the poem is either a drowning body or a person dying of thirst. The poem
stutters and stops; it floods and withholds: ("www   w a wa / w a wa t / er ")
(3). The spaces between letters on the page suggest the fluid environment in
which bodies disperse.

By drawing a parallel between the text and the ship's cargo hold, Philip portrays the legal decision as an environment in the broad sense of that term: a
physical space in which the poetic speaker dwells. In "Notanda" she compares
the process of mimetic writing in relationship to the built environment of the
ship itself: "I would lock myself in this text in the same way men, women, and
children were locked in the holds of the slave ship *Zong*" (192). The outer "word
store" simultaneously enables and imprisons the in-dwelling voice of the poem.

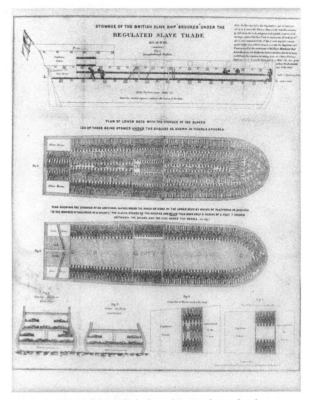

Fig. 7.1. Stowage of the British slave ship *Brookes* under the regulated slave trade act of 1788. Library of Congress Rare Book and Special Collections Division Washington, DC.

Parts of the poem visually evoke the tight space of the cargo hold (figs. 7.1 and 7.2), the geometry of arranged bodies, the shape of the ship, the exterior that *contains* individuals—bodies, words, "silences."

The poem writes against this containment: as *Zong!* progresses, Philip breaks up the legal language of her word store and reorganizes the letters to create a new lexicon, which includes words from French, Spanish, Dutch, Yoruba, Shona, and various kind of patois.

I mutilate the text as the fabric of African life and the lives of these men, women and children were mutilated. . . . I murder the text, literally cut it into pieces, castrating verbs, suffocating adjectives, murdering nouns, throwing articles, prepositions, conjunctions overboard, jettisoning adverbs: I separate subject from verb, verb from

of

water

day one . . .

for sustenance

water

day

one . . .

one day's

water

day

one . . .

sour

water

day

one . . .

three butts good

of voyage

(a month's)

Thandiwe Lukman Babuh Lüc Sikumbuso

11.

Fig. 7.2. Page from M. NourbeSe Philip's *Zong!* Published by
Wesleyan University Press. Used by permission.

object—create semantic mayhem, until my hands bloodied, from so much killing and
cutting, reach into the stinking, eviscerated innards. (193)

Analyzing her process of "unlocking" the hidden word store of the legal text,
Philip describes a revenge poetics in which the legal text seems like a group of
bodies and then a single body. There is no bleaker artistic imprisonment, no
greater catastrophe than this one—the poet inside the body of enslaving discourse, replicating its murderous logic. Evoking and transforming this violence
becomes the poem's curiously optimistic project. Philip's mutilation of the words
does not merely repeat but also expands, explodes, dismantles, sinks, and disperses the "tight space" of language. By the end of the poem the words spread
out; they are pale, overlapping, they fill the page. They become, a "surrounding

atmosphere"—not the tight space of the legal text or cargo hold but another kind of linguistic ecology in which we immerse ourselves.

When I taught this poem for the first time, students remarked that because of the radical juxtaposition of multiple languages and the breaking up of words into what at first seems like nonsense, the later sections of the poem evoke experiences of the people on the ship who would have been disoriented and confused. My students were alienated by words they could not pronounce or translate. Few of them did the work of flipping to the glossary as they read at home, they admitted. More were willing to experience the poem as a form of disorientation, to allow the poem to work on them, or not. Philip describes something similar in her writing process. Early on, she writes in "Notanda," "the poems resist my attempts at meaning or coherence" (195). So we might describe this as a kind of ecomimetic violence.

But the poem stops short of resting in the "illusion of a false immediacy" between experience and representation that Morton defines as characteristic of ambient poetry (182). Even as the poem disrupts meaning and breaks down artifice so as to create an apparently authentic immersion in violence, the framing devices of the book—Philip's essays, her word store, the glossary, and the legal text—reinscribe the dichotomy between inside and outside. These materials suggest a "reality" out there, in the "actual" record of the case, even a "real world" in which Philip composes the poem and keeps a journal about her composition: "It is June—June 15, 2002 to be exact, a green and wet June in Vermont." Morton might describe this as a "medial statement," drawing our attention to the environment in which the artist creates and potentially maintaining the fiction of a "real nature."[4] In this way, ambient poetics often seem to deny the existence of the boundary they mark, and thus to naturalize the aesthetic. But in Philip's poem the medial reminders of that boundary instead keep alive the subject, specifically the black subject, within the very "atmosphere" of her supposed erasure.

Further, if the legal environment and ship deny the agency of the enslaved, Philip's claim to spiritual inspiration by an African ancestor allows her to mark the violent suppression of black agency while also evoking non-European sources of lyric subjectivity. As I've already suggested, Philip authorizes the legal word store as an "environment" outside the world of the poem, generating an automatic writing exercise that would at first appear to minimize the subjectivity of the author or even speaker. In the first cycle of poems, which is the part of the book derived exclusively from the legal text, there appears to be no lyric speaker. Syntax subordinates the "me in/become"(18) But *Zong!* adds a third term to the binary of inside and outside by insisting up upon yet another source of "the real": on its cover and title page, the book purports to be written "as told to the author by Setaey Adamu Boateng." In printing the text of the legal decision and naming the spiritual ancestor who speaks through the poet, Philip gestures toward competing, indeed incongruous, notions of "the real," inserting, disintegrating, and displacing multiple subjects into and from the discourse of environmental immersion.

Through simultaneous, opposite structures of containment Philip creates an expansive "environment" that both surrounds and includes us. Distressed that ship logs did not contain the names of the Africans on board, Philip prints a list of names derived from Yoruba, Shona, Ibo, and other African languages at the bottom of each page, visually manifesting the drowning of the African bodies in the book's first major section, "Os." The named Africans are submerged, but they also become the environment in which Philip surrounds the legal text, reversing the outside/inside structure that frames the entire book. Immersion in this environment endangers "Rufaro, Uwimano, Kesi, Zuwena," but the poem spatially reorganizes the relationships among different categories of people, insisting upon the human dimension otherwise excised from the legal text. Two of the most prominent words in the text are the word "in" and forms of "to be"; structures of immersion and the ontology of the enslaved Africans necessarily coexist in the poem.

If the alternating structures of immersion cause us to question the division between inside and outside in the early pages of *Zong!*, subsequent sections appear to break the boundary down entirely. In "Dicta," the final subsection of "Os," the names have vanished but the line that separated them from the main part of the page remains. In *Sal* and the subsequent sections, the line between the legal language and the dead Africans disappears altogether as the poem becomes increasingly fragmented; words from African languages as well as names of women and men become part of the discourse of the poem. Marking "inside/ outside," inverting inside/outside, and then dissolving the boundary at the very moment of voicing black language and inserting black names, Philip structurally emphasizes the interrelatedness but not the interchangeability of black and white subjects and their environment.

Reading the poem aloud together, my students heard something that undermined the all-too-easy thesis that their experience of disorientation immersed them in the experience of the enslaved people aboard the ship: they heard the voice of a lyric speaker which punctures the illusion of "ambience." In the third section, *Zong!* evokes a surprising subject: a white European man, perhaps the captain or a member of the crew who participated in the murder, whose addressee is Ruth, a "she negro," in his words, whom he either murders, loves, or rapes. This speaker voices the closest thing to a narrative of the violence of the transatlantic slave trade:

                                               pan of pain that
                        is s
                                    pain a round
          the globe *mi orbe*
                        de oro bring   the slop pail pin
                              her hold her
                                               legs wide wet
          her throw   water the shelves   a mess i
                had an eye   a very good

        eye   for   negroes i grade (108–109)

But this speaker—here a human trafficker and rapist—is more than a despicable narrator from whom the poem distances us ironically. He is consumed by his own sin. But more importantly, he is "many-voiced" (205). Morton writes, "If we are ever able to achieve ecology without nature, it will be difficult, if not impossible, and even undesirable, to achieve ecology without a subject" (182–83). By splintering the discourse of the white male subject, Philip's poem suggests instead that we must achieve ecology with subjects plural.

The poem implicates us collectively in the making of catastrophe. Recounting the scene of the poem's central crime, the speaker begs,

                                    ease my
                  mind ruth she was   too thin hang
                                         him over
                        board throw her (110)

Even as the speaker attempts to absolve himself through Ruth, commanding her to "ease my / mind," he also tries to imagine "the ne / gro in me" and the "song in negro." In spite of the expansive Whitmanian tone, the line break in the middle of the first instance of the word "ne / gro" suggests the sharp split between the speaker and the other. And a desire for song—our own, perhaps—splits the speaker's dominant imperative voice into others. Other narratives overtake this primary speaker's telling, most notably an African's narrative of capture, which repeats itself at various points in the poem:

$$\begin{matrix}
& \text{it was it} & & \text{real master sir} & \\
\textit{me i} & & \textit{beg you you} & & \textit{write fo mi you} \\
& \textit{say ayo dem} & & \textit{cam fo me in} & \\
& & \textit{de field me run (105)} & &
\end{matrix}$$

Thus, even if Philip often suggests in "Notanda" that the text is automatic, the poem reads instead as a collection of collectively produced competing narratives. If at first Philip resists meaning making, later, "in the discomfort and disturbance created by the poetic text, I am forced to make meaning from apparently disparate elements. . . . And since we have to work to complete the events, we all become implicated in, if not contaminated by, this activity" (198).

Self-implication is not only an ethical stance but an ecological one, insofar as the poem produces a structure of interconnection among and between its subjects and their environment, what I have named a "lyric ecology." I've said that my students began to hear, in the later sections of the book, the voice of a lyric subject. But they also began to hear, in each other's voices, the multiple voices in the poem. Describing his own experience teaching this poem, Fred Moten has suggested that "one person can't read this poem; it has to be read symphonically" (*Social Text* Thirtieth Anniversary Panel Discussion). Perhaps it is this symphonic subjectivity that properly historicizes the ecology of the slave ship. Reading *Zong!* as ecological in this broader sense brings me back to my original supposition that the catastrophic imagination does not so much represent the tornado or the earthquake as it concatenates and collects the voices of others.

One broader contention of this book is that lyric poetry in particular can house this sort of collection because of its capacity to encompass the disjunctive ecologies, temporalities, and materials of diverse postslavery landscapes. But as Evie Shockley has argued, the poem does not "produce a representation or experience of wholeness out of the voices and fragments" ("Going Overboard," 795). Instead, *Zong!* collects the sounds of catastrophe, and it also requires us to reimagine the technology of the printed page, as well as the technicity of reading. Should we read down the page, across it, or both? Must we repeat words to make the syntax work? How can we read the fragmented words? Philips's own experience with transformed and transformative readings of the poems over many years testifies to the difficulty of answering these questions.[5] To some degree, Moten's notion of symphonic or choral reading renders these problems moot: multiple overlapping readings allow for distinct and simultaneous answers to these questions. Out loud, the competing and collaborating voices of the *Zong!* come alive. And in a sense the bodies come alive too. Moten, in this poem as elsewhere, *hears* the black operation he sometimes calls optimism as collective sonic experience.[6]

But why, then, a poetry that draws our attention so to the page and the computer that produced it? The turn toward print experimentation by Philip and other black diasporic writers extends the mediating work of other vernacular forms within poetry—from oral storytelling to song. The very last section of the poem is nearly unreadable. In an accompanying essay Philip writes that these overlapping, faded texts originated in computer-generated error (206). The function here is not only to exhume the bodies of the dead but also to generate an archive—partial, fragmentary, and diffuse—of the cultures and communities whose loss Philip marks. To mark that loss, Philip draws, leaves behind, erases, and then returns the line between what surrounds and what is. Through this multilayered archive the poem operates on the structures of containment while generating forms of black being.[7] The technological turn toward the archive is an ecological one, an attempt to build an environment, a fragmentary and diffuse one, for the relationships of the future.

Poetry embodies the future tense as a cultural form that always seems to produce the remainder between the materiality of the printed text and the aurality of song. Ambient poetry, in other words, has a visual as well as a sonic register, which in Philip's case has everything to do with preserving the past for the future. Philip describes having written *Zong!* out of the need to "account" for something—the challenge of telling a story that cannot be told. By attending to the poem as ecological, I hope to have turned our attention from the narrative problem of telling toward a consideration of the poem as an archive of relation and disavowal.

THE ECOLOGY OF BLACK OPTIMISM

I conclude by returning to Danticat's *Create Dangerously*, which draws our attention to the interconnectedness of human suffering in the context of catastrophe and to its national contours. In "Another Country," a reflection on U.S. press coverage of Hurricane Katrina, Danticat critiques Americans' shock at the resemblance of U.S. poverty to that of developing nations and our willingness to name Haiti as the sign of all that "we" are not. Danticat calls for an American catastrophic imaginary and, simultaneously, insists on its diasporic shape:

> Among the realities brought to light by Hurricane Katrina was that never again could we justifiably deny the existence of this country within a country, that other America, which America's immigrants and the rest of the world may know much more intimately than many Americans do, the America that is always on the brink of humanitarian and ecological disaster. No, it is not Haiti or Mozambique or Bangladesh, but it might as well be. (113)

Danticat's assertion that America "might as well be" a developing nation seems to be a lament or critique; in spite of being a "first-world" nation, she argues, the existence of "that other America" testifies to the failure of the United States to utilize its first-world resources in such a way as to mitigate humanitarian and ecological disaster. But this critique contains within it as well a sense of possibility in the suggestion that acknowledging "Haiti or Mozambique or Bangladesh," indeed looking beyond the boundaries of the nation, might entirely transform our response to disaster. The threat that the United States might not be the United States contains within it a promise.[8]

The tension between curse and promise that characterizes Danticat's critique of U.S. society parallels a tension that has informed this study and that is also the source of a central debate within black studies scholarship regarding the tenacity of Orlando Patterson's idea of "social death" in the present—a debate in which Philip's *Zong!* has served as an important resource.[9] *Cultivation and Catastrophe* has sought common ground between the emphasis on social death as definitive of modern blackness and the insistence that, as Moten puts it, "a complete, which is to say a lyric, *lysis* of our living flesh and earthly sociality, which is often taken for a morbid body or a morbid universe, requires us to recognize that blackness is not reducible to its social costs; it is also manifest in a set of benefits and responsibilities" ("Blackness and Nothingness (Mysticism in the Flesh)," 774).[10] An ecological frame makes clear the need for both understandings of sociality. In black literature, even into and beyond the twentieth century, tropes of cultivation describe and give shape to the resilience, persistence, and progress of black cultures. But writers also describe the experience of the break that was the middle passage and the ensuing constraint, dehumanization, and suffering of plantation slavery and its afterlives as catastrophic; if not an irremediable wound or trauma, then a dramatic turning. This book has been concerned with mapping not one or the other of these historical experiences of black engagement with the earth, but the coexistence and interexistence of these apparently opposite types of lyric ecology.

Black environmental writing not only asserts forms of social life in the face of social death but also posits black survival as a potential corrective against apocalyptic environmentalism. Recent work on the meaning of the Anthropocene, the widely accepted scientific theory that we are in an age of unprecedented human agency in geological history, has created the sense that it is urgent to rethink the scale for perceiving forms of human freedom in humanities-based inquiry. In the process, scholars are questioning the long-standing importance of subjectivity and other discourses of the human in humanistic fields of postcolonial and race studies. For Dipesh Chakrabarty it is the sudden awareness of climate change, marked in part by the release of the 2007 (and now the 2013) report of the Intergovernmental Panel on Climate Change, that should prompt a reconsideration of the nature/culture binary.[11] Extending Chakrabarty's work, Ian Baucom likewise locates the need for a paradigm shift in the humanities in response to recent scientific research:

> While the questions the interdisciplinary humanities have been asking have been fundamentally epistemological or representational, the questions the life sciences are now forcing are fundamentally ontological, questions of the nature of being, questions above all, of the nature of human being as a particular form of life among other forms of life. ("The Human Shore," 6)

While some channels of academic discourse may reflect the pattern Baucom identifies, it is also the case that black diasporic writers have been theorizing the "nature of being" for some time. In black writing we find a long engagement with ontological questions raised precisely by matters of spatiotemporal scale that Baucom now calls for as part of humanistic study.[12] In other words, the thinkers Baucom cites as his point of departure, those who have taken up "the literary, legal, and archival realm of recorded human history"—Walcott, Glissant, NourbeSe Philip, Morrison—already "speak . . . of the transcoded-circum-Atlantic histories of Africa, the Americas, the Caribbean Europe . . . with natural history also in mind" ("The Human Shore," 4). In fact, the chronotopes of natural history have driven and given shape to changing concepts of black ontology and black freedom, just as black optimism has embodied, responded to, defined, and transformed ecological thought.

We can understand the figure of the ship as a structure of cultivation and catastrophe if we juxtapose the slave ship *Zong* against what many see as a modern-day ark, artist Mark Bradford's post-Katrina installation, *Mithra* (2008) (see fig. 7.3). As a physical structure that gets dismantled in *Zong!*'s visual economy, the environment that enslaves African bodies but also the word store that unlocks their voices, the slave ship adrift in the middle passage is the sign of so-

Fig. 7.3. Mark Bradford, *Mithra* (2008). Photo: Courtesy the author and Hauser & Wirth.

cial death and also of passage itself, of rupture and continuity. Bradford's *Mi-thra*, aground in the Lower Ninth Ward of New Orleans, posits itself as a kind of life raft, the sort of help that New Orleans residents cried out for from cell phones and rooftops.[13] Built from plywood shipping containers and weathered posters, the ship became a centerpiece of Prospect.1, the contemporary art biennial launched in New Orleans in 2009. Of the title of the piece, Bradford has cited Mithra's association in Zoroastrian tradition with agricultural fecundity. Hence his decision to situate the work in what he describes as the "scorched earth" of the Lower Ninth Ward: "I was really sort of looking forward and making a proposition that humanity would spring from the earth and that life continues" (audio commentary on *Across Canal* and *Mithra*). Bradford thus explicitly frames the project as a work of cultivation. The torn and faded posters pasted on the wood panels testify to the consequences of disaster for art, archives, and the people who make them, but Bradford's reuse of the posters also asserts the generative possibilities of catastrophe. As the very form of black optimism in the face of catastrophe, *Mithra* brought viewers over the course of one hundred days to look upon the scorched earth it proposed to transform. The ship reminds us of the critical need to listen to catastrophe's sound, indeed to make the sound, even as we imagine something growing from that ground.

Notes

Introduction

1. The montage visually echoes images of the victims of an earlier hurricane, the 1928 Florida hurricane, which intrudes in Zora Neale Hurston's *Their Eyes Were Watching God* and which I take up in chapter 5.

2. I discuss these theories later in the introduction and also in the coda.

3. I take for granted the understanding of black diaspora that has been in circulation for over a decade, ever since Brent Edwards historicized diaspora in relationship to pan-Africanism and black Atlanticism, foregrounding both its specificity as a term denoting difference and its elasticity as a term that extends beyond the specific geography of the Atlantic. Most important for my purposes is Edwards's rejection of diaspora as either a name for an originary scattering from Africa (or a corollary fantasy of return) or an outward reach grounded in a U.S. exceptionalist framework. Building on Edwards's work as well as other recent formulations of diaspora as cultural practice, this book shows that the network of sites of diasporic cultural practice extends beyond metropolitan spaces. While I share Edwards's view that we must not take Gilroy's Atlantic as a singular or totalizing "heuristic" for framing blackness, I maintain that specific and diverse Atlantic ecologies (the plantation, e.g.) and processes (the hurricane, e.g.), have shaped theorizations of transnational, national, regional, and communal belonging (and unbelonging) in modern black literature. Edwards most fully elaborates his theory of diasporic practice in in *The Practice of Diaspora*, but he also provides a more detailed history of the term in "The Uses of Diaspora." Related texts include Gilroy, *The Black Atlantic*, Stephens, *Black Empire*, and DeLoughrey, *Routes and Roots*.

4. Whereas for Pinto, the turn to form involves collecting texts under the rubric of difficulty, I take up related questions of dislocation as part of lyric poetry's history as a genre.

5. See Jackson, *Dickinson's Misery*, and "Who Reads Poetry?"

6. I am grateful to one of the anonymous readers of this book for inspiring the definition of the book's imaginative region I offer in this paragraph.

7. Attending to the key term "nature" rather than geography, Evie Shockley similarly demonstrates that nature and aesthetics alike are "culturally specific" ideas we have developed, constructed, and maintained, often in historical ways that make it difficult for black writers to approach or engage nature and difficult for critics to see the ways in which they do so. Her readings of the poetry of Anne Spencer, Ed Roberson, and Will Alexander work against this problem, demonstrating how black poets "negotiate the perceived distance between 'black poetry' and 'nature poetry'" (*Renegade Poetics*, 121, 145). For a very different account of why geography must be denaturalized in order to theorize diaspora, see Pinto, *Difficult Diasporas*.

8. See Ramazani, *A Transnational Poetics*, 14.

9. In recent years, however, scholars have begun to take up the ecological and geographic implications of Wynter's work more fully, in particular Katherine McKittrick, whose edited volume of essays on Wynter fills a crucial gap and whose "Plantation Futures" emphasizes Wynter's role in decolonizing what McKittrick calls "plantation logic" (3, 8, 10–11). In a collective project undertaken in *Small Axe* of reading and responding to Wynter's 934-page unpublished manuscript "Black Metamorphosis," a group of scholars has underscored the hemispheric reach of Wynter's theories and illuminated the relationship between Wynter's early essays and her more recent work on the limits of Western humanism. See Kamugisha, "'That Area of Experience That We Term the New World,'" Kamugisha, "The Black Experience of New World Coloniality," Cunningham, "The Resistance of the Lost Body," Eudell, "From Mode of Production to Mode of Auto-Institution," McKittrick, "Rebellion/Invention/Groove," Scott, preface, and Thomas, "Marronnons / Let's Maroon."

10. I'm drawing on the foundational use of the terms "deterritorialized" and "reterritorialized" by Deleuze and Guattari in *Anti-Oedipus* and the recent elaboration of the concept of deterritorialization by Arjun Appadurai in "Disjuncture and Difference in the Global Cultural Economy." However, as I demonstrate through my reading of *BIM* and *Phylon* in chapter 2, the deterritorialization of black literature—the abstraction of labor, money, ideas, bodies, and culture from local sites—can sometimes serve national aims rather than the globalization that Appadurai suggests it serves.

11. See DeLoughrey, "Yam, Roots, and Rot," 59.

12. It should be noted, however, that this "shift" between *Caribbean Discourse* and *Poetics of Relation* is more stark in the English translations than in the French originals. As Paul Gilroy has pointed out, J. Michael Dash's translation of *Caribbean Discourse* omits—among other things—a note in which Glissant refers explicitly to Deleuze and Guattari's concept metaphor of the rhizome (*The Black Atlantic*, 31). The fact of this note supports my claim that there is continuity in thought between the two works. For a more detailed discussion of the omission of this note and its implications for the status of nationalism, regionalism, and diasporic scale, see Hantel, "Rhizomes and the Space of Translation."

13. See Morton, *Ecology without Nature*, 31–32.

14. Glissant wrote the majority of the essays in *Caribbean Discourse* in the 1970s. The section titled "Sameness and Diversity and Techniques" from which this quotation is drawn was delivered at colloquia sponsored by the magazine *Liberté* that were held at Boston University between 1974 and 1975.

15. Christina Sharpe uses the phrase "in the wake" as the title of her recent book to suggest the literary, cultural, and activist work that must be done in full awareness of the violent history of middle passage and that must also honor the work of those who came before.

16. As a third way between Gilroy's complaint that J. Michael Dash's translation caribbeanizes what we should otherwise understand as a global text (*The Black Atlantic*, 31) and Joan Colin Dayan's rejoinder that we must properly understand *Caribbean Discourse* in relationship to the specific materiality of Martinique ("Paul Gilroy's Slaves, Ships, and Routes," 10), Max Hantel has drawn our attention to the volume's publication context, highlighting the English-speaking American audience for *Caribbean Discourse* as crucial to understanding the politics of its translation and "retelling" ("Rhizomes and the Space of Translation").

17. The schedule for the "literary seminars & symposia" is listed in "Souvenir Program: Carifesta '76 Jamaica," 1976, 46, University of West Indies Special Collections.

18. Although in the New Beacon edition of *History of the Voice* quoted here, Brathwaite refers to "pentameters," in *Roots* he or an editor corrects the reference to read "pentameter." I refer to the New Beacon monograph edition of the essay except where otherwise noted because it is the longest version of the text and includes Brathwaite's bibliography, which I understand as a crucial part of his archival project. The essay was published earlier under a different title, "English in the Caribbean:" in the volume *English Literature: Opening Up the Canon,* as transcribed by Houston Baker from the Harvard lecture at the 1979 English Institute, and then circulated in Jamaica and likely elsewhere in the Caribbean as a mimeographed and bound Savacou Working Paper under the title *Nation Language Poetry.* The essay was also included in Brathwaite's *Roots,* a volume first published in Cuba by Casa de Las Américas (1986) and then in the United States by University of Michigan Press (1992). This publication history begins to suggest the outernational significance of Brathwaite's thinking and the importance of oral presentation, conversation, transcription, and revision for his theories of poetry and ecology as well as for his poems. These are questions I take up in greater detail in chapter 6. For a discussion of the medium of the transcribed lecture as a "tidalectic" space, see Reckin, "Tidalectic Lectures."

19. In spite of this translation, until Matthew Hart's recent *Nothing But Nations of Poetry,* few accounts of "dialect" or "vernacular" in American literature—from Gates's landmark *Signifying Monkey* to Michael North's *Dialect of Modernism*—have seriously engaged Brathwaite's theory of poetic language, although some accounts of contemporary poetry, such as Nathaniel Mackey's *Discrepant Engagement,* contextualize Brathwaite's thinking transnationally.

20. This tension is embodied in the important anthropological debates at the beginning of the twentieth century between Melville Herskovitz and E. Franklin Frazier.

21. For a partial account of this debate see Moten, "Black Op," Moten, "Blackness and Nothingness (Mysticism in the Flesh)," Sexton, "People-of-Color-Blindness Notes on the Afterlife of Slavery," and Sexton, "The Social Life of Social Death." I return to these questions and some of these texts in the conclusion.

22. In his famous 1965 essay "Is Uniformitarianism Necessary?," Stephen Jay Gould questions the doctrine of geological time that had reigned for a hundred years. The theory of "punctuated equilibrium" as a description of evolutionary and ecological change replaced uniformitarianism, the theory formulated in the late eighteenth century and codified by Charles Lyell in the 1830s that posited that the earth changes gradually rather than as a result of dramatic events. Gould's paradigm shift has been the widely accepted model for thinking about evolutionary time since 1972, when Niles Eldredge and Gould published their article "Punctuated Equilibria."

23. See McKittrick, "Plantation Futures," and Sharpe, *In the Wake.*

24. Drawing on Brathwaite's "geopoetic" theory of tidalectics, DeLoughrey similarly emphasizes the implications of the oceanic chronotope in the Caribbean for the structure and form of the modern (*Routes and Roots,* 51–96).

25. See Ramazani, *The Hybrid Muse,* and Edwards, "The Specter of Interdisciplinarity." Ramazani has already outlined several potential approaches to a deeper study of poetry in postcolonial literary studies. He challenges T. S. Eliot's description of poetry as "stubbornly national" as well as representations of contemporary poetry as, on the one hand, especially personal and as, on the other, bereft of subjectivity. He contends that poetry's formal characteristics may render it "a less transparent medium by which to recuperate the history, politics, and sociology of postcolonial societies" but that they contribute to the representation of cul-

tural hybridity. Ramazani emphasizes metaphor, irony, and lingusitic hybridity as the constitutive features of poetry's contribution to the discourse of "split cultural experience." As a caveat, Edwards acknowledges that scholars in recent years have paid increasing critical attention to individual authors, particular issues, and particular regional contexts (including the Caribbean) for postcolonial poetry, as well as to poetic manifestations of the relationship between postcoloniality and Euromodernism. Nonetheless, he argues, we have yet to theorize adequately "the relation between postcoloniality and poetics in the broader sense" (190).

26. *Cultivation and Catastrophe* builds on important recent scholarship by Evie Shockley (*Renegade Poetics*), Meta Jones (*The Muse Is Music*), and Anthony Reed (*Freedom Time*), as well as earlier work by Elizabeth Alexander (*The Black Interior*; "New Ideas about Black Experimental Poetry"), Aldon Nielsen (*Black Chant*), Nathaniel Mackey (*Discrepant Engagement*) and others that place poetry at the center of black studies, illuminating our conceptions of the avant-garde and of musicality in poetry. More recently there has emerged a robust discourse—much of it taking place on social media—that conversely locates contemporary poetry by black writers and other writers of color at the center of thinking about American poetry, particularly American avant-garde poetry. Two examples are John Keene's blog critique of the new lyric studies, "'White Silences',," and Dorothy Wang's introduction to her excellent book on Asian American poetry, *Thinking Its Presence*.

27. In the preface to *Blue Fasa*, his new book of poetry (a continuation of the work in *Splayed Anthems*), Mackey reminds me of this sonic basis for thinking about lyric poetry. Referring to the vibration of a stringed instrument, he writes in the preface that it "brings multiple senses of string into play. It reminds us, for one, of something I've been unable to forget, that the root of the word *lyric* is the lyre, the musical instrument the ancient Greeks accompanied songs and recitations with. It's not that I've wanted to forget, though at times I've wondered if it were something I'd made up or being misinformed about, the lyric of late being so widely equated with phanopoetic snapshot, bare-bones narrative, terse epiphany and the like much more than with music, signaling an ongoing split between poetry and musicality perhaps."

28. In her 1976 essay on ethnopoetics born of the conference of the same name, Wynter describes poetry (in all caps) as an "alternative mode of cognition suppressed in ourselves" ("Ethno or Socio Poetics," 83), much like the buried yam awaiting harvest. I'm not claiming that poetry adequately accounts for or replicates the ritual context Wynter describes or that it relates us more authentically to the "earth." Some poets in the 1960s and 1970s were interested in these possibilities, but Wynter warns of the danger of this kind of latter-day primitivism in her remarks on ethnopoetics. Wynter's essays, with the epigraphs from Jonkonnu and other songs, reflect the uneasiness of sonic transcription.

29. Here and throughout the book I take seriously critiques of the overemphasis on cosmopolitanism and travel in postcolonial and black literary study, a critique that has prompted, for example, Elizabeth DeLoughrey's important reclamation of the indigenous as a category for study in the context of the Caribbean and more broadly her insistence that we think "roots" and "routes" together in her study of the oceanic (*Routes and Roots*).

CHAPTER 1. Cultivating the New Negro

1. See Tolson, "Claude McKay's Art," 289. See also Giles, *Claude McKay*, 67.

2. Maxwell, introduction; Cooper, *Claude McKay*. Tyrone Tillery, who contends that McKay found the morals *too* lax at Tuskegee, is an exception (*Claude McKay*, 21).

3. McKay was not the only Jamaican who sought out the "Tuskegee wizard." Marcus Garvey likewise wrote to Washington shortly before his death to schedule a visit to Tuskegee for the purposes of lecturing on the activities of the Universal Negro Improvement Association (Garvey to Washington, April 12, 1915, Booker T. Washington Papers, Library of Congress). Robert A. Hill, Marcus Garvey, and Universal Negro Improvement Association. *The Marcus Garvey and Universal Negro Improvement Association Papers: 1826–August 1919.* University of California Press, 1983: 116.

4. Houston Baker, for instance, in his reconsideration of the figure of Washington in *Turning South Again* radically contrasts Washington's advocacy of what Baker calls "domesticated immobility" (60) with Benjamin's cosmopolitan flâneur, whom Baker sees as the ultimate figure of Afro-modernity. Here, Baker departs from his earlier position in *Modernism and the Harlem Renaissance*, in which he argued that Washington is modern "because he earnestly projected the flourishing of a southern, black Eden at Tuskegee—a New World garden to nurture the hands, heads, and hearts of a younger generation of agrarian black folk in the 'country districts'" (37). In *Modernism and the Harlem Renaissance* Baker reads this southern flourishing as a kind of synecdoche for "the growth and *survival* of a nation" (37) a precursor for the later flourishing of "national culture" that would define the New Negro Movement.

5. This is not to say that Du Bois necessarily celebrated cities in contrast to rural agricultural places. Although it is beyond the scope of the current work, it would be worth considering the various ways in which Du Bois saw the "gloomy soil" of the South repeated in forms of urban life.

6. See Baker, *Turning South Again*, 63.

7. It is through this lens that Bone reads McKay's oeuvre as a largely unintegrated vacillation between the "picaresque" and the "provincial" (*Down Home*, 159–70).

8. A group of more recent critics have pointed to georgic, as opposed to pastoral, as a useful category for thinking about African American representations of nature, insofar as georgics emphasize the value (and often the inequities) of agricultural and intellectual labor. See Collins, "Risk, Envy and Fear in Sterling Brown's 'Georgics,'" Finseth, *Shades of Green*, 229–45, Tobin, *Colonizing Nature*, chap. 1, and Ronda, "'Work and Wait Unwearying.'" There is also a resurgent interest in "black nature," evidenced by the 2010 poetry anthology of that name edited by Camille T. Dungy, a 2005 volume titled *Caribbean Literature and the Environment* edited by Elizabeth M. DeLoughrey, Renée K. Gosson, and George B. Handley, and recent criticism by Britt Rusert ("Black Nature"), Sandy Alexandre ("Richard Wright's Haikus"), and Evie Shockley (*Renegade Poetics*).

9. Foundational texts in this regard include Antonio Benítez-Rojo's *The Repeating Island* and Glissant's *Poetics of Relation*. More recent work in cultural geography, such as Katherine McKittrick's "Plantation Futures," extends these themes.

10. Virginia Jackson in part blames Cleanth Brooks and Robert Penn Warren's midcentury textbook *Understanding Poetry* and New Criticism more broadly for dehistoricizing poetry under the sign of lyric through their emphasis on "poetry as a thing in itself worthy of study" (qtd. in Jackson, *Dickinson's Misery*, 10). At the same time, Jackson and Prins argue in the *Lyric Theory Reader*, critics of the New Criticism get caught in the same logic of lyric abstraction. As I have suggested elsewhere, their historicization of the critique of the "lyric I" as a late twentieth-century phenomenon among mostly white scholars and avant-garde poets elides an earlier cultural critique of the lyric subject. The tension between the idea of poetry as "a thing in itself" and poetry as a thing in the world has been driving debates about the func-

tion and meaning of lyric (and other poetry) for black poets and black readers since at least the late nineteenth century, when Paul Laurence Dunbar, for example, donned the poetic mask of dialect to speak to white audiences ("Blueprints for Negro Reading"). If the lyric has become a fictive "catch-all" for poetry, I'm interested in how that category has continued to give meaning to black poetics as a genre associated with containment, with the construction of ahistorical subjectivity, and with the line between music and text. Thus I don't attempt to rehistoricize either lyric or lyric reading but rather to show how reading something we might (even in a suspended sort of way) call lyric poetry allows us to theorize what Glissant calls "nonhistory." To some extent my readings in this chapter and throughout *Cultivation and Catastrophe* attempt to reverse the alienation of the lyric referent—that is, to recognize as material the ecologies in black poetry that have often been understood as purely metaphorical.

11. To do so is to complicate the sharp divide between the provincial poems from *Songs of Jamaica* (1912) and the "picaresque" lyrics from *Harlem Shadows* (1922).

12. Practices of subsistence gardening among enslaved Africans in the West Indies did travel with them to parts of the United States along with, in some cases, West Indian crops. The gardens of enslaved African Americans did not always form the basis of alternative economies (although they did so in places like the Chesapeake Bay area and South Carolina), but like the Jamaican provision ground they often provided links to West and Central African ecology and culture and could be the basis for control over time and space, if not capital ("Gardens"). I highlight the mobility of McKay's modern poetic "garden" in this chapter, therefore, not to underscore the specificity of the Jamaican provision ground but rather to demonstrate the resilience, mobility, and adaptability of modern aesthetic practices in the diaspora. See also Simon Gikandi's discussion of the South Carolina "task system" as a form of temporal agency among enslaved laborers (*Slavery and the Culture of Taste*, 244).

13. See Tobin, *Colonizing Nature*, 62–63.

14. "What would appear to have been the shallow memory of slaves and their descendants was also what enabled the dialectic of remembering and forgetting. The shallowness of memory and the thinness of genealogy would give slaves a space for maneuver; to have a shallow memory was to be liberated from the burden of genealogy; without concrete claims to historical antecedence, slaves could be free to imagine an alternative world of space and play. In turn, loose ties to the past would enable the symbolic inversion of the meaning of work and time in the plantation" (*Slavery and the Culture of Taste*, 246). Within this debate over "memory as history," Patterson, Craton, and Gikandi are all speaking in part of continuity in relation to Africanist survivals. Building on Gikandi's argument that a black aesthetic emerges precisely where the connection to African tradition is most tenuous, I wish to demonstrate that even in the absence of an explicit engagement with Africa, an aesthetic of fragmentation similarly animates McKay's memory.

15. Indeed, as I argue in the introduction, I believe that Wynter's theorization of the provision ground ultimately paves the way for such a theoretical possibility.

16. See also Edwards, *The Practice of Diaspora*; Maxwell, *New Negro, Old Left*; James, *A Fierce Hatred of Injustice*; and Pederson, "The Tropics in New York."

17. In the Jamaican press, immediately following the publication of *Spring in New Hampshire*, a correspondent opined that "the impassioned revolutionary poems find no place"; rather "the remainder of the poems are concerned with the beauties of nature, with yearning for his Jamaica home" ("More Poems by Claude McKay"). Recent critics maintain the dichot-

omy between radicalism and nature. George Hutchinson, for instance, emphasizes McKay's nostalgia in "The Tropics in New York," arguing that "whereas his poems set in Jamaica often concerned black urban life there and protested the conditions of the lower classes," after he moved to the United States, "Jamaica became the rural, even pastoral, 'motherland.'" (*The Harlem Renaissance in Black and White*, 414). See also Hathaway, "Exploring 'Something New.'"

18. On the relationship between McKay's poems and white liberalism, see North, *The Dialect of Modernism*, 292–93.

19. McKay to Hughes, March 30, 1928, Langston Hughes Papers, James Weldon Johnson Collection, Beinecke Rare Book and Manuscript Library.

20. McKay to Hughes, April 3, 1928?, Langston Hughes Papers, James Weldon Johnson Collection, Beinecke Rare Book and Manuscript Library.

21. See Warner, *Publics and Counterpublics*.

22. McKay to Hughes, March 30, 1928, Langston Hughes Papers, James Weldon Johnson Collection, Beinecke Rare Book and Manuscript Library.

23. See Cooper, *Claude McKay*, 214–16; Edwards, *The Practice of Diaspora*, chap. 4; and Ramesh, *Claude McKay*, chap. 5.

24. For an index of *Public Opinion*'s literary publications see Dalleo, "The Public Sphere and Jamaican Anticolonial Politics."

25. Whether or not Churchill actually quoted from McKay's poem is a subject of debate, but many critics claim that Churchill recited the poem in 1939 before the House of Commons to encourage the armed forces. Lee Jenkins has documented the difficulty of confirming this oft-repeated story. As Jenkins's analysis attests, the persistence of the story within the criticism and the struggles over the content of this radical yet universal poem indicate most of all the faulty logic of conscripting McKay into a single literary, national, or political milieu ("'If We Must Die'").

26. See McKay, "Claude McKay Defends Our Dialect Poetry."

27. McKay to McKay, 1929, Claude McKay Papers, Beinecke Rare Book and Manuscript Library. Letters from McKay's relatives underscore the poet's continued financial and intellectual involvement with his family after his supposed detachment from Jamaica.

28. McKay's brother Tommy and sister Rachel describe their gratitude for money to support the girls' educations (McKay to McKay, 1929; Cooper to McKay, June 23, 1929, Claude McKay Papers, Beinecke Rare Book and Manuscript Library).

29. See also Redcam, "Appreciation of the Poems of Claude McKay," and "McKay's Latest."

30. Locke omits "Subway Wind" from the anthology.

31. See North, *The Dialect of Modernism*, 105–10.

32. Ralph Ellison would most famously evoke the yam as a madeleine of the American South in *Invisible Man* (263–67).

33. James accounts for both Kamau Brathwaite's condemnation of McKay's European meter and Jamaican icon Louise Bennett's literary sense of empowerment in response to McKay's poems (*A Fierce Hatred of Injustice*, 140–51). See also Cooper, *Claude McKay*, 35–38, and North, *The Dialect of Modernism*, 100–123.

34. North, *The Dialect of Modernism*, 100–123; Giles, *Claude McKay*.

35. See, for example, McKay's "Claude McKay Defends Our Dialect Poetry."

36. Like "The Tropics in New York," this poem was included in major anthologies. After

publication first in *Spring in New Hampshire* (1920), then in *Harlem Shadows* (1922), it was republished in James Weldon Johnson's *Book of American Negro Poetry* (1922; 1931) and Countee Cullen's *Caroling Dusk* (1927). The poem's inclusion in these contexts further underscores the sense in which diverse landscapes defined "American Negro Poetry" during this period.

37. See Goodman, *Georgic Modernity and British Romanticism*, 31.

38. "Sweet potatoes were sparingly used for human consumption. . . . But now the food of hogs was fit for gods" (292–93).

39. See Pederson, "The Tropics in New York," 259.

40. For a discussion of Caribbean ambivalence in relationship to staple foods, see Franklyn, "Grenada, Naipaul, and Ground Provision."

41. North claims that in the shift from quatrain to quatrain of "The Tropics in New York," "the particular language of the colony" represented by the list of fruits "loses out to the generalized language of empire" (*The Dialect of Modernism*, 112).

42. See Pederson, "The Tropics in New York," 259.

43. North contends that the poem rehearses the minstrel cliché of a displaced African longing for his home, demonstrating McKay's "commoditization" (*The Dialect of Modernism*, 113). This line of thinking depends on a reading of contemporary English and Anglo-American responses to the poems, which indeed confirm that the poem "fed this market" for the minstrel cliché. But the broader publication context of McKay's work, at home in Jamaica and in the black diaspora, encourages us to challenge this view and helps unshackle the poems from the confining embrace of white linguistic appropriation.

44. I am referring to modernist free verse poetry—for example, some of the poems in Jean Toomer's *Cane* (1923)—to blues poems like those of Langston Hughes, and more broadly to what Zora Neale Hurston referred to as "characteristics of negro expression" and Hughes as "racial art." But it is true that at the time when McKay was writing *Harlem Shadows*, U.S. poets like Toomer, Anne Spencer, Georgia Douglas Johnson, and Countee Cullen demonstrated a similar interest in European forms, the sonnet among them. McKay was not exceptional in this regard, and, arguably, the Harlem Renaissance did not become associated with the rejection of European forms until the Black Arts Movement retroactively reclaimed some of its poets. Nor do I wish to suggest that his poetry falls on one side of a sharp boundary between what Houston Baker has termed the "deformation of mastery" and "the mastery of form" (*Modernism and the Harlem Renaissance*, xvi). What is important, rather, is that McKay's turn to the sonnet indexes both a generational engagement with and a generational suspicion of European forms among African American poets.

45. Critics of McKay's nature poems and critics of nature poetry within the black diasporic tradition have variously echoed this rhetoric of shame.

46. In *My Green Hills of Jamaica* McKay tells a story about planting that is nearly an allegory for the relationship Brathwaite would later elaborate between English prosody and the Caribbean landscape. "When the British started to send us agricultural instructors to show the peasants how to till the soil, these men protested against the burning of the debris. They said that the debris would enrich the soil and should be plowed under. Well, some of the peasants followed their advice and when they did their planting, the leaves of what they had planted were consumed by worms as soon as they had grown a few inches. Those who insisted on burning this debris found that their planting had developed very healthily. The agricultural instructors made their mistakes. I remember one of them telling a peasant that the young

cocoa plant that he had uprooted would not grow. The peasant insisted that it would and planted it. The next year, when the instructor returned, he found a flourishing cocoa tree" (28–29).

47. My purpose in underscoring this connection is not to perform such critical shaming but rather to show how the poets themselves were engaged in shaming (or at least critiquing) the pastoral and to emphasize that their engagement with lyric forms was crucial to this process. If, as some critics have contended, McKay is a romantic poet by virtue of his education and his formal practices, his European romanticism affords him access to a Jamaican poetics and to the Jamaican landscape, "because, of all the poets I admire, major and minor, Byron, Shelley, Keats, Blake, Burns, Whitman, Heine, Baudelaire, Verlaine and Rimbaud and the rest— it seemed to me that when I read them—in their poetry I could feel their race, their class, their roots in the soil, growing into plants, spreading and forming the backgrounds against which they were silhouetted" (*A Long Way from Home*, 27). McKay claims that the mimetic potential of the sonnet specifically resides in its capacity to make us feel the poet's race and class, along with the poet's "roots in the soil." Thus if both the sonnet and the soil might engender forms of lyric shame, their association with one another provides McKay with an opportunity for innovation.

48. Distinguishing himself from scholars who read McKay's use of the sonnet as a kind of "mask" (xxxv) Maxwell points out that the sonnet is "born in medieval Italy but dispersed throughout more of the modern world than any other type of Western lyric" (xxxvi).

49. Glissant's poetics of relation also involves a revision of the trope of the "root" into a discourse of the rhizome, which might grow in an errant way away from or without a singular source (21).

50. Although he would eventually write poems in Jamaican dialect, McKay's initial education at the hands of his brother Uriah Theodore immersed him in English poetry.

51. There are poems in *Harlem Shadows*, such as "North and South," that fit this description. The coexistence of nostalgia and critique in McKay's oeuvre suggests on a larger scale the complexity with which he represents the Jamaican landscape in individual poems.

52. The term "trade winds" has not always been associated with commerce. The phrase originally developed from "to blow trade," meaning to blow in a regular or predictable way (monsoon winds), but eighteenth-century etymologists likely began to associate "trade winds" with the commercial routes of the Atlantic, at which point the expression developed its current association with commerce generally and (for African diasporic writers in particular) with the Atlantic slave trade which depended on these winds. This double sense of "trade" is resonant in a poem that juxtaposes the regularity of its meter and form against both the suffering of captivity and the possibility of errant imagination.

53. See James, *A Fierce Hatred of Injustice*, 111.

54. Baker defines "radical marronage" as the project of forming a communal national identity in the context of flight, marginality, or "frontier" culture. It's notable that the term Baker chooses to define "our first national book" is in fact a term borrowed from the Caribbean context.

55. See Huggins, *Harlem Renaissance*, and Michaels, *Our America*, 87. Recent criticism further excavates the relationship between nationalism and radicalism in the period. See Dawahare, "The Specter of Radicalism in Alain Locke's The New Negro," Foley, *Spectres of 1919*, and Maxwell, *New Negro, Old Left*.

56. I address these ideas more fully in chapter 2, where I consider the way black writers claim the landscape using the terms of indigeneity to forward the explicitly nationalist aims of postwar West Indian periodicals.

57. In her reading of Langston Hughes's editorial work on *New Negro Poets: USA*, Elizabeth Alexander highlights the "consolidating" and "distilling" work of the editor as a creative practice, making visible those "aesthetic and political choices" which, she points out "come to appear inevitable" and are "made invisible" by our reading and critical practice (*The Black Interior*, 24–25). Alexander demonstrates how the art of picking and choosing was itself a way of telling a coherent story about cultural identity as expressed through poetry. But in making visible Locke's "editorial hand" we are faced with competing stories: the story he tells in the editorial essays that frame the anthology as a whole and its various sections and the stories of the anthology's various contents, as well as the histories of their assemblage, revision, and recombination within the *New Negro* and its predecessor, "Harlem: Mecca of the New Negro," the special issue of *Survey Graphic*.

58. While eschewing "100-percent Americanism," Foley argues, Negro nationalism of this period derives from a cultural pluralism that would "at once maintain separate national identities and enhance loyalty to the newly gained capitalist nation" (*Spectres of 1919*, 169).

59. Braddock in particular shows how both African and African American cultural practices shaped European modernism (180) and in turn (through his original reading of Countee Cullen's "Heritage") how modernism mediates between the African past and the American present.

60. George Hutchinson describes the story as a "complicated and intriguing case of the American pan-African reach of *The New Negro*," because of the internationalism and multiracialism of the characters (and population of Colón during the building of the Panama Canal), the way the story subverts certain white American expectations of racial clarity, and the status of the work as an "anti-imperialist" response to colonial narratives. Hutchinson observes that Walrond's story seems a response Conrad's *Heart of Darkness* "from the other side of the 'veil.'" (*The Harlem Renaissance in Black and White*, 409).

61. According to Brittan "the physical work of connection means dredging underworlds," and Colón is a terminus, "the site of remains, material obstructions, and breaks in the line" ("The Terminal," 297).

62. Miss Bruckner's body itself is described in relationship to excessive and ruptured cultivation processes. She has "oxen hips, long, pliable hands, roving, sun-staring breasts. . . . Upon the yellow stalk of her being there shot up into mist and crystal space a head the shape of a sawed-off cocoanut [sic] tree top" ("Tropic of Death," 117). As the madame of a bordello at this meeting place of East and West, described in racially and nationally ambiguous terms with even more ambiguous daughters, Miss Bruckner is the very sign of overproduction.

63. Within the volume of *The New Negro*, Walrond's story functions as a hinge between the fiction and poetry sections and between Bruce Nugent's strangely primitivist fragmentary portrait of "Sahdji," "a little African girl, delightfully black" (113) and the poems of Countee Cullen which begin the poetry section. As such, the piece functions as a transition between regions—East Africa in the case of the Nugent piece and Harlem in the case of Cullen's poems—as well as between the genres through which, to cite the title of Locke's essay, "The Negro Youth Speaks" (among them Nugent's and Walrond's fragmentary, elliptical prose, on the one hand, and Cullen's compressed, lyrical sonnets, on the other).

64. Perhaps the historicist turn to a print cultural context itself betrays a version of lyric shame.

65. See Glissant, *Poetics of Relation*, 70–71.

CHAPTER 2. Cultivating the Nation

1. The piece carries no attribution in the issue but has been identified as Rohlehr's work on the Savacou website; see www.savacoupublications.com/journals---out-of-print.

2. In his history of Caribbean poetry, Edward Baugh similarly notes both the "great wave of migration from the West Indies to the so-called mother country" that took place after the war and, on the other hand, "the indigenizing of . . . poetry" during this period, "a matter of straightforward declarations of the beauty and difference of the local landscape and its people" (*Derek Walcott*, 240–41). Building on Baugh's observation of this duality, I would argue that such "indigenizing" was hardly straightforward, given its paradoxical coexistence with the stream of emigration. This chapter attempts to account for the complex heterogeneity of West Indian literary "indigenization."

3. For a detailed discussion of the publication context of this issue and the critical response to it, see Donnell and Welsh, *The Routledge Reader in Caribbean Literature*, 286–89.

4. In her elegant reading of the CAM archive, drawing on the previous work of Anne Walmsley, Nadia Ellis punctures the narrative of the movement's coherence, marking disaffiliation as a central feature of diasporic intimacy. As Ellis puts it, "The Caribbean Artists Movement consolidated West Indian literature in England, but it also dramatized the complexities of West Indian literary identity at this time, a decade after Caribbean writers were supposed to have created it" (*Territories of the Soul*, 70). Walmsley's account of the *Savacou* special issue likewise notes the ideological schisms inside the journal while also emphasizing the absolutely necessary "act of creativity" that was Caribbean Artists Movement's formation (*The Caribbean Artists Movement*, 261–66, 304). It is possible that the difficulty these voices have in "taking root" together has something to do with their removal from their live sources—that we can't hear poets breathe, or watch their bodies, or see them together. In the removal of *Savacou* from its scenes of place making, the journal performs a kind of formal echo of the removal of its writers from their scenes, their landscapes (a possibility underscored by the fact that the Caribbean Artists Movement was at first an expatriate enterprise initiated by writers living in London).

5. For a discussion of the critical history of this term see Deleuze and Guattari, *Anti-Oedipus* and Appadurai, "Disjuncture and Difference in the Global Cultural Economy."

6. Lloyd Brown would later underscore the distinction between what he calls "the old-fashioned Caribbean pastoral" and a more robust representation of landscape "as a living symbol of the West Indian's historical experience and sense of identity" (*West Indian Poetry*, 65). Brown contends that during this period, 1940 to 1960, in which *BIM*, *Kyk -Over-Al*, and other local literary publications emerged, "the old-fashioned Caribbean pastoral ceases to be the dominant poetic mode" (65). But even as he identifies an alternative landscape poetry more closely integrated with a new nationalist politics, he also bemoans that the old pastoral "does not disappear altogether" (65) .

7. This is not to say that Roach did not concern himself with literary "geography" in any of its forms. His most well-known poem, "I Am the Archipelago" stunningly dramatizes the very

juxtaposition between the constricting "island of my skin" and the expansive possibilities of the sea.

8. In McKittrick's view, "inevitable black-death" constrains and limits this assertion of black subjectivity and black life within the context of the plantation as a possibility for the future. She suggests that urban "black life" might be somewhat freer from this inevitable foreclosure, although it, too, is haunted by plantation logic. I take up Afro-pessimist thought in greater detail in the coda to this book, but in this chapter I wish to underscore and describe the sorts of possibilities that writers at midcentury imagined, even while marking the constraints on that imagination.

9. It would be wrong to proceed without noting that the *Savacou* special issue featured poetry by several by-then well-established talents, including Derek Walcott, Martin Carter, Mervyn Morris, and Dennis Scott. But I have attended instead to some of the more contested (or unnoticed) works in part because I address poetry by the "twin peaks of West Indian poetry" (Walcott and Brathwaite) at length elsewhere in this book and in part because what interests me is the unevenness of periodical publication.

10. Deleuze and Guattari embrace what they call the "willed poverty" of minor literature (19). They sideline mastery and talent, foregrounding instead "common action" (17). Their view of "minor literature" contrasts with, for instance, that of Cary Nelson, who wants to break down the major/minor distinction in the service of a broader politics of recovery. In *Repression and Recovery,* Nelson is concerned with the way various kinds of archival reading, including periodical reading, produce a marginal or minor literature in need of recovery and restoration in a U.S. context. Nelson contends that attending to the minor offers us a more rigorously historical view of a given period—in this case modernism—but his concern is ultimately to challenge the designation of the minor *as such.* Further, Nelson wishes to challenge the aesthetic judgments of the political as minor and restore to political writings a more central place in the canon (*Repression and Recovery*, 29).

11. Matthew Hart observes a similar issue with the identification of "synthetic vernaculars" as "minor," pointing out that in the Deleuzian sense this would be a problematic designation given the "rootedness" of the former in particular places and the insistence of Deleuze and Guattari on the "deterritorialization" of minor literatures (*Nations of Nothing but Poetry*, 38).

12. Dance, *Fifty Caribbean Writers*, 130, 91; Baugh, "A History of Poetry," 239.

13. It is conceivable that Collymore's use of the word "queer" references sexual difference, given that by 1942, the year "The Catt" was published, the term "queer" had, according to the *OED*, already acquired the meaning of "homosexual" in British and U.S. English. But in the context of Caribbean literature this meaning is unlikely: recent scholars on queer Caribbean literature and culture note that this word was not in circulation in Caribbean communities to describe nonheterosexual identities or practices until very recently. Instead, Collymore's use of the term most likely suggests abstract difference and idiosyncrasy. See Tinsley, *Thiefing Sugar*, 6–7, and Glave, "Whose Caribbean?," 68on3.

14. If Cary Nelson is thinking "minor literature" as part of a national canon, the concept has been thoroughly transnationalized by Deleuze and Guattari, for whom the very concept of the "minor" is a transnational one. In *Kafka: Toward a Minor Literature,* Deleuze and Guattari direct us toward a familiar parallel between literature that has been, as they term it, "deterritorialized" in a literal sense (German literature in Czechoslovakia) and that which has been deterritorialized more abstractly: the "strange and minor uses" of deterritorialized language,

they write, "can be compared in another context to what blacks in America today are able to do with the English language" (17).

15. Locke, "Self-Criticism: The Third Dimension in Culture," 391.

16. See Lawrence Jackson's excellent and thorough discussion of the special issue of *Phylon* in *The Indignant Generation*, his book on this transitional period. Jackson documents the turn toward the expectations of the (white) mainstream, documenting at every turn how tenuous was the grasp of black writers on mainstream inclusion (331–33).

17. Jackson notes that Nick Aaron Ford's contribution to the volume contends that there was still work to be done in the realm of propaganda (*The Indignant Generation*, 333–34). In his series of responses in *Masses & Mainstream*, "Which Way for the Negro Writer," Lloyd Brown also vehemently challenged the embrace of universalism by many of his generation, and defended a specifically black literature, in part by underscoring the global reach of black writing (*The Indignant Generation*, 348, and Washington, *The Other Blacklist*, 42–45).

18. For Foreman (who had been an advisor to President Roosevelt), industrial reform and integration of the unions were necessarily linked ("The Decade of Hope," 145–46).

19. Tolnay, "The African American 'Great Migration' and Beyond," 210. Isabel Wilkerson notes that by 1970 "six million black southerners" had "left the land of their forefathers and fanned out across the country," although Tolnay's data suggest a smaller figure of 4.5 (*The Warmth of Other Suns*, 7).

20. In the United States, the midcentury brought no boom in publications as the 1920s had. According to Lawrence Jackson a shortage of paper during the war (and the publication's increasing conservatism) led to the decline of *Opportunity*, and new publications were slow to fill the void. At the same time many black writers were finding spaces in mainstream publication from which they had previously been excluded, as the contributors to the 1950 special issue of *Phylon* attest (*The Indignant Generation*, 125). In a different vein, Aldon Nielsen has marked the emergence of periodicals associated with a poetic avant-garde, including Russell Atkins's *Free Lance* (first published in the same year as the *Phylon* new writing issue) and, in the 1960s, *Dasein*. For Nielson, who acknowledges the indebtedness of the "radical formalism" in these pages to Brooks's "metrical formalism," these black avant-gardes offer a refreshing alternative to the constraints imposed by the commitment to "standard British metrical forms" in many of the poems in *Phylon* (*Black Chant*, 45, 39). While I don't entirely disagree with Nielson's assessment of *Phylon*'s early decades, I wish to resist this version of "lyric shame" (which I have called "colonial lyric shame" in chapter 1, building on the insights of Gillian White) by considering such constraints in relationship to the transnational geography of the plantation and its after life.

21. Brooks would considerably modify this opinion later in her career. Although she always maintained that "a poet has a duty to words . . . and it's too bad to just let them lie there without doing anything with and for them," she recognized that a shift in audience for black poets (that is, from white readers to black readers) and the changing political climate made space for a different kind of poetry (interview with George Savros, 3).

22. In 1980, taking issue with Cedric Robinson's challenge to his authenticity as a white, non-native historian of Africa prone to excessive comparison of Scottish and African diasporas, Shepperson would insist on "how important poetry has been to me during my career as a professional teacher of history," citing his own poems of 1950 and 1951. Shepperson's perplexing implication is that to attend to his poetry as well as his poetry criticism (such as his "very

short study of some aspects of Herman Melville and the great Scottish nationalist poet Hugh MacDiarmid") would be to justify or rationalize his theory of history against Robinson's criticism. While it is impossible to imagine how such attention could possibly produce a "'native' theory of history" such as that for which Robinson calls, what I wish to draw attention to here is the way Shepperson establishes poetry as an important genre of culturally specific history. George Shepperson, "Ourselves as Others: Some Comments on Cedric Robinson on George Shepperson," *Review (Fernand Braudel Center)* 4, no. 1 (July 1, 1980): 80. Cedric Robinson, "Notes toward a 'Native' Theory of History," *Review (Fernand Braudel Center)* 4, no. 1 (July 1, 1980): 45–78.

23. It seems likely that this is one of the poems to which Shepperson refers in his 1980 rejoinder to Robinson when he states the significance of poetry for his work as a historian. The footnote reads simply: "Cf. George Shepperson, poems (1950 and 1951)" ("Ourselves as Others," 79).

24. A note tells us the poem was composed "in 1944, but never published," before its appearance in Phylon.

25. Shepperson, "Rain."

26. See McCracken, "Malawi and the Poetry of Two World Wars."

27. In the 1990 essay Shepperson also reprints another poem, one in which he has attempted to collect Askari songs for readers "unacquainted with Malawian soldiers at war in Burma" ("Malawi and the Poetry of Two World Wars," 147).

28. See Lee, "Criticism at Mid-Century," 393.

29. In the same issue of *Phylon* Hugh Gloster similarly evokes the "ghetto" as the limited sphere of propaganda for the black writer, contending that propaganda "has helped certain critics and publishers to lure him into the deadly trap of cultural segregation by advising him that the black ghetto is his proper milieu and that he will write best when he is most Negroid" ("Race and the Negro Writer," 369).

30. Trotter offers a useful intellectual history of the developments in migration studies in the introduction to his edited collection.

31. Dan Jaffe, "Gwendolyn Brooks: An Appreciation from the White Suburbs," in *On Gwendolyn Brooks: Reliant Contemplation*, ed. Stephen Caldwell Wright (University of Michigan Press, 2001), 52.

32. D. H. Melhem, *Gwendolyn Brooks: Poetry and the Heroic Voice* (University Press of Kentucky, 2015), 95.

33. In his essential literary history of the Black Arts Movement, James Edward Smethurst points out that Brooks was not always seen as fully radicalized in her efforts. But as he documents, her various affiliations, teaching practices, and writing over a long stretch of time demonstrate a "sense of deep political commitment to the community" and great respect for the younger, more grassroots, local movements around her. What Smethurst so powerfully shows us is that Brooks's politics were rooted in her *local* community (*The Black Arts Movement*, 211–12). Washington similarly argues that unearthing Brooks's ongoing (if often submerged) alliances with the political left disrupts progressive narratives of Brooks's "supposedly sudden and unprecedented conversion to blackness and radicalism" (177) after the second Fisk Black Writers' Conference in 1967 (*The Other Black List*, 165–204).

34. See McKittrick, "Plantation Futures," 11–12.

35. See Brooks's account in her 1971 *Essence* interview with Ida Lewis, reprinted in Brooks, *Report from Part One*, 167.

36. John Lowney has demonstrated how *In the Mecca* "contests the dominant discourse of urban decline," offering a detailed discussion of the racialized dimension of that discourse itself as a basis for his analysis of the poem ("'A Material Collapse That Is Construction,'" 4).

37. Alexander usefully cites Robert Hayden's resistance to "the riot-squad of statistics" (*The Black Interior*, 47).

38. See Alexander, *The Black Interior*, 43–58, and Clarke, "The Loss of Lyric Space and the Critique of Traditions in Gwendolyn Brooks's 'In the Mecca.'" Brooks herself, while marking a shift in her interests, style, and audience after the Fisk conference, refused this distinction in her interview with George Stavros. "No I have not abandoned beauty, or lyricism, and I don't consider myself a polemical poet. I'm a black poet, and I write about what I see, what interests me, and I'm seeing new things" (5).

39. In chapter 3 I argue that for Walcott the specific spaces of black diasporic life necessitate the kind of re-sensitization that lyric makes possible.

40. See Walker, "New Poets," 348.

CHAPTER 3. Cultivating the Caribbean

1. See King, *Derek Walcott*, 369.

2. See Benítez-Rojo, *The Repeating Island*, esp. 61–81, in the chapter "From the plantation to the Plantation," in which Benítez-Rojo relates the acculturation process to the epoch in which the plantation takes hold in a given island space.

3. It is in this final scalar adjustment that my analysis departs most sharply from the useful archipelagic frame Benítez-Rojo has drawn around the Caribbean; as the previous chapters of *Cultivation and Catastrophe* have demonstrated, I understand the repetition and fragmentation of colonial structures to be features of modern (not only postmodern) literature.

4. The poets themselves, while full of mutual respect, have also noted the distinction between them, Walcott referring to Brathwaite's "mission-school melancholy" ("Tribute Flutes," 44) and Brathwaite to Walcott's humanism (see Ismond, "Walcott versus Brathwaite," 228). For a thorough discussion of the critical positions on this divide, see Ismond, "Walcott versus Brathwaite." Ismond defends Walcott's "Western humanism" while upholding a common distinction between Brathwaite's radical content and Walcott's elegant forms and between Brathwaite's populism and Walcott's privacy.

5. Brathwaite's explication of his volume's title foregrounds the complexity of the roots metaphor. He opens the collection by outlining his concern with what he describes as the dichotomy between migratory and rooted sensibilities in relationship to the Caribbean: "The dichotomy, I think, is still there. . . . It comes, in a way, as an almost physical inheritance from Africa where in nature, drought and lushness, the flower and the desert, lie side by side. It is a spiritual inheritance from slavery" (*Roots*, 29). Brathwaite essentializes the "physical inheritance from Africa." However, perhaps surprisingly to critics (Walcott included) who would emphasize Brathwaite's Africanism as a singular, constraining worldview, Brathwaite himself highlights indeterminacy over certainty. "In nature" he finds not the rooted fullness of African experience but the dialectic between "drought and lushness, the flower and the desert."

6. Clifford turns to the term "routes" as a way of promoting "a view of human location as constituted by displacement as much as stasis."

7. I do not attempt to categorize works as "pastoral," "antipastoral," or "georgic" in part because of self-conscious resistance to these traditions among some of the poets. These categories are nonetheless useful to my consideration of the role of labor in cultivation, as well as

to my interest in genre. Leo Marx's distinction between simple and complex pastoral (*The Machine in the Garden*) and Timothy Sweet's argument that the georgic rather than the pastoral is the mode that engages the economic relationship between humans and the environment (*American Georgics*) are both ways of naming and reorganizing the relationship between nature and culture. The legacy of slave labor in particular transforms this relationship during the twentieth century.

8. In spite of Grainger's attempts to replicate the taxonomic order of the georgic, the brutal context of plantation slavery fragments that order. For a fuller discussion of the disintegration of poetic form in *The Sugar-Cane* in the context of emerging empirical science see Rusert, "Plantation Ecologies: The Experimental Plantation in and against James Grainger's *The Sugar-Cane*."

9. Walcott notes that, "A culture, we all know, is made by its cities" ("The Antilles," 71).

10. Breslin's analysis of history in Walcott's oeuvre draws on Glissant's notion of a "non-history" that describes historical consciousness as a series of overturnings rather than a continuous or gradual relationship to time.

11. As Brent Hayes Edwards defines the term, which he has extracted from Claude McKay's autobiography, a "bad nationalist" is "a subject that is mobile and loosely transnational" (*The Practice of Diaspora*, 239).

12. In part because of the large place *Omeros* has taken up in the criticism, much has been written about Walcott's engagement with the European classical tradition of epic, which critics have identified as one of Walcott's central preoccupations.

13. Patricia Ismond declares that "The Star-Apple Kingdom" is "more significant" than "The Schooner Flight" because in her view the former is "Walcott's most conclusive statement on history and politics in the region," even as she acknowledges that the latter is better "structured." Thus her lengthy reading of the poem, while a refreshing exception to the general rule of brief mention in relation to larger works, focuses on the intertwining of the political and personal narratives as the poem's "essential meaning" and largely ignores the poem's formal and generic qualities, beyond establishing metaphor as a "point of entry" to narrative and characterization (*Abandoning Dead Metaphors*, 249).

14. See http://www.thecaribbeanwriter.org for Fleming's interview with Walcott.

15. See Jameson, "Third World Literature in the Era of Multinational Capitalism." For different reasons, Jahan Ramazani has convincingly argued that Walcott's later poem *Omeros* belies Jameson's claim that third-world texts "are to be read as what I will call national allegories" ("Third World Literature in the Era of Multinational Capitalism," 69). But Ramazani distinguishes *Omeros*, in which Walcott addresses the history of West Indian suffering, from Walcott's earlier condemnations of what Walcott regards as a literature of "victimization." Ramazani argues that the metaphor of the wound and the figure of Philoctete in *Omeros* allow Walcott to take up the mantle of Caribbean suffering without claiming a unique status (*The Hybrid Muse*, 49–71). "The Star-Apple Kingdom" similarly evokes the history of Caribbean suffering in relationship to transcultural experience. However, the figure of the epic hero who embodies the wounded trope that is central to this process in *Omeros* remains unavailable to this shorter poem, in spite of its apparent focus on a single character.

16. "History of Jamaica House," http://www.opm.gov.jm/JamaicaHouse.

17. Elizabeth A. Wilson makes a similar point in her critique of Claire Malroux's French translation of "The Star-Apple Kingdom." Specifically, Wilson demonstrates how Malroux's

choice of "palatiales" for "Great House" fails to convey the suffering associated with the landscape of slavery ("Translating Caribbean Landscape," 21–22).

18. Walcott's critique of tourism for its perpetuation of the destructive ecological effects of the plantation economy has been unearthed by George Handley, who cites Walcott's objections to tourist development in St. Lucia in the 1990s and his dismay at the "miamification" of the archipelago ("Derek Walcott's Poetics of the Environment in The Bounty," 202–4). My reading of "The Star-Apple Kingdom" suggests that even earlier in his career Walcott had linked excessive environmental control and ill-planned agricultural development with the failures of social, political, and economic transformation.

19. Although critics likewise celebrate the Adamic impulse of Walcott's poetry as its most revelatory quality, George Handley has similarly observed that the "numinous" runs the risk that "poetry will function as a neocolonial Adamic possession of the land" (New World Poetics, 3) and Paul Breslin recognizes the "fool's errand" of trying to unlock this particular paradox in Walcott's writing (Nobody's Nation, 6).

20. "Appropriating a Western icon of suffering and refashioning a polysemous and multiparented trope, Walcott's Omeros, together with the poetry of Goodison, Brathwaite, p'Bitek, and Ramanujan, champions a postcolonial poetics of affliction that obliterates the distinction between 'victim's literature' and its supposed opposite" (Ramazani, The Hybrid Muse, 71).

21. As I note in chapter 2, Stewart's discussion centers on both Walcott and Gwendolyn Brooks—both are black diasporic poets writing not only after war but after slavery, colonialism, and Jim Crow violence.

22. I'm referring to the racially oppressive class distinctions Hurston must accept in order to advertise her prospect to Hughes: "They say they do not mind Negroes having the plat, but NO niggers. They do not want the property to lose its value. I mean the adjacent property" (Zora Neale Hurston, 145).

23. In her letter, she points out to Hughes that "everybody down here is dead broke" (145) and that this is why the white community would allow an African American writer to buy land. Likely, the collapse of land values after the 1928 Florida hurricane (as well as an earlier storm in 1926), devastating the economy well beyond the region (and contributing to the subsequent stock market crash and nationwide depression), played a part in the economic microdepression Hurston describes. "For all they [the rest of the country] cared," writes Robert Myckle, "the state could be given back to the Seminoles" (Killer 'Cane, 215).

CHAPTER 4. Continuing Catastrophe

1. I derive this outline of the events surrounding the flood from John M. Barry's Rising Tide, a history of the river, the flood, and the effects of the flood on U.S. political, social and economic life. See also Rozario, The Culture of Calamity, 143–50, and Mizelle, Backwater Blues. I use the term "refugee" advisedly. In the aftermath of Hurricane Katrina in 2004, its use by politicians and journalists rightly outraged many commentators, who objected to the classification of U.S. citizens as "refugees," given the contemporary association of that word with international migrants fleeing political violence or environmental catastrophe. The rejection of that term has been an important assertion of the rights of black citizenship (I address the complexity of this response in somewhat more detail in the coda to this book). Here I use the term to echo its historical usage in The Crisis and also because the black survivors of the Mis-

sissippi river floods already were denied full legal citizenship, which dramatically affected their experience of the disaster.

2. While these reports are unsigned, David Levering Lewis attributes them to Du Bois, given that he was the editor of *The Crisis* (*W.E.B. Du Bois*, 801n11). Susan Scott Parrish, however, in her riveting cultural history *The Flood Year 1927* (published just as this book was going to press), attributes the series on the Red Cross to the NAACP investigator herself (116–19).

3. See Evans, "High Water Everywhere," 5–9, and Mizelle, 33–41.

4. For the reference to the refugee camps as slave camps, see Du Bois, "Flood."

5. Class difference, however, is a significant dimension in how we might perceive the way *The Crisis* participates in creating this narrative. If the reporting in *The Crisis* identifies the ecological, environmental and social conditions that produce the need for migration for a large mass of workers, the advertisements I've described here identify enticements and opportunities in the North for a smaller elite. Farah Jasmine Griffin has also usefully distinguished between the blues (as artistic vehicles primarily concerned with entertainment and pleasure) and letters by migrants (as documents concerned with the conditions of everyday life), although both, along with sociological accounts, contribute to her overall emphasis on the agency of migrants (*"Who Set You Flowin'?,"* 23).

6. "Approximate" would also be a good way of understanding the relationship between what Brathwaite calls "nation language"—which approximates the hurricane, according to Brathwaite, because it "largely ignores the pentameter" of English verse—and English. In charting out this relationship, Brathwaite describes and then pulls back from or modifies a series of likenesses: "English it may be," "the words, as you hear them, might be English," "it may be in English," but "it is not English" (13). Brathwaite acknowledges the proximity but not an identity between nation language and English. The language also brings the English and the "African" into proximity, simultaneity. Brathwaite's repetition and hesitation reflects the uneasy relationship between the colonial language and nation language as he imagines it, but it also suggests the approximate quality of nation (and nature) itself.

7. See Lamothe, *Inventing the New Negro*, 45.

8. "Conceptual umbrella" is Griffin's term (*"Who Set You Flowin'?,"* 4); she approaches visual, musical, and literary texts under this rubric.

9. Ellison's formulation is as much about literary genre as it is about music, or rather it names the interpenetrating relationship between the two. As Edwards has argued, Ellison's use of the word "lyrically" to describe the way the blues work draws our attention to transcription as a major preoccupation of modern poetry ("The Seemingly Eclipsed Window of Form," 583). Ellison's description of the blues also suggests a powerful parallel between the challenge of transcribing "those blasting pressures" of social and environmental catastrophe and the challenges of transcribing one artistic form into another: chronicle into lyric, lyric into blues, blues into lyric.

10. See Griffin, *"Who Set You Flowin'?,"* 19–20.

11. See Evans, "High Water Everywhere," 13–14. See also Albertson, *Bessie*, 150.

12. See David Evans's account of another Crosby/Whiteman recording from the same period, "Mississippi Mud," whose lyrics associate such idyll with "the darkies" who "beat their feet on the Mississippi mud" ("High Water Everywhere," 15).

13. See Albertson, *Bessie*, 148.

14. I'm referring to the title of the Langston Hughes poem and his 1949 collection of the same name, with illustrations by Jacob Lawrence.

15. Although Brown does not refer directly to the relative mobility of white evacuees, the scene in the cabaret echoes the historical contrast between white freedom and black constraint. In his cultural history of the floods, Robert Mizelle offers an especially harrowing account of how "efforts to undermine movement were painfully connected to the reinscription of power over black bodies through labor" (*Backwater Blues*, 36).

16. See also Mark Sanders's interpretation of the road as "a road *through* modernism" (*Afro-Modernist Aesthetics and the Poetry of Sterling A. Brown*, 91).

17. Nixon perhaps too easily attributes the "representational bias against slow violence" to a generically "speedy" way of living, having to do with attention spans and computer screens. He admirably wishes to make invisible violence visible by increasing attention to a different kind of time, but in doing so he also waxes nostalgic for "slower" forms of experience and representation (*Slow Violence and the Environmentalism of the Poor*, 12–13).

18. See Griffin, "*Who Set You Flowin'?*," 19, and Lamothe, *Inventing the New Negro*, 92.

19. Parrish points out how the flood itself was inherently collective, insofar as the physical conditions for evacuees forced them into intensely "public" situations (*The Flood Year 1927*, 143). Where Parrish argues that Smith refrains from "blaming" the floods on human behavior (142), by placing "Back-Water Blues" in the context of Smith's other flood blues I hope to underscore the connection in Smith's lyrics between the slow violence of Jim Crow and the catastrophic violence of the floods.

20. Ellison, Ralph, "Richard Wright's Blues," 78–79. "Chronicle, N," *OED Online* (Oxford University Press, March 2012), http://www.oed.com/view/Entry/32576.

21. Through a reading of two other Bessie Smith songs, Griffin cites natural disasters as one of the primary reasons for leaving the South chronicled in blues migration narratives (*"Who Set You Flowin'?,"* 19–21).

22. Smith, like Crosby, recorded "Muddy Water" before the defining event of the Mississippi floods, the April 1927 levee break in Arkansas which would leave hundreds of thousands homeless, destroy whole farms for the season, and give rise to a racist system of "concentration camps" and enforced recovery labor. Soon after its release, however, Columbia Records marketed the song alongside "Back-Water Blues" as a response to the flood conditions (Evans, "High Water Everywhere," 14).

23. Evans's research into the particularities of the state response to the Nashville flood demonstrates effectively that in that local context, disaster relief was not a "racialized" matter, because existing housing inequalities in Nashville were part of ongoing problems—what I have called "continuing catastrophe." Far from refuting "racial" readings of the song, however, his exhaustive discussion of the multiple contexts in which it has been performed, produced, and heard, as well as his acknowledgment of the slippage between the different kinds of catastrophe effecting poor black communities—a thematic Smith's song explicitly takes up—indicates the power of anachronism in the flood songs ("Bessie Smith's 'Muddy Water,'" 25–29).

24. See Bhabha, *The Location of Culture*, 340.

25. Here my reading departs from those who understand the poem as an homage to Rainey's status as a priestess whose singular voice speaks for and bears witness to the people, or, as Mark Sanders puts it, who becomes "the speaking subject, taking over the poem and thus embodying the ritual" (*Afro-Modernist Aesthetics and the Poetry of Sterling A. Brown*, 66). See also Rowell, "Sterling A. Brown and the Afro-American Folk Tradition," 141.

26. These writings have been collected in Brown's *A Negro Looks at the South*. John Edgar

Tidwell and Mark Sanders argue in the introduction to their edition of *A Negro Looks at the South* that *Southern Road* and the prose writings alike construct the figure of the witnessing artist who "traverses the Southern landscape in an effort to collect and recollect the diversity of Southern black life" (12). Joanne Gabbin (*Sterling A. Brown*, 87–89) and David Anderson ("Sterling Brown's Southern Strategy," 1023) have drawn attention to Brown's appreciation of rural, geographic isolation as a productive ground for folk art, even as they both acknowledge his commitment to adapting and transforming folk forms so as to preserve them in an increasingly urban society.

CHAPTER 5. Collecting Catastrophe

1. This collecting likely formed the basis for Hurston's production of Bahamian music in her New York City musical production *The Great Day*. See Kraut, *Choreographing the Folk*.

2. See Mitchell, "The West Indian Hurricane of September 10–20, 1928." Robert Mykle acknowledges the hurricane's transatlantic journey in a far more problematic way in the prologue to his nonfiction *Killer 'Cane*, entitled "Out of Africa," in which he describes the storm as a "perfect killer," "spawned in the heat of Africa" and poised to destroy its own "native sons" (xvi).

3. See Monge, "Their Eyes Were Watching God," 129. I credit Monge's excellent article with pointing me toward the American Folklife Center at the Library of Congress, where tapes of these songs are archived, and providing detailed bibliographic information for the songs. The transcriptions here are my own.

4. There are no early recordings of Roberts's version of the song to substantiate his status as the composer, but according to Sam Barclay Charters, who recorded Roberts in 1958 in Andros, Roberts worked aboard the ship until a week before it sank, and "John Roberts . . . composed PYTORIA. . . . And John remembered that the Pytoria sank on Wednesday and on Sunday morning '. . . I had my song ready.'" ("Liner Notes"). See also "Run Come See," *Traditional Ballad Index*, www.csufresno.edu/folklore/ballads/FSWB058.html.

5. See Bone, "The (Extended) South of Black Folk." Bone is primarily responding to Hazel Carby's *Cultures in Babylon*. Although Bone's characterization of Florida and the Bahamas as part of the "extended U.S. South" remains U.S.-centric, his argument provides crucial material context that counters Carby's critique of the novel as a nostalgic displacement of the historical realities of the great migration.

6. To read the novel as such would be to remain confined in what Brathwaite, during the same period in which he wrote *History of the Voice*, terms "the pessimistic/plantation view of society," a "system" or "model" that uncritically subsumes Caribbean history and cultural production to the space and history of slavery ("Caribbean Man in Space and Time," 202).

7. I am referring here to Fred Moten's method of reading and listening as an improvisational practice that allows us to hear the speech of the subaltern subject as broken. See *In The Break*.

8. I have in mind Moten's discussion of "the radical segregation of prophecy and description" in *Invisible Man* (*In the Break*, 68).

9. For more on the connection between Janie's development as a character and the symbolic function of trees, see Sivils, "Reading Trees in Southern Literature." For the temporality of black modernity in relation to Hurston, see Duck, *The Nation's Region*.

10. See Carby, "The Politics of Fiction, Anthropology, and the Folk." Leigh Ann Duck makes a more complex argument about the novel's temporality, allowing that Hurston's novel

is "centrally concerned with modernization" (*The Nation's Region*, 132). Whereas Duck, however, insists that Hurston's modernization of the folk ultimately consists of transforming folk pleasure into individual experience (through the bourgeois form of the novel), I argue that the disruptive experience of catastrophe foregrounds collective experience.

11. See Bone, "The (Extended) South of Black Folk."

12. Gates convincingly argues that free indirect discourse in Hurston's novel constitutes "a mediating third term" between mimesis and diegesis (215). Gates's influential reading is particularly important for his attention to how Hurston's narrative strategy allows the voice of the transcendent self to extend beyond the individual. It is notable, however, that although he acknowledges Hurston's work as an anthropologist, to which he attributes her acquisition of an "oral base," Gates does not account for the unmistakable presence of nondiscursive sound within the structure of the novel.

13. See Lamothe, *Inventing the New Negro*, and Retman, *Real Folks*. Dance scholar Anthea Kraut's rich history of Hurston's work as a choreographer (*Choreographing the Folk*) assembles an archive of the performances of African diasporic music Hurston staged in New York during this period and has noted in that context some important biographical connections between this work and *Their Eyes*. More recently Daphne Brooks ("'Sister, Can You Line It Out?'") has analyzed Hurston's vocal performances as sociopolitical phenomena that invert the relationship between informer and informed in anthropological practices, and Alexandra Vazquez ("Listening in the Cold War Years") situates Hurston as a foremother of a diasporic female performance tradition in Florida. These scholars have helped me to define the archive of Hurston's musical performance that forms the basis of my interpretation of music's irruption within *Their Eyes Were Watching God*.

14. According to my research, the June recording session—of Hurston's own voice, "collected" by Herbert Halpert and Stetson Kennedy, playing back songs she had herself collected in the field—is Hurston's last for the Federal Writers' Project and her only recording after submitting the proposal.

15. According to a note on the published letter, "Corse forwarded Hurston's letter to Henry Alsberg, director of the Federal Writers' Project, and asked if he could loan the Florida project the recording machine he had in his office" (*Zora Neale Hurston*, 415).

16. See Baucom, "History 4°," Baucom, "The Human Shore," Chakrabarty, "The Climate of History," Chakrabarty, "Postcolonial Studies and the Challenge of Climate Change," and Heise, *Sense of Place and Sense of Planet*.

CHAPTER 6. Collecting Culture

1. See "Gleaner Top Ten."

2. Citations of the lyrics of this song refer to my own transcription, adapted in part from the following website: "Lloyd Lovindeer Wild Gilbert Lyrics," accessed April 22, 2012, www .6lyrics.com/wild_gilbert-lyrics-lloyd_lovindeer.aspx. I am grateful to Stephen Russell, who pointed me toward this song, assisted with the transcription, and talked with me about its literal and figurative meanings.

3. See Treaster, "In Storm's Aftermath, Jamaica Seeks Visitors," and Treaster, "Jamaica Reviving after Hurricane but Food Shortages Are Predicted."

4. Glissant's remark comes from "The Quarrel with History," a response to Eddie Baugh's essay "The West Indian Writer and His Quarrel with History," which was presented as part of the same Carifesta symposium as the first iteration of Brathwaite's *History of the Voice* (60, 61n.1)

5. See McSweeney, "Poetics, Revelations, and Catastrophes."

6. Most historians and political theorists attribute Edward Seaga's loss of the prime ministry to Michael Manley in 1989 to Seaga's handling of posthurricane conditions.

7. See Walker, "Twenty-One Years after Gilbert." Lovindeer had been performing and deejaying since the seventies, but "Wild Gilbert" made him into a national figure.

8. The longevity of the power outage he experienced likely owed to his particular location. According to some reports, 80 percent of the people had power restored within two months (Treaster, "In Storm's Aftermath, Jamaica Seeks Visitors").

9. See Stanley-Niaah, "Negotiating a Common Transnational Space," 764. For the connection between earlier cultural forms and dancehall, see also Stanley-Niaah, *DanceHall*.

10. Lovindeer's emphasis on cultural survival divorced from the question of agricultural survival thereby anticipates some of the crucial questions about urban poverty, global inequalities, and nationalist ideology that would emerge in very different ways in the wake of Hurricane Katrina (2004) and the Haiti earthquake (2010).

11. See Dawes, *Natural Mysticism*, 264.

12. Dancehall music commonly alludes melodically or lyrically to music from the United States; one example is Yellowman's "Starting All over Again," which remakes the romantic 1972 soul hit by Mel and Tim as a hopeful, nationalist postdisaster call to action.

13. Although beyond the scope of my argument here, one major challenge to this commonplace lies in the major political upheaval that ensued after the hurricane, which ultimately resulted in the ousting of Edward Seaga as prime minister. In a broader context, Rebecca Solnit has argued in *A Paradise Built in Hell* that while governments often fail in the aftermath of disaster, communities come together in surprising ways.

14. See Cooke, "'Wild Gilbert.'"

15. In her reading of "'Wild Gilbert,'" for instance, Carolyn Cooper describes the access that wealthier Jamaicans had to generators (unlike Lovindeer's speaker "inna my room inna dark") because of their ability to travel to Miami (*Noises in the Blood*, 170).

16. I borrow the term "instrumental migrations" from the title and theorization of an earlier version of the monograph that would eventually become Vazquez's *Listening in Detail*.

17. Lovindeer complains that "in Jamaica the charts are corrupt" (Cooke, "'Wild Gilbert'").

18. See Cooke, "'Wild Gilbert.'"

19. See KC, "'Wild Gilbert'" Singer Brings 'ha-Pee-Ness' to Music."

20. In this sense, environmental catastrophe produces conditions that reverse the common assumption of a dichotomy "between the archive of supposedly enduring materials (i.e., texts, documents, buildings, bones) and the so-called ephemeral repertoire of embodied practice/knowledge (i.e., spoken language, dance, sports, ritual)." See Diana Taylor, *The Archive and the Repertoire*, 19.

21. Brathwaite's use of the word "timehri"—an indigenous word referring to rock paintings —indicates his concern with the preservation not only of sound but of the visual markers of culture.

22. Although Brathwaite's presentation itself is missing, this archive contains all of the other presentations from the Literature of the West Indies symposium at Carifesta '76. This archive, housed in a small space in the back of the campus radio station and operated by a limited number of staff, is an immensely important repository of Caribbean cultural memory.

23. It should be clear by now that I don't believe poetry is supplemental to music or sound for Brathwaite. Rather, I agree with Anthony Reed, who, in his fine recent reading of Sycorax

Video Style in *Shar* and Brathwaite's other poems of the same period, points out how video style "synthesizes techniques of orality and visuality in ways that upset the critical tendency to privilege the former" (*Freedom Time*, 60). Like both Reed and Carrie Noland, I also wish to challenge the tendency to interpret Brathwaite's investment in technology, text, and graphics as an attempt to transcribe oral communication. Where both Noland and Reed treat the synthesis in these later poems as a departure from the elaboration of "nation language" in *History* (which, according to Noland privileges "live presence" ["Remediation and Diaspora," 81, 77]), however, I see the development of video style as continuous with the already elastic notion of language in the essay.

24. My use of lyric necessarily extends the term beyond its association with brevity and compression. *Shar* sprawls visually, and some have treated it as epic, but the poem also eschews narrative structure, its song irrupting from within a historical break.

25. In reading the poem of catastrophe as a re-creation of the archive, I am an extending Joyelle McSweeney's general observation that Brathwaite's poems often function in this way, in her excellent interview with him, "Poetics, Revelations, and Catastrophes."

26. See Rigby, "Publishing Brathwaite," 711. Rigby, one-time editor of the British journal the *Page*, notes, for instance, that "the significance of Brathwaite's adventures with the Apple Mac become apparent when you try to publish them. The introduction to 'I Cristobal Colon' was centered and in a standard, Times-ish face: we could enter it into our system and get a strong *approximation*. The main body of the text was in a face to which we had no access, and even if we had, our host paper would have had copyright permission on the software. It was a typeface we couldn't *mimic*, yet it was integral to the feel and to the conceit of the poem" (711, emphasis mine). Rigby describes a typesetting process curiously akin to the oral-textual and environmental-literary transcription processes Brathwaite has described in *History of the Voice* and elsewhere.

27. Most famously, in 2001 Brathwaite republished his trilogy *Mother Poem, Sun Poem*, and *X/Self* as *Ancestors*, noting that the poems "have been enlarged, recast, and greatly revised by the Author for the 2001 single volume New Directions edition. The text has been photo-offset to incorporate 'Sycorax video style' type as developed by the author." See the copyright page of *Ancestors*.

28. On the one hand, Savory argues that the computer "bridges the gap between the world of orality and the world of reading" but, on the other, she maintains that "we are still reading, and it is still a book. Therefore, the condition of a book's creation is still dependent on the publisher and the market place" (217).

29. Here, Savory is using the terms of the debate Brathwaite stages with Shakespeare's *The Tempest* in his *X/Self*. In this poem Brathwaite joins a lineage of Caribbean writers, notably Aimé Césaire and George Lamming, who embrace Caliban as a resistant colonial subject/ex-slave challenging the authority of the colonizer, cast in this reimagined drama as Prospero.

30. For a detailed discussion of the effects of Gilbert on Jamaican libraries, particularly the Norman Manley Law Library, see Aarons, "Hurricanes and Disaster Response."

31. See Eyre, "Jamaica."

32. See Barker and McGregor, "Land Degradation in the Yallahs Basin, Jamaica," and Weis, "Beyond Peasant Deforestation," 302–3. Barker and McGregor have described the process by which the techniques of coffee monoculture plantations from the period of slavery has resulted in modern land degradation in Jamaica. According to Tony Weis, the problem is not merely individual peasants' resistance to ecologically sustainable practices but also the con-

tinuation of colonial land use policies that the logic of the international neoliberal framework encourages and that shapes Jamaica's economy (and therefore ecology).

33. See "Fig Tree." *The Barbados Museum & Historical Society*. Accessed November 4, 2016. http://www.barbmuse.org.bb/web/?s=fig+tree.

34. See Bhabha, *The Location of Culture*, 364.

35. Heise importantly acknowledges that "hybridity, diaspora, and marginality sometimes turned into quasi-essentialist categories themselves" but contends that such categories may be required in certain "particular and historical contexts" (5) in order to end a stalemate between global and local approaches to culture.

36. See David Scott's introduction to the special issue of *Small Axe* dedicated to black archives for one take on black archival practice as something other than "a domain of positivity, of pure materiality" (vi).

37. Brathwaite has recently gone back to Barbados, describing his reverse migration as being "returned to the Plantation poorer, more bereft, than when i left." In this letter dated September 23, 2011, to his friend and Internet chronicler Tom Raworth, Brathwaite recounts his concern over preserving his archives. Returning to Barbados, Brathwaite seeks an idealized "pasture" in which to write. For the text of this letter see http://tomraworth.com/SCPCL.pdf. For the online archive of Brathwaite's struggle to relocate and rebuild his archive in Barbados, see http://tomraworth.com/wordpress.

CODA. Unnatural Catastrophe

1. For a detailed reading of Turner's painting as allegory for the middle passage and representative of nineteenth-century "liberal cosmopolitism," see Baucom, *Specters of the Atlantic*, 264–96.

2. For Sharpe, Oloudah Equiano, and other abolitionists, the case became fodder for their arguments. In *Specters of the Atlantic*, Baucom argues that the event and its representations constitute the basis for modern ideas of capital, ethical spectatorship, and temporality.

3. See Weskett, *A Complete Digest of the Laws, Theory and Practice of Insurance*, 525, and Walvin, *Black Ivory*, 17.

4. According to Morton medial statements are key devices of ecomimesis from Thoreau to Denise Levertov. The problem with ambient poetics, he argues, is not so much the existence of that boundary as the attempt to deny its existence—to naturalize the aesthetic (38). At the same time, Morton holds out the possibility of what he calls a radical ecomimesis, which would acknowledge, in his words, "irreducible otherness, whether in poetics, ethics, or politics" (151).

5. See the archive of some of these readings hosted by Penn Sound: http://writing.upenn.edu/pennsound/x/Philip.php.

6. More recently, Moten has turned to *Zong!* as a text that helps us elaborate the ways in which "modernity . . . is a socioecological disaster that can neither be calculated nor conceptualized as a series of personal injuries" ("Blackness and Poetry").

7. As Anthony Reed has argued, Philip's project is not so much a work of recovery but of "fabrication." Whereas Reed sees the "fabrication" as a mode of "witness" I see it instead as an archival gesture (*Freedom Time*, 55). Philip's *Zong!* may be one model in response to Stephen Best's inquiry about how we can think future blackness apart from the project of recovery. Although Philip's poem is concerned with the past of enslavement and the middle passage—

making precisely the sort of historicist move that Best challenges—the poem's fragmented archive also documents what Best calls the "nonrelationality between the past and the present" ("On Failing to Make the Past Present," 455).

8. Danticat's refusal of the first-world exceptionalism of the United States forms an important basis for countering the otherwise reasonable discomfort produced by the use of the term "refugee" to describe survivors of domestic disasters. See chapter 4, note 1.

9. See Sharpe, "Black Studies," and Moten, "Blackness and Poetry."

10. The participants in this debate between Afro-pessimism and black optimism themselves identify much "common ground" between their positions and reject an absolute opposition. Jared Sexton, for instance, insists that the affirmation of blackness as "pathological being" does not negate "social life" but rather constitutes a commitment "to living a black social life under the shadow of social death" ("The Social Life of Social Death," 27). Responding to Sexton, Moten concedes that "I am totally with him in locating my optimism in appositional proximity to his pessimism even if I would tend not to talk about the inside/outside relationality of social death and social life" ("Blackness and Nothingness (Mysticism in the Flesh)," 773). In an interview in a recent issue of *Rhizome* devoted to thinking about Afro-pessimism, Christina Sharpe acknowledges, too, that "there is room for theorizing joy. . . . But I don't think you can theorize joy or even pleasure under certain kinds of extreme force unless you are marking them as simply the absence of force." For Sharpe it is the process of "wake work" that allows progress against the "hold" of black suffering (Terrefe, "What Exceeds the Hold?"). All of these discussions—perhaps by virtue of being discussions—mark the duality of living and making art in the aftermath of enslavement. Scholars debate which discursive gesture (expression of optimism or pessimism) merits greater force in the articulation and definition of black being against a pervasive ideology of black nonbeing. Equally important, particularly for Afro-pessimist thinkers, is the *particularity* of black suffering in relationship to other forms of rupture, containment, or enslavement.

11. Indeed, Chakrabarty goes so far as to suggest that we may be on the edge of a "new universal history" in light of the shared inter-special catastrophe that is global warming ("The Climate of History," 222). See also his "Postcolonial Studies and the Challenge of Climate Change."

12. Recent work in early American literary studies by Christopher Iannini (*Fatal Revolutions*), Britt Rusert ("The Science of Freedom"; *Fugitive Science*), and Monique Allewaert (*Ariel's Ecology*) on natural science, "fugitive science," and Atlantic embodiment, respectively, underscores the connections among the ontological, epistemological, and representational realms in early American racial discourse. If natural science and race science were uncomfortably linked in early America (although, as Rusert aptly demonstrates, there was also a powerful antiracist science during this period), then perhaps in the twentieth century we would expect a resistance to thinking black ontology in relationship to ecology. My research suggests, however, that in spite of the destructive history of race science and the perceived need to prove the humanity of black diasporic subject, the intersection between ontological thought and ecological thought continues to concern black writers well into our current century.

13. Bradford has also documented this phenomenon in "Help Us," a rooftop installation visible from Google Earth.

Bibliography

Aarons, John A. "Hurricanes and Disaster Response: Lessons Learned in Jamaica from 'Gilbert.'" In *Preparing for the Worst, Planning for the Best: Protecting Our Cultural Heritage from Disaster*, ed. Johanna G. Wellheiser, Nancy E. Gwinn, and Walter de Gruyter, 117–25. The Hague: International Federation of Library Associations and Institutions, 2005.

Adorno, Theodor. "Lyric Poetry and Society." Trans. Bruce Mayo. *Telos* 20 (Summer 1974): 52–71.

Albertson, Chris. *Bessie*. Revised and Expanded Edition. New Haven, CT: Yale University Press, 2005.

Alexander, Elizabeth. *The Black Interior: Essays*. Saint Paul, MN: Graywolf Press, 2004.

———. "New Ideas about Black Experimental Poetry." *Michigan Quarterly Review* 50, no. 4 (2011): 598.

Alexandre, Sandy. "Richard Wright's Haikus: Nature Poetry as a State of Black Culture." Paper presented at the Futures of American Studies institute, Dartmouth College, June 26, 2010.

Allewaert, Monique. *Ariel's Ecology: Plantations, Personhood, and Colonialism in the American Tropics*. Minneapolis: University of Minnesota Press, 2013.

Anderson, Benedict. *Imagined Communities: Reflections on the Origin and Spread of Nationalism*. 1983. New York: Verso, 2006.

Anderson, David. "Sterling Brown's Southern Strategy: Poetry as Cultural Evolution in Southern Road." *Callaloo* 21, no. 4 (1998): 1023–37.

Appadurai, Arjun. "Disjuncture and Difference in the Global Cultural Economy." *Theory, Culture, and Society* 7, no. 2 (1990): 295–310.

Baker, Houston A. *Modernism and the Harlem Renaissance*. Chicago: University of Chicago Press, 1987.

———. *Turning South Again: Re-thinking Modernism / Re-reading Booker T*. Durham, NC: Duke University Press, 2001.

Baker, Houston A., and Leslie A. Fiedler, eds. *English Literature: Opening Up the Canon*. Baltimore, MD: Johns Hopkins University Press, 1981.

Baraka, Amiri. "Look for You Yesterday, Here You Come Today." In *The LeRoi Jones/Amiri Baraka Reader*. New York: Thunder's Mouth Press, 1991. 11–14.

———. *See also* Jones, Leroi.

Barker, David, and Duncan F. M. McGregor. "Land Degradation in the Yallahs Basin, Jamaica: Historical Notes and Contemporary Observations." *Geography* 73, no. 2 (1988): 116–24.

Barker, David, and David Miller. "Hurricane Gilbert: Anthropomorphising a Natural Disaster." *Area* 22, no. 2 (1990): 107–16.

Barnes, W. Therold, and Frank A. Collymore. Forward. *BIM* 3, no. 9 (1949): 1.

Barry, John M. *Rising Tide: The Great Mississippi Flood of 1927 and How It Changed America*. New York: Simon and Schuster, 1998.

Baucom, Ian. "History 4°: Postcolonial Method and Anthropocene Time." *Cambridge Journal of Postcolonial Literary Inquiry* 1, no. 1 (2014): 123–42.

———. "The Human Shore: Postcolonial Studies in an Age of Natural Science." *History of the Present* 2, no. 1 (May 15, 2012): 1–23.

———. *Specters of the Atlantic: Finance Capital, Slavery, and the Philosophy of History*. Durham: Duke University Press, 2005.

Baugh, Edward. *Derek Walcott*. Cambridge: Cambridge University Press, 2006.

———. "A History of Poetry." In *A History of Literature in the Caribbean*, ed. A. James Arnold, Vera M. Kutzinski, and Ineke Phaf-Rheinberger, 2:227–82. Amsterdam: John Benjamins, 2001.

———. "The West Indian Writer and His Quarrel with History." 1977. *Small Axe* 16, no. 2 (2012): 60–64.

Bell, Bernard W. *The Afro-American Novel and Its Tradition*. Amherst: University of Massachusetts Press, 1987.

Benítez-Rojo, Antonio. *The Repeating Island: The Caribbean and the Postmodern Perspective*. Trans. James E Maraniss. Durham, NC: Duke University Press, 1996.

Berlant, Lauren. *Cruel Optimism*. Durham, NC: Duke University Press, 2011.

Best, Stephen. "On Failing to Make the Past Present." *Modern Language Quarterly* 73, no. 3 (2012): 453–74.

Bhabha, Homi K. *The Location of Culture*. London: 1994. Routledge, 2004.

Bone, Martyn. "The (Extended) South of Black Folk: Intraregional and Transnational Migrant Labor in Jonah's Gourd Vine and Their Eyes Were Watching God." *American Literature: A Journal of Literary History, Criticism, and Bibliography* 79, no. 4 (2007): 753–79.

Bone, Robert. *Down Home: A History of Afro-American Short Fiction from Its Beginnings to the End of the Harlem Renaissance*. New York: Putnam, 1975.

Botkin, B. A., ed. Introduction to *Folk-Say: A Regional Miscellany*, vol. 2, 15–18. Norman: University of Oklahoma Press, 1930.

Braddock, Jeremy. *Collecting as Modernist Practice*. Baltimore, MD: Johns Hopkins University Press, 2012.

Brathwaite, Edward Kamau. "Caribbean Man in Space and Time." In *Carifesta Forum: An Anthology of 20 Caribbean Voices*, ed. John Hearne, 199–208. Kingston: Produced for Carifesta '76 for the Institute of Jamaica and Jamaica Journal, 1976.

———. *See also* Brathwaite, Kamau.

———. "English in the Caribbean: Notes on Nation Language and Poetry, an Electronic Lecture." In *English Literature: Opening Up the Canon*, ed. Leslie A. Fiedler and Houston A. Baker Jr., 15–53. Baltimore, MD: Johns Hopkins University Press, 1981.

———. *History of the Voice: The Development of Nation Language in Anglophone Caribbean Poetry*. London: New Beacon Books, 1984.

———. *Nation Language Poetry*. Savacou Working Paper 5. Mona, Jamaica: Savacou Publications, 1982.

———. *Our Ancestral Heritage: A Bibliography of the English-Speaking Caribbean Designed to Re-*

cord and Celebrate the Several Origins of Our Structural, Material and Creative Culture and to Indicate How This Is Being Used by Us to Mek Ah-We. Mona, Jamaica: Savacou Publications, 1976.

Brathwaite, Kamau. *Ancestors: A Reinvention of Mother Poem, Sun Poem, and X/Self*. New York: New Directions, 2001.

———. *The Arrivants: A New World Trilogy*. New York: Oxford University Press, 1988.

———. "Cultural Lynching or How to Dis. Man. Tle the Artist (Letter to Tom Raworth)," September 23, 2011. http://tomraworth.com/SCPCL.pdf.

———. "The Lass Days of KB and CowPastor Vandal: My Emmerton 2005," March 15, 2005. http://tomraworth.com/wordpress.

———. *Roots*. Ann Arbor: University of Michigan Press, 1993.

———. *Shar/Hurricane Poem*. Mona, Jamaica: Savacou Publications, 1990.

Brathwaite, Kamau, and Nathaniel Mackey. *conVERSations with Nathaniel Mackey*. New York: We Press/Xcp: Cross-Cultural Poetics, 1999.

Breslin, Paul. *Nobody's Nation: Reading Derek Walcott*. University of Chicago Press, 2001.

Brooks, Daphne. "'Sister, Can You Line It Out'? Zora Neale Hurston and the Sound of Angular Black Womanhood." *Amerikastudien/American Studies* 54, no. 4 (2010): 617–27.

Brooks, Gwendolyn. *Annie Allen*. New York: Harper and Row, 1968.

———. "Beverly Hills, Chicago." In *Blacks*, 128–29. Chicago: Third World Press, 1987.

———. "the birth in a narrow room." In *Blacks*, 83. Chicago: Third World Press, 1987.

———. *Conversations with Gwendolyn Brooks*. Ed. Gloria Jean Wade Gayles. Jackson: University Press of Mississippi, 2003.

———. Interview with George Stavros. *Contemporary Literature* 11, no. 1 (1970): 1–20.

———. "In the Mecca." In *Blacks*, 401–33. Chicago: Third World Press, 1987.

———. *In the Mecca*. New York: Harper and Row, 1968.

———. "Poets Who Are Negroes." *Phylon* 11, no. 4 (1950): 312.

———. *Report from Part One*. Detroit: Broadside Press, 1972.

Brown, Lloyd. "Which Way for the Negro Writer." *Masses and Mainstream* 4, no. 3 (March 1951): 53–63.

———. "Which Way for the Negro Writer? II." *Masses and Mainstream* 4, no. 4 (April 1951): 50–59.

Brown, Lloyd Wellesley. *West Indian Poetry*. Boston: Twayne, 1978.

Brown, Sterling A. "The Blues as Folk Poetry." In *Folk-Say, a Regional Miscellany*, vol. 2, ed. B. A. Botkin, 324–39. Norman: University of Oklahoma Press, 1930.

———. "Cabaret (1927, Black & Tan Chicago)." In *The Collected Poems of Sterling A. Brown*, ed. Michael S. Harper, 111–13. Evanston, IL: Triquarterly Books, 1996.

———. "Ma Rainey." In *The Collected Poems of Sterling A. Brown*, ed. Michael S. Harper, 62–63. Evanston, IL: Triquarterly Books, 1996.

———. "Ma Rainey." In *Folk-Say: A Regional Miscellany*, vol. 2, ed. B. A. Botkin, 276–78. Norman: University of Oklahoma Press, 1930.

———. *A Negro Looks at the South*. Ed. John Edgar Tidwell and Mark A Sanders. Oxford: Oxford University Press, 2007.

———. *Southern Roads*. New York: Harcourt, Brace, 1932.

Cameron, Sharon. *Lyric Time: Dickinson and the Limits of Genre*. Baltimore, MD: Johns Hopkins University Press, 1979.

Carby, Hazel V. *Cultures in Babylon: Black Britain and African America*. London: Verso, 1999.

———. "The Politics of Fiction, Anthropology, and the Folk: Zora Neale Hurston." *History and Memory in African-American Culture*, ed. Geneviéve Farber and Robert O'Meally, 28–44. New York: Oxford University Press, 1994.

Carrie, Noland. "Remediation and Diaspora: Kamau Brathwaite's Video Style." In *Diasporic Avant-Gardes*, ed. Carrie Noland and Barrett Watten, 77–97. New York: Palgrave Macmillan, 2009.

Chakrabarty, Dipesh. "The Climate of History: Four Theses." *Critical Inquiry* 35, no. 2 (2009): 197–222.

———. "Postcolonial Studies and the Challenge of Climate Change." *New Literary History* 43, no. 1 (2012): 1–18.

Chang, Kevin O'Brien, and Wayne Chen. *Reggae Routes: The Story of Jamaican Music*. Philadelphia: Temple University Press, 1998.

Charles, John C. "What Was Africa to Him? Alain Locke, Cultural Nationalism, and the Rhetoric of Empire during the New Negro Renaissance." In *New Voices on the Harlem Renaissance: Essays on Race, Gender, and Literary Discourse*, ed. Australia Tarver and Paula C. Barnes, 33–58. Madison, NJ: Fairleigh Dickinson University Press, 2005.

Charters, Sam Barclay. "Liner Notes." In *Music of the Bahamas*, vol. 2: *Anthems, Work Songs and Ballads*. Smithsonian Folkways, 1959.

Clarke, Cheryl. "The Loss of Lyric Space and the Critique of Traditions in Gwendolyn Brooks's 'In the Mecca.'" *Kenyon Review* 17, no. 1 (1995): 136–47.

Clifford, James. *Routes: Travel and Translation in the Late Twentieth Century*. Cambridge, MA: Harvard University Press, 1997.

Collins, Michael. "Risk, Envy and Fear in Sterling Brown's 'Georgics.'" *Callaloo* 21, no. 4 (1998): 950–67.

Collymore, F. A. "The Catt." *BIM* 1, no. 1 (1942): 52–53.

Cooke, Mel. "'Wild Gilbert'—a Song for All Seasons." *Sunday Gleaner*. March 14, 2010. http://jamaica-gleaner.com/gleaner/20100314/ent/ent5.html.

"Coolie Labour in the West Indies." *Gleaner*. February 10, 1913.

Cooper, Carolyn. *Noises in the Blood*. Durham, NC: Duke University Press, 1995.

Cooper, Wayne F. *Claude McKay: Rebel Sojourner in the Harlem Renaissance*. Baton Rouge: Louisiana State University Press, 1987.

Crichlow, Michaeline A. *Negotiating Caribbean Freedom: Peasants and the State in Development*. Lanham, MD: Lexington Books, 2005.

Cullen, Countee. *Caroling Dusk: An Anthology of Verse by Negro Poets*. New York: Harper & Brothers, 1927.

———. "Fruit of the Flower." In *The New Negro*, ed. Alain Locke, 132. New York: Simon and Schuster, 1925.

Cunningham, Nijah. "The Resistance of the Lost Body." *Small Axe* 20, no. 1 (2016): 113–28.

D'Aguiar, Fred. *Feeding the Ghosts*. New York: HarperCollins, 2000.

Dalleo, Raphael. "Another 'Our America': Rooting a Caribbean Aesthetic in the Work of José Martí, Kamau Brathwaite and Édouard Glissant." *Anthurium* 2, no. 2 (2004): Article 1. http://scholarlyrepository.miami.edu/anthurium/vol2/iss2/1

———. *Caribbean Literature and the Public Sphere: From the Plantation to the Postcolonial*. Charlottesville: University of Virginia Press, 2011.

———. "The Public Sphere and Jamaican Anticolonial Politics: Public Opinion, Focus, and the Place of the Literary." *Small Axe* 14, no. 2 (2010): 56–82.

Dance, Daryl Cumber. *Fifty Caribbean Writers: A Bio-Bibliographical Critical Sourcebook*. Westport, CT: Greenwood, 1986.

Danticat, Edwidge. *Create Dangerously: The Immigrant Artist at Work*. Princeton, NJ: Princeton University Press, 2010.

Dawahare, Anthony. "The Specter of Radicalism in Alain Locke's The New Negro." In *Left of the Color Line: Race, Radicalism, and Twentieth-Century Literature of the United States*, ed. Bill V. Mullen and James Smithurst, 67–85. Chapel Hill: University of North Carolina Press, 2003.

Dawes, Kwame Senu Neville. *Natural Mysticism: Towards a New Reggae Aesthetic in Caribbean Writing*. Leeds, UK: Peepal Tree, 1999.

Dayan, Joan. "Paul Gilroy's Slaves, Ships, and Routes: The Middle Passage as Metaphor." *Research in African Literatures* 27, no. 4 (1996): 7–14.

Deleuze, Gilles, and Félix Guattari. *Anti-Oedipus: Capitalism and Schizophrenia*. Trans. Robert Hurley, Seem Mark, and Helen Lane. Minneapolis: University of Minnesota Press, 1983.

———. *Kafka: Toward a Minor Literature*. Minneapolis: University of Minnesota Press, 1986.

DeLoughrey, Elizabeth M. *Routes and Roots: Navigating Caribbean and Pacific Island Literatures*. Honolulu: University of Hawai'i Press, 2007.

———. "Yam, Roots, and Rot: Allegories of the Provision Grounds." *Small Axe* 15, no. 1 (2011): 58–75.

DeLoughrey, Elizabeth M., Renée K. Gosson, and George B. Handley, eds. *Caribbean Literature and the Environment: Between Nature and Culture*. Charlottesville: University of Virginia Press, 2005.

Diaz, Junot. "Apocalypse: What Disasters Reveal." *Boston Review*, June 2011. http://boston review.net/junot-diaz-apocalypse-haiti-earthquake.

DJ Culture Norm. "Lake Shady Reggae," 2011. http://www.lakeshady.com/reggae.

Donnell, Alison, and Sarah Lawson Welsh, eds. *The Routledge Reader in Caribbean Literature*. New York: Psychology Press, 1996.

Dover, Cedric. "These Things We Shared: An Appendix." *Phylon* 14, no. 2 (1953): 145–46.

Du Bois, W. E. B. "Flood." *The Crisis*, July 1927, 168.

———. "The Flood, the Red Cross, and the National Guard." Pt. 1. *The Crisis*, January 1928, 5–7, 26–28.

———. "The Flood, the Red Cross, and the National Guard II." *The Crisis*, February 1928, 41–43, 64.

———. *The Souls of Black Folk*. Ed. Brent Hayes Edwards. 1903. New York: Oxford University Press, 2007.

Duck, Leigh Anne. *The Nation's Region: Southern Modernism, Segregation, and U.S. Nationalism*. Athens: University of Georgia Press, 2006.

Dungy, Camille T., ed. *Black Nature: Four Centuries of African American Nature Poetry*. Athens: University of Georgia Press, 2009.

Edwards, Brent Hayes. *The Practice of Diaspora: Literature, Translation, and the Rise of Black Internationalism*. Cambridge, MA: Harvard University Press, 2003.

———. "The Seemingly Eclipsed Window of Form: James Weldon Johnson's Prefaces." In *The Jazz Cadence of American Culture*, ed. Robert O'Meally, 580–601. New York: Columbia University Press, 1998.

———. "The Specter of Interdisciplinarity." *PMLA: Publications of the Modern Language Association of America* 123, no. 1 (2008): 188–93.

———. "The Uses of Diaspora." *Social Text* 19, no. 1 (2001): 45–73.

Edwards, Bryan. *The History, Civil and Commercial, of the British Colonies in the West Indies.* 3rd ed. Vol. 2. London: Printed for John Stockdale, 1801.

Eldredge, N., and S. J. Gould. "Punctuated Equilibria: An Alternative to Phyletic Gradualism." In *Models in Paleobiology*, ed. T. J. Schopf, 82–115. San Francisco: Freeman, Cooper, 1972.

Ellis, Nadia. *Territories of the Soul: Queered Belonging in the Black Diaspora.* Durham, NC: Duke University Press, 2015.

Ellison, Ralph. *Invisible Man.* 1952. New York: Random House, 1995.

Ellison, Ralph. "Richard Wright's Blues." In *Shadow and Act*, 77–94. New York: Quality Paperback Book Club, 1964.

Eudell, Demetrius L. "From Mode of Production to Mode of Auto-Institution: Sylvia Wynter's Black Metamorphosis of the Labor Question." *Small Axe* 20, no. 1 (2016): 47–61.

Evans, David. "Bessie Smith's: The Story behind the Song." *Popular Music* 26, no. 1 (2006): 97–116.

———. "High Water Everywhere: Blues and Gospel Commentary on the 1927 Mississippi River Flood." In *Nobody Knows Where the Blues Come From: Lyrics and History*, ed. Robert Springer, 3–75. Jackson: University Press of Mississippi, 2007.

Eyre, Lawrence Alan. "Jamaica: Test Case for Tropical Deforestation?" *Ambio* 16, no. 6 (1987): 338–43.

Finseth, Ian Frederick. *Shades of Green: Visions of Nature in the Literature of American Slavery, 1770–1860.* Athens: University of Georgia Press, 2009.

Foley, Barbara. *Spectres of 1919: Class and Nation in the Making of the New Negro.* Urbana: University of Illinois Press, 2003.

Foreman, Clark. "The Decade of Hope." *Phylon* 12, no. 2 (1951): 137–50.

Frankenfield, H. C. "The Floods of 1927 in the Mississippi Basin." *Monthly Weather Review*, October 18, 1927, supp. 437–452.

Franklyn, David Omowalé. "Grenada, Naipaul, and Ground Provision." *Small Axe: A Caribbean Journal of Criticism* 11, no. 1 (2007): 67–75.

Gabbin, Joanne V. *Sterling A. Brown: Building the Black Aesthetic Tradition.* Westport, CT: Greenwood Press, 1985.

"Gardens." In *World of a Slave: Encyclopedia of the Material Life of Slaves in the United States.* Westport, CT: Greenwood, 2012.

Gates, Henry Louis, Jr. *African American Lives.* Pleasantville, NY: Kunhardt Films, 2006.

———. *African American Lives 2.* New York: PBS, 2008.

———, ed. *The Classic Slave Narratives.* New York: Mentor, 1987.

———. *Faces of America.* PBS, 2010.

———. Introduction to *The Classic Slave Narratives*, ed. Henry Louis Gates Jr., ix–xviii. New York: Mentor, 1987.

———. *The Signifying Monkey: A Theory of Afro-American Literary Criticism.* New York: Oxford University Press, 1988.

Gates, Henry Louis, Jr., and Evelyn Brooks Higginbotham, eds. *African American Lives.* New York: Oxford University Press, 2004.

Gikandi, Simon. *Slavery and the Culture of Taste.* Princeton, NJ: Princeton University Press, 2011.

Giles, James Richard. *Claude McKay.* Boston: Twayne Publishers, 1976.

Gilroy, Paul. *The Black Atlantic: Modernity and Double Consciousness.* Cambridge, MA: Harvard University Press, 1993.

Glave, Thomas. "Whose Caribbean?* An Allegory, in Part." *Callaloo* 27, no. 3 (2004): 671–81.

"Gleaner Top Ten." *Daily Gleaner*, November 4, 1988, 10.

Glissant, Édouard. *Caribbean Discourse: Selected Essays*. Trans. J. Michael Dash. Charlottesville: University Press of Virginia, 1989.

———. *Poetics of Relation*. Trans. Betsy Wing. Ann Arbor: University of Michigan Press, 1997.

Gloster, Hugh M. "Race and the Negro Writer." *Phylon* 11, no. 4 (1950): 369–71.

Goodman, Kevis. *Georgic Modernity and British Romanticism: Poetry and the Mediation of History*. Cambridge: Cambridge University Press, 2004.

Gould, Stephen Jay. "Is Uniformitarianism Necessary?" *American Journal of Science* 263, no. 3 (1965): 223–28.

Grainger, James. *The Sugar-Cane*. In *Poetics of Empire: A Study of James Grainger's "The Sugar Cane"* (1764), ed. John Gilmore, 91–197. London: Athlone, 2000.

Griffin, Farah Jasmine. *"Who Set You Flowin'?" The African-American Migration Narrative*. New York: Oxford University Press, 1995.

Handley, George. "Derek Walcott's Poetics of the Environment in *The Bounty*." *Callaloo: A Journal of African Diaspora Arts and Letters* 28, no. 1 (2005): 201–15.

———. *New World Poetics: Nature and the Adamic Imagination of Whitman, Neruda, and Walcott*. Athens: University of Georgia Press, 2010.

Hantel, Max. "Rhizomes and the Space of Translation: On Édouard Glissant's Spiral Retelling." *Small Axe: A Caribbean Journal of Criticism* 17, no. 3 (2013): 100–112.

Hardt, Michael, and Antonio Negri. *Commonwealth*. Cambridge, MA: Belknap Press of Harvard University Press, 2009.

Hart, Matthew. *Nations of Nothing but Poetry: Modernism, Transnationalism, and Synthetic Vernacular Writing*. New York: Oxford University Press, 2010.

Hathaway, Heather. "Exploring 'Something New': The 'Modernism' of Claude McKay's Harlem Shadows." In *Race and the Modern Artist*, ed. Josef JaÐab, Jeffrey Melnick, and Heather Hathaway, 54–68. New York: Oxford University Press, 2003.

Heap, Brian. "Songs of a Surrogate Mother: The Nursery Rhyme in Caribbean Culture." *Caribbean Quarterly* 43, no. 4 (1997): 26–36.

Hegel, G. W. F. *The Philosophy of History*. Trans. John Sibree. Mineola, NY: Dover Publications, 1956.

Heise, Ursula K. *Sense of Place and Sense of Planet: The Environmental Imagination of the Global*. New York: Oxford University Press, 2008.

Herron, Carolivia. "Saving the Word." In *Shar / Hurricane Poem*. Mona, Jamaica: Savacou Publications, 1990.

Higman, B. W. *Slave Population and Economy in Jamaica, 1807–1834*. Kingston, Jamaica: University of the West Indies Press, 1995.

Hill, Mozell C., and M. Carl Holman. Preface. *Phylon* 11, no. 4 (1950): 296.

Hill, Robert A., Marcus Garvey, and Universal Negro Improvement Association. *The Marcus Garvey and Universal Negro Improvement Association Papers: 1826–August 1919*. University of California Press, 1983.

Himes, Joseph S., Jr. "Changing Structure of Negro-White Relations in the South." *Phylon* 12, no. 3 (1951): 227–38.

Hoffmann, Léon-François. "The Climate of Haitian Poetry." *Phylon* 22, no. 1 (1961): 59–67.

Howarth, Peter. "The Modern Sonnet." In *The Cambridge Companion to the Sonnet*, ed. A. D. Cousins and Peter Howarth, 225–44. Cambridge: Cambridge University Press, 2011.

Huggins, Nathan Irvin. *Harlem Renaissance*. New York: Oxford University Press, 1971.

Hughes, Langston. "Drums." In *The Collected Poems of Langston Hughes*, ed. Arnold Rampersad and David Roessel, 543–44. New York: Random House, 1994.

———. "An Earth Song." In *The New Negro*, ed. Alain Locke, 142. New York: Simon and Schuster, 1925.

———. "The Negro Artist and the Racial Mountain." *Nation*, June 23, 1926, 692–94.

———. "The Negro Speaks of Rivers." In *The New Negro*, ed. Alain Locke, 141. New York: Simon and Schuster, 1925.

———. "The Negro Spirituals. In *The New Negro*, ed. Alain Locke, 199–213. New York: Simon and Schuster, 1925.

———. "Some Practical Observations: A Colloquy." *Phylon* 11, no. 4 (1950): 307–11.

Hurston, Zora Neale. "Characteristics of Negro Expression." 1934. In *Hurston: Folklore, Memoirs, and Other Writings*, 557–808. New York: Library of America, 1995, 830–846.

———. *Dust Tracks on a Road*. 1942. In *Hurston: Folklore, Memoirs, and Other Writings*, 557–808. New York: Library of America, 1995.

———. "Proposed Recording Expedition into the Floridas," 1939. Florida Folklife, WPA Collections, 1937–42, Library of Congress, Washington, DC.

———. *Their Eyes Were Watching God: A Novel*. 1937. New York: Perennial Library, 1990.

———. *Zora Neale Hurston: A Life in Letters*. Ed. Carla Kaplan. New York: Anchor Books, 2003.

Hutchinson, George. *The Harlem Renaissance in Black and White*. Cambridge, MA: Belknap Press of Harvard University Press, 1995.

Iannini, Christopher P. *Fatal Revolutions: Natural History, West Indian Slavery, and the Routes of American Literature*. Chapel Hill: University of North Carolina Press, 2012.

Ismond, Patricia. *Abandoning Dead Metaphors: The Caribbean Phase of Derek Walcott's Poetry*. Kingston, Jamaica: University of the West Indies Press, 2001.

———. "Walcott Versus Brathwaite." In *Critical Perspectives on Derek Walcott*, ed. Robert D Hamner, 220–36. Washington, DC: Three Continents Press, 1993.

Jackson, Blyden. "An Essay in Criticism." *Phylon* 11, no. 4 (1950): 338–43.

Jackson, Lawrence P. *The Indignant Generation*. Princeton, NJ: Princeton University Press, 2011.

Jackson, Virginia. *Dickinson's Misery: A Theory of Lyric Reading*. Princeton, NJ: Princeton University Press, 2005.

———. "Who Reads Poetry." *PMLA: Publications of the Modern Language Association of America* 123, no. 1 (2008): 181–87.

Jackson, Virginia, and Yopie Prins, eds. *The Lyric Theory Reader: A Critical Anthology*. Baltimore, MD: Johns Hopkins University Press, 2013.

———. General introduction to *The Lyric Theory Reader: A Critical Anthology The Lyric Theory Reader: A Critical Anthology*, ed. Virginia Jackson and Yopie Prins, 1–8. Baltimore, MD: Johns Hopkins University Press, 2013.

Jaffe, Dan. "Gwendolyn Brooks: An Appreciation from the White Suburbs." In *On Gwendolyn Brooks: Reliant Contemplation*, ed. Stephen Caldwell Wright, 50–59. Ann Arbor: University of Michigan Press, 2001.

"Jamaica Poet Praised." *Gleaner*. September 15, 1919.

James, Winston. *A Fierce Hatred of Injustice: Claude McKay's Jamaica and His Poetry of Rebellion*. London: Verso, 2000.

Jameson, Frederic. "Third World Literature in the Era of Multinational Capitalism." *Social Text* 15, no. 3 (1986): 65–88.

Jenkins, Lee M. "'If We Must Die': Winston Churchill and Claude McKay." *Notes and Queries* 50, no. 3 (2003): 333–37.

Johnson, James Weldon. *The Book of American Negro Poetry.* 1992. New York: Harcourt, Brace, and Company, 1931.

———. Introduction to *The Collected Poems of Sterling A. Brown*, ed. Michael S. Harper, 16–17. Evanston, IL: Triquarterly Books, 1996.

Jones, Leroi. *Blues People: Negro Music in White America.* 1963. New York: Harper Perennial, 1999.

———. *See also* Baraka, Amiri.

Jones, Meta DuEwa. *The Muse Is Music: Jazz Poetry from the Harlem Renaissance to Spoken Word.* University of Illinois Press, 2013.

Kamugisha, Aaron. "The Black Experience of New World Coloniality." *Small Axe* 20, no. 1 (2016): 129–45.

———. "'That Area of Experience That We Term the New World': Introducing Sylvia Wynter's 'Black Metamorphosis.'" *Small Axe* 20, no. 1 (2016): 37–46.

KC. "'Wild Gilbert' Singer Brings 'ha-Pee-Ness' to Music." *Sunday Gleaner*, February 11, 2007.

Keene, John. "'White Silences': The Lyric Theory Reader Panel @ ACLA 2014." *J'S THEATER*, March 22, 2014. http://jstheater.blogspot.com/2014/04/white-silences-lyric-theory-reader .html.

Kraut, Anthea. *Choreographing the Folk: The Dance Stagings of Zora Neale Hurston.* Minneapolis: University of Minnesota Press, 2008.

Lamothe, Daphne Mary. *Inventing the New Negro: Narrative, Culture, and Ethnography.* Philadelphia: University of Pennsylvania Press, 2008.

Lawrence, Jacob, and Langston Hughes. *One-Way Ticket.* New York: Knopf, 1949.

Lee, Spike. *When the Levees Broke: A Requiem in Four Acts.* Los Angeles: HBO, 2006.

Lee, Ulysses. "Criticism at Mid-Century." *Phylon* 11, no. 4 (1950): 328–37.

Lewis, David Levering. *W. E. B. Du Bois: A Biography.* New York: John McCrae, 2009.

Ligon, Richard. "A True and Exact History of the Island of Barbados." 1657. In *Caribbeana: An Anthology of English Literature of the West Indies 1657–1777*, ed. Thomas W. Krise, 16–30. Chicago: University of Chicago Press, 1999.

Locke, Alain, ed. "Harlem, Mecca of the New Negro." Special issue, *Survey Graphic* 6, no. 6. (1925).

———, ed. *The New Negro.* New York: Albert and Charles Boni, 1925.

———. "The New Negro." In *The New Negro*, ed. Alain Locke, 3–16. New York: Albert and Charles Boni, 1925.

———. "Negro Youth Speaks." In *The New Negro*, ed. Alain Locke, 47–53. New York: Albert and Charles Boni, 1925.

———. "Self-Criticism: The Third Dimension in Culture." *Phylon* 11, no. 4 (1950): 391–94.

Lowney, John. "'A Material Collapse That Is Construction': History and Counter-Memory in Gwendolyn Brooks's *In the Mecca.*" *MELUS* 23, no. 3 (1998): 3–20.

Mackey, Nathaniel. *Blue Fasa.* New York: New Directions, 2015.

———. *Discrepant Engagement: Dissonance, Cross-Culturality, and Experimental Writing.* Tuscaloosa: University of Alabama Press, 2000.

———. "An Interview with Kamau Brathwaite." In *The Art of Kamau Brathwaite*, ed. Stewart Brown, 13–32. Bridgend, Mid-Glamorgan, Wales: Seren, 1995

———. *Paracritical Hinge: Essays, Talks, Notes, Interviews.* University of Wisconsin Press, 2005.

Martin, John Bartlow. "The Strangest Place in Chicago." *Harper's*, December 1950, 86–97.

Marx, Leo. *The Machine in the Garden: Technology and the Pastoral Ideal in America*. New York: Oxford University Press, 2000.

Matthews, Mark. "Guyana not Ghana." *Savacou* 3–4 (1970): 153.

Maxwell, William J. Introduction to *Complete Poems*, by Claude McKay, ed. William J. Maxwell. Urbana: University of Illinois Press, 2004.

———. *New Negro, Old Left: African-American Writing and Communism Between the Wars*. New York: Columbia University Press, 1999.

McClintock, Anne. *Imperial Leather: Race, Gender, and Sexuality in the Colonial Contest*. New York: Routledge, 1995.

McFarlane, J. E. Clare. *A Literature in the Making*. Kingston, Jamaica: Pioneer Press, 1956.

———. *Voices From Summerland: An Anthology of Jamaican Poetry*. London: Fowler Wright, 1921.

McKay, Claude. *Banana Bottom*. 1933. New York: Harvest Books, 1974.

———. "Boyhood in Jamaica." *Phylon* 14, no. 2 (1953): 134–46.

———. "Claude McKay Defends Our Dialect Poetry." *Gleaner*. June 7, 1913.

———. "Flame-Heart." In *Complete Poems*, ed. William J. Maxwell, 155. Urbana: University of Illinois Press, 2004.

———. "Governor's Salary." *Gleaner*, February 10, 1913.

———. *Harlem Shadows: The poems of Claude McKay*. New York: Harcourt, Brace, 1922.

———. "If We Must Die." *Public Opinion*, April 8, 1939.

———. "Like a Strong Tree." In *The New Negro*, ed. Alain Locke, 134. New York: Simon and Schuster, 1925.

———. *A Long Way from Home*. New York: L. Furman, 1937.

———. *My Green Hills of Jamaica: And Five Jamaican Short Stories*. Kingston: Heinemann, 1979.

———. "My Mountain Home." In *Complete Poems*, ed. William J. Maxwell, 80. Urbana: University of Illinois Press, 2004.

———. "North and South." In *Complete Poems*, ed. William J. Maxwell, 159. Urbana: University of Illinois Press, 2004.

———. "Quashie to Buccra." In *Complete Poems*, ed. William J. Maxwell, 19–20. Urbana: University of Illinois Press, 2004.

———. *Songs of Jamaica*. Kingston, Jamaica: Aston W. Gardner, 1912.

———. *Spring in New Hampshire and Other Poems*. London: Grant Richards, 1920.

———. "Subway Wind." In *Complete Poems*, ed. William J. Maxwell, 178. Urbana: University of Illinois Press, 2004.

———. "The Tropics in New York." In *Complete Poems*, ed. William J. Maxwell, 154. Urbana: University of Illinois Press, 2004.

———. "The Tropics in New York." *Liberator* 3, no. 5 (1920): 48.

"McKay's Latest." *Gleaner*, July 4, 1929.

McKittrick, Katherine. *Demonic Grounds: Black Women and the Cartographies of Struggle*. Minneapolis: University of Minnesota Press, 2006.

———. "Plantation Futures." *Small Axe* 17, no. 42 (2013): 1–15.

———. "Rebellion / Invention / Groove." *Small Axe* 20, no. 1 (2016): 79–91.

———. *Sylvia Wynter: On Being Human as Praxis*. Durham, NC: Duke University Press, 2014.

McSweeney, Joyelle. "Poetics, Revelations, and Catastrophes: An Interview with Kamau Brathwaite." *Rain Taxi Review Online Edition*, Fall 2005. www.raintaxi.com/poetics-revelations-and-catastrophes-an-interview-with-kamau-brathwaite.

McTair, Roger. "Notes Toward a Final Belief." *Savacou* 3–4 (1970–71): 95.

Melhem, D. H. *Gwendolyn Brooks: Poetry and the Heroic Voice*. Lexington: University Press of Kentucky, 2015.

Michaels, Walter Benn. *Our America: Nativism, Modernism, and Pluralism*. Durham, NC: Duke University Press, 1995.

Mitchell, Charles L. "The West Indian Hurricane of September 10–20, 1928." *Monthly Weather Review* 56, no. 9 (1928): 347–350.

Mizelle, Richard M. *Backwater Blues: The Mississippi Flood of 1927 in the African American Imagination*. Minneapolis: University of Minnesota Press, 2014.

Monge, Luigi. "*Their Eyes Were Watching God*: African-American Topical Songs on the 1928 Florida Hurricanes and Floods." *Popular Music* 26, no. 1 (2007): 129–140.

"More Poems by Claude McKay." *Gleaner*, October 26, 1920.

Morton, Timothy. *Ecology without Nature: Rethinking Environmental Aesthetics*. Cambridge, MA: Harvard University Press, 2007.

———. *Hyperobjects: Philosophy and Ecology after the End of the World*. Minneapolis: University of Minnesota Press, 2013.

Moten, Fred. "Blackness and Nothingness (Mysticism in the Flesh)." *South Atlantic Quarterly* 112, no. 4 (2013): 737–80.

———. "Blackness and Poetry." *Evening Will Come: A Monthly Journal of Poetics*, no. 55 (2015). www.thevolta.org/ewc55-fmoten-p1.html.

———. "Black Op." *PMLA: Publications of the Modern Language Association of America* 123, no. 5 (2008): 1743–47.

———. *In the Break: The Aesthetics of the Black Radical Tradition*. Minneapolis: University of Minnesota Press, 2003.

———. *Social Text* Thirtieth Anniversary Panel Discussion. Social Text Collective, November 13, 2009, New York.

Mullen, Harryette. "African Signs and Spirit Writing." *Callaloo* 19, no. 3 (1996): 670–89.

Mykle, Robert. *Killer 'Cane: The Deadly Hurricane of 1928*. New York: Taylor Trade Publishing, 2006.

Nelson, Cary. *Repression and Recovery: Modern American Poetry and the Politics of Cultural Memory*. Madison: University of Wisconsin Press, 1991.

Nielsen, Aldon Lynn. *Black Chant: Languages of African-American Postmodernism*. New York: Cambridge University Press, 1997.

Nixon, Rob. *Slow Violence and the Environmentalism of the Poor*. Cambridge, MA: Harvard University Press, 2011.

North, Michael. *The Dialect of Modernism: Race, Language, and Twentieth-Century Literature*. New York: Oxford University Press, 1994.

Nugent, Bruce. "Sahdji." In *The New Negro*, ed. Alain Locke, 113–14. New York: Albert and Charles Boni, 1925.

Parrish, Susan Scott. *The Flood Year 1927: A Cultural History*. Princeton: Princeton University Press, 2017.

———. "Zora Neale Hurston and the Environmental Ethic of Risk." In *American Studies, Ecocriticism, and Citizenship: Thinking and Acting in the Local and Global Commons*, ed. Kimberly N. Ruffin, 21–36. New York: Routledge, 2013.

Patterson, Anita Haya. *Race, American Literature and Transnational Modernisms*. Cambridge: Cambridge University Press, 2008.

Patterson, Orlando. *Slavery and Social Death*. Cambridge, MA: Harvard University Press, 1982.

Pederson, Carl. "The Tropics in New York: Claude McKay and the New Negro Movement." In *Temples for Tomorrow: Looking Back at the Harlem Renaissance*, ed. Geneviève Fabre and Michel Feith, 259–269. Bloomington: Indiana University Press, 2001.

Philip, M. NourbeSe. *Zong!* Middletown, CT: Wesleyan University Press, 2008.

Phillips, James. "Democratic Socialism, the New International Economic Order, and Globalization: Jamaica's Sugar Cooperatives in the Post-Colonial Transition." *Global South* 4, no. 2 (2010): 178–96.

Philosopher. "Growing Citrus Fruits In This Island For The Markets Abroad." *Gleaner*, July 4, 1929.

Pinto, Samantha. *Difficult Diasporas: The Transnational Feminist Aesthetic of the Black Atlantic*. New York: New York University Press, 2013.

Posmentier, Sonya. "Blueprints for Negro Reading: Sterling Brown's Study Guides." In *A Companion to the Harlem Renaissance*, ed. Cherene Sherrard-Johnson, 119–36. Hoboken, NJ: Wiley-Blackwell, 2015.

Price, Ernest. "Effects of Disaster." *Gleaner*, January 5, 1913.

Ramazani, Jahan. *The Hybrid Muse: Postcolonial Poetry in English*. Chicago: University of Chicago Press, 2001.

———. *A Transnational Poetics*. Chicago: University of Chicago Press, 2009.

Ramesh, Kotti Sree. *Claude McKay: The Literary Identity from Jamaica to Harlem and Beyond*. Jefferson, NC: McFarland, 2006.

Reckin, Anna. "Tidalectic Lectures: Kamau Brathwaite's Prose / Poery as Sound Space." *Anthurium: A Caribbean Studies Journal* 1, no. 1 (2003): Article 5.

Redcam, Tom. "Appreciation of the Poems of Claude McKay." *Gleaner*. January 5, 1913.

Reed, Anthony. *Freedom Time: The Poetics and Politics of Black Experimental Writing*. Baltimore, MD: Johns Hopkins University Press, 2014.

Retman, Sonnet H. *Real Folks: Race and Genre in the Great Depression*. Durham, NC: Duke University Press Books, 2011.

Rigby, Graeme. "Publishing Brathwaite: Adventures in the Video Style." *World Literature Today: A Literary Quarterly of the University of Oklahoma* 68, no. 4 (1994): 708–14.

Roach, Eric. "I Am the Archipelago." In *The Flowering Rock: Collected Poems, 1938–1974*, 135–36. Leeds: Peepal Tree, 1992.

———. "A Type Not Found in All Generations." *Trinidad Guardian*, July 14, 1971, 6–8.

Roach, Joseph R. *Cities of the Dead: Circum-Atlantic Performance*. New York: Columbia University Press, 1996.

Roberts, Brian Russell. "Archipelagic Diaspora, Geographical Form, and Hurston's *Their Eyes Were Watching God*." *American Literature* 85, no. 1 (2013): 121–49.

Robinson, Cedric. "Notes toward a 'Native' Theory of History." *Review (Fernand Braudel Center)* 4, no. 1 (1980): 45–78.

Rohlehr, Gordon. "The Problem of the Problem of Form." In *The Shape of That Hurt and Other Essays*, 1–65. Port-of-Spain: Longman Trinidad, 1992.

———. "White Fridays in Trinidad." *Savacou* 3–4 (1970–71): 18–24.

Ronda, Margaret. " 'Work and Wait Unwearying': Dunbar's Georgics." *PMLA* 127, no. 4 (2012): 863–78.

Rowell, Charles H. "Sterling A. Brown and the Afro-American Folk Tradition." *Studies in the Literary Imagination* 7, no. 2 (1974): 131–52.

Rozario, Kevin. *The Culture of Calamity: Disaster and the Making of Modern America*. Chicago: University of Chicago Press, 2007.

Rusert, Britt. "Black Nature: The Question of Race in the Age of Ecology." *Polygraph: An International Journal of Culture & Politics* 22 (September 2010): 149–66.

———. *Fugitive Science: Empiricism and Freedom in Early African American Culture*. New York: New York University Press, 2017.

———. "Plantation Ecologies: The Experimental Plantation in and against James Grainger's The Sugar-Cane." *Early American Studies: An Interdisciplinary Journal* 13, no. 2 (April 23, 2015): 341–73.

———. "The Science of Freedom: Counterarchives of Racial Science on the Antebellum Stage." *African American Review* 45, no. 3 (September 22, 2012).

———. "Shackled in the Garden: Ecology and Race in American Plantation Cultures." PhD diss., Duke University, 2009.

Sanders, Mark A. *Afro-Modernist Aesthetics and the Poetry of Sterling A. Brown*. Athens: University of Georgia Press, 1999.

Savory, Elaine. "Returning to Sycorax/Prospero's Response: Kamau Brathwaite's Word Journey." In *The Art of Kamau Brathwaite*, ed. Stewart Brown, 208–30. Bridgend, Mid-Glamorgan, Wales: Seren, 1995.

———. "Toward a Caribbean Ecopoetics: Derek Walcott's Language of Plants." In *Postcolonial Ecologies: Literatures of the Environment*, ed. Elizabeth M. DeLoughrey and George Handley. New York: Oxford University Press, 2011.

Scott, David. *Conscripts of Modernity: The Tragedy of Colonial Enlightenment*. Durham, NC: Duke University Press, 2004.

———. Introduction. Special issue, Archaeologies of Black Memory. *Small Axe* 12, no. 2 (2008): v–xvi.

———. Preface. Special issue, Sylvia Wynter's "Black Metamorphosis." *Small Axe* 20, no. 1 (2016): vii–x.

Sexton, Jared. "People-of-Color-Blindness: Notes on the Afterlife of Slavery." *Social Text* 28, no. 2 (2010): 31–56.

———. "The Social Life of Social Death: On Afro-Pessimism and Black Optimism." *InTensions*, no. 5 (Fall/Winter 2011): http://www.yorku.ca/intent/issue5/articles/jaredsexton .php.

Sharpe, Christina. "Black Studies." *Black Scholar* 44, no. 2 (2014): 59–69.

———. *In the Wake: On Blackness and Being*. Durham, NC: Duke University Press, 2016.

Shelton "Shakespear" Alexander. "Will You Be There." In *When the Levees Broke: A Requiem in Four Acts*, directed by Spike Lee. Los Angeles: HBO, 2006. Film.

Shepperson, George. "Ethiopianism and African Nationalism." *Phylon* 14, no. 1 (1953): 9–18.

———. "Malawi and the Poetry of Two World Wars." 1990 Reprinted, *Society of Malawi Journal* 53, nos. 1–2 (2000): 143–55.

———. "Ourselves as Others: Some Comments on Cedric Robinson on George Shepperson." *Review (Fernand Braudel Center)* 4, no. 1 (1980): 79–87.

———. "Pan-Africanism and 'Pan-Africanism': Some Historical Notes." *Phylon* 23, no. 4 (1962): 346–58.

———. "Rain." *Phylon* 12, no. 2 (1951): 171.

Shockley, Evie. "Going Overboard: African American Poetic Innovation and the Middle Passage." *Contemporary Literature* 52, no. 4 (2011): 791–817.

———. *Renegade Poetics: Black Aesthetics and Formal Innovation in African American Poetry*. University of Iowa Press, 2011.

Singh, Nikhil Pal. *Black Is a Country: Race and the Unfinished Struggle for Democracy*. Cambridge, MA: Harvard University Press, 2004.

Singleton, John. "A General Description of the West-Indian Islands." In *Caribbeana: An Anthology of English Literature of the West Indies 1657–1777*, 262–314. Chicago: University of Chicago Press, 1999.

Sivils, Matthew Wynn. "Reading Trees in Southern Literature." *Southern Quarterly: A Journal of the Arts in the South* 44, no. 1 (2006): 88–102.

Smethurst, James. *The Black Arts Movement: Literary Nationalism in the 1960s and 1970s*. Chapel Hill: University of North Carolina Press, 2005.

Smith, Neil. "There's No Such Thing as a Natural Disaster." *Understanding Katrina: Perspectives from the Social Sciences*, June 11, 2006. http://understandingkatrina.ssrc.org/Smith.

Smith, Neil. *Uneven Development: Nature, Capital, and the Production of Space*. 3rd ed. Athens: University of Georgia Press, 2008.

Solnit, Rebecca. *A Paradise Built in Hell: The Extraordinary Communities That Arise in Disaster*. New York: Viking, 2009.

"Souvenir Program: Carifesta '76 Jamaica," 1976. University of West Indies Special Collections, Kingston, Jamaica.

Spillers, Hortense J. *Black, White, and in Color: Essays on American Literature and Culture*. Chicago: University of Chicago Press, 2003.

Stanley-Niaah, Sonjah. *Dancehall: From Slave Ship to Ghetto*. Ottawa: University of Ottawa Press, 2010.

———. "Negotiating a Common Transnational Space." *Cultural Studies* 23, no. 5 (2009): 756–74.

Stephens, Michelle Ann. *Black Empire: The Masculine Global Imaginary of Caribbean Intellectuals in the United States, 1914–1962*. Durham, NC: Duke University Press, 2005.

Stewart, Susan. *Poetry and the Fate of the Senses*. Chicago: University of Chicago Press, 2002.

St. John, Bruce. "West Indian Litany." *Savacou* 3–4 (1970–71): 82.

Sweet, Timothy. *American Georgics: Economy and Environment in Early American Literature*. Philadelphia: University of Pennsylvania Press, 2002.

Sylvia Wynter. "Ethno or Socio Poetics." *Alcheringa: Ethnopoetics* 2, no. 2 (1976): 79–94.

———. "Jonkonnu in Jamaica." *Jamaica Journal* 4, no. 2 (1970): 34–48.

———. "Novel and History, Plot and Plantation." *Savacou* 5 (1971): 95–102.

Terrefe, Selamawit. "What Exceeds the Hold? An Interview with Christina Sharpe." *Rhizome*, no. 29 (2016): DOI: 10.20415/rhiz/029.e06.

Thomas, Greg. "Marronnons / Let's Maroon: Sylvia Wynter's 'Black Metamorphosis' as a Species of Maroonage." *Small Axe* 20, no. 1 (2016): 62–78.

Tidwell, John Edgar, and Mark A Sanders. Introduction to *A Negro Looks at the South*, ed. John Edgar Tidwell and Mark A Sanders, 3–15. Oxford: Oxford University Press, 2007.

Tillery, Tyrone. *Claude McKay: A Black Poet's Struggle for Identity*. Amherst: University of Massachusetts Press, 1991.

Tinsley, Omise'eke Natasha. *Thiefing Sugar: Eroticism between Women in Caribbean Literature*. Durham, NC: Duke University Press, 2010.

Tobin, Beth Fowkes. *Colonizing Nature: The Tropics in British Arts and Letters, 1760–1820*. Philadelphia: University of Pennsylvania Press, 2005.

Tolnay, Stewart E. "The African American 'Great Migration' and Beyond." *Annual Review of Sociology* 29 (2003): 209–32.

Tolson, Melvin B. "Claude McKay's Art." *Poetry* 83, no. 5 (1954): 288–89.

Toomer, Jean. *Cane.* New York: Boni and Liveright, 1923.

Treaster, Joseph B. "In Storm's Aftermath, Jamaica Seeks Visitors." *New York Times*, November 10, 1988.

———. "Jamaica Reviving after Hurricane but Food Shortages Are Predicted." *New York Times*, September 20, 1988.

Trotter, Joe William. Introduction to *The Great Migration in Historical Perspective: New Dimensions of Race, Class, and Gender*, ed. Joe William Trotter, 1–21. Bloomington: Indiana University Press, 1991.

Vazquez, Alexandra T. "Listening in the Cold War Years." Paper presented at the American Studies Association, Baltimore, MD, October 21, 2011.

———. *Listening in Detail: Performances of Cuban Music.* Durham, NC: Duke University Press, 2013.

———. "Musical Recourses, Mystical Qualities: Cuba Linda Lifts the Studies Protocol." In Instrumental Migrations: The Critical Turns of Cuban Music. Unpublished manuscript, 2009.

Wade, Betsy. "Practical Traveler; An Update on Jamaica: Services Intact If Frayed." *New York Times*, December 18, 1988.

Walcott, Derek. "The Antilles: Fragments of Epic Memory." In *What the Twilight Says: Essays*, 65–84. New York: Farrar, Straus and Giroux, 1998.

———. "The Caribbean: Culture or Mimicry?" In *Critical Perspectives on Derek Walcott*, ed. Robert D Hamner, 51–57. Washington, DC: Three Continents Press, 1993.

———. "Forty Acres." In *White Egrets: Poems*, 75. Farrar, Straus and Giroux. 2011.

———. Interview with Carrol B. Fleming. *Caribbean Writer* 7 (1978): 52–61. http://www.thecaribbeanwriter.org.

———. Interview with J. P. White. In *Conversations with Derek Walcott*, 151–74. Jackson: University Press of Mississippi, 1996.

———. "The Muse of History." In *What the Twilight Says: Essays*, 36–64. New York: Farrar, Straus and Giroux, 1998.

———. "The Schooner Flight." In *Collected Poems, 1948–1984*, 345–61. New York: Farrar, Straus and Giroux, 1986.

———. "The Sea Is History." In *Collected Poems, 1948–1984*, 364–67. New York: Farrar, Straus and Giroux, 1986.

———. "The Star-Apple Kingdom." In *Collected Poems, 1948–1984*, 383–95. New York: Farrar, Straus and Giroux, 1986.

———. *The Star-Apple Kingdom.* New York: Farrar, Straus and Giroux, 1979.

———. "Tribute Flutes." In *Critical Perspectives on Derek Walcott*, ed. Robert D. Hamner, 41–44. Washington, DC: Three Continents Press, 1993.

Walker, Karyl. "Twenty-One Years after Gilbert." *Jamaica Observer Limited*, September 13, 2009.

Walker, Margaret. "A Litany from the Dark People." *Phylon* 13, no. 3 (1952): 252–53.

———. "New Poets." *Phylon* 11, no. 4 (1950): 345–54.

Walmsley, Anne. *The Caribbean Artists Movement, 1966–1972: A Literary and Cultural History.* London: New Beacon Books, 1992.

Walrond, Eric. "The Palm Porch." In *The New Negro*, ed. Alain Locke, 115–26. New York: Albert and Charles Boni, 1925.

Walvin, James. *Black Ivory: A History of British Slavery*. London: HarperCollins, 1992.

Wang, Dorothy. *Thinking Its Presence: Form, Race, and Subjectivity in Contemporary Asian American Poetry*. Stanford, CA: Stanford University Press, 2015.

Ward, Edward. "A Trip to Jamaica." In *Caribbeana: An Anthology of English Literature of the West Indies 1657–1777*, 77–92. Chicago: University of Chicago Press, 1999.

Warner, Michael. *Publics and Counterpublics*. Brooklyn, NY: Zone Books, 2002.

Warren, Kenneth W. *What Was African American Literature?* Cambridge, MA: Harvard University Press, 2011.

Washington, Booker T. *Up from Slavery*. New York: Oxford University Press, 2009.

Washington, Mary Helen. *The Other Blacklist: The African American Literary and Cultural Left of the 1950s*. New York: Columbia University Press, 2014.

Weheliye, Alexander G. *Phonographies: Grooves in Sonic Afro-Modernity*. Durham, NC: Duke University Press, 2005.

Weis, Tony. "Beyond Peasant Deforestation: Environment and Development in Rural Jamaica." *Global Environmental Change* 10, no. 4 (2000): 299–305.

Weskett, John. *A Complete Digest of the Laws, Theory and Practice of Insurance*. London, 1781.

White, Gillian. *Lyric Shame: The "Lyric" Subject of Contemporary American Poetry*. Cambridge, MA: Harvard University Press, 2014.

Wilkerson, Isabel. *The Warmth of Other Suns: The Epic Story of America's Great Migration*. New York: Vintage, 2011.

Williams, Raymond. *Keywords: A Vocabulary of Culture and Society*. New York: Oxford University Press, 1976.

Wilson, Elizabeth A. "Translating Caribbean Landscape." *Palmipsestes* 12 (2000): 15–29.

"Work in Progress." *BIM* 3, no. 11 (1950): 237.

Wright, Richard. "Between Laughter and Tears." *New Masses*, October 5, 1937, 25–26.

———. "Down By the Riverside." In *Uncle Tom's Children*, 62–124. New York: Perennial, 1993.

Discography

Atkinson, Lily Mae. *God Rode on a Mighty Storm*. Frederica, Georgia, 1935. AFS 327 A. American Folklife Center, Library of Congress, Washington, DC.

Beach Boys. *Kokomo*. 1989. Vol. Still Cruisin'. Capitol B-44445.

Brathwaite, Edward Kamau. *History of the Voice, Q & A*. 1976. Library of the Spoken Word, University of West Indies, Mona.

Crosby, Bing (Paul Whiteman orchestra). *Muddy Water*. Written and Composed by DeRose, Peter, Harry Richman, and Jo Trent. 1927. Victor 7820508.

DeRose, Peter, Harry Richman, and Jo Trent. "Muddy Water." 1927.

Hurston, Zora Neale, and Carita Doggett Corse. *Evalina*. 1939. 3144B:4. Florida Folklife, WPA Collections, 1937–1942, Library of Congress, Washington, DC.

Jenkins, Viola. *The West Palm Beach Storm*. Gainesville, Florida, 1937. AFS 977 A. American Folklife Center, Library of Congress, Washington, DC.

Lovindeer, Lloyd. *Wild Gilbert*. 1988. Kingston, Jamaica: Sounds of Jamaica.

Odetta, and Larry Mohr. *Run, Come See Jerusalem*. 1954. Vol. Tin Angel. Fantasy Records EP-4017.

Roberts, John. *Pytoria (Run, Come See Jerusalem)*. 1959. Vol. Music of the Bahamas, Anthems, Work Songs and Ballads. Smithsonian Folkways, Library of Congress, Washington, DC.

Smith, Bessie. *Back-Water Blues*. 1927. Columbia 14195-D.

———. *Homeless Blues*. 1927. Columbia 14260-D.

———. *Muddy Water (A Mississippi Moan)*. Written and Composed by DeRose, Peter, Harry Richman, and Jo Trent. 1927. Columbia 14197-D.

Various Artists. *Evalina*. 2002. Vol. Deep River of Song, Bahamas 1935, Ring Games and Round Dances. Rounder Select.

Washington, George, and unidentified group of Negro convicts. *In That Storm*. Gainesville, Florida, 1936. AFS 715 A & B. American Folklife Center, Library of Congress, Washington, DC.

Index

Page numbers in *italics* indicate figures.